Blue-Collar Workers in Eastern Europe

Blue-Collar Workers in Eastern Europe

Edited by
JAN F. TRISKA
CHARLES GATI

London
GEORGE ALLEN & UNWIN
Boston   Sydney

George Allen & Unwin (Publishers) Ltd,
40 Museum Street, London WC1A 1LU, UK

George Allen & Unwin (Publishers) Ltd,
Park Lane, Hemel Hempstead, Herts HP2 4TE, UK

Allen & Unwin Inc.,
9 Winchester Terrace, Winchester, Mass 01890, USA

George Allen & Unwin Australia Pty Ltd,
8 Napier Street, North Sydney, NSW 2060, Australia

First published in 1981

British Library Cataloguing in Publication Data

Blue-collar workers in Eastern Europe.
  1. Labor and laboring classes – Europe, Eastern – Political
  activity – Congresses
  2. Europe, Eastern – Politics and government – 1945 –
  Congresses
  I. Triska, Jan F   II. Gati, Charles
  323.3   HD8378

ISBN 0-04-321027-9
ISBN 0-04-321028-7 Pbk

Set in 10 on 11 point Times by Gilbert Composing Services,
Leighton Buzzard, and printed in Great Britain
by Richard Clay (The Chaucer Press) Ltd, Bungay, Suffolk.

Contents

Acknowledgements

The editors are pleased to acknowledge their gratitude to the Dickinson Memorial Symposium Fund, the Otis Castle Fund, and the Center for Russian and East European Studies, all of Stanford University, and to the International Ladies' Garment Workers' Union and American Federation of Labor/Congress of Industrial Organizations, whose financial assistance made it possible to hold the May 1980 conference on East European workers at Stanford University. Most contributions to this book were originally presented at that conference.

Stanford students helped to organize and run the conference. They had taken seminars and written research papers on topics discussed at the conference. Subsequently, they commented on the studies now presented here. This was a new pedagogical experience for all of us, students and scholars alike, and we have learned from it.

We also wish to thank Ms Betty J. Herring, secretary of the Center for Russian and East European Studies at Stanford, for her helpful assistance with the conference and the book, and the staff of the Research Institute on International Change at Columbia University for expert help and cooperation.

Washington, DC   JAN F. TRISKA
New York   CHARLES GATI
November 1980

Introduction

Authors and editors intend their books to fill a gap in the literature. This book is no exception. It deals with the conditions, attitudes and political disposition of the East European industrial working class, a subject which has not received proper attention from Western scholars. Although many books and articles have become available over the years about intellectuals and about the peasantry of Eastern Europe, no systematic treatment of the East European proletariat – the professed mainstay of the political order in communist polities – has yet been published.

The editors and contributors to this book seek to provide the reader with information about and analysis of the East European blue-collar workers. Their interpretations often vary, but they agree that the topic is intellectually challenging as well as politically relevant. For the central question posed in the book has to do not only with the status of the workers, but with their increasingly assertive voice for economic and political change, particularly in Poland. As Sol C. Chaikin, President of the International Ladies' Garment Workers' Union, noted in his address to the Stanford University conference on the East European proletariat in May 1980, up to now, the leadership of the dissident movements in Eastern Communist countries has devolved upon the intellectuals and social philosophers and religious activists of uncommon courage. They have of late, however, been joined by workers of varied background.

The chapters that make up this book fall into three categories. Some are issue-oriented and analytical, dealing with the role, economic condition, attitudes, social and demographic characteristics, and political involvement of the industrial proletariat. They are followed by case studies of specific tendencies and problems in the several East European countries. Finally, two chapters focus on the policy implications of the workers' assertiveness, assessing international influences in general and the policy options and dilemmas of the Soviet Union and the West in particular.

In his introductory chapter, SEYMOUR MARTIN LIPSET draws on Marx, the sociologist, and his analysis of the relationship between economic and political forces and the proletariat's struggle for socialism, to discuss the industrial proletariat in comparative perspective. This involves looking at class politics in relation to industrialization, assuming that the class struggle is deeply affected by the technological period at hand, be it preindustrial, industrial, or, as many countries are today, postindustrial.

Marx and his followers believed that socialism would emerge in the most developed capitalist country, specifically the United States. Of course, this expectation came to naught. But if we assume an apolitical sociological Marxist approach, then the United States should show to others how they will develop politically as they become more advanced industrially. The data have borne this out; the more explicit forms of class consciousness have been declining, and class is less important as a source of political struggle than it once was. Moreover, Marx's theory has been confounded since communist revolutions have succeeded in preindustrial, agrarian societies.

If the Marxist theory of proletarian revolution has been proved incorrect, a related aspect and prediction of historical materialism has been verified in events and processes which have occurred in the countries that call themselves socialist or communist. Marx argued that socialism or equality could only be established in highly developed industrial nations, on the premise that inequality was the result of scarcity. If revolution did not occur in the highly developed nations, Marx warned, 'all the filthy business would necessarily be reproduced'. This, of course, has happened in the socialist countries. There, workers face experiences comparable in the West some time ago, but they lack the protection of workers' parties and unions. As Jan Machajski and Robert Michels have recognized, workers require the erection of class defense organizations to protect them against the new ruling class.

The rapid pace of communist-sponsored industrialization in Eastern Europe during the first decades after World War II, argues PAUL M. JOHNSON, led to an extremely rapid increase in the numbers of manual workers. Most of the increase was accomplished by the large-scale recruitment of youths from a peasant background, who experienced the move to urban employment as upward social mobility. The inundation of working-class ranks by these poorly educated and organizationally inexperienced urban migrants helps to account for the success of the communist regimes in maintaining working-class conformism despite disorienting change and often severe material deprivations. More recently, the slowing in the rates of social mobility, the consolidation of an increasingly hereditary, better-educated and more organizationally sophisticated manual working stratum, and the necessary changeover from 'extensive' to 'intensive' economic growth, may lead workers to be more assertive and less amenable to manipulation. While development of a revolutionary political stance by workers may be regarded as unlikely, communist authorities will probably find it necessary to create more effective institutional guarantees for workers against adverse economic policies. The authorities may even resign themselves to the likelihood of more frequent instances of working-class protest against specific decisions.

ALEX PRAVDA examines the political involvement of workers in Hungary, Poland and Czechoslovakia. While interest in politics is relatively high, knowledge is poor, especially among unskilled groups. Workers seem attached to the security and welfare aspects of the existing systems and willing to tolerate a paternalistic state in return for socialist welfare benefits. At the same time, many cleave to notions of social justice and personal liberty and have an instrumental attitude to authority. Skilled workers in particular tend to adapt and bend the rules to maximise personal benefit; hence the term 'adaptive workers' is used to describe this influential group of working-class opinion-leaders.

The second part of the chapter contrasts the impressive rates of participation in official social and political organizations with the widespread cynicism and passivity that characterizes workers' organizational activity. And since many workers seem far from satisfied with the way in which official organizations represent their interests, they frequently articulate their demands by informal means ranging from slowdowns to strike action. While such informal activity can create situations of 'dual power' in Hungary and Czechoslovakia, it tends to help prevent tensions from developing into open conflict. However, with all these regimes beset by increasing economic constraints, informal activity tends to assume a more radical and disruptive role.

According to ELLEN TURKISH COMISSO, some light can be shed on the difficulties the Yugoslav League of Communists (LCY) has in recruiting blue-collar workers by examining its role within the Yugoslav self-managed firm. In that context, the roots of the LCY's recruitment dilemma seem to lie in a lack of incentives for blue-collar workers to pay the costs of political action that party membership entails for them. When workers as a group derive benefits from party actions, the benefits take the form of 'public goods' which accrue to the work collective as a whole or to workers in general, regardless of party affiliation. Thus, workers are implicitly encouraged to assume the position of 'free riders', especially given that the party's ability to perform its tasks in the firm require it to be as responsive to the demands of non-members as to those of its own activists. At the same time, the LCY's political responsibilities and the means it has to fulfill them in the enterprise both restrict the resources the party branch has at its disposal and limit the ways it can allocate them. The result is that, as individuals, workers – in contrast to managerial personnel — are unlikely to profit from whatever non-collective benefits party membership can carry. Indeed, given the presence of self-management bodies with real decision-making power, even opportunities to exercise political influence in the firm are quite independent of party membership, and especially so for blue-collar workers.

JACK BIELASIAK contrasts the communist regimes' goals concerning mass participation with the actual extent of workers' participation in economic and political institutions. The governments' emphasis in the 1970s on 'socialist democracy' was motivated by the need for identification with the proletariat at a time of increasing turbulence among the workers, the concern with economic efficiency due to productivity problems, and the necessity of assuring social integration at a time of greater socioeconomic complexity. The aim was to increase workers' satisfaction through a sense of involvement in neighborhood and workplace issues. Despite the rhetoric of socialist democracy, the evidence reveals that mass participation is low, largely symbolic, and does not significantly increase grassroot influence on economic and political decisions. The ability of the working class to make decisions that affect their work and life environment remains very limited, and the majority feel that participation is not efficacious and does not increase their impact on policy. For that reason, despite the verbal commitments to and symbolic innovations in mass participation, the hope of the communist leaders that pseudoparticipation will diffuse the discontent of the workers appears unwarranted.

LAURA D'ANDREA TYSON examines how aggregate economic difficulties, resulting from an interaction between deteriorating external conditions and internal economic weaknesses, have influenced the realization of economic goals important to workers in Eastern Europe during the 1970s. Case studies of Hungary and Poland, analyzed in a simple economic framework relating internal economic performance and worsening balance-of-payments constraints, indicate that these difficulties have necessitated sacrifices on all the major goals valued by workers, with the exception of the goal of full employment.

WALTER D. CONNOR maintains that workers constitute one class among others in East European societies – not *the* 'leading class' of regime rhetoric. The creations of the process of socialist industrialization, East Europe's working classes face the issues of power; to advance their 'interests', however defined, *versus* the regime, and, perhaps, *versus* other classes.

Workers possess both assets and liabilities in the area of power: among the former, their numbers, their critical functions when taken as a mass, and the never-revoked regime decree that they are the leading class. Their liabilities, however, also derive from the large numbers and difficulties in independent organization in a repressive environment, as well as the logical strain in elaborating a counterideology to the one that already 'exalts' them, and the limited frame of reference and analytic capacity which in a general way distinguishes them from the intelligentsia.

Worker *action* in the past has been at times direct and even violent, but also generally episodic and uncoordinated with the actions of the dissident intellectuals. Regimes have been largely successful thus far, by manipulating consumption policy and offering opportunities for upward mobility, in blunting worker protest. But future prospects depart from the past record in at least two respects: in a worsening economic environment, the regime can no longer guarantee the maintenance of a constant, if moderate, growth in levels of consumption to meet workers' material expectations, *nor* can high rates of upward mobility be maintained in now-mature economies to draw off pressure by offering the prospect of individual advancement out of the working class for many of the ambitious and dissatisfied. Thus arises the prospect of a more class-conscious socialist working class, protesting *as* workers against slow growth, inflation and shortages, and of potentially critical instability in regime–society relations.

J. M. MONTIAS deals with the several strikes, riots and other disturbances in Eastern Europe from a comparative perspective. With regard to the causes of these events, the author seeks 'to isolate plausible connections, to develop simple conjectures relating observed conditions and their presumed effects, mindful that these propositions cannot be rigorously tested at the present time'. Among his conclusions are the following: that strikes are more likely to occur if the country has a past history of successful civil protests, if the government is not determined to repress the strike immediately and at any cost, and if the regime is unwilling to make prompt concessions or reforms aimed at pacifying potential insurgents. The author also suggests that, while the primary demands made by strikes are economic, secondary demands regarding workers' participation and representation play an important subsidiary role in the interaction between the authorities and the strikers.

JAN B. DE WEYDENTHAL is concerned with the political significance of workers' unrest in Poland. The main difficulties, he argues, result from the absence of political institutions which could adequately represent the socio-economic interests of the workers. As long as the government fails to allow for the creation of permanent institutional channels through which the workers could defend their economic interests, periodic outbursts of protests will continue to erupt from time to time. Such persistent threats of disruption undermine the effectiveness of government operations and endanger its stability.

The basic thesis of GEORGE KOLANKIEWICZ is that the 1980 events in Poland represent a reaction by the working class to the moral disintegration of socialist society. Corruption and mismanagement, lack of discipline, and social pathology are symptomatic of a society which had lost all sense of normative order, within the economic and social spheres as well as in political life. The broad-based action of the working-class strike committees in the summer of 1980, including as they did staunch Roman Catholics, party members and trade union activists, makes plain that to term this development as anything other than a 'moral revolt' would be to miss the point. Underlying these events were political, social and economic policies which were ill-conceived, poorly executed and ultimately disintegrative.

Although there is a hidden conflict between the ruling class and the workers in Czechoslovakia, and the workers possess a revolutionary potential for overthrowing their rulers, successful workers' revolutions have not taken place, writes JIRI VALENTA. There can be no successful workers' revolt without the support of the intellectuals and no revolutionary attempt of the intellectuals can succeed without the workers' support. So far, with their policies of embourgeoisement, the ruling elite has succeeded in appeasing significant sectors of the working class and has isolated the intelligentsia. While the high cost of energy; the significant hard-currency debt; increasingly severe shortages; and inflation may serve as a catalyst for future worker dissatisfaction, external factors, primarily the Soviet occupation, limit the extent of worker unrest.

IVAN VOLGYES deals with the development and bifurcation of the working class in Hungary. He notes the creation of a new type of working class, the lumpenproletariat, as a stratum and value-determinant for society. And he contends that as economic problems are causing serious problems for the elite, the elite must rely on this stratum to counteract the traditional working class and its demands upon the elite for a greater share of the political power.

Because industrial labor's participation is linked to the principal rationale for party dictatorship, both an increasing level and improved quality of workers' involvement are expected as socialism progresses, argues DANIEL NELSON. The success or failure of structures and processes for worker involvement is, therefore, a 'stake' invested by the party – an investment it *must* make not simply because of its Marxist heritage, but also because the economic plan it pursues requires higher workers' productivity. Romanian workers see the limits on their participation and understand differences between their material interests and party goals. Therefore, the party's 'solutions' to the destabilizing impact of socioeconomic change in Romania may exacerbate the instability. Developed socialism as found in European communist states embodies a dialectic of its own making – where socioeconomic policies foster increased demands which cannot be met but which, when not ameliorated, encourage further demands. The occupational category for which Marx originally spoke has often been among the most vehement in confrontations with communist parties. Developed socialism in communist Europe has meant the rise of conflict between the proletariat and its erstwhile vanguard.

An analysis of labor in Yugoslavia is provided by BOGDAN DENITCH. Yugoslav sociopolitical conditions, including labor relations, significantly differ from the rest of Eastern Europe. Specifically, the Yugoslav League of Communists takes less direct responsibility for day to day economic decisions, and hence for the settlement of worker–management disputes, than other East European communist parties do. The result of this policy has been a conscious decision to grant workers a role in managing the economy on the local level and to allow the workers, however grudgingly, the practice, if not the right, to strike. Indeed, two of the important characteristics of Yugoslav society today are the so-called self-management system, signified by the workers' councils, and the increasing number of strikes which are openly and frequently analyzed in books and articles by Yugoslav social scientists.

According to JAN F. TRISKA, strikes in Soviet-dominated Eastern Europe reveal a deep, progressive alienation between the social forces in postindustrial socialist societies and obsolete political structures. Socialism has not abolished class antagonism, economic oppression and class struggle, because it has failed to update and accommodate the functional requisites of its own development. Soviet policy choices in Eastern Europe are limited by Soviet fear of social consequences of political change in the area. And that has been the Soviet dilemma all along: how to deal with political change without harming the Soviet-type socialist order in Eastern Europe. In the future, given the multiple pressures for change – workers' restiveness, nationalism, economic scarcities, and human rights activisim and intellectual dissidents, to name the major ones – the Soviet Union may well experience for the first time a serious sustained threat to its role in Eastern Europe.

CHARLES GATI seeks to analyze the evolution of Western policies and alternative approaches toward Eastern Europe in general and toward the region's industrial proletariat in particular. He provides a survey and an evaluation of the policies and dilemmas of the governments of the United States and of Western Europe as well as such non-governmental institutions as labor unions and the West European communist parties. He offers the conclusion that, while the East European workers' struggle for independent trade unions and improved living conditions has brought Western applause and genuine expressions of solidarity, Western governments are none the less committed to pursuing the 'higher' goal of détente with the Soviet Union, the presumed precondition of which is the stability of Eastern Europe.

1 Industrial Proletariat in Comparative Perspective

SEYMOUR MARTIN LIPSET

Introduction

Much of the recent discussion of the politics of advanced industrial or postindustrial societies has focused on the emergence of an oppositionist intelligentsia, one based on the well-educated strata, which resembles in its behavior that of the intelligentsia of the Czarist Empire or the less developed nations. This group seemingly has become the most dynamic agent of change, taking over the role assigned by Marxism for the proletariat. Writing in 1960, C. Wright Mills sharply criticized those who continue to regard the working class as a continuing agency of radical change. He minced no words in pointing to 'the really impressive historical evidence that now stands against this expectation', 'a legacy from Victorian Marxism that is now quite unrealistic'. He proposed that those on the left direct their attention to 'the cultural apparatus, the intellectuals – as a possible, immediate, radical agency of change' (Mills, 1970, p. 256).

The loss of faith in the working class of technologically advanced society created by their relative political passivity, ironically, has been countered by the behavior of workers in Eastern Europe, from the revolt in the German Democratic Republic in 1953 to the Polish strikes of 1980. To what extent do Marxian beliefs about the relationship between economic and political developments and the proletariat's struggle to achieve socialism hold up in the late twentieth century? To evaluate the usefulness of Marxian analysis, it is necessary to distinguish between Marx as a chiliastic revolutionary, convinced of the outcome of the class struggle under capitalism, and Marx the sociologist, whose propositions and analytic methodology still furnish important insights, even though events have sharply challenged his political expectations.

To do this involves looking at class politics in relation to industrialization, assuming that the stratification system and the class struggle are deeply affected by the technological period at hand, whether it be preindustrial, industrial, or, as many countries are today, postindustrial. The chapter first deals with Marxist assumptions about the relationship of economic development to the politics of industrial nations. It then turns to a discussion of the effects of 'postindustrial' technology on political conflict. These sections are followed by an examination of some consequences of inequality in socialist nations.

Historical Materialism and the Class Struggle

Marx's concept of historical materialism is central to his theory of social change. It assumes that the economic and technological forces are primary, or the base, and that politics and values are functionally derivative, or the superstructure. Given this postulate, he believed that the socialist movement, and ultimately the proletarian revolution, would develop with the growth of capitalist industrialization. The common experience of economic exploitation would lead the workers to class consciousness and to the realization that they must join together to overthrow capitalism. The prediction that socialism was inevitable rested on the further belief that the workers would become the large majority of industrial society, and that once this majority became class-conscious it would necessarily triumph. Of course the argument was buttressed by Marx's economics which held that capitalism, as an economic system, would break down once it had brought society to a high level of industrialization.

Following this logic, Marx believed that the most developed society should have the most advanced set of class and political relationships. As he put it in the *Capital,* 'The country that is more developed industrially only shows, to the less developed, the image of its own future' (Marx, 1958, pp. 8–9). This meant that socialism as a movement and ultimately as a social system would emerge most strongly and triumph first in the most developed capitalist country, which, from the late nineteenth century on, has been the United States.

Many Marxists, therefore, repeatedly looked to America as the country that would show others the way to socialism, in spite of the glaring weakness of socialist parties in the United States. As Howard Quint points out, they 'found the United States, of all the countries in the world, most ripe for socialism, not only in the light of Marxian law of economic development, but also by the express opinion of Friedrick Engels' (Quint, 1953, p. 380). Karl Kautsky, considered the leading Marxist theoretician in the German Social Democratic Party, announced in 1902 that 'America shows us our future, in so far as one country can reveal it at all to another'. He elaborated this view in 1910, anticipating the 'sharpening of class conflict more strongly' there than anywhere else (Moore, 1970, pp. 58, 102). The British Marxist H. M. Hyndman noted in 1904 that 'just as North America is to-day the most advanced country, economically and socially, so it will be the first in which Socialism will find open and legal expression' (Moore, p. 77). Werner Sombart emphasized this point in his classic book on American socialism written in 1906:

If . . . modern socialism follows as a necessary reaction to capitalism, the country with the most advanced capitalist development, namely the United States, would at the same time be the one providing the classic case of Socialism, and its working class would be supporters of the most radical of Socialist movements. (Sombart, 1976, p. 15)

Maxim Gorki, who supported the Bolsheviks from 1903 on, wrote in 1906 of his conviction that 'socialism would be realized in the United States before any other country in the world' (Good, 1979, p. 231). August Bebel, the political leader of the German Social Democrats, in an interview in the American socialist paper, *Appeal to Reason,* stated unequivocally in 1907, 'You Americans will be the first to usher in a Socialist Republic'. His belief, at a time when his party was already a mass movement with many elected members of the Reichstag, and the American Socialist Party had secured less than 2 percent of the vote, was based on the fact that the United States was 'far ahead of Germany in industrial development'. He reiterated this opinion in a second interview in 1912, when the discrepancy between the strength of the two movements was even greater, saying that America would 'be the first nation to declare a Co-operative Commonwealth' (Moore, 1970, pp. 78–9). The French socialist Paul Lefargue, who was also Marx's son-in-law, paraphrased Marx on the flyleaf of his book on America by asserting that 'the most industrially advanced country shows to those who follow it on the industrial ladder the image of their own future' (Moore, p. 91).

American Marxists, though perhaps more aware of the problems facing their movement than were their European comrades, also recognized that the assumptions of historical materialism required that the United States should be in the lead (Quint, 1953, pp. 380–81). Thus, at the 1904 Amsterdam Congress of the Socialist International, which was attended by representatives of much stronger European parties, the leader of the Socialist Labor Party, Daniel De Leon, regarded by Lenin as the one creative American Marxist theorist, reported that 'taking into consideration only certain cardinal principles, the conclusion cannot be escaped that America is the theatre where the crest of capitalism would first be shorn by the falchion of socialism' (De Leon, 1904, p. 133). Shortly thereafter, De Leon proclaimed to the 1906 convention of the Industrial Workers of the World (IWW): 'If my reading of history is correct, the prophecy of Marx will be fulfilled and America will ring the downfall of capitalism the world over' (Young, 1976, p. 344).

The desire to see their theoretical anticipations confirmed led Marxists to draw enthusiastic, but inevitably exaggerated, conclusions that the American workers were finally awakening and that a mass socialist movement was on its way. Yet, these expectations came to naught. Max Beer, whose fifty-year career in international socialism included participation in the Austrian, German and British parties, described the anxiety and embarrassment created by the weakness of socialism in America before World War I:

The attitude of American Labour appeared to stand out as a living contradiction of the Marxian theory that the concentration of capitalist production, and attendant proletarization of the masses,

was necessarily bound to lead to class struggles and to the formation
of an independent Labour movement with Socialist aims and ends . . .
Was the generalization faulty, or were there forces in operation that
neutralized it? (Beer, 1935, pp. 109–10)

The problem, summed up by Beer, is still present, although since 1917 and
the Russian Revolution there has been little discussion of the implications
for Marxist theory of the weakness of socialism in the United States. In
effect, latter-day Marxists have simply chosen to ignore the clear
implications of historical materialism. One exception was Leon Trotsky,
who, in an essay on Marxism written for an American audience in 1939,
explicitly faced up to the issue. He quoted Marx's statement that the most
developed country 'only shows to the less developed the image of its own
future' and then wrote, 'Under no circumstances can this thought be taken
literally' (Trotsky, 1939, pp. 38–9). (As we have seen, Marxists did take it
literally before 1917.)

If we consider the logic implicit in an apolitical sociological Marxism
and return to the proposition that the most advanced country shows to the
less developed ones the image of their own future, then it should follow that
the social, political and ideological relationships which actually have
emerged in the United States should show to other countries how they will
develop. American politics, far from being backward and behind the
politics of Europe, actually must be regarded as more advanced. Other
countries should begin to resemble the United States as they become
industrialized and affluent, rather than America take on the forms of less
industrialized and poorer countries.

This is not the place to go into an analysis of 'Why no socialism in the
United States', a topic I have elaborated on elsewhere (Lipset, 1976, 1977,
1979). It is worth noting, however, that the evidence and arguments
presented by a large number of scholars suggest that socialist class politics,
as it developed in Europe, was less an outgrowth of capitalist social
relations than of preindustrial, feudal society, which explicitly structured
relationships according to fixed, almost hereditary, social classes. Hence,
the emerging working class reacted to the political world in such terms.
Walter Dean Burnham has aptly summarized this overall thesis: 'No
feudalism, no socialism: with these four words one can summarize the basic
sociocultural realities that underlie American electoral politics in the
industrial era' (Burnham, 1974, p. 718).

The severe social strains of early rapid industrialization in societies that
took class for granted brought about working-class political action. And as
Lenin, Kautsky, and others (Lenin, n.d., p. 51; Moore, 1970, p. 110; Lipset,
1977, pp. 58–9) have commented, many of the European working-class
parties came into being in the struggle for democracy, a factor absent in the
American case, where the workers benefited from the 'free gift of the ballot'
(Commons, 1926, p. 5; Perlman, 1928, pp. 167–8).

As the industrial nations thrived economically, the rigid preindustrial
social class lines gradually broke down in most of Europe. This
development weakened the correlation between class position and party

allegiance (Abramson, 1971; Butler and Stokes, 1976; Hildebrandt and Dalton, 1978). The socialist parties moved away from Marxism to become more 'catch-all' in order to appeal across class lines, especially to the burgeoning new middle class. This phenomenon has been documented for many European socialist and social democratic parties (Kirchheimer, 1966; von Beyme, 1978; Minkin, 1978; Myers, 1970; Hancock, 1972).

In fact, it is possible to argue that the assumptions of an apolitical historical Marxism have been borne out; the more explicit forms of class consciousness that existed in Europe have been declining, and class is less important as a source of political struggle in advanced industrial society than it once was. Figure 1.1 shows the trend in class voting for Sweden, Germany, Great Britain and the United States from 1952 to 1980. The Alford Index used here is the difference between the proportions of the manual workers and the non-manual workers who vote for the left party (Alford, 1963). Therefore, the higher the number, the greater is the correlation between class and party preference. As Figure 1.1 documents, there has been a discernible decline in class voting across a number of advanced industrial countries.

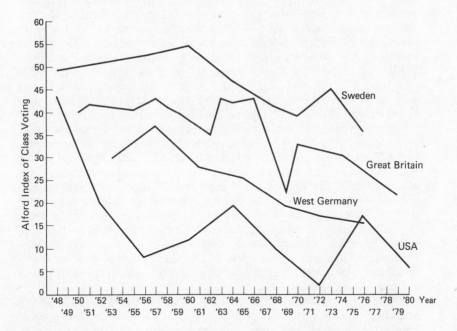

Figure 1.1　*The trend in class voting in four Western democracies, 1948–80.*

Sources: British Data 1950–70, Books and Reynolds (1975); British Data 1974, 1979, calculated from Finer (1980).
Swedish Data, Stephens (1980).
German Data, Hildebrandt and Dalton (1978).
American Data, 1948–72, Abramson (1978); American Data 1976–80 calculated from results of CBS–*New York Times* Election Day Exit Polls.

Writing in the mid-1960s the German-American Marxist Herbert Marcuse emphasized that the historical record indicated that affluent capitalism had eliminated all but the slightest possibility for radical protest from the working class. He commented that,

> in the capitalist world, there are still the basic classes [capitalists and workers] . . . but an over riding interest in the preservation and improvement of the industrial *status quo* unites the former antagonists in the most advanced areas of contemporary society. (Marcuse, 1964, pp. xii–xiii)

French Marxists Lucien Goldman and Henri Lefebvre criticized Marcuse, arguing that his interpretation was not 'correct as far as it applies to the European countries; but . . . it is possible that his analysis might very well be true of America'. Marcuse replied with the classic Marxist historical materialist position, 'that, since the United States is economically more advanced than the European countries, it cannot be long before the phenomena . . . spread to western Europe' (Mallet, 1975, p. 48).

Of course, one may point to the fact that parties which call themselves Marxist hold power in many countries, and there are still mass 'Marxist' (communist) parties in some Western industrialized countries. But as we know, communist revolutions have succeeded in preindustrial, agrarian societies – in Czarist Russia, in China, in Vietnam. The large communist parties of Europe took root primarily in what were then the more economically backward nations of Southern Europe, especially France and Italy. Marxism clearly failed or declined greatly in the more industrialized nations of Northern Europe.

No crueler joke has been played in history, and no theory has been more confounded, than that of Marxism, as it became the banner for movements in predominantly rural societies. As Marcuse stressed in 1969, 'revolution is not on the agenda' of the advanced Western industrial states, while the combination of the necessary 'subjective factor' (political consciousness) and the 'objective factor' ('the support and participation of the class which is at the base of production') only 'coincide in large areas of the Third World' (Marcuse, 1969, p. 56). Marx's fundamental premise has been totally refuted by history. Regimes identified as socialist or communist have come to power on the shoulders of the peasants of poor under-developed economies. Socialist revolutions have occurred, but they have not been Marx's revolutions.

It should be noted, of course, that Marx (and others) was right in assuming that occupational position would be a major determinant of political orientation and class organization in industrial society. In all democratic nations, including the United States, there has been a correlation between socioeconomic status and political beliefs and voting (Lipset, 1981). The less privileged have supported parties that have stood for greater equality and protection against the strains of a free enterprise economy through government intervention. Trade unions have gained strength in all industrialized nations. The state has become more powerful and has used its power to redistribute wealth and income. But such politics is not Marxist politics. The presence of parties and unions representing the less privileged in democratic politics has served to stabilize these societies, to help win the allegiance of the proletariat to their national systems. To paraphrase Disraeli, workers have been 'angels in marble', prospective supporters rather than the 'gravediggers of capitalism' (McKenzie and Silver, 1968, p. ii; Korpi, 1978, pp. 1–2).

Postindustrial Society

The changes in the class and political relations of developed societies may be analyzed within the framework of an apolitical Marxism, that is, the assumption that the level of technology will determine their forms. Some contemporary analysts have suggested that these systems are passing into a new stage, which, for want of a better name, they call postindustrial (Bell, 1973; Touraine, 1971; Gershuny, 1978).

These societies are postindustrial because the trends analyzed by Marx – increasing involvement of the labor force in the industrial productive apparatus, the growth of factories, large farms, etc. – have ended. Tertiary service occupations rather than production jobs are growing rapidly. The proportion and, in some countries, the absolute number of manual workers is declining. The occupations that are expanding are white-collar, technical, professional, scientific and service oriented. The class structure now resembles a diamond bulging at the middle much more than a pyramid. High levels of education are needed for such societies and the number of students has increased many times. Education, science and intellectual activities have become more important.

Western scholars such as Daniel Bell, Zbigniew Brzezinski, John Kenneth Galbraith and Alain Touraine, and Eastern scholars such as Radovan Richta and his associates in the Czechoslovak Academy of Sciences, and Soviet analysts such as P. N. Fedoseev and V. Kosolapov, have stressed the extent to which theoretical and scientific knowledge have become the principal source of social and economic change, altering social structure, values and *mores*, developments that have given considerable prestige and power to the scientific technological elites (Galbraith, 1958, 1967; Bell, 1973; Brzezinski, 1970; Touraine, 1971; Gershuny, 1978; Richta *et al.,* 1968; Gouldner, 1979; Bruce-Briggs, 1979). Soviet scholars and political leaders speak of the Scientific-Technological Revolution, a concept closely akin to that of the postindustrial society (Ferkiss, 1979, pp. 97–9). In the words of the Russian sociologist Fedoseev, it 'is a sweeping qualitative transformation of productive forces as a result of science being made the principal factor in the development of social production' (Fedoseev, 1975, p. 152; Ferkiss, 1979, p. 97). Richta *et al.* noted in 1968 that

science is emerging as the leading variable in the national economy . . .
There are signs of a new type of growth, with a new dynamic

stemming from continual structural changes in the productive forces, with the amount of means of production and manpower becoming less important than their changing quality and degree of utilization. (Richta *et al.,* 1968, p. 39)

They pointed to 'a relative decline in the amount of labor absorbed by industry and associated activities' and the prospect that the tertiary sector will encompass 40–60 percent of the national labor force in industrial countries in the coming decades, as is already the case in the United States (Richta *et al.,* pp. 120–24; Cameron, 1976, pp. 17–47; La Porte and Abrams, 1976, pp. 28–36; Gershuny, 1978, pp. 92–136; Gouldner, 1979, p. 15; Pollard, 1979, pp. 17–47). Touraine, though still a supporter of left-wing causes in France, suggests that the basis of power in the West has changed as a result of the trends. 'If property was the criterion of membership in the former dominant class, the new dominant class is defined by knowledge and a certain level of education' (Touraine, 1971, p. 51; Gouldner, 1979, p. 83).

Much of the analysis of postindustrial society may be seen as congruent with, or derivative from, the Marxist orientation of historical materialism, which is based on the methodological premise that the principal determining factor in social development is change in the technological structure, that the cultural and political superstructures vary with level of technology (Ferkiss, 1979, pp. 66–8). This is not surprising, since a number of the key figures in this approach are socialists or neo-Marxists, such as Daniel Bell, John Kenneth Galbraith, Alain Touraine and Radovan Richta. The emerging strata of postindustrialism – whose roots are in the university, the scientific and intellectual worlds, and who are heavily represented in the public sectors and in the professions – have developed their own distinctive values. According to Ronald Inglehart, these 'postmaterialist' values (labeled 'postbourgeois' in his original formulation) are related to 'self-actualization' needs (aesthetic, intellectual, belonging and esteem). These values manifest themselves in a desire for a less impersonal, cleaner, more cultured society, a freer personal life, and democratization of political work and community life. Such concerns run counter to those that dominate among the traditional classes of industrial society, which are more preoccupied with satisfying material needs, namely, sustenance and safety. For people with these objectives, the most salient concerns are a high standard of living, a stable economy, economic growth, an enduring family life, fighting crime and maintaining order (Inglehart, 1971, 1977, 1979).

Another student of changes in values, Scott Flanagan, has reconceptualized and broadened the distinctions. He suggests that advanced technology has led to change from traditional consciousness to libertarian consciousness, shifting 'along four dimensions: frugality versus self-indulgence, pietism versus secularism, conformity versus independence and devotion to authority versus self-assertiveness' (Flanagan, 1980, p. 274). Inglehart has also noted that these value changes are related to the general climate of affluence and absence of major wars.

The generations that came of age during the post-World War II era hold vastly different values from the previous cohorts, who were reared in economic scarcity and experienced severe economic depressions and international conflicts. While there is a generational effect, postbourgeois values are clearly much more common among better-educated and wealthier individuals (Inglehart, 1971, 1979).

These formulations are important, although some of their assumptions about the decline of materialistic concerns may be questioned. Alan Marsh, in an analysis of British data, finds that the postmaterialists are not personally antimaterialistic. His research shows no differences between the materialists and the postbourgeois on concerns about 'not having enough money, or financial debt, or needing extra income'. What differentiates the two groups for Marsh is simply their political ideologies, not their attitudes toward materialism. 'Postbourgeois groups', notes Marsh, 'are distinguished from Acquisitives by their relative youth, wealth, and education *and by their concern for ideology'* (1975, p. 28).

The Politics of Postindustrialism

Regardless of what we call this change in orientations, it has profoundly affected the political arena. As Inglehart has stated,

> The political implications of these hypotheses are significant. First, they imply that rising prosperity would not bring an end to political conflict, as the 'End of Ideology' thesis seemed to promise – even though this thesis was partially correct, in that rising prosperity apparently did bring a decline in traditional forms of social class conflict. What this thesis failed to anticipate, however, was that new grounds for conflict are likely to emerge, as new goals come to the fore. (Inglehart, 1979, pp. 210–11).

The basic political division of industrial society was materialist, a struggle over the distribution of the wealth and income that exists side by side with the continuing religious, ethnic and regional conflicts surviving from the preindustrial world (Lipset and Rokkan, 1967). But postindustrial politics is increasingly concerned with non-economic or social issues – a clean environment, a better culture, equal status for women and minorities, the quality of education, international relations, greater democratization, and a more permissive morality, particularly as affecting familial and sexual issues.

These concerns have produced new bases for political cleavage which vary from those of industrial society and have given rise to a variety of 'single-issue' protest movements. Since the existing political parties have found it difficult to link positions on the new issues to their traditional socioeconomic bases of support, party loyalties and even rates of voting participation have declined in many countries. In effect, cross-pressures deriving from differential commitments to economic and social values have reduced the salience of loyalty to parties, previously tied largely to the structural sources of cleavage in industrial society.

The reform elements concerned with postmaterialist or social issues largely derive their strength not from the workers and the less privileged, the social base of the left in industrial society, but from segments of the well-educated, and affluent, students, academics, journalists, professionals and civil servants. The New Left, the New Politics, the Green parties, receive their support from such strata. Most workers, on the other hand, remain concerned with material questions. Less educated, less cosmopolitan, less affluent, less secure, they are also more traditional, more conservative in their social views.

There are now two lefts, the materialist and the postmaterialist, which are rooted in different classes. A conflict of interest has emerged between them with respect to the consequences of policies that affect economic growth. The materialist left wants an ever-growing pie so the less privileged can have more, while the postmaterialists are more interested in the quality of life. As black political scientist Willard Johnson argues, the postmaterialist left

> is guilty of debating the issues in terms of values that, for all their humaneness, ignore the concerns of the poor . . . No doubt their concerns feed on a genuine consideration for the quality of life, but they seem to me mistaken about the contribution material goods can make to it. (Johnson, 1973, p. 174)

Or, as the late Anthony Crosland, Cabinet member in various British Labour governments, contended, those who seek to limit growth to protect the environment are 'kindly and dedicated people. But they are affluent, and fundamentally, though of course not consciously, they want to kick the ladder down behind them' (Crosland, 1974, pp. 77–8).

Both lefts are often in the same party, democratic, social democratic, even communist, as in Italy, but they have different views and interests. One commentator sees a parallel between these two lefts and the conflict between Marx and the utopian socialists; that is, they both favor equality but dispute over the role of economic development in attaining it (Watts, 1979). The New Politics intelligentsia does not like trade unions which, like business, it considers materialistic rather than public-interested. Some workers move right as a result, over to more conservative groupings which espouse growth, a competitive mobile society, and retain beliefs in traditional social values. The left, however, picks up support from the growing ranks of the intelligentsia. Thus, as mentioned earlier, the correlations between class and party voting have been reduced.

In line with the classic logic of historical materialism, as the most developed nation the United States should be among the first to exhibit the characteristic politics of postindustrialism. The record would seem to sustain the assumption. As the French political analyst Jean-François Revel pointed out in 1971,

one of the most striking features of the past decade is that the only
new revolutionary stirrings in the world have had their origin in the
United States . . . I mean the complex of new oppositional
phenomena designated by the term 'dissent'. (Revel, 1971, p. 6)

A critical intelligentsia, based on the new middle class, emerged as early as
the 1950s, with the formation of the 'reform' movement within the
Democratic Party, and constituted the beginning of what was subsequently
labeled the New Politics. 'The appearance of significant numbers of
college-educated, socially mobile, issue-oriented voters in urban and
suburban reform clubs was noted by political observers in New York,
California, Wisconsin, Missouri and elsewhere' (Kirkpatrick, 1979, p. 43).

The 1960s witnessed the full-flowering of the New Politics in the form of
opposition to the Vietnam War, struggles for civil rights, women's and
gays' liberation, and environmentalism, as well as the emergence of new
lifestyles. Jeane Kirkpatrick emphasizes the way

the involvement of basic cultural symbols in the political arena has
become a regular feature of our politics. As *avant garde* culture
spread through rising college enrollments, the electronic media, and
mass-circulation magazines, anti-bourgeois attitudes . . . became the
bases of the anti-establishment politics of the 1960s . . . It is now clear
that the assault on the traditional culture was mounted by young and
not-so-young representatives of the relatively privileged classes,
while the basic institutions of the society were defended by less-
prosperous, less-educated, lower-status citizens. (Kirkpatrick, 1979,
p. 44-5)

The conflict between the New Politics left and the traditional working-
class-based left has occurred largely within the Democratic Party. Its
defeats in the presidential elections of 1968 and 1972 can be attributed in
part to the split between the old left and new left. As noted in Figure 1.1,
class voting in the United States fell in 1952 and 1956, rose in 1960 and
1964, declined to an almost negligible level in 1968 and 1972, increased in
1976 and fell off again in 1980. Since 1952, the Democrats have won every
election in which class voting has increased. In 1952 and 1956, the defeated
Democratic candidate for President was Adlai Stevenson, who has often
been called the initiator of the New Politics phenomenon in America. He
consciously sought to avoid the New Deal economic and class conflict
issues and emphasized cultural and social concerns.

Class voting moved up somewhat in 1960, largely reflecting John F.
Kennedy's special appeal to less-privileged Catholic ethnic voters. It rose
dramatically in 1964, when Senator Goldwater, the Republican nominee,
advocated repeal of many of the welfare state and pro-trade union policies,
while Lyndon Johnson was emphasizing New Deal reform measures. In
1968 Hubert Humphrey, a New Dealer, was the Democratic candidate for
the Presidency, but he lost votes to the left and the right because of the
saliency of non-economic issues. Many blue-collar voters supported

George Wallace, reacting against Humphrey's stand on civil rights, while the New Politics left, who had voted for Eugene McCarthy or Bobby Kennedy in the primaries, refused to back Humphrey because of his lack of commitment to ending the war in Vietnam, and his links to the old politics.

These factors continued to affect electoral behaviour in the ensuing decade. In 1972 the New Politics left won the Democratic Party nomination for its candidate George McGovern, but was defeated soundly in the general election. McGovern was the first Democratic Presidential nominee since the 1920s not to receive the support of the labor movement, as blue-collar voters deserted the Democrats to vote for Richard Nixon, who campaigned for traditional values and law and order. The split between the two lefts in the Democratic Party can be seen in the epithet the Humphrey trade union-based wing of the party circulated, depicting McGovern as the candidate of 'amnesty, abortion and acid'. Four years later, however, the Democrats were able to win back the White House, when both major parties nominated candidates who were identified as social conservatives. Thus, many workers who had voted previously for Nixon or Wallace returned to the Democratic line to support Jimmy Carter.

The Democratic nomination contest in 1980 was, in some part, a fight between Jimmy Carter, viewed as socially conservative, and a New Politics challenger, Edward Kennedy, who also sought to appeal to workers and minorities on economic issues. The opinion surveys reported a strong relationship between socioeconomic status and candidate preference, with the less privileged and the older voters supporting the incumbent and the more affluent, better-educated and younger people backing his opponent. The postmaterialist elements found both major party nominees, Reagan and Carter, objectionable. As of mid-summer 1980, they were supporting an independent alternative, John Anderson, whose campaign stressed social liberalism. In a full-page advertisement in the *New York Times* of 27 June 1980 (p. 22E), the Anderson campaign organization called for support because of their candidate's record on five issues: protecting the environment, civil rights, the Equal Rights Amendment, federal funds for abortions for the poor and reduction of excessive government regulations. The opinion polls reported that Anderson's strength (around 22 percent in July) consisted largely of college graduates, professionals, Jews and self-identified liberals (Ladd and Ferree, 1980). Survey data also indicated that Anderson's followers were much more socially liberal than Carter's supporters. The trade unions, on the other hand, were strongly opposed to Anderson, and endorsed the Democratic nominee, whose strength came disproportionately from the older, less-educated, poorer and working-class sections of the population.

In the 1980 elections themselves, class factors once again became less important as Anderson's support dropped off rapidly, following a pattern typical of third party candidates in the United States. Differences in party orientation toward social issues were more important than in 1976. The Republicans explicitly rejected many of the social programs of the New Politics, the Equal Rights Amendment, government financing of abortions for poor people, and measures such as busing designed to foster racial integration. Ronald Reagan linked his campaign to the efforts of highly moralistic evangelical religious groups opposing politicans who favored the new social permissiveness.

Although Jimmy Carter tried to avoid being identified with the social policies advocated by the New Politics wing of his party, he could not openly repudiate them and hope to retain their support. Hence, social issues played a somewhat greater role in the outcome of the 1980 election than they had four years earlier.

As Revel has stressed, the new American style of activism, single-issue movements and radical cultural politics spread during the 1960s to other parts of the developed world, which were entering the stage of postindustrialism. Campus-based protest occurred in all the European countries. Sizeable left-wing tendencies rooted in the new middle-class groups challenged the moderate union-based leadership of the socialist parties. But these developments were

> imitations of the American prototype, or extensions of it, and subsequent to it. European dissenters, who represent the only force which has been able to rouse both the Left and the Right, the East and the West, from their academic torpor, are the disciples of the American movements. (Revel, 1971, pp. 6–7)

In Sweden, the Social Democrats, who actively pursue pro-growth measures as the best way to achieve a better, more equitable world, have been weakened by the nuclear power debate. In the late 1970s, while a number of intellectuals and the youth within the party were anti-nuclear, the trade unions adamantly favored building more nuclear power plants (Zetterberg, 1978, p. 35). This division seriously hampered the party's election efforts, thus contributing to its first defeat in forty-four years. The principal victor in terms of electoral gains was the Centre Party, the most active anti-growth, anti-nuclear party. A number of analysts, both journalists and scholars, attributed the defeat to the Social Democrats' support of nuclear power (Abrahamson, 1979, pp. 30–31; Korpi, 1978, pp. 90, 271, 306, 330–31). Hans Zetterberg has summarized the problem that nuclear power posed for the Social Democrats:

> Swedish voters had difficulty fitting the atom power issue into their habitual political patterns of thought. Young leftists considered that the Centre Party atom power policy lay to the left of the Social Democrats. The usual left–right line-up between the parties broke down on the atom power issue: Centre took a left view and the Social Democrats a more rightist one. (Zetterberg, 1978, p. 36)

This conflict has yet to subside. The Social Democrats remained divided during the nuclear power referendum campaign in March 1980. A number of leading party intellectuals openly supported the most anti-nuclear alternative on the ballot, siding with the Centre Party. This division within the left has affected support for the labor movement. A general strike called by the labor federation (LO), in May 1980, was supported by only 25 percent of those polled in a national survey, although the Social Democratic and Communist vote is normally close to 50 percent. Political observers reported that reactions to the strike were affected by the pronuclear role of the labor movement in the referendum debate. At the height of the strike a leading left-wing intellectual and environmentalist published an article in the country's major newspaper criticizing the union movement for its crass materialism, for engaging in 'nothing more than a bid for a still higher living standard in a country already boasting one of the world's highest' (Noble, 1980, p. 1).

In France, the difference between the two lefts was in many ways responsible for the collapse of the *Union de la Gauche* and its *Programme Commun* in the 1970s. Initially conflicts over postmaterialist issues made the forming of a coalition among leftist parties difficult. The socialists and the CFDT union, both of which gained many supporters among the new middle class, were extremely critical of the communists and the Common Program. The main points of disagreement surrounded the role of the state and nationalization in furthering the interests of the working class, with the CFDT taking the position that the communists were 'much too state-oriented, the *Programme Commun* presupposes that a decisive social and political change will result merely from the nationalization of the leading companies by the state'. They also differed about growth:

> The *Programme Commun,* states the CFDT, is based upon the same logic as the type of economic growth proposed by the capitalist theorists: the exclusive criteria of a high level of production and profit. Now since 1970, the CFDT has come out in favour of a 'new type of growth' which is more qualitative than quantitative. (Lavau, 1978, p. 453)

While the socialists and communists maintained an uneasy alliance until the election in 1978, these differences proved fatal to the Union of the Left. Jean-Louis Moynet, a secretary of the communist-dominated CGT union, explained the electoral failure of the communists as flowing from 'the stubbornness and intransigency of the Communists and the CGT concerning the minimum wage, nationalizations, or even concerning their lack of interest in such issues as women's rights, ecology, the nuclear threat and education' (Lavau, p. 451). A French communist historian, Jean Ellenstein, also argued in 1978 that his party had lost support because of its failure to emphasize the social issues. He noted that prospective supporters

> have not always been at ease with the 'proletarian' style adopted by the Communist Party in its electoral campaign . . . They are increasingly concerned with qualitative problems, even if some quantitative problems continue to exist. ('Editorial', 1978, p. 264)

A study of German electoral behavior points to similar phenomena in that country. During the Weimar Republic and in West Germany in the

1950s, traditional class divisions determined the support for left and right parties, while 'the issues which divided the groups were primarily economy and security related'. Starting in the 1960s, the new middle class, civil servants and salaried people, developed 'a liberal position on New Politics [social] issues', while the old middle class, the self-employed, remained conservative on 'the New as well as the Old [materialistic] Politics'. The workers, however, began to 'move in the opposite direction from the new middle-class, from a Left stance in the conflicts of the Old Politics, to a more conservative position on the New Politics issues'. Hildebrandt and Dalton anticipate that 'as postmaterialist concerns and values become more predominant in politics and more salient to growing portions of the German electorate, the traditional bourgeois/proletariat cleavage should continue to decline in importance and clarity' (Hildebrandt and Dalton, 1978, pp. 87–9).

Comparable processes have been at work in Japan, which has moved more rapidly than other countries from a preindustrial to an industrial to a postindustrial society. Many Japanese, although experiencing the advantages of rapid growth, have become increasingly disturbed by its social costs. As of 1971,

> seven times as many people in Japan regarded environmental pollution as the top-priority task for the nation as those who considered further economic growth the most important national business. The number of consumer protests . . . rose twenty-seven fold between 1962 and 1970, and protest and petitions about pollution doubled during a recent three-year period. (Tsurutani, 1976, p. 105).

The *benefits* of successful industrialization, as Taketsugu Tsurutani points out, are selective and class-related, while 'the *costs* of industrialism . . . tend to be egalitarian, catholic, indiscriminate, hence cross-stratal in nature' (Tsurutani, 1977, p. 48):

> Indeed, petrochemical smog, for instance, does not know the difference between upper-middle class children and working-class children . . . the rich and the not-so-rich alike love fish in Japan, but fish, in all too many cases, are poisoned by chemical waste that industrial plants so callously disposed of into all convenient bodies of water. (p. 50)

Scott Flanagan, analyzing Japanese electoral opinion data, concludes that

> the increasing importance of value issues appears, in part, to be responsible for the weakening association between occupational class and voting behavior. Since economic and value cleavages are cross-cutting, a third dimension that measures the relative salience of value issues was necessary to predict voting choices more accurately. I have shown that those voters who are cross-pressured by their value preferences and occupational class will tend to vote in line with their value preferences if they place greater stress on nonmaterial priorities

and value issues, and with their occupational class if they attach greater importance to material priorities and economic issues. (Flanagan, 1980, pp. 201–2)

Curiously, the prototypical country with respect to the breakdown in class-linked politics has been Denmark. There 'the relative number of workers voting for the Social Democrats declined from 80% in 1957 to 39% in 1973 . . . and the Conservatives who were supported by 39% of all employers in 1957 were down to 9% in . . . 1973' (Pedersen, 1979, pp. 43–4). Support for the two small New Left socialist parties 'nowadays is not . . . characterized by close communications with the working class. Voters for these parties are younger; they are better educated than the average voter; quite a few of them are still in the process of educating themselves for academic or semi-academic positions . . .' (Pedersen, 1979, p. 49). As Mogens Pedersen emphasizes:

> In a comparative perspective it can be argued that this development, the basic feature of which is the decomposition of the traditional class-based party system, does not differ from the development in other European systems, at least not with regard to the character and the direction of the change. Everywhere social class tends to lose in importance. (Pedersen, 1979, p. 44)

What do these trends portend for working-class influence and power? The answer, in part, hinges on whether postmaterialistic politics is a short-run or a long-term phenomenon. If prosperity is the most important variable in the emergence of these new values, then we can expect them to decline if the economy becomes seriously troubled. Yet evidence from West Germany suggests that even with the economic decline of the 1970s, the New Politics has a firm foundation (Hildebrandt and Dalton, 1978). As Max Kaase and Samuel Barnes argue, postmaterialism

> displays too much of a structural component, and therefore permanence, to be considered just a fad of the young. [F]uture politics will be increasingly Postmaterialist politics. [T]hat . . . does not imply that material values are not relevant; they will continue to be so. The point is that Postmaterialist values become relatively more important, and here is where we see potential sources of strain for post-industrial societies. (Kaase and Barnes, 1979, pp. 524–5)

If postmaterialist politics is a structural phenomenon related to the shifting occupational structure, support for the New Politics should increase since there is a growing number of jobs outside of the industrial sector, whose holders will presumably be more disposed to oppose growth.

But beyond the staying power of the New Left, it is important to note that the classic political division of industrial society still predominates in affecting partisan support. The electorate of the left comes largely from the working class and the more deprived, while the conservative parties are based on the more affluent strata. Organized labor has gained a new source of influence through an increasing involvement in the economic planning process in a number of advanced industrial societies (Schmitter, 1974; Coombs, 1978). Many elites in these countries currently see economic growth as their *raison d'être* and need organised labor to sustain it (Putnam, 1977). In any case, the working class will continue to maintain socioeconomic leverage through what Finer calls their 'power to disrupt' (Hayward, 1980).

It is far from certain, however, that the two lefts will oppose each other at the ballot box. Touraine believes that the new middle strata which he describes as a 'new working class' will support radical politics. He sees them as increasingly alienated, reduced in status and subject to capitalist controls, much like the proletariat. As a result they will cooperate with the manual working class (Touraine, 1971). Inglehart has also noted,

> There can be acute strains between an older Left that emphasizes economic gains for the working class, and a newer Left that is more concerned with life-style changes, with qualitative rather than quantitative gains. But both factions share a common concern with social change in an egalitarian direction, and precisely because the goal of equality appeals to different groups for different reasons, it may serve as a bond that holds the Left together. (Inglehart, 1977, p. 366)

Flanagan estimates that over the long run, the influences which press new middle-class elements to move to the left on social issues should be stronger than those which dispose working-class traditionalists to switch to the right (Flanagan, 1980, pp. 202–203).

Michael Harrington, President of the Democratic Socialist Organizing Committee in the United States, has suggested the possibility of a coalition between the two lefts. He hopes that a middle ground can be found: 'not either cancerous growth or no growth, but . . . planned growth on a human scale' (Harrington, 1980, p. 325). Certainly, not all environmental efforts are zero-sum games. Concern about pollution and toxic waste disposal, as evidenced in the Love Canal tragedy in New York, is an example of an issue that cuts across the two lefts. Indeed, some leaders in each group, realizing that they need each other for political strength, try to endorse policies of concern to the other. Environmentalists for Full Employment publicly backed both the full employment and labor law reform bills (Harrington, p. 309; Vogel, 1978, p. 70), and efforts at consumer protection have brought the unions and the New Politics together in the United States (Vogel, p. 70). Yet there remain more divisive areas than mediating ones; fundamental differences exist on such issues as foreign policy, nuclear energy, social and moral concerns, as well as the profound distrust the different types of people in the two lefts feel toward each other. In essence the future depends on the degree of flexibility and compromise shown by ideologically different groups who have the pursuit of greater equality as common ground.

Inequality under Socialism

If the Marxist theory of proletarian revolution has been confounded, and disconfirmed by the pattern of politics in different countries, it should be noted that a related aspect and prediction of historical materialism has been verified in events and processes which have occurred in the countries which call themselves socialist or communist. Marx assumed that socialism as a system, a relatively egalitarian society, could only be established in highly developed industrial nations. His premise for this was the belief that inequality, intense stratification, was a result of scarcity. Marx argued that in systems that did not produce enough economic goods for all to live well, inequality and class exploitation must exist, that the dominant position-holders in such societies would necessarily take a disproportionate share of the goods for themselves. The basic condition for equality, according to Marx, is abundance, having enough goods so that, if shared, all can live very well. The historically progressive task of capitalism was not only to create the working class, which would eventually overthrow it, but also to produce the advanced technology and affluence necessary for socialism. Hence, socialism is impossible until economic abundance exists.

Marx, as we know, wrote polemically against those who believed that socialism could occur prior to abundance. He described such socialists as 'utopians' (Marx, 1933, pp. 237–40). His brand of socialism was 'scientific' because it was premised on historical materialism, on relating social forms or systems to appropriate material conditions. Now what would happen if socialists tried to create socialism under 'utopian' conditions, if they overthrew capitalism before it had exhausted its historical mission to create an advanced affluent industrial system? His answer in *The German Ideology* was clear. In order to build socialism it is necessary to have

> a great increase in productive power, a high degree of its development . . . [T]his development of productive forces . . . is absolutely necessary as a practical premise: for the reason that without it only *want* is made general, and with *want* the struggle for necessities and all the old filthy business [the German word was 'Scheisse'] would necessarily be reproduced. (Marx and Engels, 1947, pp. 24–5)

Trotsky discussed this passage, in *The Revolution Betrayed,* in his effort to explain why Stalinism occurred and resulted in a system of intense inequality (Trotsky, 1937, pp. 56–64).

In other words, efforts to create an egalitarian society under conditions of economic scarcity must fail, must result in a new system of exploitation, of class domination. As Rosa Luxemburg described the contradiction, 'elementary conceptions of socialist politics and an insight into their historically necessary prerequisites force us to understand that under such fatal conditions even the most gigantic idealism and the most storm-tested revolutionary energy are incapable of realizing democracy and socialism but only distorted attempts at either' (Luxemburg, 1961, p. 28). This is, of course, what has happened in the less-developed countries which have become communist. They cannot be workers' states, for they are class-ridden societies. As one pair of scholars from Eastern Europe has stated it, there is merely the emergence of 'the next class' (Konrad and Szelenyi, 1979).

Karl Wittfogel has taken this analysis one step further by drawing on another category in Marx's writings, the concepts of Asiatic society and Oriental despotism (Wittfogel, 1957). Wittfogel notes that Marx described a societal system, which had existed in certain Asian states in which large irrigation works were a prime condition for agriculture. In these societies, the state rather than private property was the key source of class rule. The state became powerful and maintained control because only a strong state could establish and allocate water resources. The ruling class was the group which controlled the state. Such systems were highly centralized, despotic and sharply stratified. Using Marxist categories, Wittfogel argues that communist societies should be seen as forms of Oriental despotism; their characteristics, class and political relations, resemble those described by Marx as inherent in Asiatic systems.

Wittfogel points to indications that Lenin, who knew his Marx, was consciously worried that the Soviet Union was becoming an Oriental despotism, that he had helped to create a new exploitative regime. He quotes a speech Lenin delivered on 20 April, 1921, at the 10th Party Congress, in which he said: 'Socialism is better than capitalism, but capitalism is better than medievalism, small production, and a bureaucracy connected with the dispersed character of the small producers.' Lenin then observed that the roots of bureaucracy in the Soviet Union were 'the fragmented and dispersed character of the small producer, his poverty, the lack of culture'. To understand Lenin's implications, Wittfogel notes that 'the initiated will recall Marx's and Engels' view that self-sufficient, dispersed and isolated communities form the solid and natural foundation of Oriental despotism'. And Wittfogel concludes, 'in Aesopian language he was obviously expressing his fear that an Asiatic restoration was taking place and that a new type of Oriental despotism was in the making' (Wittfogel, 1957, pp. 399–400).

At the same 1921 party congress, Lenin advocated independent trade unions, which would have the right to strike, to protect the workers against the bureaucracy which dominated industry and the state. This suggests his concern over the potential of the new communist bureaucracy to exploit the Russian people. In a passage that the compilers of the latest official Moscow edition of his party congress speeches have seen fit to edit out, Lenin stated,

> Ours is a workers' government with a bureaucratic twist. Our present government is such that the proletariat, organized to the last man, must protect itself against it. And we must use the workers' organizations for the protection of the workers against their government. (Gordon, 1941, pp. 88–9)

Lenin, of course, cannot be exempted from responsibility for the creation of the oppressive Soviet state. He was warned by Trotsky in 1903 that his highly centralized party structure would lead to a 'pseudo-Jacobin dictatorship over the masses', which would end with the use of the 'guillotine' to eliminate dissidents. Trotsky prophesied that the Leninist seizure of power would result in a situation in which the 'organization of the Party would take the place of the Party itself; the Central Committee takes the place of the organization; and finally the dictator takes the place of the Central Committee' (Wolfe, 1955, p. 253). The martyred leader of the abortive German communist revolution, Rosa Luxemburg, anticipated in 1918 that the curtailment of the rights of opposition in the Soviet Union would result in a totally repressive society, 'in which only the bureaucracy remains as the active element' (Luxemburg, 1961, p. 76). As she noted, 'without a free and untrammelled press, without the unlimited right of association and assembly, the rule of the broad masses of the people is unthinkable' (Luxemburg, pp. 66–7).

In taking these positions Trotsky and Luxemburg were closer than Lenin to the classic Marxist orientation. Thus, Friedrich Engels had explicitly written, 'if anything has been established for certain, it is this, that our party and the working class can achieve rule only under the form of the democratic republic. This is even the *specific form* for the dictatorship of the proletariat' (Marx and Engels, 1934, p. 486). On the same page of the edition of the Marx–Engels *Correspondence* from which the Engels statement is taken, the Russian editors inserted a comment by Lenin from his book, *State and Revolution,* in which he reported that Engels had said 'the democratic republic is the *nearest approach* to the dictatorship of the proletariat'. The Stalinist editors noted that this formulation constituted a 'revision of Marxist views about democracy'. It is clear that Lenin changed Engels's formulation, possibly to deny that the specific form of a state dominated by the workers should be a democratic republic.

Thus, we see that Marx's theory of historical materialism relied on advanced industrial systems to generate the conditions under which the working class would come to power and a free, egalitarian, socialist society could flourish. Capitalism led to a highly efficient, very productive industrial society. The workers in the most industrialized countries have not turned to revolutionary socialism, however, but rather to labor party and trade union action to improve their life situation. 'Marxists', on the other hand, have taken power in preindustrialized, poverty-stricken societies and, as Marx anticipated, have revived 'the old filthy business', whether one wants to call their nations Oriental despotisms or not.

The 'New Class' in Socialist Society

The communist countries are also experiencing the strains flowing from inequality and the rapid growth of scientific and technological professions. As already demonstrated in a number of East European countries, as well as the Soviet Union itself, considerable discontent and protest exists among the well-educated strata (Richta *et al.,* 1968, p. 233; Lipset and

Dobson, 1972). Workers have engaged in strikes and in protest movements, sometimes in alliance with segments of the intelligentsia and student population, although, as the chapters in this book by Connor and Valenta indicate, there is a considerable gap in the concerns of the different strata. At the moment, however, most are in the stage of industrialization. Hence, their workers face experiences comparable to those in the West some time ago, but they lack the protection of workers' parties and unions. As a number of socialist intellectuals have recognized, they require the erection of class defense organizations to protect them against the socialist bureaucrats or the new ruling class.

At the turn of the century, a Polish revolutionary and former Marxist, Jan Machajski, 'produced what might be called a Marxist interpretation of Marxism' (Bruce-Briggs, 1979, p. 12). He argued that the triumph of socialists would bring about a society controlled by the educated classes who would exploit the underprivileged strata. And, Machajski suggested, concepts of participatory democracy, of control of the machinery of complex industrial society by the masses, were utopian and would only serve to conceal the fact that socialism would be severely stratified with respect to power and privilege (Machajski, 1937; Nomad, 1961, pp. 96–117; Nomad, 1964, pp. 103–108, 201–206; Avrich, 1965, pp. 66–75; Shatz, 1967, pp. 45–57; and Bruce-Briggs, 1979, pp. 12–14).

Some years later, in 1911, the German sociologist, Robert Michels, while still a member of the Social Democratic Party, published his classic work, *Political Parties,* which elaborated on the structural determinants of 'oligarchy' in all political parties and types of societies. He concluded that a socialist revolution would necessarily result in a

> dictatorship in the hands of those leaders who have been sufficiently astute and sufficiently powerful to grasp the sceptre of dominion in the name of socialism . . . The socialists might conquer, but not socialism, which would perish in the moment of its adherents' triumph. (Michels, 1962, pp. 348, 355)

More recently, while discussing the objectives of the postmaterialist protestors of contemporary society, Alan Marsh revived Machajski's theme that the populist slogans of radical elites are expressions of their feeling that they, rather than older dominant groups, should be in power. He argues that postmaterialist 'radicalism' is a response to the 'power-frustration experienced by many young middle-class Europeans who are excluded from the exercise of such power and from positions of high social respect'. By speaking out 'against their class interests they ... also acquire a reputation for altruism', but he suggests, congruent with Machajski's analysis of the objectives of the radical mandarins of the Czarist Empire, what they are seeking is power and status for themselves (Marsh, 1975, pp. 29–30).

These analyses, of course, parallel the interpretation which Marxists and others have given of the role of the democratic and egalitarian ideologies of the American and French Revolutions in legitimating bourgeois class rule.

Given the impossibility of abolishing the structural causes of class domination, Machajski argued that the only honest position for anyone interested in improving the position of the masses is to help them resist those in power through organizations independent of the state and dominant class. Michels also emphasized the need to help 'the masses, so that they might be enabled, within the limits of what is possible, to counteract the oligarchic tendencies'. He called for support of oppositionist movements 'as contributing to the enfeeblement of oligarchic tendencies', as long as the groups do not take power:

> Democracy is a treasure which no one will discover by deliberate search. But in continuing our search, in laboring indefatigably to discover the undiscoverable, we will perform a work which will have fertile results in a democratic sense. (Michels, 1962, pp. 368–9)

It should be noted that a few of the contemporary postmaterialists implicitly take a position close to that advocated by Machajski and Michels. Organizations such as the civic initiative groups in West Germany or Acorn in the United States seek to work with underprivileged people outside of the electoral process so that, regardless of which political party holds office, they can continue to press for increased rights and representation.

The analyses of Machajski and Michels implied that Marx was a political 'utopian' in the sense in which he, himself, used the word. They believed that the structure of large-scale society makes a non-exploitative egalitarian system impossible, that it requires a domineering class which uses its power to enhance its privileges. But at the same time, they agreed with his method of analysis. Michels explicitly accepted the Marxist materialist conception of history. As he emphasized, his own approach as elaborated in *Political Parties*

> completes that conception and reinforces it. There is no essential contradiction between the doctrine that history is the record of continued class struggles and the doctrine that class struggles invariably culminate in the creation of new oligarchies which undergo fusion with the old. The existence of a political class does not conflict with the essential content of Marxism, considered not as an economic dogma, but as a philosophy of history. (Michels, 1962, p. 354)

Although contemporary Marxists have chosen to ignore Machajski and Michels, it is worth noting that a leading theoretician of the Russian Communist Party, Nicolai Bukharin, in his book, *Historical Materialism*, published in 1925, discussed Michels's ideas and acknowledged both their intellectual importance and the possibility that Michels might turn out to be correct. Bukharin agreed that in 'the *transition period* from capitalism to socialism, i.e., the period of the proletarian dictatorship . . . there will inevitably be a tendency to "degeneration", i.e., the excretion of a leading stratum in the form of a class-germ'. But he countered Michels with the argument:

> This tendency will be retarded by two opposing tendencies; first, by the growth of the productive forces; second, by the abolition of the educational monopoly. The increasing reproduction of technologists and of organizers in general, out of the working class, will undermine the possible new class alignment. The outcome of the struggle will depend on which tendencies turn out to be stronger. (Bukharin, 1925, pp. 309–11)

The chapters in this book as well as a myriad of scholarly analyses demonstrate which tendency has won out (Lane, 1971; Parkin, 1971; Matthews, 1972; Lipset and Dobson, 1973; Yanowitch and Fisher, 1973; Lapidus, 1978; Connor, 1979; and McAuley, 1979). In the words of Tito's former second-in-command, Milovan Djilas, 'the Communist revolution, conducted in the name of doing away with classes, has resulted in the most complete authority of any single new class. Everything else is a sham and illusion' (Djilas, 1957, p. 36).

In the final year of his life, Leon Trotsky faced up to the possibility that Marxism might be a utopian doctrine, that the working class of advanced industrial societies, the countries which had the prerequisites for building socialism, were incapable of taking or holding power. If the revolution did not occur in the Western developed world, then, as his biographer and follower, Isaac Deutscher, summed up Trotsky's views,

> the Marxist view of capitalist society and socialism must be admitted to have been wrong, for Marxism had proclaimed that socialism would either be the work of the proletariat or it would not be at all. Was Marxism then just another 'ideology' or another form of the false consciousness that causes oppressed classes and their parties to believe that they struggle for their own purposes when in truth they are only promoting the interests of a new, or even of an old, ruling class? Viewed from this angle, the defeat of the pristine Bolshevism would indeed appear to be of the same order as the defeat of the Jacobins – the result of a collision between Utopia and a new social order – and Stalin's victory would present itself as a triumph of reality over illusion. (Deutscher, 1963, p. 467)

Or in Trotsky's words, if the 'proletariat should actually prove incapable of fulfilling the mission placed on it by the course of development, nothing else would remain except only to recognize that the socialist programme, based on the internal contradictions of capitalist society, ended as a Utopia' (Trotsky, 1966, p. 11).

Trotsky did not put off the test of the Marxist hypothesis to the far-off future. Rather recognizing that the record of left-wing failures in industrial societies argued for the negative, he stated unequivocally that World War II, which had just begun, presented the 'decisive test'. As Deutscher notes,

'He defined the terms of the test with painful precision . . . a matter of the next few years' (Deutscher, 1963, p. 468). If World War II did 'not lead to proletarian revolution in the West, then the place of decaying capitalism would indeed be taken not by socialism, but by a new bureaucratic and totalitarian system of exploitation', based on state power (p. 467).

Trotsky, unfortunately, was not allowed by Stalin to live long enough to react to the continued failure of Marxism in developed societies and the expansion of communist bureaucratic rule in less developed nations. He retained his faith in Marxism and the revolution through to his assassination in August 1940. His movement has continued to the present, seemingly unconcerned with the fact that the date for Trotsky's final test has long passed. Isaac Deutscher, in words reminiscent of Trotsky's own reaction to the implications of American developments for Marx's theory, describes Trotsky's specification of a decisive test of the Marxist hypothesis as 'one of those overemphatic and hyperbolic statements . . . which taken literally leads to endless confusion' (Deutscher, 1963, p. 467).

But it should be noted that Trotsky left specific advice to revolutionaries as to what they should do if Marxism turned out to be Utopian. His recommendation was the same as those proposed by Machajski and Michels, support the masses against the oppressors. 'It is self-evident that a new "minimum" programme would be required for the defense of the slaves of the totalitarian bureaucratic society' (Trotsky, 1966, p. 11).

In the contemporary world to think of 'proletarian class struggle' is to focus on the position of the workers in Eastern Europe. The 'revolution' has come and gone, and they are now beginning, in political circumstances almost inconceivable in Marx's day, to find ways in which to develop yet again, class-consciousness and class organization under the alien conditions of state socialism. Ironically, as the Polish strikes demonstrate, the usefulness of Marx's sociological insights concerning the way the social situation of the industrial proletariat enables them to organize more effectively against their oppressors than does that of any other class, has been demonstrated by events in the communist world.

Note: Chapter 1

I am deeply indebted to Stephen Stedman for research assistance and intellectual advice and to Brenda McLean for helping make the language more intelligible.

References: Chapter 1

Abrahamson, D., 'Governments fall as consensus gives way to debate', *Bulletin of the Atomic Scientists,* vol. 35, no. 9, 1979, pp. 30–7.

Abramson, P. R., 'Social class and political change in Western Europe: a cross-national longitudinal analysis', *Comparative Political Studies,* vol. 4, no. 2, 1971, pp. 131–55.

Abramson, P. R., 'Class voting in the 1976 election', *Journal of Politics,* vol. 40, no. 4, 1978, pp. 1066–72.

Alford, R., *Party and Society: The Anglo-American Democracies* (Chicago, Ill.: Rand McNally, 1963).

Avrich, P., 'What is machaevism?', *Soviet Studies,* vol. 17, no. 1, 1965, pp. 66–75.

Barnes, S. H., Kaase, M., *et al., Political Action: Mass Participation in Five Western Democracies* (Beverly Hills, Ca.: Sage, 1979).

Beer, M., *Fifty Years of International Socialism* (London: Allen & Unwin, 1935).

Bell, D., *The Coming of Post-Industrial Society* (New York: Basic Books, 1973).

von Beyme, K., 'The changing relations between trade unions and the Social Democratic Party in West Germany', *Government and Opposition,* vol. 13, no. 4, 1978, pp. 399–416.

Books, J. W. and Reynolds, J. B., 'A note on class voting in Great Britain and the United States', *Comparative Political Studies,* vol. 8, no. 3, 1975, pp. 360–75.

Bruce-Briggs, B., 'An introduction to the idea of the new class', in B. Bruce-Briggs, ed.; *The New Class* (New Brunswick, NJ: Transaction, 1979), pp. 1–19.

Brzezinski, Z., *Between Two Ages: America's Role in the Technetronic Era* (New York: Viking, 1970).

Bukharin, N., *Historical Materialism. A System of Sociology* (New York: International Publishers, 1925).

Burnham, W. D., 'The United States: the politics of heterogeneity', in R. Rose, ed., *Electoral Behaviour* (New York: Free Press, 1974).

Butler, D. and Stokes, D., *Political Change in Britain,* 2nd ed. (New York: St Martin's Press, 1976).

Cameron, D. R., 'Postindustrial change and secular realignment' (PhD dissertation University of Michigan, 1976).

Commons, J. R., 'American labor history: introduction', in J. R. Commons *et al.,* eds, *History of Labor in the United States,* Vol. I (New York: Macmillan, 1926), pp. 3–21.

Connor, W. D., *Socialism, Politics and Equality* (New York: Columbia University Press 1979).

Coombs, D., 'Trade unions and political parties in Britain, France, Italy and West Germany', *Government and Opposition,* vol. 13, no. 4, 1978, pp. 485–95.

Crosland, A., *Socialism Now* (London: Cape, 1974).

De Leon, D., *Flashlights of the Amsterdam Congress* (New York: New York Labor News, 1904).

Deutscher, I., *The Prophet Outcast* (London: Oxford University Press, 1963).

Djilas, M., *The New Class* (New York: Praeger, 1957).

'Editorial', *Government and Opposition,* vol. 13, no. 3, 1978, pp. 261–40.

Fedoseev, P. N., 'The social significance of the scientific and technological revolution', *International Social Science Journal,* vol. 27, 1975, pp. 151–62.

Ferkiss, V., 'Daniel Bell's concept of post-industrial society: theory, myth, and ideology', *Political Science Reviewer,* vol. 9, 1979, pp. 61–102.

Finer, S. E., *The Changing British Party System, 1945–1979* (Washington, D C: American Enterprise Institute, 1980).

Flanagan, S. C., 'Value change and partisan change in Japan: the silent revolution revisited', *Comparative Politics,* vol. 11, no. 3, 1979, pp. 253–79.

Flanagan, S. C., 'Value cleavages, economic cleavages, and the Japanese voter', *American Journal of Political Science,* vol. 24, no. 2, 1980, pp. 177–207.

Galbraith, J. K., *The Affluent Society* (Boston, Ma.: Houghton Mifflin, 1958).

Galbraith, J. K., *The New Industrial State* (Boston, Ma.: Houghton Mifflin, 1967).

Gershuny, J., *After Industrial Society?: The Emerging Self-service Economy* (London: Macmillan, 1978).

Good, J. E., 'Strangers in a strange land: five Russian radicals visit the United States' (PhD dissertation, Washington, DC: American University, 1979).

Gordon, M., *Workers Before and After Lenin* (New York: Dutton, 1941).

Gouldner, A. W., *The Future of Intellectuals and the Rise of the New Class* (New York: Seabury, 1979).

Hancock, M. D., *Sweden: The Politics of Post-Industrial Change* (Hinsdale, Ill.: Dryden Press, 1972).

Harrington, M., *Decade of Decision: The Crisis of the American System* (New York: Simon & Schuster, 1980).

Hayward, J., 'Trade unions and their politico-economic environments: a preliminary framework', *West European Politics,* vol. 3, no. 1, 1980, pp. 1–10.

Hildebrandt, K., and Dalton, R. I., 'The new politics: political change or sunshine politics?', in M. Kaase and K. von Beyme, eds., *Elections and Parties: Sociopolitical Change and Participation in the West German Federal Election of 1976* (Beverly Hills, Ca.: Sage, 1978), pp. 69–96.

Inglehart, R., 'The silent revolution in Europe: intergenerational change in post-industrial societies', *American Political Science Review,* vol. 65, no. 4, 1971, pp. 991–1017.

Inglehart, R., *The Silent Revolution: Changing Values and Political Styles among Western Publics* (Princeton, NJ: Princeton University Press, 1977).

Inglehart, R., 'Value priorities and socioeconomic change', in S. H. Barnes *et al.,* eds., *Political Action: Mass Participation in Five Western Democracies* (Beverly Hills, Ca.: Sage, 1979), pp. 305–43.

Johnson, W. R., 'Should the poor buy no growth?', *Daedalus,* vol. 102, no. 4, 1973, pp. 165–90.

Kaase, M. and Barnes, S. H., 'In conclusion: the future of political protest in Western democracies', in S. H. Barnes *et al,* eds, *Political Action: Mass Participation in Five Western Democracies* (Beverly Hills, Ca.: Sage, 1979), pp. 523–37.

Kirchheimer, O., 'The transformation of Western European party systems', in J. La Palombara and M. Weiner, eds, *Political Parties and Political Development* (Princeton, NJ: Princeton University Press, 1966), pp. 177–200.

Kirkpatrick, J. J., 'Politics and the new class', in B. Bruce-Briggs, ed., *The New Class?* (New Brunswick, NJ: Transaction, 1979), pp. 33–49.

Konrad, G. and Szelenyi, I., *The Intellectuals on the Road to Class Power* (New York: Harcourt, Brace, Jovanovich, 1979).

Korpi, W., *The Working Class in Welfare Capitalism: Work, Unions and Politics in Sweden* (London: Routledge & Kegan Paul, 1978).

Ladd, E. C. and Ferree, G. D., 'John Anderson: candidate of the new class?', *Public Opinion,* vol. 3, no. 3, 1980, pp. 11–15.

Lane, D., *The End of Inequality?: Stratification under State Socialism* (London: Penguin, 1971).

Lapidus, G. W., *Women in Soviet Society: Equality, Development and Social Change* (Berkeley, Ca.: University of California Press, 1978).

La Porte, T. and Abrams, C. J., 'Alternative patterns of postindustrialism: the California experience', in L. N. Lindberg, ed., *Politics and the Future of Industrial Society* (New York: McKay, 1976), pp. 19–57.

Lavau, G., 'The changing relations between trade unions and working-class parties in France', *Government and Opposition,* vol. 13, no. 4, 1978, pp. 437–58.

Lenin, V. I., *On Britain* (Moscow: Foreign Languages Publishing House, n.d.).

Lipset, S. M., 'Radicalism in North America: a comparative view of the party systems in Canada and the United States', *Transactions of the Royal Society of Canada,* series 4, vol. 14, 1976, pp. 19–55.

Lipset, S. M., 'Why no socialism in the United States?', in S. Bialer and S. Sluzar, eds, *Sources of Contemporary Radicalism,* Vol. I (Boulder, Co.: Westview, 1977), pp. 31–149, 346–63.

Lipset, S. M., 'American exceptionalism', in M. Novak, ed., *Capitalism and Socialism: A Theological Inquiry* (Washington, DC: American Enterprise Institute, 1979), pp 34–52.

Lipset, S. M., *Political Man* (Baltimore, Md: Johns Hopkins University Press, expanded edn, 1981).

Lipset, S. M. and Dobson, R. B., 'The intellectual as critic and rebel: with special reference to the United States and the Soviet Union', *Daedalus,* vol. 101, no. 2, 1972, pp. 137–98.

Lipset, S. M. and Dobson, R. B., 'Social stratification and sociology in the Soviet Union', *Survey,* vol. 88, no. 3, 1973, pp. 114–85.

Lipset, S. M. and Rokkan, S., 'Cleavage structures, party systems, and voter alignments: an introduction', in S. M. Lipset and S. Rokkan, eds, *Party Systems and Voter Alignments: Cross-National Perspectives* (New York: Free Press, 1967), pp. 1–67.

Luxemburg, R., *The Russian Revolution* (Ann Arbor, Mi.: University of Michigan Press, 1961).

McAuley, A., *Economic Welfare in the Soviet Union: Poverty, Living Standards, and Inequality* (Madison, Wi: University of Wisconsin Press, 1979).

McKenzie, R. and Silver, A., *Angels in Marble: Working Class Conservatives in Urban England* (London: Heinemann, 1968).

Machajski, J. W., 'On the expropriation of the capitalists', in V. F. Calverton, ed., *The Making of Society* (New York: Random House, 1937), pp. 427–36.

Mallet, S., *Essays on the New Working Class* (St Louis, Mo.: Telos Press, 1975).

Marcuse, H., *One-Dimensional Man* (Boston, Ma.: Beacon, 1964).

Marcuse, H., *An Essay on Liberation* (Boston, Ma.: Beacon, 1969).

Marsh, A., 'The silent revolution, value priorities, and the quality of life in Britain', *American Political Science Review,* vol. 69, no. 1, March 1975, pp. 21–30.

Marx, K., *Selected Works,* Vol. I (New York: International Publishers, 1933).

Marx, K., *Capital,* Vol I (Moscow: Foreign Languages Publishing House, 1958).

Marx, K. and Engels, F., *The German Ideology* (New York: International Publishers, 1947).

Marx, K. and Engels, F., *Writings on the Paris Commune* (New York: Monthly Review Press, 1971).

Matthews, M., *Class and Society in Soviet Russia* (New York: Walker, 1972).

Michels, R., *Political Parties: A Sociological Study of the Oligarchical Tendencies of Modern Democracy* (New York: Free Press, 1962).

Mills, C. W., *Power, Politics and People. Collected Essays of C. Wright Mills,* ed. I. L. Horowitz (New York: Oxford University Press, 1970).

Minkin, L., 'The party connection: divergence and convergence in the British labour movement', *Government and Opposition,* vol. 13, no. 4, 1978, pp. 458–85.

Moore, R. L., *European Socialists and the American Promised Land* (New York: Oxford, 1970).

Myers, F. E., 'Social class and political change in advanced industrial societies', *Comparative Politics,* vol. 2, no. 3, 1970, pp. 389–412.

Noble, D., 'Sweden struggles to end crippling strike', *Guardian* (London), 9 May, 1980, p. 1.

Nomad, M., *Aspects of Revolt* (New York: Noonday, 1961).

Nomad, M., *Political Heretics* (Ann Arbor, Mi.: University of Michigan Press, 1963).

Nomad, M., *Dreamers, Dynamics and Demagogues* (New York: Waldon, 1964).

Parkin, F., *Inequality and the Political Order* (London: McGibbon & Kee, 1971).

Pedersen, Mogens N., 'Denmark: the breakdown of a working multiparty system' (unpublished paper, Odense University, Odense, Denmark).

Perlman, S., *A Theory of the Labor Movement* (New York: Macmillan, 1928).

Pollard, S., 'The rise of the service industries and white collar employment', in B. Gustafsson, ed., *Post-Industrial Society* (New York: St Martin's Press, 1979), pp. 17–43.

Putnam, R. D., 'Elite transformation in advanced industrial societies: an empirical assessment of the theory of technocracy', *Comparative Political Studies,* vol. 10, no. 3, 1977, pp. 383–413.

Quint, H. H., *The Forging of American Socialism: Origins of the Modern Movement* (Indianapolis, Ind.: Bobbs-Merrill, 1953).

Revel, J.-F., *Without Marx or Jesus* (Garden City, NY: Doubleday, 1971).

Richta, R. *et al., Civilization at the Crossroads. Social and Human Implications of the Scientific and Technological Revolution* (White Plains, NY: International Arts and Humanities Press, 1969).

Schmitter, P., 'Still the century of corporatism?', *Review of Politics,* vol. 36, no. 1, 1974, pp. 85–131.

Shatz, M., 'Jan Waclaw Machajski: the conspiracy of the intellectuals', *Survey,* no. 62, 1967, pp. 45–57.

Sombart, W., *Why Is There No Socialism in the United States?* (White Plains, NY: International Arts and Sciences Press, 1976).

Stephens, J. D., 'Social class, contextual effects and party preference; theoretical approaches and some evidence from the Swedish case' (unpublished paper, 1980).

Touraine, A., *The Post-Industrial Society: Tomorrow's Social History: Classes, Conflicts, and Culture in the Programmed Society* (New York: Random House, 1971).

Trotsky, L., *The Revolution Betrayed: What Is the Soviet Union and Where Is It Going?* (Garden City, NY: Doubleday, Doran, 1937).

Trotsky, L., *The Living Thoughts of Karl Marx* (New York: Longmans, Green, 1939).

Trotsky, L., *In Defence of Marxism* (London: New Park Publications, 1966).

Tsurutani, T., 'Japan as a postindustrial society', in L. Lindberg, ed., *Politics and the Future of Industrial Society* (New York: McKay, 1976).

Tsurutani, T., *Political Change in Japan: Response to Postindustrial Challenge* (New York: McKay, 1977).

Vogel, D., 'The new class: conservatism's chimerical villain', *Working Papers for a New Society,* vol. 5, no. 4, 1978, pp. 68–71.

Watts, N. S. J., 'Post-material values and political change: hypotheses for comparative research' (paper presented, 2nd Annual Meeting of International Society of Political Psychology, Washington, DC, 1979).

Wittfogel, K., *Oriental Despotism* (New Haven, Cn: Yale University Press, 1957).

Wolfe, B. D., *Three Who Made a Revolution* (Boston: Beacon, 1955).

Yanowitch, M. and Fisher, W. A., *Social Stratification and Mobility in the USSR* (White Plains, NY: International Arts and Sciences Press, 1973).

Young, J. D., 'Daniel De Leon and Anglo-American socialism', *Labor History,* vol. 17, no. 3, 1976, pp. 329–51.

Zetterberg, H., 'The Swedish election of 1976' (paper presented, 9th World Congress of Sociology, Uppsala, Sweden, 1978).

2 Changing Social Structure and the Political Role of Manual Workers

PAUL M. JOHNSON

Introduction

Classical Marxist theory casts the industrial proletariat in the starring role in the drama of human history. Generated and shaped by the inexorable operation of the historical laws of motion of capitalist systems, the working class, in its struggle for its own emancipation from exploitation, was to provide the social power-base and the sense of conscious purpose whereby the capitalist mode of production would be abolished and the foundations for a classless communist social order established.

In an ironic inversion of the materialist conception of history, communist parties have thus far normally come to power in predominantly agrarian societies where industrialization under bourgeois auspices had been absent or seriously retarded and where therefore the industrial proletariat had been small, fragmented, poorly organized and, hence, relatively powerless. Only in two of the present-day communist-party-ruled countries – Czechoslovakia and the German Democratic Republic – did manual workers outnumber the peasantry to become the largest social category in the population prior to the establishment of the regime (see Table 2.1). And only in the case of Czechoslovakia can it be plausibly maintained that the principal political muscle for the foundation of the new order was provided by industrial workers (rather than foreign troops and/or a predominantly peasant guerrilla army).

Viewed from one perspective, Leninism represents a theoretical reformulation of Marxism to confront the practical problems entailed in carrying out premature socialist revolution in underdeveloped societies – primarily by reassigning the historical tasks of the numerically insufficient, organizationally inchoate and ideologically muddled manual workers to an elite corps of disciplined and ideologically advanced professional revolutionaries organized along military-bureaucratic lines in a highly centralized 'party of a new type'. After seizing state power from an old regime debilitated by disastrous foreign wars and/or peasant rebellion, communist party regimes characteristically have turned their formidable organization prowess to the task of mobilizing available human and material resources for a sustained program of forced industrialization aiming at the most rapid possible transformation of the social and economic structure. In effect, the political 'superstructure' of the dictatorship of the proletariat suspends itself in mid-air through sheer

Table 2.1   *Estimated Composition of Population by Occupational Groups*

Country	Manual Workers (%)	Non-manual Employees (%)	Peasants (%)	Other (%)
East Germany				
1939 *	56	18		26
1970 *	45	39	13	3
Czechoslovakia				
1930 *	57	7	22	14
1950 *	56	16	20	8
1961 *	56	28	14	2
1970 *	60	27	11	2
1975 *	61	28	9	2
Hungary				
1949 *	39	11	39	11
1960 *	55	16	26	3
1970 *	55	22	21	2
1973 *	56	23	19	2
Poland				
1931 †	26	4	61	9
1950 †		45	53	2
1960 †	34	18	44	4
1970 †	41	23	34	2
1972 †	42	23	33	2
Bulgaria				
1956 †	16		64	
1965 †	27		41	
1975 †	42			
Yugoslavia				
1961 †	22	19	57	2
1971 †	30	24	43	3
Romania				
1956 *	20	9	68	3
1964 *	33	10	55	2
1966 †	26	19	55	–
Albania				
1950 *	11	10	74	5
1960 *	29	11	59	1
1971 *	34	13	53	–
1975 *	36	14	50	–

* by predominant source of family income – entire population;
† by occupation of the individual – economically active population only.
Sources: See note 1, p. 41.

willpower while constructing its own socioeconomic 'base' after the fact. Far from the socialist revolution arising out of the maturation of the working class, the working class in most of the present socialist countries owes its very existence and character to the consciously chosen policies (and, of course, the unintended byproducts) of the ruling communist party leadership.

Thus, the first point to be kept in mind in any consideration of the contemporary role of the East European workers in political life is that we are dealing in most cases with social groupings that have undergone explosive growth in the very recent past and in many respects are still very much *in statu nascendi*. The years since World War II (and especially the years since the adoption of Soviet-style economic planning, administrative mechanisms and policy priorities around 1949–50) have been characterized by marked changes in the occupational structure of the population involving the massive outflow of the rural peasant population into newly created jobs in the urban economy. Table 2.1, which displays estimates of the 'class structure', and Table 2.2, which displays the declining proportion of the economically active population involved in agricultural production, convey a rough idea of the magnitude and rate of change in social structure during the process of 'building socialism'. Inspection of the tables quickly reveals that, while the largest proportional shifts have taken place in the initially most backward regions (the Balkan countries), even the already highly developed countries of East Germany and Czechoslovakia underwent important changes in occupational structure under communist auspices. While in the GDR and Czechoslovakia the fastest growth was in the numbers of non-manual employees, there was also sizable new rural to urban migration in the 1950s and early 1960s. The GDR's shift out of agriculture of 'only' about 0·6 percentage points per year still involved the movement of about 100,000 peasants and family members a year into the cities and towns. For Bulgaria, the average annual change of about 1·6

Table 2.2 *Percentage of Labor Force Employed in Agriculture*

Country	About 1930	1950	1960	1970	1978
East Germany	–	24	18	13	10
Czechoslovakia	37	38	26	19	11
Hungary	53	49	37	25	17
Poland	64	56	47	39	32
Bulgaria	80	73	57	47	36
Yugoslavia	78	70	58	50	40
Romania	–	74	66	49	40
Albania	–	85	71	66	62

Source: *FAO Production Yearbook*, various years; Paul F. Myers, 1974, pp. 468–9; *Annuarul Statistic al Republicii Socialiste Romania*, 1975.

percentage points reflected an influx of about the same absolute numbers, but drawn from a population of not quite half that of the GDR and arriving in an initially much smaller urban sector. In Eastern Europe, as elsewhere in the world, peasant migrants to the cities and towns found work in the overwhelming majority of cases as unskilled or semiskilled manual workers rather than in white-collar or skilled blue-collar occupations.

The impact of rapid occupational mobility patterns on both the size and the composition of the manual working class has been quite striking throughout the region, with the relative magnitude of the effects being inversely proportional to the initial size of the working-class population at the beginning of accelerated industrialization. In the more developed countries, like the GDR and Czechoslovakia, which already had large and relatively skilled industrial workforces before World War II, the numerically substantial influx of former peasants was still outnumbered by the second-and third-generation workers long established in the cities and towns. In the less-developed countries to the south and east, the small prewar working classes were very quickly submerged in the peasant flood. The most extreme case was that of Albania, where the number of non-agricultural manual workers rose from an estimated 55,000 in 1950 to 154,000 in 1960, and on up to 307,000 in 1970, about a sixfold increase in only twenty years, less than a generation (Bardhoshi and Kareco, 1974, p. 187).

Poland's pattern of occupational mobility may be taken as something like a representative median case for the eight European people's democracies, since it ranked fourth in the proportion of its agricultural population in both 1950 and 1970, and its proportions very closely approximated the mean for the group in both years. The number of non-agricultural manual workers in Poland grew from about 2·7 million in 1950 to 4·2 million in 1960, and amounted to almost 6·3 million in 1970, for an average rate of increase over the twenty-year period of about 4·3 percent per annum that more than doubled the size of the Polish working class.[2] In a sample surveyed in 1963, about 50 percent of factory workers and about 60 percent of construction workers consisted of people who had lived in rural areas up to at least the age of 14 years.[3] As of 1960, there were even 700,000 'peasant workers' employed in Polish industry who still continued to live on and to cultivate small farms in their spare time (Turski, 1965, pp. 107–108). By 1974, the number of these hybrid 'peasant-worker' commuters had grown until they numbered nearly 1 million (Wiatr, 1974, p. 129), which is to say, about 15 percent of the working class.

The varying relative importance of upwardly mobile peasants in the composition of the working class can be roughly assessed on a comparative basis by utilizing East European sociological research on father-to-son intergenerational occupational mobility (see Table 2.3). Although differences in the dates of the surveys and in their methodologies make precise comparison impossible, the general picture that emerges is quite clear. At the time of the respective surveys (roughly the late 1960s and early 1970s), an absolute majority of workers in Hungary, Yugoslavia, Bulgaria, Romania, and no doubt (though precise data are lacking)

Table 2.3 *Distribution of Blue-Collar Workers by Father's Occupation (Male Workers Only)*

Country	% with peasant fathers	% with worker fathers	% with non-manual fathers
Czechoslovakia (1967)	37·5	53·6	8·9
Poland (1972)	43·6	50·4	6·0
Hungary (1973)	54·0	42·8	3·2
Yugoslavia (1962)	55·8	34·8	9·4
Bulgaria (1967)	61·5	33·3	6·2
Romania (1970)	65·4	30·5	4·1

Source: Connor, 1979, pp. 119–23.

Albania, were people who had grown up in peasant families. Only in Poland, Czechoslovakia and, presumably, the GDR did 'hereditary' proletarians constitute a bare majority of the blue-collar ranks (and in Poland this threshold evidently had only very recently been crossed).

The implications of this massive influx of peasants into urban manual occupations for the political role of the working class during the first generation of the communist regime have been both numerous and important. Let us suggest just a few of the more interesting ones. It should be stressed that the move from the village to the town or city represented an enormous change in nearly every aspect of the lives of those involved. It was not simply a case of changing one 'job' for another. An enormous gulf separated the relatively 'modern' lifestyle of the industrial centers from the age-old patterns and traditions of the relatively isolated peasant communities. The urban migrant left behind the emotional support and the economic security (however tenuous) provided by multibonded ties of familial relationship and lifelong acquaintance for the anonymity and impersonality of a life among strangers. Instead of the relatively self-sufficient patterns of consumption characteristic of subsistence agriculture and handicraft production, he now found it necessary to depend for his necessities upon decisions about mass production of commodities made by remote economic planners and upon his capacity to acquire the cash to purchase them by selling his labor. Instead of the autonomous, self-scheduled and periodically varied patterns of work characteristic of small-scale agriculture, he now had to accustom himself to the unfamiliar discipline of the foreman, the punch-clock and a minutely specialized and routinized task on the assembly line. With his skills as a farmer and husbandryman essentially useless in his new setting, and lacking in formal education, he almost necessarily had to settle for the low wages and often unpleasant working conditions of an unskilled or semiskilled laborer; yet at the same time the example of his acquaintances and the proximity and visibility of amenities and 'luxury' commodities almost unknown in the village stimulated him toward acquisitiveness and a consumption-oriented mentality that linked the sense of self-worth with the outward trappings of material prosperity. When he married, the patterns of family life were apt to be very different from those of the extended family of his childhood, especially in the likely event that the wife continued to be employed outside the home after marriage and, thus, maintained her economic independence. With the constraints of immediate and constant supervision of family elders and an intimate village community largely removed, traditional religious, social and moral values had a tendency to erode, and the new worker was apt to find himself cross-pressured by the often conflicting values advocated by peers and by communist authorities. In short, the peasant-turned-worker found himself confronted with a range of changes in his familial, social, economic and cultural environments nearly as all-encompassing as those he might have encountered as an emigrant to a foreign country. He was faced with a task of acculturation and adaptation that would require years at best and that might never be fully accomplished in his lifetime.

The difficulties that can arise from large-scale shifts of peasant populations into urban environments are well known to us because of the prominence of such factors in the accepted explanations for political instability in contemporary Third World countries. The stresses of early urbanization and industrialization have historically been associated with the growth of militant oppositionism by labor as well as with such symptoms of social pathologies as increased rates of alcoholism, violent crime, juvenile delinquency, family instability, mental disorders and suicide. None of these phenomena have been wholly absent under the communist regimes in Eastern Europe (the propagandistic disclaimers of regime apologists notwithstanding), but the most noteworthy fact is not so much that such negative phenomena existed as it is that they have not been much more widespread. The high degree of success of the communist regimes in maintaining relative social integration and a high degree of working-class political conformism is no doubt explicable in part by the high repressive capability which was skillfully used whenever necessary, but surely there was much more to it than this.

It seems that the major factors encouraging working-class political conformism in Eastern Europe, despite the unsettling effects of rapid industrialization, have been three: the alleviation of the material insecurity of the working class through economic policies that abolished the threat of cyclical unemployment; the high rate of upward social mobility, which created a situation in which a large fraction of the working class evaluated their situation as having been greatly improved in comparison with their former rural impoverishment; and the effectiveness of the regimes' efforts at resocialization of workers through intensive and consciously coordinated 'mobilizational' techniques.

The fact that classical Stalinist' economic development strategy emphasized extraordinarily high savings and investment rates to the detriment of immediate improvements in the living standard of the masses is well known and widely emphasized in the Western literature. In the early 1950s, this went so far in at least some countries that average wages in industry actually declined, as has subsequently been acknowledged even by. some of the regimes' official statistical agencies (as in Hungary and Poland). What is less commonly given due weight in Western analyses, is that even during these most trying of times very large numbers of workers could reasonably evaluate their material positions as improved either because they no longer had to face periodic layoffs or unemployment (particularly a gain for unskilled workers), or simply because the gap between rural and urban incomes and living standards was historically so very large that mobility from the former to the latter could almost completely overshadow the effects of near-stagnant wages for those newly arrived from the country. It was primarily the small core of long-time proletarians in skilled or highly skilled occupations who would have experienced the most palpable deprivation, since they had not historically suffered overmuch from unemployment and had been around when wages were higher. And even here there was something of a safety-valve provided by the massive recruitment of the most militant and politically conscious opinion-leaders from the factory floor to fill essentially white-collar administrative positions in the burgeoning party, trade union and state bureaucracies. Whatever the psychic traumas of transition to an urban working-class way of life, it would seem likely that the experience of upward social mobility was in the vast majority of cases sufficiently satisfying on balance to make the beneficiaries somewhat reluctant to question the authority of the regime that had made it all possible.

The extreme emphasis that communist regimes give to efforts at socializing and resocializing the population into acceptance of officially approved values, beliefs and attitudes has also received a good deal of attention in the Western literature, as has their proclivity for dragooning virtually the entire population into membership in a wide variety of tightly controlled and ideologically sanitized mass organizations. The image sometimes conveyed by Western commentators tends to be one that concentrates a bit too exclusively on certain (admittedly important) aspects of this machinery of mobilization. The aspects principally discussed are the prevalence of artificially 'preachy' attempts either to inculcate abstract Marxist-Leninist doctrine, or to exhort the masses to specific practical actions through boosterism and sloganeering, and the subtle Machiavellian use of the network of mass organizations in a 'pre-emptive' way in order to short-circuit the spontaneous efforts of the masses to seek out or form responsive associational interest groups to articulate their possibly dangerous demands or grievances.

What tends to be underplayed is perhaps the less explicitly political, but none the less vital, functions of general guidance and education carried on by the pervasive network of formal organizations and face-to-face agitation. More important to stability than political indoctrination may have been the more general socialization of rural migrants and younger workers into the sociocultural values and behaviour patterns vital to the regime for the successful functioning of its industrial workforce: coming to work regularly, on time, and sober; maintaining a steady and acceptably rapid pace of work; striving to improve skills, productivity and quality of performance; responsiveness to the direction of superiors and cooperativeness with fellow workers; observance of norms forbidding theft or embezzlement of productive resources, and so on. Viewed in the context of an industrial system that offered considerable potential for many workers to improve their material well-being, it becomes apparent that the manipulative efforts of the regimes' mobilizational network was successful to the extent that it engaged individual interests by teaching workers the rules of the game that it was necessary to know in order to get along (and get ahead) in the unfamiliar urban-industrial *milieu.*

Because of the existence of various and overlapping organizations promoting a relatively integrated and coherent set of goals and values covering virtually every sphere of the citizen's economic, social and cultural activities, successful adjustment was greatly facilitated. The new worker simply could not long remain in doubt as to what was expected of him in various situations. Centralized regime control not only of most agencies of socialization and mass communications, but also of the process of allocating most social and economic benefits, coupled with an efficient system of surveillance, made it possible to an extent unparalleled in more pluralistic societies consistently to reward conformism of all kinds (including political conformism) and to punish deviance. While members of the 'old' working class may very likely have felt little need for the kind of guidance provided by the regimes' agencies (and indeed, probably already had a pretty good grasp of what its immediate interests were that conflicted at times with party policies), it seems not at all implausible that many of the less sophisticated former peasants would accept it without much resistance and even with some gratitude. Lacking much previous experience with associational interest-group activity or free trade unions because of their rural backgrounds, they might not object too much to the 'mobilized' character of participation in the mass organizations, so long as activists maintained a basically paternalistic *modus operandi.*

Thus, the political role of the working class in European communist countries has indeed been shaped in very important ways by the circumstance that most of these countries have been undergoing rapid industrialization, which created a working class numerically dominated by upwardly mobile ex-peasants anxious to integrate themselves into urban life and predisposed by reason of their relative success (as well as by reason of a certain political passivity and naïveté springing from their rural upbringing) to be basically supportive of the regime and of its leaders. But if the first point to bear in mind is *the rapidity of past socioeconomic changes,* surely the second and equally important point to consider is that for each country *this transformation is a one-time-only historical phenomenon* that necessarily gives way to a rather different situation.

Eventually the great pool of redundant agricultural manpower drawn upon by Stalinist industrialization policies to swell the industrial laborforce is absorbed, the growth rate of the working class slows markedly, and an increasing proportion of the new entrants must necessarily be recruited from among the city-bred children of the existing workers. This has been the situation for quite some while in the GDR and Czechoslovakia, as we have seen already. Hungary's manual workforce has grown very little since about 1960. While Poland still has considerable potential reserves of manpower in the rural economy, the policy dilemmas involved in trying to release them more rapidly for urban employment (which would require either a willingness to allow the predominantly private, uncollectivized farmers to accumulate much larger capital stocks or the political will to push through a belated collectivization drive) will likely tend to inhibit rural out-migration, particularly as lagging food production is a principal political problem of the regime. Even in the less developed Balkan countries, where the processes of urbanization and industrialization presumably still have a good way to run and substantial rates of growth in the working class can be expected, a somewhat slower pace seems to be already in evidence.

One implication of this is that the composition of the working classes in Eastern Europe is shifting from predominantly rural in origins to predominantly urban in origins. While the complexity of such a transition makes prediction hazardous, it is at least not implausible to expect this to have certain consequences. For one thing, the question 'what have you done for us *lately*?' is apt to arise more and more frequently as the 'heroic' period of socialist industrialization, with its rapid rates of social mobility, recedes more and more into the past. A declining proportion of the workforce who have experienced radical social mobility suggests that average working-class incomes and perquisites would need to rise more rapidly than in the past in order to maintain the same levels of support and sweet reasonableness. The recent narrowing of urban–rural income and educational differentials, especially in the more developed countries of the region, suggests the same thing, since there is evidence that workers have in the past derived a certain psychic satisfaction from being able to compare themselves favorably with the peasantry.[4] Moreover, an urbanized, acclimized and better-educated workforce with greater experience in (and aptitude for) organizational activities may prove to be more assertive in promoting its self-interest and less amenable to manipulation by party-controlled *cadres* in the trade unions and factory youth organizations. This may be particularly critical as the growing emphasis of the party on educational credentials as a criterion for advancement to administrative positions makes it less and less possible to find positions into which to co-opt an increasingly large number of manual workers manifesting both organizational talents, and the desire to put them to political or economic use.

A third point to bear in mind is that the decline in the rates of expansion of the urban industrial workforce that we have been discussing is part of a much broader set of changes in economic system dynamics that is likely to have a number of additional, indirect implications for the overall situation in which East European workers find themselves.

As East European economists have been telling us *ad nauseam* since about the mid-1960s, East European socialist systems are passing (or are about to pass, or at least eventually must pass) through a transition between the 'extensive' and 'intensive' stages of socialist economic development. In their view, the near-exhaustion of underemployed rural manpower that can be shifted at low opportunity cost to more productive employment in industry (and the more or less concurrent completion of the process of recruiting housewives into paid employment outside the home) has very serious implications for the overall rate of growth of national income. The high growth rates of the past were based principally on the large quantitative increases in the laborforce (for which the high investment rates made it possible to build new factories and other capital facilities). With these so-called 'extensive' growth factors now much more limited, growth rates may be expected to fall unless it is possible to compensate by a new reliance on the so-called 'intensive' growth factors – improvements in the amount of value produced per unit of (human and non-human) input in the productive process.

Since the 1960s, this new imperative to cultivate the intensive growth factors has provided a theoretical basis to justify a great variety of changes and proposed changes in both macroeconomic policy and the organizational framework of economic planning and management, at least in the more developed countries of the region. Among other things, the line of analysis suggests the desirability of improving microeconomic efficiency through a more exacting manipulation of the system of material incentives to tie personal incomes of workers and managers more closely to economic performance criteria (such as profitability), encouraging the more economic utilization of factors of production (including labor), reallocating human and non-human resources from less productive branches of industry to more productive ones, taking fuller advantage of the principles of specialization and comparative advantage through expansion of foreign trade, and accelerating the rate of technological innovation in the production process. All of these changes have important and potentially adverse implications for the affected workers.

In the first place, slowing of the pace of economic growth implies that resources for allocation to consumption will also grow more slowly unless the rate of investment declines (which would be difficult to reconcile with the need for investment in upgrading capital's technological level and shifting resources into new areas of more efficient production). This occurs precisely at the stage when, as we noted earlier, the rate of social mobility upward from the peasantry is decreasingly significant in encouraging working-class support, and when accordingly it becomes important to deliver measurable improvements in average wages at a somewhat more rapid rate than heretofore. The constructive way to meet this problem is by taking steps to improve overall productivity per worker and paying wage increases out of the resulting surplus. However, there are competing uses for the national resources other than wage increases (notably, higher defense expenditures, wages and salaries in the 'non-productive' sectors, investment), making it difficult to allocate sufficient resources to wage increases for them to satisfy aspirations.

Moreover, many of the measures put forward as methods of enhancing productivity are themselves likely to have an adverse effect on the interests of manual workers in other ways. Wage and bonus systems tying worker incomes more closely to personal output and enterprise profitability diminish the worker's ability to predict his future income and expose him to fluctuations and risks he might well prefer not to take, particularly if his income is on the low side in the first place. Managerial bonus sytems based on profitability may encourage administrators to undertake measures to 'sweat' the workers by increasing the pace of work, cracking down on slack work discipline, and even firing redundant labor. The allocation of premia and bonuses, intended to reward individuals' extra contributions to productivity, may be abused by foremen or section leaders to play favorites or extort kickbacks. Similarly, macroeconomic decisions to reallocate resources from less profitable to more profitable branches of the economy necessarily entail a 'redeployment' of labor, which at a minimum will be disruptive of established habits and personal relationships, and which may well involve the necessity for retraining in new skills, loss of seniority benefits, employment in a less convenient location (perhaps even necessitating locating a new apartment in an ultratight housing market), etc. In short, the traditional assurance of stability and security in the workplace in exchange for political conformity and minimally satisfactory work habits seem increasingly likely to be seriously eroded in the necessary push to improve productive efficiency.[5]

It would seem, then, that there are a number of established long-term trends that appear to be working in the direction of a less conformist and less passive role for workers than has heretofore been the norm in Eastern Europe, particularly in the more developed countries of the bloc. The established ideology emphasizing the leading role of the working class and the proletarian character of the state makes it particularly difficult for the party to denounce any such aspirations as illegitimate without serious risk of undermining the basic legitimating myths of their own regime, yet the party leaders are scarcely likely to renounce many of their own decision-making prerogatives in favor of any sort of proletarian populism. Does this mean, then, that the long-awaited final crises of communism are imminent? Is Trotsky's predicted 'third revolution', in which the workers rise up to smash the bureaucratic state built by Stalin, around the corner?

Probably not. It is a perennial error of future-casters to extrapolate seemingly 'hard' social or economic trends in a linear fashion indefinitely into the future, while systematically underestimating both the adaptive capacities of political systems, and their capabilities for reshaping their socioeconomic environment. While the events of the 1960s and 1970s would seem to confirm the existence of a tendency for workers to engage more frequently in opposition against particularly unpleasant or ill-timed policy initiatives of the party leadership (witness the problems encountered in Czechoslovakia and Hungary in implementing features of the 1960s economic reforms (Johnson, 1978, pp. 281–347) as well as the Polish events of 1970 and 1976), it is important to note that such oppositional activity has generally been reactive in nature, with little indication of lasting organization or of any broadly based alternative program. Moreover, the protests have tended to be basically issue-specific in nature and not obviously motivated by radically revolutionary sentiments – although in the case of Poland in 1970 the failure to make timely concessions and (especially) the decision by Gomulka to use force led to the discrediting of the chief policy-makers as well. There has been no reliable indication that any substantial number of workers has reached the point of rejecting the basic institutions of the postwar communist regimes, though there are obvious signs that many would like to see a few reforms made as expedients to secure the protection of their perceived interests.

The usual pattern of regime responses to working-class strikes or other non-violent protests in the past seems to have been remarkably effective: a prompt show of concern by top party leaders, followed by quick concessions or at least a review of the offending lower-level decision, the removal of a few unpopular lower-echelon officials – followed up a few weeks or months later by the quiet arrest, firing or transfer of the ringleaders of the protest. It may be that in the future this tactic will begin to wear thin, especially if (as in Poland in 1970 and 1976) the immediate issue stimulating the protest is a national policy rather than a local decision; yet it is far from certain that such politically foolish tactics as making all price hikes effective nationwide on the same day at five-year intervals are necessarily dictated by fundamental features of the regime or inevitable historical trends.

What seems more likely is a modest expansion of institutionalized opportunities for particularly active or interested workers to involve themselves in low-level decision-making, along with, perhaps, a stoic acceptance by the political leadership that they will have to put up with somewhat more frequent complaints, criticisms and even protests from workers without assuming the motivations to be subversive. Yugoslav workers' councils come first to mind, but the model need not be such a radical one. Limited decentralization of decision-making to specialized economic managers may provide a welcome degree of insulation for the top leaders, particularly if they are also careful to build in channels of appeal to safeguard workers from the most serious consequences of managerial decision-making. The 'suspensory veto' power delegated to the (still tightly controlled) trade unions in Hungary is an example of a very limited reform that seems to have had important positive effects in winning worker acquiescence for the 1968 economic reforms.

It does seem likely that East European policy-makers will come to feel increasingly constrained in the kinds of policy choices open to them in some fields. The desire to avoid trouble will in particular be a potent influence in consumer pricing decisions and overall wages policy decisions. Policy options involving the 'redeployment of labor' are particularly sensitive and difficult to implement, if Hungarian experience is a reliable guide. This certainly does not mean that it will be impossible to implement unpopular decisions, but it does suggest that policy-makers will increasingly find it prudent to supplement them as much as possible with measures to alleviate at least the worst hardships and thereby to minimize the adverse reactions in advance. Maintaining paternalistic authority while limiting severely the real potential for mass participation may very well turn out to be a viable strategy, but it will require the leadership to cultivate most carefully the image of thoughtful and caring patrons.

Notes: Chapter 2

1 Sources for Table 2.1 are: East Germany – Krejči (1976, p. 83); Czechoslovakia – Krejči (1972, p. 43) and *Statisticka Ročenka ČSSR* (1972, p. 103; 1976, p. 88); Hungary – *Statistical Yearbook of Hungary* (1975, p. 35); Poland – Zagorski (1976, p. 20); Bulgaria – estimated from data in the ILO's *Yearbook of Labor Statistics* (1960, pp. 44–5; 1977, pp. 254–5; 1979, pp. 112–13); Yugoslavia – estimated from data in the ILO's *Yearbook of Labor Statistics* (1969, pp. 254–5; 1977, pp. 282–3); Romania – estimated from data in the ILO's *Yearbook of Labor Statistics* (1977, pp. 278–9), Murgescu, Costin *et al.,* as cited in Chirot (1978, p. 469); Albania – Prifti (1978, p. 61) and Pano (1979, p. 206).
2 Estimates of the numbers of manual workers were calculated by combining information from several sources. Data on their proportions in the economically active population were taken from Zagorski (1976, p. 20). These were multiplied by the numerical estimates of total economically active population in *Rocznik Statystyczny* (1973, p. 2). The figure for 1950 comes from Vaughan (1971, p. 324).
3 *Rocznik Statystyczny* (1964), as cited in Vaughan (1971, p. 325).
4 It is perhaps significant that growing resentments against *'nouveau riche'* peasants on the part of urban workers were regarded as sufficiently serious to justify a major ideological campaign in Hungary during the early 1970s, approximately the time when average rural and urban incomes reached parity, according to official statistics.
5 For a dissident's particularly lurid (but insightful) account of the adverse effects of NEM policies as applied in one Hungarian factory, see Haraszti (1978). For a more dispassionate sociological analysis, see Hethy and Mako (1971, 1974).

References: Chapter 2

Bardhoshi, Beshim, and Kareco, Theodhor, *The Economic and Social Development of the People's Republic of Albania During Thirty Years of People's Power* (Tirana: '8 Nentori' Publishing House, 1974).
Chirot, Daniel, 'Social change in communist Romania', *Social Forces,* vol. 62, no. 2, 1978.
Connor, Walter D., *Socialism, Politics and Equality* (New York: Columbia University Press, 1979).
Haraszti, Miklos, *A Worker in a Worker's State* (New York: Universe Books, 1978).
Hethy, Lajos, and Mako, Csaba, 'Obstacles to the introduction of efficient money incentives in a Hungarian factory', *Industrial and Labor Relations Review,* vol. 24, July 1971, pp. 541–53.

Hethy, Lajos, and Mako, Csaba, 'Work performance, interests, powers, and environment – the case of cyclical slowdowns in a Hungarian factory', *European Economic Review,* vol. 5, no. 2, 1974, pp. 141–57.

Johnson, Paul M., *Political Development, Penetration, and the Politics of Economic Policy in the European Communist States* (PhD dissertation, Stanford University) (Ann Arbor, Mi.: University Microfilms International 1978).

Krejči, Jaroslav, *Social Change and Stratification in Postwar Czechoslovakia* (New York: Columbia University Press, 1972).

Krejči, Jaroslav, *Social Structure in Divided Germany* (New York: St Martin's Press, 1976).

Murgescu, Costin, Grigorescu, C., Retegan, G., and Trebici, U., 'Influences of the process of industrialization on social mobility – on Romanian data', *Romanian Journal of Sociology.* no. 4–5, 1966, pp. 181–92.

Myers, Paul F., 'Population and labor force in Eastern Europe', in US Congress, Joint Economic Committee, *Reorientation and Commercial Relations of the Economies of Eastern Europe* (Washington, DC: US Government. Printing Office, 1974).

Pano, Nicholas, 'Albania', in T. Rakowska-Harmstone and A. Gyorgy, eds, *Communism in Eastern Europe* (Bloomington, In: Indiana University Press, 1979).

Prifti, Peter, *Socialist Albania Since 1944* (Cambridge, Ma.: MIT, 1978).

Turski, R., 'Chlopi-Robotnicy', in Adam Sarapata, ed., *Socjologiczne problemy przedsiebiorstwa przemyslowego* (Warsaw: Ossolineum, 1965).

Vaughan, Michalina, 'Poland', in M. Archer and S. Giner, eds, *Contemporary Europe: Class, Status, and Power* (London: Weidenfeld & Nicolson, 1971).

Wiatr, Jerzy, 'Polish society', in Ewa Trzeciak and Janusz Wankowicz, eds, *Poland: A Handbook* (Warsaw: Wydawnictwo Interpress, 1974).

Zagorski, Krzysztof, 'Changes of socio-occupational mobility in Poland', *Polish Sociological Bulletin.* no. 2, 1976.

3 Political Attitudes and Activity

ALEX PRAVDA

Introduction

This chapter is about the political involvement of workers in the communist states of Eastern Europe. It is concerned with both the psychological and behavioral dimensions of that involvement. Given the highly inclusive nature of politics in communist states, we treat as political attitudes and actions that have a bearing on the authoritative allocation of values. By workers is meant manual workers outside of agriculture. Just as we realize that these are not a hermetically sealed group – the boundaries that divide them from the peasantry at one end and white-collar groups at the other are often fuzzy – so we are aware that blue-collars are internally differentiated along lines of education and skill. Indeed, it is one of the objectives of this chapter to examine the ways in which such differences affect political involvement. To keep the chapter within manageable bounds, three East European countries are focused on: Czechoslovakia, Poland and Hungary. Not only do these countries provide the richest data on workers' attitudes and actions, but of all the states in the region they are the three in which workers have played the most conspicuous political role.

The chapter falls into three parts. The first is concerned with how workers see politics, the regime and their own role within the polity. A descriptive analysis of workers' attitudes, values and opinions is combined with an attempt to identify those features of their political outlook that distinguish them from white-collar groups. The second part considers workers' participation in official social and political organizations and movements. We attempt to assess the quantitative and qualitative aspects of such participation and investigate the relative importance of socioeconomic and organizational factors in shaping these. The subject of the final part of the chapter is the interplay between official and informal political activity at enterprise level. Under the heading of informal activity is included all activity that is not officially sponsored, but is autonomous, spontaneous and even illegitimate in nature. Finally, we examine the politicization of workers' demands and actions in Poland in an attempt to assess the factors underlying this process and their significance for the region as a whole. It is hoped that an examination of the above aspects of workers' political involvement might help to shed light on the validity of three contending interpretations of this group's general position and role in communist states: the official party claim that workers constitute the leading political class in these societies; the concept developed by David Lane with reference to the Soviet Union of the well-socialized worker, thoroughly 'incorporated' into the system (Lane and O'Dell, 1979, pp. 41-5); and finally, Konrad and Szelenyi's view of workers in these states as a class exploited by the intelligentsia through the mechanisms of rational redistribution (1979, pp. 228-30).

Before proceeding to examine workers' political involvement, something should be said about the data on which the observations are based. Comparison between blue-collar groups in different countries has to rely on evidence that is not strictly comparable. National surveys are extremely rare, and even those at local and factory level do not cover many of the most interesting questions because of their obvious political sensitivity. And where sensitive questions are included, the results may well be distorted by respondent's inhibitions and by the adjustment of published data. None the less, the published material relating to workers' political involvement provides a fund of evidence that is well worth examining.

Workers' Political Outlook

Summarizing the findings of a recent comparative volume on political culture in communist states, Jack Gray describes political socialization as a 'depressing failure' (Gray, 1977, p. 270). Since the creation of a politically attentive, loyal, committed and competent worker is officially central to the emergence of New Socialist Man, blue-collar political interests, values and attitudes stand as an important measure of the success of the entire socialization enterprise.

Political Interest and Knowledge
With remarkable consistency, Czech, Hungarian and Polish surveys show that three out of every four workers claim to be interested in politics. Approximately a quarter of workers can be described as highly interested, just under half display mild interest, the remainder fall into the category of total indifference (Molnar *et al.,* 1970, p. 62; Gospodarek, 1971, pp. 237-40; Piekalkiewicz, 1972, pp. 48-9). Mass-media audience studies indicate analogous levels of attentiveness to political affairs. A 1967 Polish survey of newspaper readership came up with the remarkable revelation that workers paid more attention to political items than to sports news (Glowny Urzad Statystyczny, 1969, pp. 60, 62). Reassuringly, this is contradicted by what we know of workers' topics of conversation where work and sport predominate (Piekalkiewicz, 1972, p. 92; Kovacs, 1976, appendix, figures 5, 6).

The impressive levels of claimed political interest and attentiveness are not matched by political knowledge. Recent Polish evidence suggests that up to a third of those who show a general interest in public affairs know little or nothing about them (Ostrowski and Sufin, 1979, p. 157). More specifically, Hungarian research has revealed a widespread ignorance among workers of the most basic political facts. A majority of blue-collars in the late 1960s could not name the ruling party in Hungary, nor were they aware that their country bordered on a capitalist state (Kovacs, 1976, p. 227 and appendix, figure 1). In a more recent survey two workers thought that Khrushchev was a former president of the United States (*If ju Kommunista,* 1979, p. 17). Given such evidence, we are inclined to go along with one sociologist's estimate that three-quarters of workers in Budapest are very badly informed and lack the information on which to base any coherent political opinions (Kemeny, 1979, p. 77).

The disparities between interest, attentiveness and knowledge are not difficult to explain. Poor performance in answering questions about formal institutional arrangements may reflect doubts about their real importance. Moreover, a tendency to pay only cursory attention to political items may be increased by cynicism about the accuracy of the media reports. An early Polish survey found that only a handful of workers believed all that they read in the newspapers (Sicinski, 1962, pp. 70–74). Such widespread skepticism may be enhanced by relatively easy access to alternative sources of information: foreign broadcasts, visiting relatives or trips to the West. It is, thus, not particularly surprising that one Hungarian study concluded that only 5 percent of the manual workforce in the two factories under scrutiny held clear and well-informed political opinions based on 'socialist ideas' (Molnar *et al.,* 1970, p. 108).

Disappointing by the ideal standards of New Socialist Man, overall levels of political interest and information among East European workers are respectable by international comparison (Almond and Verba, 1965, pp. 45–59). What is of greater concern to us, however, is that workers in Eastern Europe, like their Western counterparts, perform less well than white-collar groups, particularly where political knowledge is concerned. In part these differences are accounted for by the strong relationship between political interest and information on the one hand, and education and skill on the other. Indeed, skill differences make a considerable impact within the blue-collar group. Highly skilled men in their thirties and forties are by far the most politically aware and, thus, exercise considerable influence over the vague and uninformed views of their less qualified and younger colleagues (Kovacs, 1976, appendix, figure 1; Kemeny, 1977, p. 71). But even the best informed of the skilled worker 'core' of opinion-leaders are concerned primarily with enterprise and local politics, and have little real interest in or idea of how things operate at national level. Along with the rest of the population, workers in Poland and Hungary probably share their Czech counterparts' general disdain for politics as such and think that most politicians are out for what they can get for themselves (Piekalkiewicz, 1972, pp. 126–7).

Orientations to Socialism
Such views of politics are not necessarily associated with weak or negative attitudes to the socialist system. Two Hungarian studies dating from the

late 1960s found that a majority of workers supported the system; interestingly, blue-collar support slightly outran that voiced by the technical intelligentsia (Kovacs, 1976, appendix, figure 14). Several kinds of attachments underlie such support. Polish evidence at least indicates strong national identity among workers (Nowak, 1962, p. 151). More than other groups, workers think that they have a stake in the system. While the majority of non-manuals in Czechoslovakia in 1967 thought that they would have fared better under the First Republic, this view was shared by only just over a third of worker respondents (Vecernik, 1969, p. 318). Workers' relatively higher perceived stake in socialism should not be seen solely or even largely in material terms. To judge from Hungarian evidence, their appreciation of the 'moral' advantages offered by the socialist system seems far to outweigh positive evaluation of its material benefits (Kovacs, 1976, p. 260). Central to these 'moral' advantages are notions of welfare, security and equality on which workers' attachment to, and conception of, socialism is based. To be sure, when asked to list the benefits of socialism Hungarian workers, especially the skilled, mention living standards, but pride of place goes to equal rights and full employment (Molnar *et al.,* 1970, p. 103). This priority seems to be shared by the Poles. According to a nationwide survey conducted in September 1979, the absence of unemployment was perceived to be the greatest single advantage that socialism had over capitalism (OBOP, 1979a). To most workers, socialism means job security and remuneration largely regardless of performance, yet it does not mean working primarily for the good of the collective. The overwhelming majority of workers place material reward and good conditions far above 'the social significance' of labor (Doktor, 1964, p. 195; Matejko, 1969, p. 463; Mod and Kozak, 1974, pp. 65, 68).

None the less, altruistic elements do appear in blue-collar concepts of socialism in the shape of a strong attachment to egalitarianism. Four out of five Polish and Hungarian workers want to see existing income differences reduced to very low levels and a small minority want to see them eliminated altogether (Blachnicki, 1977, pp. 143–8; Kolosi, 1979, p. 73). Feelings in Czechoslovakia are somewhat less intense as objective differences are smaller (*Odborar,* no. 14–15, 1968, p. 26). Technical and managerial staff, on the other hand, hold anti-egalitarian views (Blachnicki, 1977, pp. 143–8; Horvath, 1979, pp. 14–15). Underlying this division of opinion over income differentials, contending views of socialism are formed. Arguments for widening differentials are couched in terms of economic rationality, while workers justify greater equality by referring to concepts of social justice which they often reduce to the simple statement that all have 'equal stomachs'. By the same token, workers object strongly to the existence under socialism of what they see as unjustifiable privilege fomenting social tension (Malewski, 1971, pp. 20–22; Blachnicki, 1977, pp. 144–52; Kolosi, 1979, pp. 67–72).

Attached to a security and welfare concept of socialism, workers are generally mistrustful of rationalizing and marketizing reforms. Both Czech and Hungarian workers were extremely wary of the economic reform schemes of the late 1960s. Indeed, it is largely because of their concern about the effects of economic rationalization that workers tend to be unenthusiastic about allied political reforms. At the Csepel iron and steel plant in 1969 a substantial majority of workers – particularly the skilled— were critical of regime policy on both the economic and general domestic front (Kovacs, 1976, appendix, figure 17). Blue-collar conservatism might stem in part from a low level of interest in politics, but it is more deeply rooted in anxiety about economic security and stability.

Yet one cannot say that workers are set implacably against all change. Szelenyi and Konrad argue persuasively that it is in the objective interests of the working class to combat rational redistribution by helping technocratic groups to press marketizing reforms (1979, p. 230). While East European workers in general seem to have been largely unaware of such 'interests', recent Polish events suggest that they might be open to persuasion on this score. Demands voiced in August 1980 for better-qualified management and for the formulation of an economic reform program drove home the point that most workers recognize the need to eliminate inefficiency (Demands, 1980). Even skilled workers in Hungary, who are highly critical of some aspects of economic reform policy, seem willing none the less to accept a closer correspondence between wages and performance as long as extremes of inequality are reduced (Kolosi, 1979, p. 30).

Views of Authority and Power

A logical connection might be seen to exist between workers' attachment to egalitarianism and welfare socialism and a need for a state with strong regulative powers. What evidence we have suggests that workers do incline somewhat toward a strong paternalistic state to which they have a highly extractive orientation, expecting the authorities to provide the material welfare benefits they associate with socialism (Nowak, 1976, p. 290). Workers' support for the system may be seen as being conditional on its provision of these welfare benefits and rights. The exchange of working-class quiescence and support for the fulfillment of such basic rights can be conceived as constituting a 'social compact' between workers and regimes in Eastern Europe (*Pravda,* 1979, pp. 215–16). To some extent workers also seem more willing than intelligentsia groups to condone state curtailment of civil liberties. Even Czech workers in 1968 were somewhat more critical than their higher-educated counterparts of press freedom and came out less strongly in favor of greater political pluralism (*Rude pravo,* 26 June 1968; Piekalkiewicz, 1972, p. 223). Such difference between blue- and white-collar views might be explained partly in terms of Lipset's (1973, pp. 120–22) emphasis on working-class tendencies to intolerance, isolation and 'the least complex alternative'. In the East European context, doubts about political pluralism might also be seen as stemming from the low credibility of political institutions. Confronted with hollow constitutional arrangements, workers set much greater store by political leaders and tend to see the regime in highly personalized terms (Piekalkiewicz, 1972, pp. 35, 37; Kemeny, 1977, p. 75).

The *relative* authoritarianism of blue-collar groups should not be allowed to obscure the fact that many workers hold opinions of a fairly liberal stamp. Nearly 60 percent of Czech workers in 1968 disagreed with the proposition that all political organizations should be subordinated to the leading role of the communist party. And only very narrow margins separated blue- from white-collar opinion on a wide range of allied issues (Piekalkiewicz, 1972, pp. 221, 223, 233). While Czech democratic traditions and the climate of 1968 may arguably make such responses an exception to East European patterns, no such factors affect Polish findings that workers have a strong attachment to personal liberty and freedom of speech. Surveys conducted in Warsaw and Kielce in the early 1970s showed that while overall blue-collar tolerance of civil rights infringement was somewhat greater than that displayed by the intelligentsia, fewer than one in four workers could be counted as authoritarian in this respect. In fact, of all the groups polled, the most strongly opposed to state restrictions of civil rights were manual workers with secondary education. The study also indicated that blue-collar liberalism may be growing: students from working-class families came out more strongly in support of civil rights than did their parents (Nowak, 1976, p. 307, table 10-9).

The apparent contradiction between workers' attachment to individual freedom and a strong paternalistic state may be accounted for in part by the peculiar nature of their attitudes to authority. This emerges clearly from Podgorecki's research into attitudes to the law in Poland. In his research he found that workers had far less respect for the law than did white-collar groups. Unskilled workers figured prominently among those who condoned violation of a law with which they disagreed; skilled workers were particularly prone to favor appearing to conform with the law while nevertheless effectively breaking it (Podgorecki, 1966, p. 110; Podgorecki, 1974, pp. 93–4). Podgorecki (1974, pp. 99–103) links workers' lower regard for the law to instrumental attitudes to moral principles as such. Skilled workers were particularly willing to adjust their principles to suit their purpose in contrast with higher-educated groups who generally adopted a principled stance. He argues convincingly that these instrumental attitudes are, in turn, associated with individualistic orientations which are characteristic of blue-collar groups. It is when these individualistic orientations confront the social norms of the enterprise and polity that regulations tend to be broken or circumvented.

The tendency to flout and defy the law may be particularly strong in Poland where many workers are not far removed from the strong individualism of the countryside. A defiant attitude to authority among unskilled Polish workers may be one of the factors underlying the high incidence of workers' riots in that country. Under non-crisis conditions workers display a readiness to break the law while appearing to conform (Honza, 1975). Such attitudes and conduct characterize what we shall refer to as the 'adaptive worker'.

The adaptive orientation to authority, centering on a strategy of maximizing benefits by circumventing regulations without openly challenging state power, is closely linked to workers' appraisal of their influence and political competence.

Despite the official image of popular sovereignty, East Europeans think that they have very little influence over policy (Ostrowski and Sufin, 1979, p. 159). Proclamations about the leading role of the working class may be a source of pride to some of its members, but fail to bolster feelings of efficacy. Workers see themselves as far less influential than non-manual groups (Malanowski, 1967, p. 346). More than any other group, workers perceived Czechoslovak society in 1967 as divided into a ruling elite and a controlled mass to which they themselves belonged (Jungmann, 1969, pp. 360, 364–70, 373). According to Hungarian evidence, the unskilled seem particularly affected by feelings of powerlessness (Horvath, 1979, pp. 12, 15). Most workers do not even consider power or authority as such a desirable value (Malanowski, 1967, p. 360; Sopuch, 1978, pp. 338–9). Partly this is due to the prejorative connotations of power as well as its distance and apparent unattainability: power and authority is something 'they' possess. Also, workers find it difficult to envisage practical ways in which power *per se,* especially political power, could help them maximize the material welfare benefits they desire (Kovacs, 1976, p. 230 and appendix, figure 4).

Yet the picture is not one of total resignation to powerlessness. Skilled workers seem aware and resentful of the inequalities in power and influence (Horvath, 1979, p. 12; Bielicki and Widerszpil, 1979, p. 82). And there is some evidence to suggest that younger, better-educated workers are more ambitious and do want a greater say in decision-making at enterprise level (Tudek, 1975, p. 297). Events can also affect views in this area. Successful crisis confrontations with the regime, such as have occurred in Poland, breed self-confidence and raise potential competence. Wasiak (1976, p. 44) attributes the high estimates of working-class influence he found among young Szczecin workers in 1975 in part at least to the 1970–71 crisis. However, the translation of such increased self-confidence into a desire systematically to curtail central government power is made unlikely by blue-collar views of the state as well as by the tendency of workers to target resentments against proximate power-holders.

The adaptive worker should not be seen as representative of *all* workers in Poland, Hungary and Czechoslovakia. As an ideal type he captures the essence of the politically salient attitudes, values and opinions of East European workers, particularly the key skilled groups. The adaptive worker has a secondary interest in national politics, his primary concern being with enterprise affairs and local conditions. Parochial in outlook, his support for the system is based on national identity and an attachment to a concept of socialism centering on security, stability and relative equality. His acceptance of a strong state is conditioned by its provision of welfare socialism and qualified by the adaptive worker's penchant to bend or circumvent the rules to preserve what he sees as personal liberty and maximize his material benefits.

From a purist socialist perspective, the adaptive worker is a token of the failure of official political socialization. He falls short of New Socialist Man in many respects, notably in his individualism, lack of social motivation and political competence. Yet, failure turns into qualified success if one considers the adaptive worker in the light of real as distinct from declared socialization objectives. What George Kolankiewicz and Ray Taras (1977, pp. 123–4) point out in the context of Poland applies to Eastern Europe in general: the authorities have long been ready to settle for far less than New Socialist Man. In many ways a parochial, welfare-centered worker is essential to political stability under the 'social compact'.

Political Participation

Participation is a more important facet of New Socialist Man from a practical standpoint than is commitment to the 'right' values. Not only is participation supposed to help inculcate those values, but it is itself a visible measure of their success (Drazkiewicz, 1974, p. 173). Above all, there is the simple fact that actions speak louder than words and that conformity of behavior is more important to political stability than uniformity of conviction. For these reasons a great deal of organizational effort is expended in communist states to ensure large-scale participation. Because of its highly mobilized nature, some observers have argued that it is not comparable with political participation in the West; but, as Jan Triska (1977, pp. 149–50) points out, the distinctions between mobilized and autonomous participation are far from straightforward and all political systems exhibit elements of both. However, communist states fall into Verba, Nie and Kim's (1978, p. 112) category of dominant institutional systems, and one of the most interesting aspects of participation, to which we devote some attention, is the relationship between levels of blue-collar participation, on the one hand, and socioeconomic and organizational factors, on the other.

Political participation in communist states can be divided into three categories. The first, which consists of occasional mass demonstrations of support, such as voting in elections, is so inclusive and undifferentiated that it has little relevance for our investigations. The second category is that of sociopolitical activity – as participation is officially termed – at the most general level of affiliation to organizations and movements, ranging from Women's Leagues through to the Communist Party. Finally there is activism which denotes the fulfillment of a regular part-time office or commission within one or more of these organizations, representative bodies or movements (Kulpinska, 1969, pp. 20–21). Activism is by far the most important measure of political participation.

Levels of Participation
General sociopolitical activity embraces up to half the population of these countries (Szanto, 1974, p. 17; Kovacs, 1976, p. 205; Ostrowski and Sufin, 1979, p. 162, table 5); this is a high level of participation by Western standards. Since social and political organizations are concentrated at the workplace, involvement here is higher still: Hungarian and Polish evidence indicates that approximately two-thirds of the laborforce are involved in some form of sociopolitical activity (Molnar *et al.,* 1970, p. 65; Przybyla

Piwko, 1977, p. 275). Most of this activity is peripherally political in nature and levels of activism are low. Perhaps one in four or five workers could be described as moderately active and only one in ten falls into the highly activist class (Widerszpil, 1965, p. 315; Molnar *et al.,* 1970, p. 201).

Activism is strongly differentiated along lines of education, skill and occupation. Kulpinska's research in Lodz in the early 1960s (1969, p. 108) revealed that workers were proportionately under-represented by a third among activists, whereas white-collars and supervisory staff were over-represented by a factor of four. The higher one goes in the factory hierarchy, the greater the likelihood of finding individuals holding key part-time posts. The author of a major study of the distribution of power and influence in Czechoslovakia in 1967 found the relationship between activism and professional position to be so strong that he described part-time functions as the 'infrastructure of authority' (Brokl, 1969, pp. 245, 262). Levels of education and skill also exercise a strong influence on activism. Skilled workers figure disproportionately among blue-collar activists, so much so that their participation rates fall not far short of those of some technical and lower supervisory groups (Kovacs, 1979, p. 83). It is the massive passivity of the unskilled workers that accounts for the gap in activism between the blue-collars as a whole and their non-manual colleagues. As many as eight out of ten unskilled workers do not take any part in sociopolitical activity (Widerszpil, 1965, p. 315; Molnar *et al.,* 1970, p. 68; Kovacs, 1976, p. 201). Apart from education, an important factor underlying such passivity is that unskilled groups include a large proportion of women. And regardless of socioeconomic resources, women seem to be approximately half as active in this respect as men (Kulpinska, 1969, p. 108; Kovacs, 1976, p. 214).

Just as psychological involvement in politics was found to be differentiated along occupational, education and skill lines, so activism appears to be strongly related to social and economic resource levels. Since the investment of time and effort involved in participating is greater than in attending to public affairs, one might expect socioeconomic-based disparities in activism to be higher. Unfortunately, we do not have the data on which to reach any firm conclusions. Broadly speaking, the correlations between activism and levels of social and economic resources do seem to be higher than in the area of psychological involvement. Yet the gap between the activism of skilled workers and the technical intelligentsia seems to be significantly smaller than that separating their levels of political interest. The relatively higher activism of the skilled also increases the distance between them and their unskilled colleagues.

A possible explanation for this apparent 'elevation' of the skilled worker group's activism is the effect of organizational factors on the rate at which the skilled convert their socioeconomic resources into political activity (Verba *et al.,* 1978, pp. 81, 112). There is no doubt that organizational involvement is positively related with activism. While this relationship is weak where trade union or Youth League membership is concerned, it is strong in the case of the party. Communists are commonly over-represented by a factor of three or more among political activists

(Malanowski, 1967, p. 342; Kulpinska, 1969, p. 108; Brokl, 1969, pp. 245, 261).

Given the Communist Party's key role in channeling political participation, one might ask whether party affiliation raises workers' activism and acts to narrow the blue-collar/white-collar opportunity gap. Party membership certainly raises blue-collar activism above the levels one would expect on the basis of their social and economic resources; Hungarian evidence suggests that skilled workers are particularly affected in this way (Kovacs, 1976, p. 214, table 24). As to the effects of party affiliation on relative levels of activity within the organization itself, Polish research, conducted some twenty years ago, found that activism differentials were only slightly lower within the party than outside its ranks. Skilled, and particularly unskilled, worker communists were still far less active than their comrades from the technical intelligentsia (Stasiuk, 1964, pp. 78–9; Bauman, 1967, pp. 167, 170). This seems to parallel Verba, Nie and Kim's conclusion (1978, p. 226) in relation to Yugoslavia, that the League of Communists 'channels political activity but draws the haves into those channels'.

Recruitment and Motivation

A major reason for the weakness of the party's effect on participation inequalities, is its selective recruitment. Although communist parties have large numbers of workers in their ranks, they still draw members disproportionately from white-collar groups. Party membership saturation varies markedly with occupation and job responsibilities: 10–15 percent among workers, 30–40 percent among the technical intelligentsia, and 50–60 percent plus among professionals (Kovacs, 1976, p. 214; *Rocznik Statystyczny,* 1979, p. 24; Ostrowski, 1976, pp. 98–9). Of all social and political organizations in Czechoslovakia in 1967 it was the Communist Party that showed the strongest correlation between membership and occupation (Brokl, 1969, p. 259; Machonin, 1969, p. 119).

Concerned with the effects of such disproportions on legitimacy and control at factory level, party leaders have in recent years stepped up worker recruitment. In Czechoslovakia great efforts have been made to recover from the slump in blue-collar membership in the early 1970s when the Czechs vied with the Mongolians for the title of least-proletarianized communist party. The drive has had some success: in 1976 workers consituted a respectable if unspectacular 35 percent of total membership (Kusin, 1978, p. 187). Relatively little seems to have come of Kadar's efforts to boost working-class presence in the party (*Nepszabadsag,* 15 March 1976), while Gierek's campaign for a more participative socialist democracy took until 1975 to make any impact on the social composition of the Polish United Workers' Party. At the end of 1979 working-class membership stood at 46 percent of the total – eight percent up on the 1970 figure (*Zycie Partii,* no. 2, 1980, pp. 12–14; Grzybowski, 1979, p. 226). In tandem with membership drives, affirmative action measures have raised blue-collar representation in party committees and assemblies as well as in other bodies such as national councils. However, executives still remain dominated by the intelligentsia (de Weydenthal, 1977, p. 351; Kovacs, 1979, p. 82).

All attempts to increase blue-collar participation through the party are beset by two problems. First, there are the basic functional requirements affecting party recruitment (Rigby, 1968, pp. 511–13). In order to perform its leading role within the political and economic system, all communist parties have to include a very large proportion of the intelligentsia elites whose knowledge, ability and authority are essential for the running of a complex system. For the intelligentsia – especially its upper echelons – party membership is largely an attribute rather than the determinant of resources and authority that they already possess (Brokl, 1969, pp. 258–9). On the other hand, for purposes of popular legitimacy and political integration, communist parties also need to recruit an elite of blue-collar groups. But given the size restrictions imposed by the vanguard concept, and the numerical expansion of strategic intelligentsia groups, there is often pressure on the room available for workers.

Even when party leaders decide – as in the Polish and Czechoslovak cases – to go all out to recruit workers and keep down non-manual numbers, they are still faced by the problem of the two groups' different propensities to join and become active members (Pomian, 1977, pp. 603, 606; Konrad and Szelenyi, 1979, pp. 179–80, 222).

For the intelligentsia – especially its technical and middle management segments – a party card is a distinct career advantage. And since white-collars are well-equipped to cope with the demands of membership, including the taking on of various part-time functions, the burdens imposed by belonging to the party appear as acceptable costs for faster career advancement.

For the skilled worker, party membership is also attractive for the chances it offers for promotion, either to lower supervisory posts or to full-time functions within the party or trade unions. One Hungarian study found that of all the groups in the factory, it was the skilled workers who gave greatest weight to political adaptability as a factor in 'getting ahead' (Kolosi, 1979, p. 75). Not that this means that all adaptive skilled workers rush to join the party – a considerable number are persuaded to do so. Moreover, a keen awareness of the political adaptability factor may make them alive to the risks involved in joining the party and falling short of expected conduct. Many others may consider the burden of party duties too heavy a price to pay for the marginal advantages offered by membership, especially if they are not ambitious to advance to supervisory posts.

Party membership probably holds out least advantage to the unskilled. A few may see party channels as a way to advance to higher ranks but the days of large-scale upward mobility through political work have gone. The advantages of political adaptability are offset by the obligations this involves. A considerable number of unskilled workers who are talked into joining the party, or harbor illusions about the advantages and duties entailed, soon leave or are expelled, usually for passivity or misconduct (often drunkenness). The high rates of attrition of blue-collar communists compound the difficulties of 'proletarianizing' the party. In recent years workers have constituted half of new recruits and two-thirds of those expelled, whereas intelligentsia attrition rates are far lower (Barat, 1970; de Weydenthal, 1977, p. 346).

In broad terms the differences in blue- and white-collar groups' perceptions of party affiliation apply to orientations to political participation in general. To be sure, our earlier discussion of reasons for joining the party omitted to mention the altruistic and collectivist socialist reasons for participating that should motivate all East European citizens to be active. And indeed, in response to questions about why they participate, roughly one in every two Eastern Europeans seem to give the 'correct' answer: socialist convictions, a wish to help the community. It would be presumptuous to discount altogether what is by far the most important single reason given for taking part in sociopolitical activity. Yet the remarkable consistency of such responses – ranging between 40 percent for the unskilled to 50 percent for the intelligentsia (Kulpinska, 1969, p. 80; Molnar *et al.,* 1970, p. 82; Kovacs, 1976, appendix, figure 15) – casts doubt on their accuracy and plausibility. Moreover, such motivation is belied by the other reasons given for participating.

Passive acceptance of participation as something into which one is talked or mobilized seems fairly widespread, especially among the unskilled, up to one in four of whom may be persuaded to take on the sociopolitical work they do (Kulpinska, 1969, p. 60; Molnar *et al.,* 1970, p. 82; Kovacs, 1976, p. 73). Predictably, persuasion plays a smaller part where non-manuals are concerned (Kovacs, 1976, appendix, figure 15).

Only a small percentage of participants – 10 percent of skilled and 18 percent of unskilled workers in one Hungarian survey (Molnar *et al.,* 1970, p. 79) – admit to seeking material benefits. Considerably more – approximately one in four workers and one in three members of the intelligentsia – mention non-material personal gain which is an acceptable cover term for career advantage (Kovacs, 1976, appendix, figure 15). Not surprisingly, careerist motives are more often attributed to others than given as the reason for one's own activity. They seem to figure importantly among skilled workers and especially among middle-ranking members of the technical intelligentsia (Kulpinska, 1969, pp. 116–30; Brokl, 1969, p. 262).

Effects of Participation

Even though most workers participate for the wrong reasons, their activity can have a positive impact on their political views and opinions. Czechoslovak and Hungarian evidence indicates higher levels of psychological involvement in politics and a greater attachment to officially approved values – as well as a greater critical awareness – among communists than among those outside party ranks (Molnar *et al.,* 1970, pp. 63–4; Piekalkiewicz, 1972, pp. 104–5). That such differences are not merely the effect of the Communist Party's occupational and educational profile is shown by Gospodarek's (1971, pp. 242–3) study of a Polish factory in 1970. He found that party membership was associated with a considerable increase in political interest, particularly among the unskilled. While political interest levels among non-communist unskilled workers were half those of their skilled colleagues, within the party the two groups showed very similar levels of interest. No such effects are linked with membership in other organizations or with sociopolitical activity in general. All in all, the instrumental orientations to participation which seem to predominate among workers and technical intelligentsia alike confirm low levels of real psychological involvement in politics. The fact that activism reflects rather than weakens established authority hierarchies must serve to reinforce workers' feelings of political incompetence.

Going through the motions of what is largely cosmetic participation serves to disassociate sociopolitical activity in workers' minds from real influence. It also helps to establish superficial, façade activism as part of normal behavior. In a sense, such socialization into hypocritical conformity aids stability and reinforces the tendencies of the adaptive worker. Yet cosmetic participation has two inherent flaws. First, the leadership cannot use workers' and others' participative conduct to gauge their real attitudes or the strength of their loyalty. Secondly, façade participation can so discredit the organizations involved that workers may resort to informal channels and methods to articulate their views.

Informal Activity

Workers' activity outside official channels can be divided into four categories. The first comprises large-scale, violent protests against regime policies that threaten the welfare concept of socialism around which blue-collar support for the system revolves. Such major protests are extremely rare: Poland is the only East European country to have experienced more than one such outbreak in the last thirty years.

Strikes, which invariably precede such protests, are more frequent, although numbers are tiny by Western standards – even Poland probably has no more than a few dozen a year. Defensive and specific in character and rarely involving more than one factory, strikes are ill-organized and short. Because of their political sensitivity, they are usually settled by management concessions within a few hours, or at the most in one or two days. The demands put forward by the Gdansk Interfactory Strike Committee in August 1980 for wider access to the media and for the release of all political prisoners (Demands, 1980) marks an important development in the politicization of the working-class protest which we examine in greater detail in this chapter. (The subject of strikes and riots is treated at greater length in the chapter by Michael Montias in this book.) Far more common a form of workers' informal activity are slowdowns or partial stoppages directed at extracting gains from management rather than protesting against certain measures. Finally, individual workers often express dissatisfaction with conditions by infringing labor discipline or by changing jobs. In assessing the political nature of these types of activity we must be careful to distinguish between the political content of demands, on the one hand, and the political significance of actions, on the other.

Even those involved in violent protest do not usually put overt political demands first. Absorption with immediate economic grievances overshadows concern with broader political questions. These are raised, if at all, in the form of slogans denouncing privilege, certain party and government leaders and the security forces. Strikers have usually concentrated almost exclusively on material issues, venturing into the political arena mainly to demand the release of arrested comrades and the punishment of local officials (Pravda, 1979, pp. 221–7).

While there is an element of deliberate and conscious avoidance of political issues by striking workers who realize that political demands would reduce their chances of success, the general economism of workers' demands also stems from their view of politics as something distant from their immediate concerns. Moreover, the personalization of political issues and the devaluation of terms such as democracy and participation severely handicap workers' political self-expression (Staniszkis, 1979, p. 179).

If we turn to the latent political content and overt political significance of informal activity, a different picture emerges. As acts directed against the authorities, and often culminating in the destruction of symbols of party and police power, workers' violent protests are clear political statements, albeit of a negative kind. They also signify a failure in communication and understanding between workers and regime, a failure which is often traceable to the malfunctioning of political organizations.

While strikes are not actually illegal, they also constitute acts of defiance of authority and signal the breakdown of normal conflict management machinery, centering on the party. By contrast, slowdowns and individual indiscipline might officially be regarded as symptoms of poor political work by party and trade unions, but in reality they are tolerated as a part of informal enterprise politics. Accommodation of informal activity of this kind, and thus of a limited exercise of workers' power and personal freedom, helps to defuse and contain conflict within politically acceptable bounds. Where workers' informal activity is not successfully incorporated, as in Poland, industrial conflict tends to spill over into the political arena.

Enterprise Politics

To understand the interaction between formal and informal activity, we must briefly examine the enterprise power structure. As the major institutional links between the factory and the wider political system, the unions and the Communist Party play a mediating role (Bilska and Flasza, 1978, pp. 14–53). Both organizations are supposed to mobilize and educate the workforce, supervise management, ensure the implementation of regime policy and reconcile interests within the enterprises. Beyond that their roles somewhat differ.

In addition to a general responsibility to help management with meeting production targets, the trade unions retain a special brief to protect workers' legal rights. They also play an important role in coordinating various forms of workers' participation in management (Bilska and Flasza, 1978, pp. 36–47). Thus, in theory, trade unions should defend workers' interests, and it is this defense role that most workers want the unions to perform above all others. Union officials, however, conceive of their role primarily in terms of administering welfare and managing labor on behalf of the director. And in practice, unions tend to give priority to production over protection of their members' interests. The evidence concerning workers' attitudes to trade unions indicates a disparity between the union's potential as representative bodies and their actual performance in this role. On the one hand, a Polish study shows that of all the organizations in the enterprise, it is the unions which command broadest blue-collar trust and are perceived as playing a significant role in settling disputes (Hirszowicz and Morawski, 1967, p. 238; Owieczko, 1966, pp. 79–85). On the other, it and other studies suggest that Polish workers harbor no illusions about the unions' production bias, nor do they exhibit much confidence in unions' capacity to get things done, ranking them well below party and management in the enterprise power hierarchy (Hirszowicz and Morawski, 1967, p. 332; Molnar *et al.,* 1970, p. 99; Owieczko, 1966, p. 79). Even in Hungary, where unions possess more extensive powers than elsewhere, a substantial majority of workers take their grievances directly to supervisors, bypassing union officials (Hirszowicz and Morawski, 1967, p. 332; Hethy and Mako, 1978, pp. 25–31). The position is clearer where bodies for workers' participation in production are concerned. These are seen as having even less influence than the unions and operating largely as vehicles for technical intelligentsia interests (Hirszowicz and Morawski, 1967, p. 290; Tudek, 1975, p. 294; Gitelman, 1977, p. 133).

The Communist Party organization has a difficult dual role to perform. At one and the same time, it is supposed to help management to fulfill production plans as well as to articulate workers' interests (Bauman, 1967, p. 58). Partly because they consider the party as a powerful force within the enterprise, workers expect it to perform both roles as well as arbitrate in disputes (Hirszowicz and Morawski, 1967, pp. 332–3; Molnar *et al.,* 1970, p. 57). But its representation and arbitration functions are vitiated by a strong identification with management. Party officials are often seen as the director's men and this impression is compounded by the strength of managerial and technical staff on the party's executive. Not that the party fails totally to serve any blue-collar group. Skilled worker communists make good use of party meetings to air their views and are strongly represented on elected committees (Dyoniziak, 1967, p. 168). Yet, the very nature of the party as a selective political organization limits its credibility as a body representing the interests of the workforce as a whole. In contrast with the considerable confidence shown in the party by a majority of communists, most non-communists regard it with mistrust (Owieczko, 1966, p. 79; *Nova svoboda,* 30 November 1967; Molnar *et al.,* 1970, p. 96; Kemeny, 1977, p. 77).

Since communists figure prominently in all other enterprise organizations, the top officials of party, trade unions and self-management bodies appear to many workers as a clique in league with management. It is within this enterprise establishment, that major decisions are taken. Some groups have access to the establishment through its constituent bodies. One

Polish study found that the technical staff used self-management bodies; skilled worker communists went through the party executive (Dyoniziak, 1967, p. 163). But the formal structure of representation effectively excluded the overwhelming majority of blue-collars outside the party.

Informal Activity and Dual Power

These outsiders can demonstrate their discontent and try to influence management in at least two ways. As individuals, workers can express their dissatisfaction with conditions by adjusting their work pace, infringing labor rules – most commonly by not turning up to work – or by changing jobs. A recent Polish survey found that nearly one in three workers thought moves of this kind were a legitimate way to respond to tension in the factory. While such action is not political in itself, it does reflect attitudes to authority and the general climate in the enterprise. High levels of indiscipline may catalyze a deteriorating situation; more often, however, this type of informal activity relieves tension by providing an outlet for the most disaffected (Pravda, 1979, pp. 219–21).

Far more significant in a political sense, is informal activity involving groups of workers. By slowing down the pace or reducing the quality of their work, teams, sections or brigades can demonstrate their dissatisfaction with work norms, bonus payments, and the like. In Hungary pressure-group activity of this kind is highly sophisticated and does not go beyond an adjustment of productivity (Hethy and Mako, 1972). In Poland, on the other hand, actual work stoppages are more common (*Robotnik,* no. 17, 17 June 1978). In either case the informal action is usually sufficient to obtain concessions, since directors are concerned with meeting plan targets and anxious to avoid open confrontation.

At the center of such pressure-group activity is a core of skilled men, usually aged between 30 and 50, who fall squarely into the adaptive worker category (Hethy and Mako, 1970, Chapters 3, 4; Kemeny, 1977, p. 78). Extremely well-informed about enterprise politics, they act as informal opinion-leaders within their respective teams or sections. With their detailed knowledge of how the factory operates – down to details of relations within the establishment elite – these workers are adept at applying just the right amount of pressure on management to achieve their ends. Such opinion-leader groups seem to include union activists and brigade leaders but not officials of any of the enterprise organizations. The core of opinion-leaders constitutes an informal elite which counters but coexists with the enterprise establishment. Its influence over workers' opinions and actions creates what Kemeny has called a system of dual power within the factory (1977, p. 78). Moreover, working through a set of informal rules and structures which run parallel to official regulations, these groups typify the approach and *modus operandi* of the adaptive worker.

The system of dual power and parallel stuctures takes the political potential out of enterprise conflicts. To a great extent it can depoliticize enterprise relations in several ways. First, in bypassing official organizational channels and dealing directly with management, informal action can take the pressure off unions and party as mediators between workers and management. No doubt this detracts from their influence and standing, but it also takes conflict management out of politically linked channels. Secondly, informal pressure-group activity provides an outlet for narrow, specific grievances, the accumulation of which might lead to much more serious tension. Closely connected with this is the fact that the accommodation, or at least toleration, of this activity by the establishment helps to avoid open confrontation involving the entire workforce. And it should be remembered that it is the size and visibility of industrial conflict that make it a political problem. The sophisticated system of informal pressure-group activity that exists in Hungarian factories – and the more general mutual accommodation that is found in Czechoslovakia – is a major reason for the absence or near-absence of strikes in those countries. By the same token, the somewhat less-developed nature of informal methods in Poland might be seen as contributing to the high incidence of open conflict.

Indeed, organizational weakness is a major reason for the inability of Polish workers to go beyond short-lived protest actions that have little long-term effect on government policy. Considerable obstacles stand in the way of the efforts to create independent working-class organizations that have been made recently by a handful of workers and dissident intellectuals. Quite apart from the constant vigilance of the police, these dissidents have to contend with more fundamental problems. The very existence of official trade unions makes the creation of independent ones extremely difficult. Despite the low popular estimation of union power, these organizations do have some support within the workforce. More importantly, official organizations, however unrepresentative, siphon off many of the most ambitious and able adaptive workers. For these reasons, rather than trying to establish free trade unions – a project that has not met with great success hitherto–it may be more practicable to use existing organizations to voice demands. Thus, the *samizdat* newsletter, *Robotnik,* has urged workers to get independent-minded candidates elected to union committees and workers' councils and transform these organizations from within (Charter, 1978, p. 7).

Yet the most formidable obstacle to any kind of radical independent working-class action is lack of solidarity. The pursuit of narrow interests by small groups of workers sectionalizes an already highly differentiated group. The very effectiveness of such actions, notably in Hungary, makes the undertaking of broader solidary protest seem unnecessary. In a wider sense, the inward-looking nature of much informal activity is closely associated with workers' general inability to grasp the full significance of the linkage between their material benefits and the general political system. The adaptive worker may resent the existence of privileged elites, occasionally he may take action to veto certain measures. But by and large, he seems satisfied with bending the rules, creating informal ones and thus adapting the system to his needs and himself to the system.

Is there any possibility that this situation might change? To start with, deteriorating economic conditions in Eastern Europe have recently compelled the authorities to try and tighten up slack discipline, over-manning and low productivity as well as to reduce price subsidies. All these moves affect important aspects of the welfare socialist system to which workers are attached. Not only might this weaken blue-collar support for the regime, but it may also reduce the scope for the accommodation of informal activity. Furthermore, as we noted earlier, young, better-educated workers seem to have a higher sense of political competence and a greater ambition to influence decision-making. Finally, as Poland has shown, confrontations with the regime engender self-confidence and might accelerate the growth of a working-class consciousness.

Given such developments – and much depends on the way in which different regimes handle the situation – dissident intellectuals who increasingly seek to build bridges with blue-collar groups might be able to radicalize and politicize the workers. But for this to happen the adaptive worker would have to be induced to go beyond adjusting the regulations and creating parallel structures and instead to try to change the *official* rules of the political game.

Poland, Politicization and the Future

Given Poland's unique record of blue-collar protest, it is worth examining the whole complex of factors underlying its development and assessing their significance for Eastern Europe. These factors fall into two categories: those operating within the enterprise and those relating to higher levels in the system.

Within the enterprise the general relationship between labor and management is an obvious factor conditioning conflict. Polish managers seem to be somewhat more inflexible and high-handed than their Czechoslovak or Hungarian counterparts. Certainly, the level of tension between workers and management seems to be higher in Poland than elsewhere in the region (Preiss, 1978, pp. 64–5; Mod and Kozak, 1974, p. 68). Moreover, mechanisms for diffusing such tension and mediating workers' demands have been particularly ineffective in Poland. Reluctant to challenge management even where workers' rights were clearly violated, Polish trade union officials have generally failed even to support those members who have taken their grievances to court (Loch, 1975). It is, therefore, not surprising to find survey evidence suggesting that four out of every five Polish workers are dissatisfied with union performance (Steszenko, 1973, p. 178).

While official Polish trade unions have been weaker than their East European counterparts, Communist Party organizations at enterprise level have been more assertive. Not only may this assertiveness have imposed greater restrictions on informal grouping than exist in Hungarian or Czech factories, it has also helped to raise tensions in labor–management relations in a different sense. Revitalization of party enterprise organizations in the 1970, however imperfect, expanded the ranks of party activists sympathetic to blue-collar interests and frustrated with management inefficiency. Many of these activists took part in the strike movements of 1970–71 and 1980 (Baluka and Barker, 1977, pp. 19–25; J. Strzelecki, *Le Soir,* 9 September 1980). The very participation of party activists in the organization of protests directed against higher authorities lends political significance to industrial conflict. It can also politicize blue-collar protests by prompting reactive action from non-communists. As we have already noted, the party is perceived by workers as a partisan organization and is viewed with mistrust by most of those outside its ranks. Political tensions of this kind are probably greater in Poland than in Hungary or Czechoslovakia; survey results indicate the existence of considerable cleavages stemming from differences in political outlook and affiliation (Nowak *et al.,* 1976, p. 340). After the initial stage of industrial action, non-communist opinion-leaders frequently come to the fore. This is politically significant in two respects. In the first place, any movement outside the control of local party members is perceived by the regime as a political threat. Quite apart from the issue of control, there is the question of the political content of actions led by non-communist workers many of whom have in the past experienced harassment at the hands of the regime. Unrestrained by the divided loyalties that beset those party activists who sympathize with workers' grievances, they tend to adopt an overtly apolitical stance which has obvious political ramifications. Throughout the events of August–September 1980 Lech Walesa, the Gdansk strike leader, took a studiedly non-partisan stand, insisting that he was interested only in defending workers' rights and so had to be independent of all political parties (*El Pais* (Madrid), 6 September 1980; *New York Times,* 27 August 1980). Such issues clearly take us beyond the enterprise sphere and into the national arena. While as individuals workers may be relatively uninterested in politics, Polish developments show how their collective outlook and action can be politicized via three vectors – economic, organizational and social – linking their immediate concerns with national politics.

That changes in the economic situation have a direct effect on blue-collar attitudes and action, almost goes without saying. Public opinion surveys show that in Poland, as elsewhere, the standard of living is the major yardstick against which regime performance is popularly measured (OBOP, 1979b, p. 2). They also show that public estimates of economic conditions are highly volatile (OBOP, 1980b, p. 4). In part this volatility stems from the discontinuity of Poland's economic development. Stagnation in the late 1960s was followed by a rapid rise in living standards in the early 1970s which declined later in the decade giving way to stagnation by 1979. Workers' expectations were, thus, raised only to be let down again. Disappointment with economic conditions has acted as a major catalyst in the politicization of enterprise-located, blue-collar protest. Each of the last three major waves of protest has been sparked by attempts to raise food prices. Since the party and government control all aspects of economic policy such protests are necessarily directed against the political authorities. Grievances relating to living standards also politicize workers' protests in as much as they provide a common cause which links blue-collar demands with the population at large and swells mass support for all aspects of workers' actions. Thus, all but a small minority of Poles approved of the July–August 1980 strikes (OBOP, 1980a, p. 1).

While the key role of economic issues in politicizing workers' outlook and action is readily visible, its operation becomes clearer when we examine the organizational vector. The highly centralized structure of the Polish economic system has made it impossible for enterprise directors to satisfy many of the material claims put by workers. Blue-collar demands, therefore, frequently have to be targeted at and against higher political authorities. Of the 11,000 demands made by Baltic coast strikers in December 1970 well over half could not be dealt with at enterprise level (Krukowski, 1971, p. 59). All of the twenty-one demands raised by the Gdansk Interfactory Strike Committee in August 1980 fell within the central authorities' sphere of competence (Demands, 1980). That these demands are conveyed to the center by way of protest action is also attributable to organizational factors. Neither the party nor the trade unions are effective channels of communication; their hierarchical structure and democratic centralist rules hamper upward articulation of blue-collar expectations and demands. Reports on rank-and-file grievances seem to be filtered out, blocked or disregarded at regional and central apparatus levels. At any rate they find little reflection in key policy decisions, especially those relating to food prices. Bureaucratic high-handedness has been expressed by a repeated failure on the part of the Polish authorities to follow Hungarian practice and give the public ample notice of and information about such unpopular measures. It is this apparent disdain for workers' opinions that engenders resentment among many who are usually not concerned with politics (Walentynowycz, 1980). Anger at the way in which party and government disregard blue-collar opinion is as important a catalyst in politicizing workers' outlook and protest as the substance of the economic measures that trigger such action.

It is precisely the shortcomings in organizational representation that have prompted the most important political demands put forward by Polish workers – the successful call in August 1980 for free, independent and self-governing trade unions. The events of 1980 are discussed in detail elsewhere in this book; for our purposes it is useful to note that the demands for free unions – and the concessions made – are highly political in at least three respects. To begin with, the very notion of self-governing trade unions existing alongside the old unions and providing 'genuine' representation of workers' interests (Protocol, 1980, p. G30) legitimizes the existence of different interpretations of working-class interests. Secondly, there is the fact that these new unions are prepared to take an adversary stand on any official policy that they see as opposing workers' interests. As it is practically impossible to draw a clear line between what is an economic policy and what is a political one, this means that such unions must be ready to pursue an independent political line, notwithstanding their self-denying ordinance regarding political activity (Protocol, 1980, p. G30).

Finally, while the new unions have pledged their allegiance to the Polish Constitution, they have been most reluctant explicitly to subordinate themselves to the party's leading role – consigning mention of the role to an annex of their statutes – and have asserted their independence of all political organizations (Plan Rozmowy, 1980, p. 6). More specifically, while rank-and-file communists may be elected to office in the new unions, party office-holders have been declared ineligible (Walesa, *Sztandar Mlodych,* 20 October 1980). The chairman of the new Solidarity unions, Lech Walesa, has reportedly even gone as far as to state that 'The Party must rule the country but in the trade unions there is no room for it' (*New York Times,* 24 October 1980).

The third and last of the vectors through which Polish workers' outlook and action has been politicized, is that of social consciousness and social relations. Demands to eliminate elite privilege in Polish society have appeared in all the waves of workers' protest to date. In August 1980 the Gdansk strikers called for an end to the special shops and other material privileges enjoyed by members of the party and police apparatuses (Demands, 1980). They also advocated the introduction of meat rationing, a demand that reflects the strong blue-collar egalitarianism we noted earlier.

Much working-class anti-elitism stems from resentment of the much higher living standards of groups who do not seem to deserve such benefits, being both underqualified and incompetent. This resentment is part of a wider blue-collar awareness of growing social differences between manual and upper white-collar managerial and ruling groups. In Poland at least, this awareness seems to have been accompanied by increasing blue-collar identification with the working class. Underpinned by declining rates of mobility and hardening lines of social distinction, the growth of working-class consciousness has been furthered by the traumas of conflict between workers and regime. It made possible and was further reinforced by the solidarity of working-class action in 1980. That the materially 'pampered' miners of Silesia came out on strike alongside their Baltic coast fellows, and that makeshift committees were able to coordinate a national general strike on 3 October 1980, must have surprised Polish politicians and sociologists alike.

In some respects the greater cohesion and self-confidence of Polish workers has lessened the importance of the last social factor operating to politicize their outlook and action: the influence of dissident intellectual groups. None the less intellectual groups have contributed to the politicization of blue-collar movements in two ways. In the first place, workers' attachment to civil liberties in 1980 was made more explicit by ties with intellectual groups and causes. Catholicism not only provided a moral corset for strikers, but also constituted the most obvious link between them and certain reformist intellectuals; together the Catholic connection produced the political demand for greater church access to the mass media put forward by the Gdansk Interfactory Strike Committee (Demands, 1980). As far as workers' links with intellectuals around the KSS-KOR (Committee for Social Self-Defense-Committee for Defense of the

Workers) is concerned, solidarity stemmed from a record of KSS–KOR support for blue-collar rights and a mutual feeling of common cause against regime repression. Such sentiments of solidarity underpinned the Gdansk strikers' commitment to intellectual dissenters' rights freely to express their opinions (Walesa, Gdansk Domestic Radio Service, 30 August 1980, Foreign Broadcast Information Service, vol. 11, no. 171, p. G6). From this commitment, in part came the most unalloyed political demands of 1980: the full implementation of constitutional civil liberties and the release of all political prisoners (Demands, 1980).

Actual direct contributions by dissident intellectuals to the political content of workers' demands are far more difficult to gauge than the general effects of solidarity between the two groups. We know that Catholic intellectuals around the journal *Wiez* acted as advisers to the Gdansk Interfactory Strike Committee (*New York Times,* 28 August 1980). Members of the KSS–KOR also played a consultative role in negotiations at Gdansk and elsewhere. More importantly, for three years the group around KSS–KOR had exercised a considerable influence on the general climate of blue-collar opinion and on the views of worker activists by way of the *samizdat* journal, *Robotnik*. Circulating in tens of thousands of copies in major industrial centers, *Robotnik* established a dialogue between intellectual and working-class dissidents, focusing blue-collar attention on questions of representation and the building up of independent workers' organizations. The most significant practical result of this new focus was the establishment of free trade union committees in Gdansk, Szczecin and Katowice in 1978 (*Labour Focus on Eastern Europe*, vol. 2, no. 3, July–August 1978, pp. 21–3). Though small in size, these committees provided many of the ideas and leaders of the mass movement for independent unions of summer–autumn 1980. In this way, intellectual influences helped catalyze the development of free trade unionism. A similar contributory role was played by intellectual advisers, who helped to sharpen and inform the political thrust of strikers' demands in August 1980. In no sense did intellectual dissidents covertly graft political demands onto 'genuine' working-class economic concerns as some conservative critics in Poland have claimed (*Trybuna Ludu,* 30–31 August 1980). Rather, intellectual influence since 1976 should be seen as helping to heighten blue-collar awareness of the linkages between the economic and political spheres.

Whatever weight one assigns to the various vectors examined, and whatever the final outcome of the events of summer 1980, the direction of developments surrounding the Polish working class over the last decade is clear: blue-collar assertiveness has become increasingly political in nature and impact. One could summarize the process by saying that the old 'social compact' has given way to a new, written social contract embodied by the agreements signed between government and strikers in August 1980.

The question remains, how significant is the Polish case for Eastern Europe in general? Clearly, Polish developments will not be duplicated elsewhere in the region; yet certain trends evident in Poland are also affecting the adaptive workers of Czechoslovakia, Hungary and even East

Germany. Rising educational levels and higher living standards fuel workers' material expectations and promote greater interest in gaining a real say in questions directly affecting blue-collar interests. This, in turn, places increasing pressure on the political organizations that are supposed to mediate and represent those interests. Even if Czechoslovak and Hungarian formal organizations operate more effectively than their Polish counterparts, workers' attitudes toward them differ more in degree than in kind. As we have seen, blue-collar involvement in formal social and political activity is very similar across national boundaries. In Hungary and Czechoslovakia management accommodation of informal activity has helped to compensate for poor organizational performance. By bending the rules and obviating the formal structures, adaptive workers in these countries have been able to obtain sufficient benefits to keep them from openly challenging and seeking to break that structure. Relatively favorable economic conditions have also helped these regimes to maintain a manageable balance between blue-collar expectations and reality. But as the economic situation deteriorates throughout the region, so the Hungarian, Czechoslovak and East German authorities will be forced to reduce the 'slack' that has long provided the scope for informal activity.

The ever-growing pressures for higher economic efficiency also pose a direct threat to the 'social compact' rights that anchor workers' attachment to the existing systems. So far leaders in all three countries mentioned have responded to these economic pressures more carefully and have handled them far more adeptly than the Poles. Either by maintaining high subsidies – in the case of Czechoslovakia and the GDR – or by introducing substantial price increases gradually and only after considerable public discussion, they have avoided open conflict with the working class and minimized the politicization of blue-collar demands. If, as seems likely, economic problems continue to worsen, only Hungary, with its relatively decentralized economic system and flexible approach to political compromise, has the capacity to absorb the social repercussions of further stringency by organizational adaptation. And even this adaptation clearly has its limits; Hungarian union officials have been highly critical of the notion of independent trade unions (Gaspar, *Nepszabadsag,* 19 October 1980). Czechoslovak or East German political and organizational elasticity is far smaller. Should living standards decline substantially and informal activity be squeezed further, workers in these countries may well turn from adaptive techniques to more open and politically challenging forms of assertiveness. Currently, latent worker–intellectual links, such as those around the Charter movement in Czechoslovakia, could conceivably catalyze the politicization of blue-collar demands as has happened in Poland. Indeed, the entire process could be accelerated by the developments in Poland. In October 1980 Czech miners reportedly went on strike demanding the right to establish independent trade unions *(Le Monde,* 22 October 1980). The Czechoslovak and East German authorities felt sufficiently concerned about the dangers of 'contagion' to clamp down on communications and travel contacts with Poland (*New York Times,* 20 November 1980). Neither Czechoslovak, nor East German, workers are likely to get free trade unions; at the time of writing (November 1980) the gains made by Polish workers remain uncertain, their future dependent on a triangular balance of forces: working-class organization and determination, the constellation of domestic political elites and the limits set by Moscow. But regardless of the outcome of this particular crisis, the development and interaction of the regional economic, social and organizational trends we have outlined will produce a new set of rules governing relations between workers and regime rules, which will require more adaptation from the political authorities than from the working class.

References: Chapter 3

Almond, G. and Verba, S., *The Civic Culture* (Boston, Ma.: Little, Brown, 1965).

Baluka, E. and Barker, E., 'Workers' struggles in Poland', *International Socialism*, January 1977, pp. 19–25.

Barat, K., *Partelet*, November 1970, cited in Radio Free Europe, 'Hungarian Background Report no. 29, 1970, pp. 8–11.

Bauman, Z., 'Social structure of the party organisation in industrial works', in J. Wiatr, ed., *Problems of Polish Political System* (Warsaw: Ossolineum, 1967), pp. 156–78.

Bielicki, W. and Widerszpil, S., '*Z problematyki przemian spolecznych w Polsce Ludowej*', *Nowe Drogi*, no. 7, 1979, pp. 74–85.

Bilska, A. and Flasza, R., *Organizacja i metody pracy spolecznej w przedsiebiorstwach* (Warsaw: Ksiazka i Wiedza, 1978).

Blachnicki, B., '*Rownosc ekonomiczna w swiadomosci pracownikow przemyslu*', *Studia Socjologiczne*, no. 4, 1977, pp. 135–53.

Brokl, V., '*Moc and socialni rozvrstveni*', in P. Machonin *et al., Ceskoslovenska spolecnost* (Bratislava: Epocha, 1969), pp. 235–64.

Charter 1978, 'Charter of workers' rights', trans. in *Labour Focus on Eastern Europe*, September–October 1978, pp. 7–8.

Demands 1980, 'New list of demands given Polish government by Gdansk strikers', *New York Times*, 29 August 1980, p. 4.

Doktor, K., *Przedsiebiorstwo przemyslowe* (Warsaw: Ksiazka i Wiedza, 1964).

Drazkewicz, J., '*Uwagi o aktywnosci spolecznej i zroznicowanie spolecznym*', *Studia Socjologiczne*, no. 4, 1974, pp. 173–90.

Dyoniziak, R., *Spoleczne uwarunkowanie wydajnosci pracy* (Warsaw: Ksiazka i Wiedza, 1967).

Dziedzic, T., '*Strwktura formalna a faktyczny system podejmowania decyzii w socjalististycznym przedsiebiorstwie przemyslowym*' (doctoral thesis, University of Warsaw, 1973).

Gitelman, Z., 'Development, institutionalization and elite–mass relations in Poland', in J. F. Triska and P. M. Cocks, eds, *Political Development in Eastern Europe* (New York: Praeger, 1977), pp. 119–46.

Glowny Urzad Statystyczny, *Oddzialywanie prasy, radia i telewizji. Wyniki badania ankietowego GUS przprowadzanego w 1967 r* (Warsaw: GUS, 1969).

Gospodarek, T., '*Z badan nad kultura polityczna w zakladach wielkoprzemyslowych*', *Studio Socjologiczne*, no. 2, 1971, pp. 235–51.

Gray, J., 'Conclusion', in A. H. Brown and J. Gray, eds, *Political Culture and Political Change in Communist States* (London: Macmillan, 1977), pp. 253–72.

Grzybowski, L., *Robotnicy in PZPR 1948–75* (Warsaw: Ksiazka i Wiedza, 1979).

Hethy, L. and Mako. C., *The Principle of Payment According to Performance, and Enterprise Interest and Power Relations* (in Hungarian) (Budapest: MTA Szociologiai Kutato Csoport, 1970).

Hethy, L. and Mako, C., 'Work performance, interests, power and environment (The case of cyclical slowdown in a Hungarian factory)', in P. Halmos, ed., *Hungarian Sociological Studies,* Sociological Review. Monograph no. 17 (Keele: Keele University Press, 1972), pp. 125–50.

Hethy, L. and Mako, C., 'Workers' participation and the socialist enterprise' (Budapest: mimeo., 1978).

Hirszowicz, M. and Morawski, W., *Z badan nad spolecznym uczestnictwem w organizacji przemyslowym* (Warsaw: PWN, 1967).

Honza, K., *'Co si mysli delnici',* *Listy,* no. 4, 1975, pp. 1–4.

Horvath, Z., 'Findings on attitudes towards social differences', *Valosag,* no. 12, 1978, trans. in JPRS, *East European Political, Sociological and Military Affairs,* no. 1643, 1979, pp. 1–16.

Ifju Kommunista, July 1979, cited in *Radio Free Europe Hungarian Situation Report,* no. 15, 1979, pp. 16–17.

Janicki, A., Szczecin Domestic Radio, 10 September 1980, trans., *Foreign Broadcasting Information Service Daily Report (Eastern Europe),* vol 11, no. 178, pp. 8–9.

Jungmann, B., *'Sebehodnoceni a sebeidentifikace',* in P. Machonin *et al.,* eds, *Ceskoslovenska spolecnost* (Bratislava: Epocha, 1969). pp. 351–76.

Kemeny, I., *'La classe ouvriere en Hongrie',* in G. Mink and J. Rupnik, eds, *Structures sociales en Europe de l'Est, No. 2: Transformations de la classe ouvriere* (Paris: Documentation française: Notes et Etudes, nos 4511–4512).

Kolankiewicz, G. and Taras, R., 'Poland: socialism for everyman', in A. H. Brown and J. Gray, eds, *Political Culture and Political Change in Communist States* (London: Macmillan, 1977), pp. 101–30.

Kolosi, T., in *Tarsadalmi Szemle,* no. 4, 1979, trans., JPRS, *East European Political, Sociological and Military Affairs,* no. 1685, 1979, pp. 65–78.

Konrad, G. and Szelenyi, I., *The Intelligentsia on the Road to Class Power* (Brighton: Harvester Press, 1979).

Kovacs, F., *A munkasosztaly politikai ideologiai muveltsegerol es aktivitasarol* (Budapest: Kossuth Kiado, 1976).

Kovacs, F., 'Examining the rapproachement of the workers and the intelligentsia', *Tarsadalom Tudomanyi Kozlemenyek,* no. 4, 1978, trans., JPRS, *East European Political, Sociological and Military Affairs,* no. 1675, 1979, pp. 79–93.

Krukowski, M., contribution in 'Discussion of December 1970 events at 11th Polish Trade Union Plenum', *Przeglad Zwiazkowy,* April 1971, trans., *Joint Publications Research Service* (East European *Political, Sociological and Military Affairs),* no. 53594, 1971.

Kulpinska, J., *Spoleczna aktywnosc pracownikow przedsiebiorstwa przemyslowy* (Wroclaw: Ossolineum, 1969).

Kusin, V. V., *From Dubček to Charter 77* (Edinburgh: Q Press, 1978).

Lane, D. and O'Dell, F., *The Soviet Industrial Worker* (London: Robertson, 1979).

Lipset, S. M., *Political Man* (Garden City, NY: Anchor Books, 1963).

Loch, J., *'Swieczka i ogarek',* *Polityka,* no. 51–2, 1975, p. 5.

MacDonald, O., 'Poland: party, workers and opposition', *Labour Focus on Eastern Europe,* May-June 1977, pp. 3–5.

Machonin, P., *'Socialni stratifikace v Ceskoslovensku',* in P. Machonin *et al., Ceskoslovenska spolecnost* (Bratislava: Epocha, 1969).

Malanowski, J., *Stosunki klasowe i roznice spoleczne w miesce* (Warsaw: PWN, 1967).

Malewski, A., 'Attitudes of employees from Warsaw enterprises toward the differentiation of wages and the social system in May 1958', *Polish Sociological Bulletin,* no. 2, 1971, pp. 17–31.

Matejko, A., 'Some sociological problems of socialist factories', *Social Research,* no. 3, 1969, pp. 448–80.

Mod, A. and Kozak, G., *A munkasok retegzodese munkaja, ismeretei es uzemi demokracia a Duna Vesmu ket gyarreszlegeban* (Budapest: Akademiai Kiado, 1974).

Molnar, L., Nemes, F. and Belane. S., *Ipari munkasok politikai aktivitasa* (Budapest: Kossuth Kiado, 1970).

Nowak, S., *'Srodowiskowe determinanty ideologii spolecznej studentow Warszawy',* *Studia Socjologiczne,* no. 2 1962, pp. 143–79.

Nowak, S. *et al., Ciaglosc i zmiana tradycji kulturowej* (Warsaw: Zaklad Metodologii Badan Socjologicznych Socjologii, Uniwersyetu Warzawskego, 1976), mimeo.

OBOP, *'Idea demokracji w opiniach spoleczenstwa'* (Warsaw: Osrodek Badania Opinii Publiczney, 1979a), typed summary.

OBOP, *35 Years of the PRL* (Warsaw: Osrodek Badania Opinii Publicznej, 1979b), mimeo.

OBOP, *Summary of Results of Poll No. 15, 1980* (in Polish) (Warsaw: OBOP, 1980a), mimeo.

OBOP, *Summary of Results of Poll No. 16, 1980* (in Polish) (Warsaw: OBOP, 1980b), mimeo.

Ostrowski, K., *'Charakterystyka skladu organizacji partynych wielkich zakladow pracy',* in A. Lopatka, J. Bluszkowski and K. Konstanski, eds, *Organizacje partyjne wielkich zakladow pracy.* (Warsaw: Ksiazka i Weidza, 1976), pp. 94–110.

Ostrowski, K. and Sufin, Z., *'Aktywnose spoleczna w swietle badan',* *Nowe Drogi,* no. 11, 1979, pp. 156–73.

Owieczko, A., *'Opinie o samorzadzie robotniczym',* *Studia Socjologiczne,* no. 3, 1966, pp. 65–99.

Piekalkiewicz, J. A., *Public Opinion Polling in Czechoslovakia, 1968–69* (New York: Praeger, 1972).

'Plan Razmowy ulkadamy wspolnie', *Polityka,* no. 44, 1980, pp. 1, 6.

Podgorecki, A., *Prestiz prawa* (Warsaw: Ksiazka i Wiedza, 1966).

Podgorecki, A., *Law and Society* (London: Routledge & Kegan Paul, 1974).

Pomian, K., *'Le parti: verites et mensognes',* *Les Temps Modernes,* November–December 1977, pp. 588–607.

Pravda, A., 'Industrial workers: patterns of dissent, opposition and accommodation', in R. L. Tokes, ed., *Opposition in Eastern Europe* (London: Macmillan, 1979), pp. 209–54.

Preiss, A., *'Przemiany styla zarzadzania ir zautomatyzowanych przedsiebiorstwach przemyslowych',* in *Kierowanie zespolami pracownicymi w organizcajach,* Prace Naukowe Instytutu Organizacji i Zazradzania Politechniki Wroclawskej, no. 18 (Warsaw: Wydawnicturo Politechnicki Wrocklawskej, 1978).

'Protocol of agreement between the government commission and the interfactory strike committee concluded on 31 August 1980 at Gdansk shipyards', *Glos Pracy,* 2 September 1980, pp. 2, 4, trans., *Foreign Broadcasting Information Service Daily Report (Eastern Europe),* vol. II, no. 176, 1980, pp. G-30-39.

Przybyla Piwko, E., *'Aspiracje i postawy spoleczno-zawodowe mlodych robotnikow przemyslowych'* (doctoral thesis, University of Warsaw).

Rigby, T. H., *Communist Party Membership in the USSR, 1917-67* (Princeton, NJ: Princeton University Press, 1968).

Sicinski, A., *'Spoleczne unwarunkowania zasiegu komunikowania w Polsce',* Studia Socjologiczno-Politiczne, no. 12, 1962, pp. 41–91.

Sopuch, K., *'Struktura spoleczna a wybor wartosci',* Studia Socjologiczne. no. 1, 1978, pp. 235–53.

Staniszkis, J., 'On some contradictions of Polish society', *Soviet Studies,* April 1979, pp. 167–87.

Stasiuk, A., *'Czynni i bierny czlonkowe partii w zakladzie przemyslowym',* Studia Socjologiczno-Politiczne, no. 16, pp. 78–94.

Steszenko, L., *Rada zakladowa—z badan w przedsiebiorstwach przemyslu terenowego* (Warsaw: Kriazka i Weldza, 1973).

Szanto, M., *Munkaiado csokkentes es eletmod* (Budapest: Akademiai Kiado, 1974).

Triska, J. F., 'Citizen participation in community decisions in Yugoslavia, Romania, Hungary and Poland', in J. F. Triska and P. M. Cocks, eds, *Political Development in Eastern Europe* (New York: Praeger, 1977), pp. 147–77.

Tudek, A., *'Wybrane problemy swiadomosci politycznej mlodych robotnikow',* in *Mlodzi robotnicy kwalifikacje, postawy, aspiracje* (Warsaw: Institut Wydawniczy CRZZ, 1975), pp. 289–98.

Vecernik, J., *'Problemy prijmu a zivotni urovne v socialni diferenciaci',* in P. Machonin *et al., Ceskoslovenska spolecnost* (Bratislava: Epocha, 1969).

Verba, S., Nie, N. H. and Kim, J. O., *Participation and Political Equality. A Seven Nation Comparison* (London: Cambridge University Press, 1978).

Walentynowycz, A., cited in J. Darnton, 'Gdansk activist doesn't mince his words', *New York Times,* 21 August 1980, p. 4.

Wasiak, K., 'Views of Szczecin youth concerning the role of social classes in Poland', *Kultura i Spoleczenstwo,* no. 2, 1976 trans., JPRS, *East European Political, Sociological and Military Affairs,* no. 1307, 1976, pp. 42–68.

de Weydenthal, J. B., 'Party development in contemporary Poland', *East European Quarterly,* Fall 1977, pp. 341–63.

Widerszpil, S., *Sklad polskiej klasy robotniczej* (Warsaw: PWN, 1965).

4 Can a Party of the Working Class be a Working-Class Party?

ELLEN TURKISH COMISSO

Introduction

One of the great political ironies of the twentieth century is the success communist parties have recruiting a working-class following when they are out of power and the difficulty they have retaining it when they control the reins of government (Tables 4.1, 4.2). In fact, in the past decade, a number of East European communist parties have literally had to embark on an affirmative action program to shore up the blue-collar contingent of their memberships (Bielasiak, 1980). The Yugoslav League of Communists (LCY) is a case in point; viewed from this perspective, it is less a case of 'exceptionalism' than a Balkan variant on a common Marxist theme.

Table 4.1 *Percentage of Blue-Collar Workers in Yugoslav League of Communists, 1946–78*

Year	Percentage of membership
1946	27·6
1952	32·2
1966	33·9
1968	31·2
1971	28·8
1973	29·1
1978	29·4

Source: 1946–71 figures: Bogdan Denitch, *The Legitimation of a Revolution* (New Haven, Ct.: Yale University Press, 1976), p. 94; 1973 figures: Radio Free Europe Research, 22 May 1974; 1978 figures: League of Communists of Yugoslavia, *The League of Communists of Yugoslavia between the Tenth and Eleventh Congresses* (Belgrade: Socialist Thought and Practice, 1978), p. 112.
Note: Official statistics, to the extent that they equate educational classification with occupation (if Zvir is at all typical, many who had 'highly skilled' qualifications were actually working as technicians, not on the machines) and often class lower technical personnel as production workers, tend to overestimate somewhat the real proportion of 'direct producers' who are party members. This is apart from the distorting effects of 'subjective factors' in the reporting of membership statistics.

Table 4.2 *Percentage of Manual Laborers in Italian Communist Party, 1948–73*

Year	Percentage of total membership	
	Urban workers	Rural workers*
1948	45·0	17·0
1950	42·0	18·0
1956	39·8	17·1
1962	39·5	12·7
1969	40·2	10·4
1973	39·5	8·0

Source: 1948–62 figures: Sidney Tarrow, *Peasant Communism in Southern Italy* (New Haven, Ct.: Yale University Press, 1967), p. 140; 1969, 1973 figures: Sezione centrale di stampa e propaganda del PCI, *Almanacco del Partito comunista italiano, 1972, 1973* (Rome: F.lli Spada Ciampino, 1972–3).

* 'Rural workers' in Italy are day-laborers *(braccianti)* on large farms; they are a propertyless group and are distinct from small peasants and sharecroppers *(mezzadri).* No such category exists in Yugoslavia. There, rural workers in large, self-managed 'industrial' farms are classed together with blue-collar workers.

In Italy, mechanization of agriculture and emigration to industrial areas has reduced the number of these workers. Thus, the drop in the relative size of their membership in the PCI should not be interpreted as disaffection.

This is not to deny the differences in ideology, organization and political role Bogdan Denitch uses to distinguish the LCY from its East European counterparts. On the contrary, it is precisely these differences which make recruiting blue-collar workers especially urgent in the Yugoslav case.

On the one hand, Yugoslav ideology differs from that of other communist parties in viewing socialist society as composed of diversified social groups that regularly come into legitimate (and occasionally, illegitimate) conflict in pursuing their respective interests (Kardelj, 1973). On the other, the Yugoslav party shares the assumption that a group's social power is reflected by the degree to which its members populate the ranks of the ruling party (Tito, 1978).

Thus, a drop in the number of blue-collar workers in the party need not be of immediate concern in a Soviet-type system, for workers' interests can theoretically be equally well represented there by members of other occupational strata employed within the state sector. Moreover, the situation can be corrected by a simple change in *cadres* policy and stepped-up recruitment efforts in the plants (Hough, 1976, 1979; McAuley, 1977). In Yugoslavia, however, workers' interests are not considered identical with those of other employees in the socialist sector, and when the proportion of manual workers in the LCY declines, the party line itself is brought into question. As Tito remarked in 1974,

Workers flocked to the League of Communists in greater numbers when it was uncompromisingly engaged in putting the socialist program of development into effect. And conversely, the workers left it when there were vacillations . . . in the implementation of the revolutionary course. In the latter situations, views typical of bourgeois society made their way into the League of Communists.

Why the party of the working class in Yugoslavia has difficulty describing itself as a working-class party is a complicated question. Some light can be shed on it by examining the role of the LCY within the Yugoslav self-managed enterprise, where it comes into direct contact with rank-and-file workers. In that context, the roots of the LCY's recruitment dilemma seems to lie in a lack of incentives for blue-collar workers to pay the costs of political action party membership entails for them. When workers as a group derive benefits from party actions, the benefits take the form of 'public goods' (Olson, 1965) which accrue to the work collective as a whole, or to workers in general, regardless of party affiliation or the lack of it. Thus, workers are implicitly encouraged to assume the position of 'free riders', especially given that the party's ability to perform its tasks in the firm require it to be as responsive to the demands of non-members as to those of its own activists. At the same time, the LCY's political responsibilities and the means it has to fulfill them in the enterprise both restrict the resources the party branch has at its disposal, and limit the ways it can allocate them. The result is that, as individuals, workers – in contrast to managerial personnel – are unlikely to profit from whatever non-collective benefits party membership can carry. Indeed, given the presence of self-management bodies with real decision-making power, even opportunities to exercise political influence in the firm are quite independent of party membership, and especially so for blue-collar workers.

The relationship between organizational role and individual recruitment in the enterprise party branch can be concretized by drawing on a case study of a Zagreb machine-tool plant done from March to September 1974. By examining some of the specific activities an enterprise party branch undertook during the study, we can get a clearer understanding of why these activities are not of a sort that would attract blue-collar workers into the party. The firm, which we shall call Zvir, manufactured and serviced machinery for a major primary-sector industry. In 1974, it employed 528 people, approximately 230 of which were skilled and highly skilled production workers. Of these, no more than 12 (5 percent) were members of the LCY at the time.

Zvir is not a 'typical' Yugoslav firm – no single enterprise could be. Nevertheless, the kinds of activities its party branch engaged in are as closely related to the structural position of the LCY as a ruling communist party in a self-managed politicoeconomic system as to the particular conditions surrounding Zvir itself. Hence, while the specific actions the Zvir LCY branch took necessarily reflect the empirical circumstances of the firm at the time, they are also specific examples of a more general pattern of activities. Likewise, the dynamics of the party's interaction with workers and management reflect such classic dilemmas of political action that it is doubtful that they are unique to Zvir.

The Organizational Actors*

The basic internal life of Yugoslav firms is characterized by the interaction of two parallel structures. One is the enterprise self-management structure, the complicated system of councils, commissions and assemblies through which the work collective – encompassing everyone employed in the firm – exercises its formal authority to make policy decisions.

The other is the firm's organizational structure, that is, the organization of work in the enterprise. The organizational structure also includes everyone in the firm, and one's place in it is simply one's job. But whereas the self-management structure is a political creation and is regulated by law, the organizational structure is a productive-technological entity and is conditioned by economic forces. And while the 'sovereign' of the self-management structure is the work collective acting as a whole in the assemblies, the firm's general director and top management stand at the apex of the organizational structure.

In theory, the self-management structure controls the organizational structure, which merely executes the former's decisions (Horvat, 1968). Supposedly, those who have power in the self-management bodies – and this should, of course, be direct production workers for the most part – have power in the organizational structure. In practice, however, the power equation is quite the opposite, and the higher-ups in the organizational structure also have the bulk of influence in the self-management bodies (Županov and Tannenbaum, 1968; Obradovic, 1972; Verba and Shabad, 1978). In short, the firm's executives tend to dominate both.

Enter the enterprise League of Communists organization. Several characteristics distinguish it from both the self-management and organizational structures. First of all, it is a voluntary organization: where one is automatically a member of the organizational structure by virtue of holding a job and part of the self-management structure through membership in a work collective, one must make a conscious decision to join the LCY. Nor is such a decision costless in terms of an individual's time, energy and freedom of action; LCY members are not only required to attend party meetings, but they are also expected to participate in other organizations as well. Hence, the LCY must induce potential members to pay the costs of political action by providing non-collective benefits, be they advancing individual careers, increasing members' status in the workplace, facilitating on-the-job performance, or providing opportunities to exert influence.

Nevertheless, the other characteristics differentiating the LCY from the self-management and organizational structures are precisely what make it difficult for the LCY to offer such individualized benefits, especially to blue-collar workers. In this regard, while the self-management and organizational structures are autonomous and contained within the individual firm, the party is an enterprise-level branch of a larger, national

* Parts of this and the following sections are excerpted from the author's recent work (Comisso, 1979).

organization. If the former tend to assert enterprise interests as over and occasionally against wider social interests, the role of the party is precisely to bring general social concerns into play in enterprise decision-making. In this way, the party supplements laws and market forces in integrating the enterprise into the larger society.

But if the party is politically responsible for bringing 'society's' concerns into the enterprise, it has no formal authority to do so; it must convince the collective to accept them. Hence, the party requires the compliance of non-members as well as members to accomplish its tasks, and so must be responsive to their preferences as well as those of its membership. Meanwhile, not only does its lack of formal authority deprive the party of control over resources with which it might reward its members (for instance, special access to influence), but its dependence on the cooperation of non-members prohibits it from discriminating too heavily in favor of its own activists in allocating the few rewards it does have at its disposal (such as time off from work for political activity).

Mediating between the enterprise and society means not only bringing outside influences to bear on internal decisions. It also entails protecting the enterprise's interests in political bodies external to it, and indeed, the party branch's ability to perform this role is a critical source of its support from the work collective as a whole. But to the degree the party is successful and able to further the enterprise's cause outside the firm, the benefits it delivers go to the work collective at large, with no special advantages accruing to party activists. The result, as we shall see below, is that blue-collar workers have scant incentives to join the League of Communists.

The League of Communists as Interest Articulator

Yugoslav market socialism is characterized both by a substantial degree of enterprise autonomy and a great deal of government intervention in both macro- and microeconomic processes. Firms, thus, seek to maximize their independence from government and political bodies so as to respond flexibly to market opportunities while maintaining their ties to political elites so as to ensure government discretion is used in their favor. Having good 'sociopolitical relations' is, therefore, as much of an economic imperative as it is politically advisable for Yugoslav enterprises.

This brings us to the first major type of grassroots party activity: the enterprise party organization's role as a pressure group on behalf of the firm with outside political bodies. Its activity here is extremely important, ranging from relatively mundane tasks such as speeding up bureaucratic procedures (for example, obtaining a building permit) to literally saving an enterprise's economic life. This, in fact, was precisely what occurred at Zvir.

In 1972, Zvir was experiencing serious economic and financial difficulties, primarily for two reasons. First, following the 1965 economic reforms, price controls had been lifted for nearly all commodities other than capital goods equipment. Zvir, producing heavy machinery, was caught in a squeeze, with its own prices frozen and the cost of its raw materials skyrocketing. Secondly, a general capital shortage caused by deflationary monetary policies (Tyson, 1977) made Zvir decide to sell its machinery on credit. But the consequence of extending credit it didn't really have was that, while the firm showed a healthy profit on paper, it lacked the liquid cash reserves to cover its own wage bill, let alone pay its rising debts to suppliers. The financial situation went from bad to worse when Zvir's bank account was 'blocked', that is, it was unable to draw on its account until it had paid back its outstanding debts and full salaries could not be paid to the laborforce in the interim.

The *impasse* was only broken when a price increase was approved by the Federal Price Commission in Belgrade and a large loan was granted by the Zagreb City Reserve Fund. The mobilization of Zvir's LCY and trade union activists, repeatedly appealing to higher bodies to 'save the firm' and prevent the party organization from being 'compromised', was a critical factor in finally securing such favorable government intervention.

The situation was described in a special issue of the factory bulletin, put out by the party secretariat in response to sharp criticisms of the party organization's apparent inability to solve Zvir's financial crisis. The party secretary's opening remarks are perhaps illustrative of the LCY branch's sensitivity to the collective's complaints:

> This is . . . in response to those comrades who, at the assembly of May 26, attacked our branch of the League of Communists on the grounds that it had not taken the necessary steps with political bodies to stabilize our situation. (*Bilten,* June 1972)

To show the party was in fact taking concrete action, a letter sent to the Croation Central Committee, on advice of the local party committee, was reprinted in full.

The letter itself detailed the firm's financial difficulties, dwelling on the technological advances Zvir had brought to its customers' industry (a major export sector) and pointing to the concern the industry felt for the solvency of its main equipment supplier. It went onto summarize the most important meetings already held to deal with Zvir's difficulties: with representatives of the Bosnian industry at the Sarajevo Economic Chamber; with the Croation Economic Chamber; with delegates of the Croation Executive Council; the republic Economic Chamber; the municipal Economic Chamber and the banks at a meeting of the republic Trade Union Council, to name just a few. The secretary even noted in the letter that two vice-presidents of the Executive Council of the Croation Parliament had singled out Zvir's 'business orientation' for special praise.

Yet although all the meetings had concluded that Zvir should be saved, the letter noted that the enterprise was still in the same financial straits it had been in at the start. The result, the party secretary warned, was that

> the position of the LC in the factory is increasingly difficult . . . [wages] have been late for months already. This time, pay was a

month late, and the director had to explain the difficulties at an assembly where he appealed for higher morale. The workers then began to ask questions: why were other structures [an allusion to government bureaucracies] paid on time? And what [were] the communists doing and to whom have they spoken about the situation? I answered that we had met with the municipal [party] committee and had tried to solve the problem there and at other meetings.

The letter concluded with a fervent appeal by the party secretary:

I managed to save the work climate for the time being, but I don't know for how long. The workers are waiting for an answer. We cannot find a way out alone, yet a solution must be found – in the name of the party's authority.

Zvir got its price increase, its bank account freed, and was further supported by an emergency loan – but at a price. We shall return with the sequel to the liquidity crisis below.

For now, the incident is illustrative of the impact of LCY responsiveness to widely felt worker grievances on its recruitment possibilities. Not only did the enterprise party branch quickly spring into action following the May assembly, not only did it feel obligated to publish a special issue of the plant bulletin to defend itself before critical workers, but it also used evidence of worker unrest successfully as a bargaining point to achieve a desirable solution to a long-standing enterprise problem. At the same time, however, it responded to workers in general, not the particular workers who were themselves party members; significantly, the secretary's letter was written in the wake of an assembly at which the entire work collective was present, not as a consequence of the party meetings at which the same complaints had undoubtedly been brought to the secretary's attention. In effect, the party proved itself more sensitive to the criticisms of rank-and-file workers, who were not party members and were perfectly willing to turn on the organization should it fail to deliver, than to warnings of worker dissatisfaction articulated by its own loyalists. For workers, the moral of the story was hardly to join the party.

Likewise, it was not party members who benefited from the loan and the price increase, but the entire enterprise workforce. For workers outside the party ranks, the enterprise party branch had simply provided a public good which they had as much right to as any party member. Thus, even effective party action gave workers slight reason to join the LCY.

Finally, the liquidity crisis resolution points up the importance of alternative channels of political influence for workers provided by the self-management bodies. Party membership was neither a requirement, nor an aid, in workers' ability to demand action at the May assembly; again, for workers this meant there were few advantages to joining it.

Party Activity inside the Enterprise: Defending Socialist Legality

The party's role as a pressure group on higher political authorities also conditions its activities within the enterprise. That is, to effectively bring influence to bear on external authorities, an enterprise party branch must have 'political credit'. Political credit is a product of several factors, not the least of which is how well an enterprise's self-management structure is operating. However, as outside bodies normally have no independent way of finding out what is going on within a firm, the only way they can judge it is by its formal compliance with the latest set of reforms. Thus, a key task of the League of Communists in the firm is superintending the formal procedures of the self-management structure.

In this regard, although the self-management structure's main lines are laid down in the laws passed by federal and republic legislatures, national and republic party organizations typically take the initiative in proposing them, while enterprise party branches are expected to play a leading role in seeing them implemented properly at the grassroots level. Thus, Zvir's LCY branch was the prime mover in setting up Basic Organizations of Associated Labor (BOAL) in the firm in early 1973; it organized the procedures to elect delegates to the commune assembly in 1974 with the new constitution's establishment of the delegate system; it called an assembly in September 1974 to explain the operation and procedures of the not-yet-established Self-Management Interest Communities.

Given the frequency of the reorganizations of the self-management bodies in Yugoslav firms, the diligent party organization has its hands full with this constant amending of formal procedures; 1974 was a particularly active year in this respect. Nevertheless, since real power in the firm tends to follow the lines of the organizational structure, the party's constant preoccupation with the legal processes of self-management is viewed by rank-and-file workers largely as a waste of time and energy. At Zvir, the intricacies of the 1974 reforms were greeted with a singular lack of interest on the part of blue-collar workers; implementing them was hardly a cause for which they would join the party. As one worker commented, 'It [the establishment of BOALs] hasn't made any difference. Who knows what it's about – it's all politics anyway.'

Such attitudes inevitably take their toll on the status of the party activist in the plant. Given the importance of 'sociopolitical relations' for an enterprise's economic welfare, the time the LCY activist spends away from his job and devotes to political concerns is actually a highly rational allocation of collective resources. Yet it is never recognized as such, and the activist's chronic political absenteeism can become a major source of irritation to his peers, who feel they are subsidizing his 'politicking' with their own labor. Rather than increasing one's status at the workplace, then, prominence in the LCY branch can have the opposite effect, as it did among Zvir's blue-collar production workers.

Getting Self-Management Moving

Mere establishment (or disestablishment) of self-management bodies does not exhaust the LCY's function in the procedural area. At Zvir, the party also felt itself responsible for seeing that the bodies operated with at least a minimum of efficiency. This activity, too, was relevant to the maintenance of political credit, especially when the outcomes of internal decisions affected external agencies.

For example, in 1974, Zvir received eleven apartments from the Zagreb Solidarity Fund. Administered by the municipal Trade Union Federation, the fund was based on contributions from local enterprises and was used to purchase housing for workers. Apartments were then allocated to the firms for distribution on the basis of need, with the criteria-defining need to be set forth in special regulations drawn up by each enterprise. At Zvir, however, the workers' council Commission on Social Standards went for months without being able to pull itself together for a meeting to draft a set of regulations. Finally, the party organization itself met on the question, and at long last the secretariat rounded up the commission members to begin work on the regulations. It is significant that the party chose the apartment regulations to act on rather than, say, the regulations on material incentives, also in sore need of revision at the time. While the incentive rules would clearly have a far more critical impact on Zvir's business success, the immediate effect of a delay in revising them would only be felt inside the firm. Although the housing question directly affected only the eleven individuals who received apartments, the delays accompanying their distribution were already being criticized by the city Trade Union Federation.

Nevertheless, if party intervention was able to move the Commission on Social Standards into drawing up an initial set of regulations for housing allocations, it by no means guaranteed a warm reception for the proposed criteria from the work collective. In fact, when a preliminary list of apartment allocations was posted, an uproar broke out, with the blue-collar production workers voicing the loudest protests. The upshot was not only that the regulations had to be rewritten and the apartments reallocated, but also that an entirely new commission had to be appointed since the original one was tainted with accusations of favoritism. The second time around, several key party leaders sat in on commission meetings to ensure that the rules were scrupulously fair and drawn up according to procedures.

If the party's role as interest articulator is illustrative of the lack of individual benefits flowing to party members from actions the party branch took on behalf of the firm, party activities geared to keeping the firm in line with general regulations and policies illustrate the costs individuals involved in enterprise politics must pay for their activism. Not only did the members of the first commission have to stay after work to draw up the regulations, but their best efforts were greeted only with criticism and even the motives of individual commission members were impugned by a rather unappreciative work collective. Since party membership normally involves an obligation on the part of the individual member to remain active in enterprise affairs, such costs can constitute a significant deterrent to assuming the burdens of political activism. At the same time, given the ease and effectiveness of criticizing from the sidelines, there is little reason for workers to want to pay these costs. And as for the party, when circumstances did place it in a position to influence the allocation of highly prized individual benefits on behalf of its members, it did not dare to do so lest it jeopardize its legitimacy in the collective altogether.

Procedures *versus* Substance: Party Relations with Management

The party's absorption with the formal structures and processes of self-management should not be equated with intervention in substantive decision-making. Although the way in which an enterprise party organization interprets and handles procedural questions may indirectly affect decision outcomes, generally its influence on the latter is relatively weak (Kilibarda, 1966; Jeličic, 1970; Rus, 1978). At Zvir, the party's lack of independent influence in substantive decisions stemmed from ideological principle; in part, it was a product of the party's need for political credit, and in part, it reflected internal divisions the party organization appeared unable to overcome.

That is, especially after the 1965 economic reforms, the Yugoslav League of Communists became increasingly committed to an ideology of 'guaranteeing the workers' right to self-manage' (namely, supervising formal procedures) and 'developing the forces of production' (namely, ensuring that firms operate efficiently). Enterprise efficiency, however, is the product of the organizational structure: how production is organized, what is produced, labor productivity, etc. Hence, it is critically affected by the quality and foresight of enterprise executives, and at Zvir, this was reflected in the almost universal sentiment held by the workers that management was responsible for how well the firm was doing. As for Zvir's party branch, since it had neither any standards of efficiency distinct from those of management, any independent way of judging whether maximum efficiency was actually being attained, nor any reason to suspect that the various measures management proposed were not, in fact, the wisest course to pursue in a given situation, it either took no position at all on proposals coming before the self-management bodies, or acted as a support group for the plans management submitted and as a mobilizing agent to help carry out decisions once they were made.

In such cases, the party's influence was inevitably more peripheral than when it itself would initiate a proposal or carry through an action. Management normally had little difficulty persuading the self-management bodies to adopt its proposals, and party contributions to the effort were marginal at most. As far as executing decisions were concerned, since the party could neither offer material incentives, nor apply disciplinary sanctions, the best it could do was exhort the collective to 'work better to complete the plan' or urge it to 'bear with the difficult situation'.

Non-intervention in the name of 'developing the forces of production' was reinforced by the party's need for political credit: it stood to reason that a party organization from a profitable, dynamic firm would be viewed far more favorably by local officials and political leaders outside the firm than an LCY branch from an enterprise constantly lagging behind in production and floundering about in a financial morass.

Quite understandably, under such conditions, a certain complementarity of interests between the enterprise party branch and management began to develop at Zvir. On the one hand, the party had a general interest in insulating the organizational structure from purely political pressures and to ensure management had a free hand to pursue the economic policies it judged best for the firm. On the other, it was in management's interest to leave the legalities of the self-management structure in the politically skilled hands of the party, while aiding it to build up its political credit outside the firm, so that in case of emergency, debts could be called in and assistance obtained. What is important to realize here is that this complementarity of interests did not arise from a 'technocratic takeover' of the LCY branch by management nor to 'illegitimate political influence' of the party in economic decision-making, but rather to precisely the opposite: as long as the party didn't trespass on management's area of expertise, and vice versa, and as long as one needed the other to deal effectively with external political forces, the situation could continue indefinitely. Thus, while most of Zvir's top executives were party members, they were hardly party activists: the vast bulk of their time was devoted to business, not political, affairs.

In fact, should one group move in too aggressively on the other's turf, or should either fail to perform well in its own area of concern, severe strains could be put on the alliance. In this regard, 1974 was a trying year at Zvir, since the vast reorganizations necessitated by the new constitution meant that heightened party activity in the procedural realm was inevitably going to spill over into business affairs. Thus, some distancing between management and party did occur at Zvir, as evidenced by the party's failure to inform the general director in advance of the elections to the self-management bodies it called in June 1974. On the one hand, the party felt itself frustrated in its attempts to restructure the decision-making process in line with the new laws (for example, Zvir proved itself unable to adopt new statutes owing to confusion between the BOAL Councils and the workers' council over where the adoption process should begin – a confusion in large part due to the absence of enterprise statutes!), and felt management's permissiveness and toleration of slack discipline was at least partially the cause. On the other hand, management felt that the large amounts of time devoted to meetings which produced no tangible results were hurting the firm's ability to meet its plan goals. The anti-technocracy campaign also took its toll, putting executives' nerves on edge and giving party militants favoring a hardline approach an incentive to attack Zvir's more liberal management.

At the same time, however, other forces continued to operate to keep party–management relations on an even keel. One was the potential threat to both posed by the possibility that members of the collective, either individually or collectively, might bring complaints to the attention of outside bodies over the heads of the enterprise politicoeconomic leadership. Normally, the effect of such a threat increased the sensitivity of both party and management to rank-and-file demands; occasionally, however, it would manifest itself as a climate in which individuals hesitated to persist in opposing particular decisions. But in general, cooperation between the LCY branch and management at Zvir was not at the expense of the rest of the work collective. Indeed, where financial aid and favors from outside were concerned, all stood to benefit from the alliance.

No surprisingly, the complementarity of interests that characterized party–management relations was reflected in party membership patterns at Zvir; executives were quite disproportionately represented in LCY ranks. Unlike blue-collar workers, for whom party membership carried few benefits they could not receive through other channels, executives both individually and as a group had a number of specific incentives to join the LCY.

First of all, while training and qualifications are the key factors affecting an executive's career in Yugoslavia, failure to join the party has a cost to it. More precisely, possessing a party card insures that only one's professional qualifications will be considered for employment and promotion; not being a party member means questions will be raised about one's political sympathies as well. In effect, if joining the party does not advance one's career, refusing to join it can hurt.

More profoundly, in a very real sense, party membership is a genuinely professional qualification for managerial personnel in Yugoslavia. Not only does it facilitate on-the-job performance, but at Zvir it was also associated with the attitudes, values and orientations needed to be an effective executive in a self-managed firm. That is, except for the relatively rare case of the complete opportunist, individuals who are in fundamental disagreement with the principles espoused by the party will not join it. Hence, executives who are party members typically do support self-management, are basically sympathetic to workers' demands, favor the resolution of conflict through discussion, and are willing to accept the constraints on their discretion, authority and salary imposed by both the internal self-management structure, and the external political environment. In short, the same qualities which make for managerial effectiveness in the labor-managed firm also make executives likely to be party members.

Furthermore, party membership itself makes an important contribution to an executive's on-the-job performance. For one thing, it is far easier for an executive who is a comrade to call on the party to mobilize the collective to complete the plan, suffer austerity in bad times, consent to controversial business policies, or simply come to work on time in the morning, than it is for an executive who is not himself an LCY member. Likewise, in the course of fulfilling the daily responsibilities of their jobs, executives come into frequent contact with local political leaders with whom common commitment to the party of the working class can form an important bond.

In addition, to the degree that party membership constitutes evidence that an executive's sympathies really do lie with the direct producers, it serves to protect managerial independence by allaying potential suspicions of external political bodies. Significantly, at the height of the 1974 anti-technocracy campaign, the Zvir party branch launched a recruitment drive among managerial personnel, largely to protect the firm from the accusation of 'technocratic-managerialism'. In doing so, it was protecting itself as much as Zvir's executive *cadres*: after all, would a party that defended the interests of the direct producers permit apolitical technocrats to assume a position of influence in the firm? Thus, it is not the dis-proportionate presence of enterprise executives in the LCY that creates the party–management *entente*; rather, the conditions – both internal and external—that create the alliance also provide the incentives attracting managerial personnel into the LCY.

Conflict and Opportunities for Influence: the Party and the Workers

For workers, in contrast, the same incentives work in the opposite direction. Whereas party membership was likely to enhance an executive's day to day performance, involvement in the political activities expected of party members carried very direct penalties for production workers. In the first place, Zvir's blue-collar machinists were paid on piece-rates, and time spent away from work to attend in-plant or out-of-plant meetings jeopardized workers' ability to meet their production quotas. The result could be a substantial loss in pay. Secondly, where executives were regularly in and out of the plant on their jobs, workers had no such mobility and, as noted above, political absenteeism was likely to be noticed and criticized by their fellows. Thirdly, whereas promotion opportunities for managerial personnel were highly contingent on performance in their present job, workers seeking to be promoted to a higher category of manual labor or out of blue-collar jobs altogether normally required additional education. Typically, this entailed attending school after work, leaving workers little free time to devote to party meetings and other such activities.

Consequently, the workers who did join the party at Zvir had done so at some sacrifice and primarily out of ideological commitment. Yet, whereas the executive's ideological commitment could legitimately be construed as part of his professional qualifications, for the worker it was not. Instead, the worker's decision to join the LCY meant assuming a 'purely political' position, with the result that LCY members at Zvir were distinguished from other production workers by their articulateness, rebelliousness and mili-tancy on behalf of workers' rights. Party members or not, they typcially led the protests when labor–management conflict occurred, regardless of the stance the party leadership took.

This brings us to the third reason for the party's lack of influence on substantive issues at Zvir: on controversial questions, its internal divisions were so severe that, as an organization, the LCY simply could not take a consistent stand at all. Here, the sequel to the 1972 liquidity crisis is illustrative.

In order to receive its loan from the Zagreb Reserve Fund, Zvir had to satisfy two conditions. First, the firm had to adopt a stabilization plan to prevent its falling into illiquidity again. Secondly, it had to take some concrete step to show it was really turning over a new leaf. The latter condition was met by the work collective's decision to work twenty-four Saturdays without pay in 1973.

The decision was certainly not made with wild enthusiasm; nevertheless, workers felt in retrospect that it was a necessary one in so far as the firm's survival was at stake. The party organization, whose activity had been so critical in securing the loan in the first place, surely made its contribution to their perceiving the situation in such dramatic terms and helped to create the climate in which the assembly had agreed to the terms of the loan.

But once the decision to work Saturdays had been made, carrying it out was far from simple. Absenteeism rose while productivity dropped; dissatisfaction among Zvir's laborforce mounted until finally a special assembly was called in November 1973 to deal with it. At that time, the workers were able to extract a promise from the general director that they would be reimbursed in 1974 for half of the 'free' Saturdays if the firm's plan had been completed.

The director's promise calmed the situation, and in the end, 94 percent of the 1973 plan was completed. The start of the new year saw an across-the-board wage increase, and it was agreed that the portion of the 1973 profit earmarked for distribution among the collective would be divided as in the past, an equal share going to each Zvir employee. Ominously, however, January and February of 1974 came and went with no word on the promised Saturdays pay. Tempers began to rise and at an assembly called in mid-March, the explosion occurred.

The essential conflict of the March assembly was between workers and management and centered around two questions. First, the workers demanded the promised backpay, while management insisted that once wages had been raised and profits distributed, there was simply no additional money to allocate any more to personal incomes. Secondly, to the degree that the workers accepted the firm's inability to pay them, they wanted to know why (in their words, 'whose fault is it?'). As they saw the problem, they had come to work on Saturdays and done their jobs; in Marxist terms, they had 'created the value' through their labor, and if it had not been 'realized', this was clearly not their fault even if they were being compelled to suffer for it. Management, on the contrary, maintained that if Zvir lack the funds to pay back the Saturdays, this was the fault of no single individual or group, but a failure of the entire work collective. As for the LCY branch, although the party leadership sided with management on both questions, party members were among the most aggressive leaders of the rank-and-file revolt.

It would take us too far afield here to examine the critical ideological issues (distribution according to work *versus* distribution according to the 'results' of work; individual *versus* collective responsibility) involved in this debate. Rather let us briefly note that it ended with a complete victory by management: the Saturdays were not paid back, nor was there any retreat from the collective responsibility position. Yet, victory did not come easily: the turbulent March assembly broke up into small groups of workers and executives arguing bitterly, without having reached any conclusion. A second assembly was called the next week, at which time the workers finally conceded. In the interim, management, the party secretariat, the trade union president and the heads of the self-management bodies conferred repeatedly to structure a meeting that would not disintegrate into the disorder which characterized the first assembly. Yet management clearly bore the brunt of the battle at both assemblies; the significance of the other groups, including the party, lay more in the fact that they provided no organized leadership or support to the rank-and-file rebellion than in their positive contribution to the management stand.

The issues surrounding the 'free' Saturdays debate illustrate another reason for the LCY's role in the firm being so much of a procedural rather than a substantive one. Namely, the cleavages occurring within the collective as a whole were simply replicated inside the party organization. Thus, the party could act as a united organization to represent the firm before external political authorities and it could stand firm on implementing decisions made by outside bodies inside the enterprise, but when an issue polarized the collective, the party also split on it. Accordingly, the party could mobilize on behalf of the initial decision to work Saturdays; its own political reliability was involved in securing compliance with the conditions laid down by outside bodies as part of the loan package. But on the Saturdays conflict, the party organization divided up along with everyone else, its leaders supporting management, its members leading the workers in opposition.

In sum, the party organization as a unified whole had no major influence on the content of decisions, because it couldn't agree itself on what those decisions should be. As far as workers were concerned, then, party membership did not make any independent contribution to the influence they exerted as a group in the firm, and Zvir's policies continued to reflect a distribution of power highly skewed in favor of management.

Nor did party membership enhance the influence workers exerted as individuals. Aside from the fact that party members led what turned out to be a losing cause in any case, their leadership role was quite independent of their party membership. More precisely, the workers who led the revolt assumed such a role because they were articulate and militant, not because they were party members. At the same time, however, the same qualities of articulateness and militancy which make some workers more active in rank-and-file protests, make the same workers more likely to be party members. The consequence for an enterprise party organization, however, is to exacerbate its tendency to fall victim to whatever divisiveness characterizes the collective as a whole.

The League of Communists and Recruitment of Blue-Collar Workers

Given the role the LCY plays within the Yugoslav firm, its difficulties in achieving a 'working-class majority' (Tito, 1978) among its membership are all too understandable. Paradoxically, they stem as much from the party's responsiveness to worker demands as from its inability to act on them, as much from the LCY's success at 'implementing the revolutionary course' as in its failure to do so.

On the one hand, the benefits workers receive from party activities accrue to them regardless of whether or not they are party members. On the other, joining the party means incurring non-trivial costs for .workers without implying additional benefits to compensate them. At Zvir, since the production worker was most directly interested in the results of self-management, that is, in the actual decisions made and carried out, rather than in the procedural forms they followed, a party organization largely concerned with structure and legalities held little appeal for him. Further, since he had a right to participate in self-management regardless of party membership, there was little cause for him to pay dues and attend extra (party) meetings to make this right effective. Indeed, in the case that he perceived his interests in contrast with a party position on a given issue, he might well be freer to push his cause as a non-member, untouched by the possible invocation of party discipline. Nor was individual influence over the decisions made in the self-management bodies increased by the simple possession of a party card, at least as far as blue-collar workers were concerned.

In addition, the voluntary nature of the League of Communists, its relatively small membership at Zvir, plus its need to maintain its political credit with outside agencies, all meant that it had to be fairly responsive to the needs of non-members as well as those of actual members. If anything, to the extent that the former, lacking the emotional and ideological ties the members often had, might be more prone to make trouble for the party outside the firm in case of prolonged dissatisfaction, the Zvir party organization in some ways had to be even more sensitive to their needs than to those of its own activists. Certainly, it could not use whatever influence it had in the enterprise to discriminate against them. Given the overall Yugoslav ideological emphasis on the need to have the support of the working class, manual and production workers could often exert as much influence on party actions from outside it as they could from within.

Finally, the party was useless as a mechanism to redress the balance of power in the enterprise; when it could have supported the workers, it either split or went along with management. Workers thus received neither collective, nor non-collective, benefits from party membership; it is hardly surprising that they did not rush to join it.

In conclusion, the Yugoslav League of Communists is neither the *deus ex machina* its right-wing critics make it out to be (Silberman, 1977), nor the revolutionary vanguard and heavy-politicizing agent its left-wing critics demand of it (Šuvar, 1968; Zukin, 1975). Nor can one find much support for the argument that it is the political arm of a 'ruling class' (Djilas, 1957):

rather than blocking the realization of the direct producers' interests out of class antagonism, the party was simply neutral with respect to many of them in the Zvir case. As a bridge organization, it was able to bring 'society's' interests into play inside the enterprise when there was agreement in the party organization itself as to what these interests were; typically, consensus was most easily arrived at on implementing laws and procedures already decided on by outside bodies. At the same time, it was an important factor keeping outside political authorities responsive to the needs of the enterprise as a whole. For the blue-collar production worker at Zvir, to the degree his interests coincided with those of society or with those of the enterprise, he could expect a good deal of responsiveness from the League of Communists; none the less, should they conflict, he could hardly turn to the party of the working class for support.

References: Chapter 4

Bielasiak, Jack, 'Workers in workers' states: mass participation in "Socialist democracy"', paper presented at Annual Meeting of Midwest Slavic Conference Cincinnati, Ohio, May 1980 (Xeroxed).

Comisso, Ellen, *Workers' Control Under Plan and Market* (New Haven, Ct.: Yale University Press, 1979).

Denitch, Bogdan, *The Legitimation of a Revolution* (New Haven, Ct.: Yale University Press, 1976).

Djilas, Milovan, *The New Class* (New York: Praeger, 1957).

Horvat, Branko, *An Essay on Yugoslav Society* (White Plains, NY: International Arts and Sciences Press, 1968).

Hough, Jerry, 'Party "saturation" in the Soviet Union', in P. Cocks, R. Daniels and N. Heer, eds, *The Dynamics of Soviet Politics* (Cambridge, Ma.: Harvard University Press, 1976), pp. 117-35.

Hough, Jerry, *How the Soviet Union is Governed* (Cambridge, Ma.: Harvard University Press, 1979).

Jeličic, Zlatko, *'Distribucija utjecaja nekih odluka u radnoj organizaciji'*, *Moderna organizacija*, no. 5-6, 1970.

Kardelj, Edvard, *Osnovni uzroci i pravci ustavnih promena* (Belgrade: Komunist, 1973).

Kilibarda, Krsto, *Samoupravljanje i Savez komunista* (Belgrade: Socioloski institut, 1966).

League of Communists of Yugoslavia, *The League of Communists of Yugoslavia between the Tenth and Eleventh Congresses* (Belgrade: Socialist Thought and Practice, 1978).

McAuley, Mary, *Politics and the Soviet Union* (New York: Penguin, 1977).

Obradovic, Josip, *'Distribucija participacije u procesu donošenja odluka'*. *Revija za socijologiju*, no. 1, 1972, pp. 15-48.

Olson, Mancur, *The Logic of Collective Action* (New York: Schocken, 1965).

Radio Free Europe Research Reports, 22 May 1974.

Rus, Veljko, 'Enterprise power structure', in J. Obradović and W. Dunn, eds, *Workers' Self-Management and Organizational Power in Yugoslavia* (Pittsburgh, Pa.: University Center for International Studies, 1978), pp. 199-218.

Sezione centrale di stampa e propaganda del PCI, *Almanacco del Partito comunista italiano, 1972, 1973* (Rome: F.lli Spada Ciampino, 1972-3).

Silberman, Laurence, 'Yugoslavia's "Old" Communism", *Foreign Policy,* no. 26, Spring 1977, pp. 3–28.

Šuvar, Stipe, *'Ne odgadati otvorenu i odlučnu bitku za samoupravljanje', Naše teme,* vol. 12, no. 3, 1968, pp. 798–838.

Tarrow, Sidney, *Peasant Communism in Southern Italy* (New Haven, Ct.: Yale University Press, 1967).

Tito, Josip B., 'The struggle for the further development of socialist self-management in our country and the role of the LCY', speech, 10th Congress of the Yugoslav League of Communists, press release, courtesy of the Yugoslav Information Service, May 1974 (multilith)

Tito, Josip, B., *The League of Communists of Yugoslavia in the Struggle for the Further Development of Socialist, Self-Managing and Nonaligned Yugoslavia* (Belgrade: Socialist Thought and Practice, 1978).

Tyson, Laura, 'Liquidity crises in the Yugoslav economy: an alternative to bankruptcy?', *Soviet Studies,* no. 29, April 1977.

Verba, Sidney and Shabad, Goldie, 'Workers councils and political stratification: the Yugoslav experience', *American Political Science Review,* vol. 72, no. 1, March 1978, pp. 80–96.

Zukin, Sharon, *Beyond Marx and Tito* (New York: Cambridge University Press, 1975).

Županov, Josip and Tannenbaum, Arnold, 'Control in some Yugoslav industrial firms', in A. Tannenbaum, ed., *Control in Organizations* (New York: McGraw-Hill, 1968), pp. 91–112.

5 Workers and Mass Participation in 'Socialist Democracy'

JACK BIELASIAK

Introduction

The riots by the Polish industrial workers in December 1970 and June 1976, the strikes by Romanian miners in August 1977, and the growing workers' dissent in Eastern Europe and the Soviet Union have focused new attention on the status and role of the proletariat in communist states. The workers' acquiescence to their economic and social conditions has given way to the articulation of demands for improvements, and even to outright rejection through violent action of governmental and party policies. Faced with the prospect of an increasingly vocal and active working class, the communist regimes have sought to assure political stability by providing for the better integration of the workers into the political system. Outstanding among these efforts, has been a new stress on the participation of the masses in policy-making, especially on decisions affecting the economic and social benefits of the workers.

The aim of this chapter is to contrast the regimes' goals concerning mass participation with the actual extent of workers' participation in the economic and political institutions of the European communist states. I will, first, address the reasons why the East European governments have selected the emphasis on mass participation as a primary political response to the workers' dissatisfaction in the 1970s. Secondly, the degree of workers' participation in political organizations and institutions will be examined, together with workers' participation in economic management. The chapter will conclude by assessing the significance of mass participation in communist states.

'Mass Participation' as Political Response

The regimes' need for identification with the proletariat at a time of increasing turbulence among the workers, the concern with economic efficiency due to growing problems of productivity, the necessity of assuring social harmony at a time of greater socioeconomic complexity, resulted in considerable pressures on the leaderships of communist states. The political response, by the East European and Soviet leaders, to the growing assertiveness of the workers and the tensions in society, was a new emphasis on citizens' involvement in policy-making. This took the form of the formulation of an ideological stage in the construction of socialism marked by the intensification of socialist democracy and mass participation (Evans, 1977; Chekharin, 1977; *World Marxist Review* (WMR) Conferences 1975, 1979). The aim was to create the impression that the communist governments were paying closer attention to the demands of industrial labor by providing new channels for popular inputs in deliberations determining the distribution of social and economic benefits. These ideological descriptions of socialist democracy were not necessarily translated into reality. Rather, the communist regimes sought to create mechanisms of mass participation which would increase a citizen's *sense* of involvement in socioeconomic affairs without significantly altering regime policy preferences. As students of political participation have pointed out (Pateman, 1970, pp. 45–84; Friedgut, 1979, pp. 48–50), an individual's sense of efficacy is improved if he has a feeling of access to the government – even if this does not lead to the satisfaction of the individual's needs. This 'pseudoparticipation' is beneficial to the political authorities by forging new links between the public and the state. The integration of the working masses into the communist societies is especially critical to the leaderships, for it involves issues of political legitimacy, economic efficiency and social integration. It is in the pursuit of these goals that communist theorists have used the rhetoric of mass participation.

The association of political legitimacy with the economic, social and political transformation of the communist societies was a significant factor in the escalation of the participatory rhetoric in the mid-1970s. The promise of an egalitarian society, where each individual could obtain similar material rewards and contribute equally to the building of a new environment, was an important feature of the socialist self-image. When the processes of economic and political development did not bring the desired egalitarian transformations, the working class acted on the belief that change would not be forthcoming without a visible expression of their demands. The most extreme articulation of workers' preferences occurred in Poland in 1970 and 1976, where labour riots and strikes forced the government to abandon previously announced economic policies (de Weydenthal, 1979). The miners' strike in the Jiu Valley in 1977 and the demands of the East German workers for wage changes did not have such an immediate policy impact, but none the less contributed to the perception of a growing workers' consciousness in the communist states (Zimmerman, 1978; Nelson, 1979). The workers in the East European states appeared to have achieved greater solidarity and political awareness, as well as the will to act in their own interests.

This fact could not be ignored by the leaderships of the communist states. A diffusion of the issue occurred throughout the region after the unrests in the Polish cities. The grievances of the labor class had to be taken seriously, and greater attention paid to the resolution of their problems.

This was necessitated in large part by the Marxist definition of political rule. The communist parties derive their rights to political primacy from their standing as 'the vanguard of the proletariat', representing the needs and the interests of the working class. Under these circumstances, political legitimacy must be assured by a continuous claim by the party of a congruence of interests between the working masses and its vanguard. To offset the mounting expressions of workers' unhappiness, the communist regimes were forced to adopt a response which would establish to a greater extent the identification of the labor class with the party. Foremost among the new policies was the promise to make workers' demands a greater part of decision-making, and thus to open channels for workers' participation in the polity (Koziolek, 1977; Dascalescu, 1978; Kalecka, 1978; *Pravda, Bratislava*, 1979). The leadership hoped that verbal commitments, labor codes and political statutes emphasizing the opportunities for worker involvement would, at least in part, resolve the newly visible schism between the state and the masses.

The renewed vigor of the mass-participation rhetoric can also be traced to the regimes' growing concerns with economic efficiency and the quality of labor's contribution to the production effort (Fusko and Perlaki, 1979; Mako and Hethy 1979; Yanowitch, 1979). In fact, improvements in labor inputs into economic growth were necessary, because part of the solution to workers' dissatisfaction was to raise the standards of living. The policy of consumerism was more difficult to pursue by the second half of the 1970s as a result of worsening international terms of trade and domestic productivity. The growth of GNP per capita slowed down markedly in 1976 or 1977 for all the East European states (Alton *et al.,* 1978, p. 16). In order to offset the declining growth rates and assure continued satisfaction within the consumer sector, the efficiency of the economy had to be improved. One obvious means was to increase the productivity of economic enterprises by aiming for better work efforts by the industrial proletariat. The emphasis on labor's participation in the management process was an effort to increase worker job satisfaction:

> We regard advancement of democracy at the factory as essential for building socialism. To begin with, this form of democracy helps to raise the standard of economic activity and manage the factory more efficiently. (Romany, 1975, p. 82)

Clearly, the stress on workers' participation in factory decisions was meant to increase the economic productivity of the enterprises and contribute to the maintenance of industrial growth. Even symbolic commitment to democracy at the factory was thought by the communist leaders to create positive links between worker and state, and to involve the former more directly and intensely in economic activities.

Modernization itself is increasingly viewed as a process necessitating and facilitating the involvement of the people in policy-making. This view was given official legitimization at the 24th CPSU Congress by Brezhnev (1971) through the enunciation of a new stage in the building of communism, that of the developed socialist society. The theme of developed socialism was then expanded to the East European states, which are currently 'building' the mature socialist society (WMR Conferences, 1975, 1979). This phase is characterized by the growth in complexity of productive forces, resulting in increased economic and social differentiation within the East European states. In turn, this signaled the recognition by socialist theorists of the existence of distinct social groups and interests under developed socialism. In 1975, for example,

> Congress XI of the Hungarian Socialist Workers' Party made a major contribution to the social guidance of the Seventies. *It accepted that conflicting human demands and interests feature even in a socialist society.* A source of this conflict is the different interests that arise from the division of labor. (Mako and Hethy, 1979, p. 298; emphasis added)

The most significant variations among the population are based on differences in occupational tasks and styles of living associated with the nature of work. These result in 'non-antagonistic' conflicts in society. 'The task of those responsible for guiding society is not to suppress these conflicts, but to reveal and solve them' (Mako and Hethy, p. 298). The principal aim, then, is to reconcile diverse social views and to establish cohesiveness through the recognition of each group's demands. To facilitate the conflict management task of the leadership, provisions for the expression of different interests must be made. The consequence has been a theoretical commitment to procedural improvements in policy-making and the introduction of new decisional methods (WMR Conferences, 1975; 1979).

In effect, the need to seek political legitimacy, increase economic efficiency and provide for social integration has led to the development of ideological concepts reflecting the contemporary concerns and goals of the Soviet and East European leaders. Paramount among the descriptive features of developed socialism is the intensification of socialist democracy, which is viewed as the principal trend in the current development of socialist political systems. This extension of socialist democracy is said to take three main forms: the improvement of already-existing patterns of representative democracy, the expansion of direct participation by the people in state administration and the intensification of workers' participation in economic management (Kerimov, 1977; Zawadzki, 1977; Nemes, 1978; Zaharescu, 1978).

Another side to the theory of developed socialism, however, limits even the theoretical extension of socialist democracy, and reinforces the view that the aim of the communist leaders is the development of pseudoparticipation. Official ideology has continued to advocate the primacy of the 'leading role of the party' and democratic centralism, as well as to point to the critical importance of the scientific and technological revolution (STR) for the 'scientific management' of socialist societies (Afanasyev, 1971; WMR Conference, 1979). The latter signifies rationalization of decision-making, so that policy is determined according to objective 'efficiency' criteria arrived at by the application of STR techniques. This process is viewed by communist ideologues as most complex: it requires careful guidance and supervision. Thus, during developed socialism the leading role of the party is further intensified. More than ever before, the function of the central political authorities is to manage the complex processes of economic and social transformation.

The implications of these views are that the leaderships are committed to maintaining control over decision-making even as opportunities for popular participation are extended. The simultaneous advocacy of socialist democracy and mass participation, on the one hand, and scientific management and the leading role of. the party, on the other, presents a problem: how can the participation of the masses be strengthened when decisions are to be made scientifically by the political center? While socialist theories claim that this contradiction can be resolved (Kalecka, 1978), how can citizens overcome the claim that the party 'knows best'? The value for the communist regimes of the contemporary ideological rhetoric on the intensification of participation and democracy lies, thus, in the fact that the experience of taking part in discussions enhances the acceptance, cooperation and satisfaction of participants (Pateman, 1970, pp. 63–4). Given the difficulties of the East European and Soviet societies in the 1970s, such pseudoparticipation on the part of the working class can signify important supports for the political legitimacy, social harmony and economic efficiency of the communist states.

Important variations in both the rhetoric and practice of popular participation exist among the communist states. Some governments appear enthusiastic in their ideological descriptions of socialist democracy, while others are much more cautious and tend to focus on the principles of the leading role of the party and scientific management. Those states, like Poland and Romania, which have witnessed considerable workers' disturbances have responded by embarking on campaigns praising new opportunities of 'self-management' through self-governing residential and workplace associations (Zawadzki, 1977, pp. 188–9; Waligorski, 1976; Nelson, 1979). However, while the operation of these organizations was expanded, their effectiveness was quickly circumscribed by continued references to the leading authority of the party and the application of democratic centralism (Ozdowski and Alexander, 1978; Nelson, 1979). Of all the socialist states, Hungary has gone furthest in the recognition of different interests among its social groups, and in the development of mass participation mechanisms for their reconciliation (Hethy and Mako, 1977; Hethy, 1979). The Hungarian trade unions' capacity to act on behalf of workers' interests is unmatched in the region, and experimentation with workers' participation in enterprises has also been significant.

The other communist states have been much more conservative in expounding the virtues of mass participation. Rather than emphasizing new forms of self-management or workplace participation, the Soviet, GDR and Czechoslovak governments refer to existing political structures as vehicles for mass involvement. The Soviets refer primarily to organs of people's administration (Kelley, 1980), while German and Czechoslovak officials continue to espouse representational participation arrangements in the form of production conferences or standing commissions (Baylis, 1976; *Pravda,* Bratislava, 1980). The style of work of these organizations is unlikely to be altered, for the party's right to control their activities remains indisputable. The greater capability of the Honecker and Husak leaderships to provide their citizens with better economic benefits, in contrast to the rest of Eastern Europe, means that they have less need to pay lip-service to the virtues of mass participation. There are, therefore, important differences even in the ideological commitment of communist regimes to the increased involvement of workers in political and workplace organizations. In all, however, there is a gap between the rhetoric and the practice of mass participation.

Workers in Political Institutions

In the 1970s the ruling communist parties have been faced with 'the dilemma of party growth' (Hammer, 1971): the *apparat* stresses the leading role of the party in the period of developed socialism, while at the same time continuing to present an image of itself as the party of the people (Rigby, 1976; de Weydenthal, 1977; Fischer, 1979). As the leading institutions in the mature socialist state, the ruling communist parties need to attract

Table 5.1 *Communist Party Memberships: Total and as percentage of Population*

	1962	1966	1971	1976	1978
Bulgaria	528,674 6·6%	611,179 7·4%	699,476 8·1%	789,796 9·0%	812,000 9·2%
Czechoslovakia	1,680,819 12·1%	1,698,000 11·9%	1,173,183‡ 8·2%	1,382,860 9·3%	1,473,000 9·7%
GDR	1,610,679 9·4%	1,750,000† 10·3%	1,909,859 11·2%	2,043,697 12·0%	2,077,262 12·4%
Hungary	498,644 5·0%	584,849 5·7%	662,397‡ 6·4%	754,353§ 7·2%	770,000 7·2%
Poland	1,270,000* 4·2%	1,848,000 5·8%	2,270,000 6·9%	2,500,000 7·3%	2,758,000 7·9%
Romania	900,000 4·8%	1,518,000† 7·8%	1,999,720‡ 9·9%	2,655,000 12·5%	2,747,000 12·6%
USSR	9,981,068 4·6%	12,357,308 5·3%	14,455,321 5·9%	15,694,187 6·2%	16,300,000 6·2%·

Source: Official figures as reported by the East European and Soviet press.
*: 1961;
†: 1965;
‡: 1970;
§: 1975.

highly educated, well-trained personnel capable of managing the modern, industrial state. Party recruitment policies must be aimed at the absorption of the while-collar strata. However, the party still derives much of its legitimacy as the representative of the working class, requiring the continued presence of the proletariat as a large proportion of party membership. The dilemma for the leadership is how to reconcile these two concerns of an elite *versus* a mass party, without expanding the size of the party to the point of eroding its vanguard status in society (de Weydenthal, 1977, p. 343; Unger, 1977, p. 314).

In general, the ruling parties have continued to stress their mass character. Table 5.1 shows that the membership of the parties as a percentage of the national populations has continued to expand since the early 1960s. The only exception occurs in Czechoslovakia between 1965 and 1971, a trend accounted for by the Prague Spring and the subsequent party purge (Wightman and Brown, 1975). There are, however, differences among the ruling parties in terms of their share within the populations. The communist parties of Romania (RCP) and East Germany (SDEP) are proportionately the largest organizations, both with over 12 percent of their country's inhabitants. The difference between these two and the other ruling parties can best be explained by the nationalistic content of the RCP's and SDEP's policies. In the case of the GDR this is due to the need to establish a separate national identity from West Germany, while in Romania such a policy is connected to the foreign policy requirements of the country and its relative autonomy within the socialist bloc. In both instances, the parties demonstrate broad popular support by emphasizing their mass character.

Throughout the region, the communist governments have sought to maintain the *image* of a party associated with the working people. Official policy statements strongly emphasize the working-class nature of the party and the need for the continuing recruitment of workers into its ranks (Gierek, 1977; WMR Conference, 1979). This view was strongly affirmed, for example, by Brezhnev (1976) at the 25th CPSU Congress:

> Under the conditions of developed socialism, when the Communist Party has become the party of the whole people, it by no means loses its class character. In its nature the CPSU was and remains a party of the working class.

The testimonial to the proletarian character of the communist parties even under the complex requirements of mature socialism is evident in the social composition trends of the ruling parties (Table 5.2). The relative percentage of workers has increased in all the parties during the past decade. While in some cases that growth has been small in terms of the overall membership, it has been more significant in the category of newly recruited candidates (de Weydenthal, 1977, pp. 344–5; Molnar, 1978, pp. 64–9; Fischer, 1979, pp. 9–11). This is clearly evident, for example, from the trends in the CPSU: the workers' representation in the total membership increased from 40·1 percent to 41·6 percent between 1971 and 1976; among

Table 5.2 *Social Composition of the Communist Parties (%)*

	Bul-garia	Czecho-slovakia	GDR	Hun-gary	Pol-and	Rom-ania	USSR
	1962		1962		1964	1960	1961
Workers	37·2	33·8			40·2	51·0	34·5
Farmers	32·1	6·2			11·4	22·0	17·5
White-collar	30·7	41·3			43·0	11·0	48·0
Others	—	18·7			5·4	16·0	—
	1966	1966		1966	1968	1965	1966
Workers	38·4	30·2		42·5	40·2	40·0	37·8
Farmers	29·2	8·1		6·0	11·4	32·0	16·2
White-collar	32·4	30·5		} 51·5	43·0	22·0	46·0
Others	—	31·2			5·4	6·0	—
	1971	1973	1970	1970	1971	1971	1971
Workers	40·1	44·1	47·1	} 42·7	39·7	43·4	40·1
Farmers	26·1	4·7	5·8		10·6	26·6	15·1
White-collar	33·8	31·6	28·1	38·1	43·6	24·0	44·8
Others	—	19·6	19·0	19·2	6·1	6·0	—
	1976		1976	1975	1975	1976	1976
Workers	41·4		56·1	} 45·5	40·9	50·0	41·6
Farmers	23·0		5·2		9·5	20·0	13·9
White-collar	35·6		20·0	46·1	43·2	22·0	44·5
Others	—		18·7	8·4	6·4	8·0	—
	1978	1977	1979	1979	1979	1978	1979
Workers	41·8	42·0	56·1	62·4	46·2	51·0	41·6
Farmers	22·4	5·3	5·2	10·8	9·4	19·0	13·9
White-collar	30·2	35·2	31·5	25·3	33·0	22·0	ca.44
Others	—	17·5	7·2	1·5	11·4	8·0	—

Source: Official figures as reported by the East European and Soviet press.

the new recruits the workers' share grew from 52·0 percent in 1966–70 to 58·6 percent in 1976 (*'KPSS v tsifrakh'*, 1978, p. 140).

Why despite the larger proportion of worker recruits does the social composition of the parties change much more gradually? In part, the answer is likely to be the higher attrition rate of this strata (de Weydenthal, 1977, p. 346), although another factor appears to be at work as well. Entrance into the party creates the conditions for workers' movement from manual labor to white-collar occupations (Unger, 1977, pp. 310–13). Workers joining the party ranks in recent times are more likely to possess secondary education, and use that as a base for further instruction. In turn, the acquisition of new skills enables them to switch into administrative jobs. Party participation, in short, is used by a number of working-class members for upward mobility. In this way at least, a congruency of interests exists between the leadership's policy of increased recruitment of the industrial labor class and the desire of workers for social and economic advancement. While the increased emphasis on mass participation has facilitated the mobility of at least some members of the working class, this is at best a minuscule segment of the blue-collar workforce. The opportunities presented for such advancement are, therefore, unlikely to diffuse the discontent generated by the inability of the vast majority of industrial labor to attain the desired social and economic mobility.

Perhaps for this reason the extension of workers' involvement in the party ranks has been paralleled by efforts to increase citizens' activism in other political institutions. This is especially evident at the local level, where mass participation is being given a significant push by the present leaders of the communist states. Indications of greater citizens' involvement exist in workers' representation on local bodies and the expansion in the scope of activities of local organizations. For example, the occupational status of deputies to local soviets in the USSR and people's councils in Poland and Bulgaria has shifted steadily in favor of workers (Zawadzka, 1976, pp. 200–201; Jasiewicz, 1979, p. 112; Friedgut, 1979, p. 168). In contrast the number of deputies whose jobs are white-collar has, for most years, decreased. Presumably the greater the number of delegates from the labor class, the more likely it is that information concerning the needs and demands of the workers will reach local policy-making institutions. In addition, local councils and public organizations have new functions aimed at expanding their influence, particularly in spheres touching directly on the citizens' lifestyle and work. Constitutional reforms and party decrees in the 1970s have stressed the creation of new forums for popular participation, the development of residential self-government and the provisions of participation opportunities in state administration (Hough, 1976; Zawadzki, 1977; Dascalescu, 1978; Nemes, 1978).

The extension of participation through organizational changes at the local level has been supplemented by the intensification of contacts between the top political leadership and the masses. This direct participation by the working class through meetings with party and state officials has developed furthest in Poland and Romania in the aftermath of the workers' strikes in 1970, 1976 and 1977 (Dascalescu, 1978; Wiatr, 1979). Regular visits by Gierek and Ceausescu to factories and towns have emerged as important features of the political system. The idea is to create a forum for the exchange of opinions between the people and high officials, and to institutionalize the process of direct consultations. In this way the aspirations of the workers are to become known to the party leadership, who can then act upon that information in the hope of avoiding another outburst of workers' dissatisfaction. This method of extensive consultation with the people through direct contacts has become a keynote in the descriptions of socialist democracy in other East European states as well (Lenart, 1978; WMR Conference, 1979).

The evidence on the nature of citizens' participation in political institutions is at best fragmentary, for we do not know what is the impact of mass participation on socialist societies. It is clear that citizens of the Soviet and East European countries have become more involved in the system as political actors through growing workers' membership in communist parties, assumption of local political positions, participation in consultative forums, and the expansion of activities of local government and public organizations. It appears, however, that official political participation remains largely *pro forma*, and that citizens have little capability to affect the policy preferences of the political authorities (Friedgut, 1979, pp. 316–25; Nelson, 1979; Bielasiak, 1980). Similarly, as we have seen, the opportunities for socioeconomic advancement presented by political activism or membership in the party remain available only to a small segment of the working class.

None the less we must recognize that while symbolic political involvement does not provide any significant substantive benefits to the masses, it can contribute to the political and economic goals of the East European and Soviet leaderships. The regimes' attempt to turn the participatory energies of the people toward their immediate environment, where the citizens' life and work are shaped, may very well create the appearance of increased control by the masses. In this way, participation at the local level or in the workplace can be used by the states to channel workers' demands into more appropriate forms of behavior.

Workers' Participation in the Workplace

The participation of workers in the management of the economy is proclaimed by communist leaders as the cornerstone of socialist democracy under developed socialism. 'The main criterion of its development is the active participation of all employees, particularly manual workers, in the governing of the country and in the management of the national economy' (Gierek, 1977; also Romany, 1975, p. 81; Dascalescu, 1978, p. 58; Beno, 1979, p. 71). The belief is that the attitudes of industrial labor can be shaped through workers' participation at the enterprise. The aims of the authorities are to stimulate economic productivity and socialize workers in support of socialism. The hope is that workplace participation will increase worker identification with production tasks and spur greater work efforts. In addition, workers' involvement in factory affairs is thought to foster attitudes favoring 'cooperation', 'collective good' and 'socialistic human relations' (Wnuk-Lipinski, 1977, p. 59; Mako and Hethy, 1979, pp. 300–302; Fusko and Perlaki, 1979, p. 283). Workers' participation is therefore a means to social integration, efficiency in production and labor's identification with the state.

The communist governments have advanced the claim that economic management provides for the direct exercise of workers' opinions in factory policy-making. Manual laborers are said to have a place alongside economic managers and political activists in voicing their preferences. Hungary, Romania and Poland are in the forefront of instituting increased participation through the formation or invigoration of workers' councils (Stefanowski, 1977; Mako and Hethy, 1979; Nelson, 1979). The leaders of the other East European countries and the Soviet Union have been more cautious, stressing the more established production conferences as a means of labor's influence over issues at the enterprise (Lane and O'Dell, 1978; Bulgarian RFE Report No. 12, 1978; Czechoslovak RFE Report No. 37,

1978; Scherzinger, 1979). All, however, claim that members of the proletariat fulfill genuine participant roles and exercise considerable authority at the workplace.

What in fact is the extent of workers' participation in the communist enterprise, and what is the effect of such involvement by labor on the perceptions and attitudes of the working class? Several sociological studies in the Soviet and East European states have investigated these issues, enabling at least some partial evaluation of workers' participation at the workplace.

Data reveal that workers have a relatively small role in factory organizations and policy deliberations, certainly in comparison to other strata in the enterprise hierarchy. In machine-building plants in the Soviet Union, the workers were systematically under-represented in the membership on enterprise committees. The coefficients of representation for the manual laborers ranged from 0·62 in party primary organizations to 0·86 in factory committees, while administrative employees and engineering-technical personnel consistently show coefficients of over-representation ranging above 1·2 (Table 5.3). Most notably, those institutions which are geared specifically to the involvement of workers in economic management still do not give advantage to that strata. Factory committees are the province of administrators, while production conferences which are more concerned with the technical issues of the planning process are dominated by the specialists. It seems logical that since membership on these institutions is so overwhelmingly slanted toward white-collar employees, they will also be able to dominate the policy discussions.

This expectation tends to be confirmed by data on the scope of participation by workers. A recent Soviet study shows that, while participation by workers in meetings was overwhelming (98 percent), it was significantly lower in terms of their work in plant committees (Table 5.4). Since meetings of factory organizations are held at least once a month and require at least 50 percent of the membership to be present, it is not surprising that almost all workers in the factories took part in such meetings over a two-year period. Soviet scholars acknowledge that within these structures 'not every worker participated actively in discussions', but claim that they directly influenced decisions through their votes (Ussenin *et al.*, 1979, p. 164). The impact of workers' opinions on the content of these deliberations is none the less low, as is evident from the involvement of manual labor in the more critical work of plant committees. Only 57 percent of the workers were active in the latter institutions, whose responsibility extends to the preparation of agenda and to the implementation of decisions. Even this form of participation is problematic as a measure of influence, for we do not know whether the workers' views prevail in the overwhelming presence of white-collar employees in these factory organizations. A Romanian study of production meetings shows that in similar circumstances the majority of workers (64 percent) do not make proposals and that only a minority of industrial employees speak out on work-related problems (Table 5.4). The

Table 5.3 *Representation Coefficients in Administrative Committees at Twenty-one Plants in the USSR, by Party Affiliation and Occupation*

Organization	CPSU	Komsomol	No Affiliation	Workers	Engineering-Technical Personnel	Employees
Party Committees	NA	NA	NA	0·62	2·40	1·22
Factory Committees	1·73	0·64	0·94	0·86	1·22	2·09
Komsomol Committee	1·60	4·02	0·0	0·86	1·24	2·13
Standing Production Conferences	2·90	0·37	0·76	0·70	2·07	1·28
People's Control Committee	2·95	0·57	0·69	0·77	1·79	1·28

Source: Calculated from Mukhachev and Borovik, 1975, pp. 33–4, in Ziegler, 1980, p. 9.

presence of management at forums appears to be an inhibiting factor in the exercise of the rights of workers.

The extent of labor's participation in factory affairs is also strongly affected by the skill levels and political commitment of the workers. Members of the communist parties have the greatest advantage in obtaining positions within enterprise organizations, and then fulfilling participatory roles in these institutions. Table 5.3 shows that the extent of representation of CPSU members in production conferences and people's control committees far exceeds those with no political affiliation: the respective representation coefficients are 2·9 and 0·7. Members of the Romanian Communist Party were consistently far more involved in enterprise assemblies than their counterparts in the Young Communist and trade union organizations (Table 5.5). In the most important of all the participatory activities – that of preparation for the session – 18·9 percent of the party activists performed that task, while only 4·4 percent of trade union members did so. Obvious differences in the scope of participation are present, and party members are able not only to dominate the discussion, but also to direct its course by better preparation (Nelson, 1979, p. 8).

Table 5.4 *Workers' Participation in Factories (%)*

Behaviour	Yes	No
Soviet Workers		
Attended worker meetings	98·0	2·0
Took part in the work of committees	57·0	43·0
Romanian Workers		
Made proposals at meetings	35·6	64·4

Source: Adapted from Ussenin *et al.,* 1979, p. 163; and Badina, 1973, p. 123, in Nelson, 1979.

Table 5.5   *Participation at a Romanian Enterprise by Political Identity (%)*

Activity	Party	Young Communist	Trade Union Only
Prepared for the assembly session	18·9	9·2	4·4
Filled a role at the session	28·1	31·8	21·4
Accomplished a task for the session	46·4	30·8	26·6
Was only present	6·6	28·2	47·6

Source: Sirbu, 1977, p. 42, in Nelson, 1979.

A similar trend is evident in conjunction with the occupational skills of factory personnel. Workers with low qualifications participated rarely in their workplace, with unskilled manual labor offering suggestions far fewer times than personnel with better occupational abilities (Shkaratan, 1973, p. 83). The potential for involving blue-collar workers in the participatory processes of their place of employment appears to be quite difficult. At the very least, under present conditions, the less-skilled workers are reluctant to take part in the management of their enterprises.

The workers' assessments of the opportunities for participation and their own willingness to take part in decision-making are, therefore, critical issues. Polish and Soviet surveys on these questions reveal some differences between workers' perceptions of the desirability of participation in general and their own personal desires to take advantage of self-management. In both instances, most of the respondents think that industrial labor should have a voice on 'most matters affecting the plant', although Soviet workers (84·8 percent) are much more committed to this than their Polish counterparts (48 percent; Table 5.6). The latter tend to favor in almost equal proportion (45 percent) a pattern that would provide participation in 'decisions only on problems affecting their work'. Polish workers seek to

Table 5.6   *Workers' Opinions on Participation*

Type of Participation	Desire to Participate (%)		Willingness to Participate (%)	
	USSR	Poland	USSR	Poland
In general plant issues	84·8	48·0	79·7	32·0
In problems affecting work only	11·5	45·0	17·4	57·0
Only when management asks	3·7	7·0	2·9	9·0
No need for participation	0	0	0	2·0

Source: Ussenin, *et al.,* 1979, p. 157; and Sarapata, 1979, p. 126.

Table 5.7 *Workers' Opinions on the Opportunity for Participation in Different Types of Decisions (%)*

Decisions Concerning	Hungary			USSR		
	Yes	No	Don't Know	Yes	No	Don't Know
Work conditions	75	24	1	97	2	1
Training selection	64	28	8	95	2	3
Allocation of overtime	61	36	3	89	6	5
Premium distribution	57	40	3	95	3	2
Job and pay categories	49	48	3	82	6	12
Promotions	48	45	7	90	5	5
Wage base and pay methods	46	52	2	77	5	17
Layoffs	45	45	10	96	2	2
Discipline	44	48	8	97	2	1
Transfers	42	52	6	90	5	5
Plan development	30	59	11	90	2	9
New machinery	24	65	11	94	2	4
Personnel planning	13	76	11	77	7	16
Hiring	11	82	7	76	8	16

Source: Adapted from Hethy, 1979, p. 307, and Ussenin *et al.,* 1979, p. 159.

have influence directly on issues that are most relevant to their employment conditions and are willing to forgo access to more general management questions. This becomes particularly evident in the expression of personal willingness to participate in policy discussions, with 57 percent of Polish labor willing to take part in work-related deliberations but only 32 percent in broader issues of enterprise direction. The contrast in the Soviet case is overwhelming, with the respective figures being 17·4 and 79·7 percent (Table 5.6). However, in both instances, there is a slippage between desire and willingness to participate in favor of decisions more immediate to work conditions; for instance, some workers whose ideal preference may be for participation on matters affecting the whole plant are none the less unwilling to devote their own efforts to that and prefer to contribute their time to questions that affect them most directly.

These preferences appear to be influenced not only by labor's self-interest in working conditions, but also by the fact that the existing situation allows for greater workers' involvement in issues bearing on conditions of employment. Hungarian and Soviet workers think that their opportunity to participate is greatest on problems concerning work conditions, job opportunities and determination of supplementary bonuses (Table 5.7). In contrast, the workers saw a significantly lower opportunity for taking an active role in topics dealing with personnel planning, production development and wage payment. It is impossible to judge whether workers' views are motivated primarily by lack of interest in the latter decisions, or by their concern that such involvement will result in unpleasant political and social consequences. Most probably both factors are at work here, for it seems obvious that on some questions (for example, pay scale) the workers have an interest in expanding their influence. Lack

Table 5.8   *'Romanian Workers' Sense of Efficacy (%)*

Evaluation	Machine Industry	Chemical Industry	Textile Industry
Proposals have an effect	59·8	60·3	66·1
Proposals have no effect	43·2	39·7	33·9

Source: Badina, 1973, p. 124, in Nelson, 1979.

of motivation, therefore, is not the sole reason why the workers are unwilling to take part in general enterprise issues. The view that the administration creates barriers to such activity without doubt causes the working class to be more cautious in its support of increased participation. The desire for workers' involvement is, thus, related to perceptions of opportunities for participation.

Labor's preparedness to take part in discussions of enterprise activities also hinges on its evaluation of the effectiveness of such participation, The Romanian study measured the sense of efficacy of those workers who participated in production meetings by offering proposals for consideration by the assembly, and found that about 60 percent of those who did so thought that their suggestions have an effect on decisions (Table 5.8). This means that even a large number of workers (approx. 40 percent) who demonstrate participatory initiative by going beyond mere attendance to make proposals do not believe that their intervention is efficacious. Furthermore, the workers who exhibit this type of participatory behavior account for only about 35 percent of all the workers who attend factory meetings (Table 5.4); it is most likely that the remaining 65 percent do not think that such actions are effective. In view of the high degree of correlation between participation and political commitment, and activism and skill level of the workers, we can conclude that the small percentage of

Table 5.9   *Participation and Job Satisfaction of Workers (%)*
            Participation in discussion of:

Evaluation of Job	Methods and Techniques			Rewards and Punishment			Premiums		
	yes	seldom	no	yes	seldom	no	yes	seldom	no
Job is interesting; I like it	66·7	15·7	17·6	52·3	15·5	32·3	31·2	10·5	58·3
Job is no worse and no better than any other	47·3	20·3	32·4	33·0	21·0	41·0	30·0	11·1	58·9
Job is not interestin; I do not like it	37·3	20·9	41·8	30·0	22·0	48·0	25·4	3·6	71·0

Source: Alekseev, 1979, pp. 92–3.

participants who view their actions as effective are the most politically engaged and the better-skilled workers.

The importance of mass participation lies principally in its supposed contributions to increases in economic productivity and the satisfaction of workers. Indeed, it does seem that participation in factory policy deliberations has a positive effect on labor's evaluation of their working and living environment. A study of a labor collective in the Soviet Union showed a strong relationship between the extent of workers' participation and their attitudes toward work (Table 5.9). Job satisfaction was positively affected by higher degrees of involvement in discussions on production methods, work discipline and the distribution of supplementary pay, although the extent of satisfaction varied considerably depending on the issue under consideration. Since the rates of participation by workers on these issues varied in that order, the extent of participation is clearly related to the working class' attitudes toward its occupational activities. Workers who participate in management issues and feel they are 'their own boss' not only find their jobs more interesting, but also derive more satisfaction from their labor activities and tend to work with more concentration and in better moods (Alekseev, 1979, pp. 94–5).

In short, increased participation in the enterprise leads the workers to carry out better their occupational tasks, to derive greater satisfaction from the work process, and to find their jobs more interesting. The consequences of such developments are bound to result in improved performance by labor in production, and therefore contribute to economic growth. Indeed, a study of this issue reports that a Czech factory's experiment with extensive workers' participation resulted in a 94 percent production increase after the first year (Fusko and Perlaki, 1979, p. 293). Similarly the workers' more positive feelings toward work are likely to contribute increased supports for the system and result in greater social stability.

These studies confirm the view that societies which provide opportunities for mass participation reap considerable economic and social benefits. Involvement of workers in factory affairs has the potential of alleviating some of the problems faced by the communist societies. However, despite claims of socialist democracy in the workplace, the regimes have not provided the working class with the opportunity to take part in the management of the enterprise. The evidence is that most workers' participation is nominal, consisting of attendance at factory meetings. Few blue-collar workers attempt to have more influence by participating in discussions and offering suggestions. The majority believe that such actions will be ineffective. Industrial labor perceives the domination of factory councils and committees by white-collar employees as a constraint on its capabilities to influence important enterprise issues.

Workplace participation in Eastern Europe and the Soviet Union, therefore, does not appear to be a useful vehicle for the increased satisfaction of workers with their work and life conditions. The regimes' attempts to use pseudoparticipation to increase economic efficiency and social harmony have not paid off, probably due to fears that the extension of such symbolic participation will lead to greater workers' demands. The consequence has been continued large dissatisfaction of workers with their jobs (Sarapata, 1979, p. 132), high labor turnover and relatively low productivity (Alton, 1977).

Conclusions

Pressures by the working class to obtain a greater voice in policy-determination are a continuing reality in the communist states. Workers' claims have been expressed through overt strikes, riots and disruptions of production, and in more covert ways which find expression primarily in work discipline problems and socially destructive behaviour. In the 1970s workers' discontent spread throughout Eastern Europe, and all the governments acted in anticipation of increasing difficulties. The regimes' concerns with economic growth, social integration and political legitimacy made it crucial to secure the cooperation of the workers. In practice, this meant that more attention had to be paid to the workers' needs and demands. The means chosen to accomplish this task were to offer inducements for mass participation in local political issues and economic questions related to the workplace.

'Socialist democracy' and experimentation with new forms of participation were aimed at providing the working class with a sense of involvement in policy deliberations. As Pateman (1970), Friedgut (1979), and others, have pointed out, even the semblance of participation can enhance an individual's satisfaction and contribute to better social harmony and economic productivity. Studies of socialist enterprises confirm this view, for the laborforce is more content when workers perceive that they have control over their working and living environments.

The problem is that the rhetoric of socialist democracy greatly surpassed the actual implementation of participation opportunities for citizens in their neighborhoods and workers in their factories. Mass participation in the communist states remains inadequate, largely symbolic and without a significant increase in grassroot influence on economic and political decisions. Workers' mobility through membership in the party and their policy impact through political activism are severely limited. Workers' involvement in economic management is low, and even this participation tends to be dominated by the most politically active and most highly skilled segments of the laborforce. The ability of the working class to make decisions that affect their work and life environment is therefore limited, and the majority feel that participation is not efficacious and does not increase their influence. Under these circumstances, despite the verbal commitments to and symbolic innovations in mass participation, the hope of the communist leaders that pseudoparticipation will diffuse the discontent of the workers appears unwarranted.

References: Chapter 5

Afanasyev, V. G., *The Scientific Management of Society* (Moscow: Progress, 1971).

Alekseev, N. I., 'The interrelationship of social factors determining work attitudes', *International Journal of Sociology,* vol. 8, no. 4, 1979, pp. 81–99.

Alton, Th. P., 'Comparative structure and growth of economic activity in Eastern Europe', in *East European Economies Post-Helsinki,* Joint Economic Committee, US Congress (Washington: Government Printing Office, 1977), pp. 199–266.

Alton, Th. P., Bass, E. M., Lazarcik, G., Staller, G. J., and Znayenko, W., *Economic Growth in Eastern Europe 1965–1977* (New York: L. W. International Financial Research, 1978).

Andorka, R., and Zagorski, K., 'Socio-economic structure and socio-occupational mobility in Poland and Hungary', in *Social Structure,* Polish Sociological Association (Wroclaw: Ossolinskich, 1978), pp. 139–59.

Baylis, Th. A., 'Participation without conflict: socialist democracy in the German Democratic Republic', *East Central Europe,* vol. 3, no. 1, 1976, pp. 30–43.

Beno, M., 'Guiding the building of a developed socialist society', *World Marxist Review,* vol. 22, no. 5, 1979, pp. 68–76.

Bielasiak, J., 'Recruitment policy, elite integration and political stability in people's Poland', in M. Simon and R. Kanet, eds, *Policy and Politics in Gierek's Poland* (Boulder: Westview, 1980).

Brezhnev, L. I., Report to 24th Party Congress, *Pravda,* 31 March 1971.

Brezhnev, L. I., Report to 25th Party Congress, *Pravda,* 25 February 1976.

Chekharin, E., *The Soviet Political System under Developed Socialism* (Moscow: Progress, 1977).

Dascalescu, C., 'Worker participation in running society', *World Marxist Review,* vol. 21, no. 11, 1978, pp. 48–59.

Evans, Jr, A. B., 'Developed socialism in Soviet ideology', *Soviet Studies,* vol. 29, no. 3, 1977, pp. 409–28.

Fischer, M. E., 'The Romanian communist party and its central committee: patterns of growth and change', *Southeastern Europe,* vol. 6, no. 1, 1979, pp. 1–28.

Friedgut, Th. H., *Political Participation in the USSR* (Princeton, NJ: Princeton University Press, 1979).

Fusko, Z., and Perlaki, I., 'Increasing the socio-economic effectiveness of socialist work groups and organizations', in C. L. Cooper and E. Mumford, eds, *The Quality of Working Life in Western and Eastern Europe* (Westport, Ct.: Greenwood, 1979), pp. 282–96.

Gierek, E., *Trybuna Ludu,* 8 April 1977.

Hammer, D. P., 'The dilemma of party growth', *Problems of Communism,* vol. 20, no. 4, 1971, pp. 16–21.

Hethy, L., 'Plant democracy and the interests of the workers in participation', in *Joint Publications Research Service,* June 1979.

Hethy, L., and Mako, C., 'Workers' direct participation in decisions in Hungarian factories', *International Labour Review,* vol. 116, no. 1, 1977, pp. 9–21.

Hough, J. F., 'Political participation in the Soviet Union', *Soviet Studies,* vol. 28, no. 1, 1976, pp. 3–20.

Hummel, L., 'Greater worker involvement in planning', in *Joint Publications Research Service,* June 1979.

Jasiewicz, K., *Role Spoleczne Radnych Wojewodzkich Rad Narodowych* (Wroclaw: Ossolinskich, 1979).

Kalecka, R., 'Stan samorzadu robotniczego', *Trybuna Ludu,* 24 May 1978.

Kelley, D. R., 'Developments in ideology', in D. Kelley, ed., *Soviet Politics in the Brezhnev Era* (New York: Praeger, 1980), pp. 182–99.

Kerimov, D. A., *Gosudarstvo, Demokratiia i Trudovoi Kollektiv v Razvoitom Sotsialisticheskom Obshestve* (Moscow: Mysl, 1977).

Koziolek, H., 'Economics and politics under developed socialism', *World Marxist Review,* vol. 20, no. 3, 1977, pp. 49–75.

'KPSS v tsitpakh', *Partinaia Zhizn,* no. 21, 1977, pp. 20–43.

Lane, D., and O'Dell, F., *The Soviet Industrial Worker* (Oxford: Martin Robertson, 1978).

Lenart, J., 'The economy and democracy', *World Marxist Review,* vol. 21, no. 7, 1978, pp. 3–14.

Mako, C., and Hethy, L., 'Worker participation and the socialist enterprise: a Hungarian case study', in C. Cooper and E. Mumford, eds, *The Quality of Working Life in Western and Eastern Europe* (Westport, Ct.: Greenwood, 1979), pp. 296–326.

Molnar, N., *A Short History of the Hungarian Communist Party* (Boulder: Westview, 1978).

Nelson, D., 'Workers in a workers' state: participatory dynamics in developed socialism' (unpublished).

Nemes, D., 'The socialist political system in Hungary', *World Marxist Review,* vol. 21, no. 11, 1978, pp. 16–25.

Ozdowski, S. A., and Alexander, S. C., 'The legal order and industrial workers in a communist enterprise: the Polish case', *Law and Society Review,* vol. 12, no. 4, 1978, pp. 545–85.

Pateman, C., *Participation and Democratic Theory* (Cambridge: Cambridge University Press, 1970).

'Portret Partii', *Zycie Partii,* no. 2, 1980, pp. 12–14.

Pravda, Bratislava, 'Participation in management', in *Joint Publications Research Service,* May 1979.

Pravda, Bratislava, 'Production councils foster worker role in management', in *Joint Publication Research Service,* February 1980.

Radio Free Europe Research, 'Sociological science and sociological research', *Bulgarian Situation Report,* no. 12, 10 July 1978.

Radio Free Europe Research, 'Twenty years of the brigades of socialist work', *Czechoslovak Situation Report,* no. 37, 17 November 1978.

Rigby, T. H., 'Soviet communist party membership under Brezhnev', *Soviet Studies,* vol. 28, no. 3, 1976, pp. 317–37.

Romany, P., 'Searching for new solutions', *World Marxist Review,* vol. 18, no. 2, 1975, pp. 79–83.

Sarapata, A., 'Polish automobile workers and automation', in J. Forslin, A. Sarapata and A. Whitehill, eds, *Automation and Industrial Workers,* Vol. 1 (Oxford: Pergamon, 1979), pp. 118–53.

Scherzinger, A., 'GDR labor conditions, characteristics, problems', in *Joint Publications Research Service,* January 1979.

Shkaratan, O. I., 'Social groups in the working class of a developed socialist society', *International Journal of Sociology,* vol. 3, no. 1–2, 1973, pp. 63–105.

Stefanowski, R., 'Workers' councils 1956–1977', *Radio Free Europe Research Background Report,* no. 160, 9 August 1977.

Triska, J. F., 'Citizen participation in community decisions in Yugoslavia, Romania, Hungary and Poland', in J. F. Triska and P. Cocks, eds, *Political Development in Eastern Europe* (New York: Praeger, 1977), pp. 147–77.

Unger, A. L., 'Soviet communist party membership under Brezhnev: a comment', *Soviet Studies,* vol. 29, no. 2, 1977, pp. 306–16.

Ussenin, V. I., *et al.,* 'Soviet workers and automation of the production process', in *Automation and Industrial Workers* (Oxford: Pergamon, 1979), pp. 154–99.

Waligorski, M., 'Samorzad mieszkancow miast', in Z. Leonski, ed., *Rady Narodowe i Terenowe Organy Administracji po Reformach* (Warsaw: PWN, 1976), pp. 147–59.

de Weydenthal, J. B., 'Party development in contemporary Poland', *East European Quarterly,* vol. 9, no. 3, 1977, pp. 341–63.

de Weydenthal, J. B., 'The workers' dilemma of Polish politics: a case study', *East European Quarterly,* vol. 13, no. 1, 1979, pp. 95–119.

Wiatr, J., 'About the sociology of power', *Polityka,* 20 January 1979.

Wightman, G., and Brown, A. H., 'Changes in the levels of membership and social composition of the communist party of Czechoslovakia, 1945–73', *Soviet Studies,* vol. 27, no. 3, 1975, pp. 396–417.

Wnuk-Lipinski, E., 'Job satisfaction and the quality of working life: the Polish experience', *International Labour Review,* vol. 115, no. 1, 1977, pp. 53–64.

World Marxist Review Conference, 'The present-day problems of socialist democracy and its perspectives', *World Marxist Review,* vol. 18, no. 2, 1975, pp. 41–83; and no. 3, 1975, pp. 101–26.

World Marxist Review Conference, 'Political system of developed socialism', *World Marxist Review,* vol. 22, no. 6, 1979, pp. 31–40.

Yanowitch, M., 'Introduction', *International Journal of Sociology,* vol. 8, no. 4, 1979, pp. vii–xiv.

Zaharescu, B., 'A new stage in the development of socialist Romania', *World Marxist Review,* vol. 21, no. 3, 1978, pp. 50–60.

Zawadzka, B., *Przedstawicielstwo w Panstwie Socjalistycznym* (Wroclaw: Ossolinskich, 1976).

Zawadzki, S., 'Demokracja a formy panstwa socjalistycznego', in A. Lopatka and Z. Rykowski, eds, *Formy Panstwa Socjalistycznego* (Wroclaw: Ossolinskich, 1977), pp. 175–90.

Ziegler, Ch. E., 'Political participation in the USSR: the workers' role in the developed socialist state', paper presented at Midwest Slavic Conference, Cincinnati, Ohio, USA, 1980.

Zimmerman H., 'The GDR in the 1970s', *Problems of Communism,* vol. 27, no. 2, 1978, pp. 1–40.

6 Aggregate Economic Difficulties and Workers' Welfare

LAURA D'ANDREA TYSON

'I wish I could afford to live as well as I do.' Janos Komlos, Hungarian humorist, quoted in *Economist*, 24 March 1979, p. 61

Introduction

During the decade of the 1970s, economic conditions throughout the world deteriorated. Both developed and less-developed economies, as well as market-capitalist and planned-socialist economies, shared in the deteriorating economic performance to some extent. Economic interdependency, the realization of postwar trends in international trade and credit relations, meant that many nations found themselves confronted with some of the same economic difficulties, despite significant ideological and systematic differences in the organization of their economies.

Among the many countries adversely affected by changes in world economic conditions were the East European nations. Always more sensitive to shocks in international markets than their Soviet neighbors, because of their smaller size and their greater openness to international trade,[1] the East European states had increased their participation in international exchange prior to the world economic disturbances beginning in 1973–4. Even though their trade participation rates (measured roughly as the ratio between the value of trade and the value of national output) remained below those of comparable market economies, they were not so small as to reduce significantly their sensitivity to international shocks. From the perspective of the East European states, such shocks took many forms in the 1970s, including a dramatic slowdown in Western demand[2] for their exports, a dramatic increase in the prices of their imports, first from Western and later from Soviet and CMEA sources, and for all of the economies except Poland, Bulgaria and perhaps Romania, a significant and persistent deterioration in their terms of trade.

These external shocks had two general effects on internal economic conditions. Deteriorating external conditions made the realization of domestic growth goals more difficult even when the slowdown was not accompanied by a deterioration in the terms of trade, as for example in Poland in most years (see Table 6.2). With export demand faltering due to external slowdowns, a country like Poland found it extremely difficult to earn enough foreign exchange from exports to finance imports and pay back credits for past imports. When manifested in part as a deterioration in the terms of trade, the external shocks produced an absolute real-income loss, meaning that not only did growth goals become more difficult to achieve, but their achievement rested on the transfer of additional real resources to the rest of the world. In effect, countries experiencing a terms of trade loss were forced to pay the equivalent of a real tax in order to maintain their imports and domestic growth at unchanged levels. How to distribute the burden of the loss across different categories of expenditure, such as investment, consumption and government expenditure, and across different groups in the population, such as farmers, industrial workers and government bureaucrats, became an important political and policy issue. And even where the terms of trade did not deteriorate, the potential slowdown in growth necessitated by external events had distributional consequences; the burden of growth reductions had to be shared by various expenditure categories and income groups.

The issue of the distributional consequences of external shocks in Eastern Europe leads to the questions that are the focus of this chapter, namely, questions about how these shocks have influenced the well-being of industrial workers. According to some observers (for example, Connor, 1979), workers in Eastern Europe have developed class characteristics and a class consciousness in recent years. Whether this is the case or not, it is certain that workers have become more assertive in their demands on East European regimes. It is also certain that these regimes base their legitimacy on the industrial proletariat on whose behalf they rule, and that this legitimacy has become more closely linked to their ability to provide certain economic desiderata, such as steady increases in the standard of living, job security and welfare benefits. Finally, as a consequence of deteriorating international economic conditions, it is certain that the realization of these desiderata has become more difficult.

The problem facing the East European regimes is how to satisfy the interests of workers under economic conditions that do not provide the wherewithal to do so, unless other significant economic goals, such as high investment rates and a reasonable balance between export receipts and import expenditures, are sacrificed to some extent. In short, the East European leaders, like the leaders in many Western economies suffering from tightening economic constraints, face tradeoffs among competing goals. Two questions make the behaviour of East European states under these circumstances particularly interesting. First, how do the systemic features of planned and socialist economies influence economic goals and the policy instruments available to realize them? Secondly, in the absence of an acceptable resolution of economic difficulties, how does the dissatisfaction of the population manifest itself to the political leaders? In the West, deteriorating economic performance frequently leads to popular dissatisfaction expressed in election results. In the East, the same dissatisfaction plays itself out in different forms of political conflict and social discontent that may have the same ultimate result – a change in leadership.

In order to focus the analysis of these questions, this chapter limits itself to a consideration of two countries, Hungary and Poland. It compares their responses to economic difficulties in the 1970s, particularly as these responses affected industrial workers. Before examining each individual country, the chapter outlines a general framework for understanding the links between internal and external economic conditions that is related to accepted theory for market economies. The framework shows how external conditions can influence various indicators of worker well-being. There follows a brief survey of how economic difficulties in each country influenced these indicators in the 1970s. Finally, the chapter ends with a discussion of possible future prospects for workers' welfare in Eastern Europe under more adverse economic circumstances.

1   External Disturbance and Macroeconomic Adjustment in the Economies of Eastern Europe: a General Framework[3]

The macroeconomic interconnections between the foreign sector and the domestic sector in an individual economy, be it of the planned or market variety, can be understood most simply in terms of what economists call the 'absorption approach'. According to this approach, links between trade flows and internal macroeconomic variables can be understood in terms of the relationship between available resources and internal demand (total expenditures or 'absorption'). Resources available for domestic use are given by output plus imports less exports; domestic use in turn is the sum of household consumption, investment in fixed or working assets (whether private or state-owned), and government expenditure. Thus, according to the absorption approach we have

(1) $A = Y + M - X$
(2) $A = C + I + G$, hence
(3) $Y - A = X - M = B = Y - (C+I+G)$

where Y = output, A = domestic utilization (absorption), X = exports, M = imports, B = balance of trade, C = consumption, I = investment and G = government expenditure.

According to these relationships, any excess of output over domestic use is available for net exports, and any excess of domestic use or absorption over production must be supplied by net imports. Suppose, then, that an economy absorbs more for domestic use than it produces so that $Y - A < O$, implying a balance-of-trade deficit $B = X - M < O$. This deficit must be financed by foreign credit until such time as either income is increased or domestic absorption is reduced to restore the trade balance.

The situation of an excess of domestic absorption over domestic output, matched by a balance-of-trade deficit, was characteristic of Eastern Europe during the 1970s, for reasons which had to do with both internal policy decisions, and external economic shocks. In Poland and Yugoslavia, for example, growth plans were predicated on a balance-of-trade deficit to be financed by borrowing from abroad. Deteriorating international conditions, which caused export performance to falter, made the actual trade deficit and the required foreign borrowing even larger than anticipated. In Yugoslavia and Hungary, the impact of the export slowdown was aggravated by a terms-of-trade loss. With import prices rising faster than export prices, an even greater volume of real exports was required to pay for the same real volume of imports. In all three countries, the interconnections between the foreign and domestic sectors was heightened by the fact that imports were largely raw materials and capital inputs required to maintain domestic production. Formally,

(4) $M = \alpha\, Y$, where α is an import coefficient relating required imports to domestic production levels.

Under these circumstances, any attempt to achieve trade balance by cutting imports meant a reduction in domestic output as well.

As the absorption model suggests, in the long run, equilibrium requires a balance between domestic output and domestic use. Trade deficits, financed by external credits, cannot persist indefinitely. Economies are forced to adjust Y or A or both to achieve trade balance. This is the crucial link between foreign shocks and domestic economic conditions – if export performance falters because of external economic conditions, or if the same volume of imports requires a larger volume of exports, then ultimately a position of balance requires some adjustment in domestic economic conditions to reduce the gap between output and absorption.

In a growing economy, this may require that output grow more quickly than absorption, thereby freeing up increments in domestic output for exports. In this case, the adjustment burden is one of slowing the growth of domestic absorption, and the distributional issue is one of determining how that slowdown is distributed among C, I and G, among groups within each expenditure category. In a static economy, adjustment may require an absolute reduction of domestic absorption, in which case the distributional issue is the tougher one of how to distribute the total cutback among C, I and G and among different groups.

In both the static and dynamic cases, moreover, macroeconomic adjustments in Y or A or both imply microeconomic adjustments, in particular, the reallocation of labor and capital from industries that decline, absolutely or relatively, to industries that expand in response to the distribution of the adjustment burden. Such microeconomic adjustments may also be required as a consequence of changing domestic relative prices reflecting a change in the terms of trade. Finally, microeconomic adjustments to move labor and capital from low– to high-productivity industries and to rationalize the use of scarce resources may also be part of policy efforts to expand Y by promoting efficiency in resource use. Whatever the cause, microeconomic adjustments (usually referred to as 'industrial adjustments' in the literature on Western economies), have potential distributional consequences – in particular for the employment security and wages of workers in declining industries and for the degree of wage-differentiation. Whether these consequences are actually realized, will depend on what kinds of government policies are introduced to promote the necessary microeconomic adjustments.

Adjustment policies in general must be shaped within the constraints set by existing goals and institutions. From the perspective of this chapter, the goals to consider are those of importance to industrial workers. In the planned economies of Eastern Europe, such as Hungary and Poland, these goals include: aggregate full employment and the related but distinct goal of individual job security; the avoidance of excess demand on markets for consumer goods and services, with attendant open or repressed inflationary pressures; acceptable differentials among wages and between wages and other incomes; and an acceptable rate of increase in real wages and the standard of living. In market economies, including the quasi-market economy of Yugoslavia, workers' goals are similar, except that the problems of excess demand and consequent inflationary pressures go beyond the market for consumer goods, since the extent of price controls and quantity rationing is much more limited than it is in planned economies.[4]

As far as economic institutions are concerned, a traditional view of planned economies suggests that adjustment will be realized by direct policy interventions on the supply side of the economy to stimulate the rate of growth of output, or to cut the rates of growth or the levels of domestic expenditure categories. Direct policies can also be used to determine the distributional impact of adjustment among groups. Consider, for example, an adjustment policy to slow the rate of growth of consumption. Such a result can be achieved by a planned reduction in the rate of growth of consumer output combined with a planned reduction in the rate of growth of money wages. In theory, since the planners have control over the composition of supply between consumption and non-consumption goods and over wages, this policy combination can be directly achieved by an adjustment in plan targets and/or enterprise incentives. Moreover, the planners' control over wages, as well as their extensive use of price-subsidy programs, allows them to determine not only the extent of the slowdown in consumption, but also its distribution among different income groups. Thus, in theory, the planned economies appear to have the instruments available to effectuate adjustment without sacrificing some of the goals deemed important to workers. In this example, the only goals affected are individual job security, since the adjustment problem may require the transfer of some workers out of consumer-goods production, and the rate of increase in the standard of living. Full employment, the avoidance of inflationary pressures on consumer and labor markets and an acceptable income distribution are all maintained. As we shall see, reality in Hungary and Poland diverges sharply from this traditional view of the adjustment process in planned economies.

In a market system, in which the scope for direct planner intevention is much more limited, as in Yugoslavia, indirect policies are usually employed to produce the desired changes in the level and/or composition of output and absorption as part of the adjustment process. Such policies usually work on the demand side of the economy. For example, tighter monetary policy may raise interest rates to cut investment or its rate of growth, or exchange-rate adjustment may be introduced to increase exports at the expense of domestic demand, or a tax increase may be engineered to cut consumption. In Yugoslavia, as in other market-oriented economies, such indirect, demand-oriented policies also tend to reduce output levels or growth rates somewhat, because of temporary rigidities in money wages and money prices. Thus, in market systems, an attempt to reduce absorption may be accompanied by a reduction in output levels or growth rates and a sacrifice of the goals of high employment and job security. In theory, at least, the direct control policies of the planned economy do not require such a sacrifice. Of course, if the planners choose to cut investment to trim total absorption while maintaining consumption, they will reduce output growth in the future; similarly, a cut in consumption may depress output if it causes workers to work less hard because of reduced incentives (the so-called 'supply multiplier effect'); and finally, if the planners try to cut imports to restore the trade balance, domestic output may fall as a consequence of limits on the availability of imported inputs for which there are no domestic substitutes (the so-called 'bottleneck multiplier effect') (Portes, 1980, p. 15). In none of these cases, however, does output or employment slow down or fall because of a policy-induced deflation of domestic demand, as frequently happens in market economies.

The potential inflationary consequences of adjustment policies also differ between planned and market systems. In market economies, an attempt to cut absorption may produce unintended inflationary and distributional consequences, as a result of successive rounds of nominal wage and price increases, reflecting the efforts of workers and profit-earners to maintain their real absorption levels. Inflationary pressure emanating from this source, is the manifestation of the struggle to distribute the adjustment burden in the market system. In theory, in planned economies, where central distributional decisions can be made – for example, by adjusting nominal wage growth to achieve the desired distribution between consumption and investment expenditures – this source of inflationary pressure does not come into play. As later sections of this chapter indicate, actual developments in Hungary and Poland have been inconsistent with this theoretical conception of how planned economies function.

As the preceding discussion suggests, deteriorating external economic conditions in the 1970s forced the East European economies to make adjustments in output and/or absorption to maintain trade balance, or in the absence of such adjustments, to borrow abroad in order to cover trade imbalances. In the following sections, the adjustment responses of Hungary and Poland will be examined with particular emphasis on how they affected the economic goals of industrial workers. These responses shared one important characteristic: the slowdowns in planned and actual growth rates and the slowdowns in absorption were insufficient to restore external balance. By the end of the 1970s, trade deficits were at record high levels, and foreign indebtedness had climbed dramatically as a result of the use of foreign credit to cover these deficits. Under these circumstances, external constraints on credit availability began to tighten, indicating that much more severe adjustment responses will be forthcoming in the 1980s, with important potential implications for worker well-being and political and social stability.

2   Economic Adjustment and Workers' Welfare in Hungary in the 1970s

When viewed from the perspective of the goals important to workers, Hungary's economic performance during most of the 1970s must be judged a success. Hungary offered its workers full employment, individual job security and rapid increases in per capita real income, real wages per employee and per capita real consumption over the 1971–8 period, as the data in Table 6.1 reveal. Moreover, the data fail to reflect the fact that both the quality and selection of consumer goods, as well as their aggregate availability, increased during the 1970s, partly in response to the greater impact of market forces on enterprise decision-making. Although aggregate performance was marred somewhat by persistent increases in consumer prices, such increases were outstripped by increases in money wages and incomes that kept the real purchasing power of worker earnings increasing at a respectable average rate of about 3·3 percent between 1971 and 1978. In addition, there is no evidence to suggest the existence of

Table 6.1   *Macroeconomic Indicators in Hungary*

	1971-5	1974	1975	1976	1977	1978	1979
Annual Percentage Change							
Real Net Material Product							
Plan	5·7	5·0	5·2	5·3	6·3	5·0	3·0*
Actual	6·3	6·9	5·4	3·0	7·8	4·0	1·5†
Industrial Output	6·4	8·1	4·7	4·6	6·6	5·2	2·5†
Agricultural Output	4·8	3·5	2·1	-2·7	10·3	2·0	0·0†
Gross Fixed Investment	7·1	9·8	14·8	-0·3	14·4	4·0	1·5†
Real Income Per Capita	4·6	6·4	4·1	0·8	4·5	3·0	—
Real Consumption Per Capita‡	4·3	5·1	4·5	1·1	4·2	2·7	—
(Alton *et al.* estimates)§	(3·5)	(5·4)	(4·1)	(1·5)	(5·0)	(2·8)	(-)
Consumer Price Index	2·8	2·2	3·8	5·0	3·9	4·6	9·0†
Money Wages per Employee*	6·2	7·1	6·6	6·6	8·5	—	—
Real Wages per Employee	3·3	5·6	3·8	0·1	3·8	3·1	—
Terms of Trade‡	-3·7	-7·5	-7·1	2·2	-3·4	-0·6	—
Balance of Trade (million $)	47	-446	-889	-607	-700	-1566*	—
Balance of Trade with Industrial West (million $)	-348	-741	-550	-674	-817	-1287	—

Sources: Unless otherwise indicated, figures are from Portes (1980).
*Figures taken from *CMEA Data, 1979,* a publication of the Vienna Institute for Comparative Economic Studies.
†Estimates taken from the *Economist* (5–11 April 1980, p. 48).
‡From Marrese (1980).
§Alton *et al.* (1979, table 4).

repressed inflationary pressures, at least in the aggregate over most of the period, although temporary shortages of some goods may have occurred, as for example during the investment boom of 1977 (Portes, 1977a, 1980). Finally, the increases in real wages occurred along with a successful policy to keep nominal income differentials in the first economy (roughly equivalent to all state sector economic activity) within politically acceptable ranges.[5]

The significance of the successful control of differentials in the 'first' economy to the workers' sense of well-being is suggested by the events of the early 1970s. As part of the reform of 1968, a conscious decision was taken to reverse, at least to a limited extent, the highly egalitarian nature of previous Hungarian incomes policies. With the new emphasis on efficiency and the use of the market in the reformed system, a greater differentiation of incomes was deemed necessary both to reward workers and managers for greater effort, and to direct labor resources to their most profitable uses. This differentiation was to occur both within the state sector of the economy, and possibly between the legal private sector and the state sector, since an expansion of some legal private activity was encouraged as part of the reform.

In the eyes of many observers (for example, Portes, 1977; Wiles, 1974), the slowdown in economic reforms that occurred after 1972 was the result of worker dissatisfaction with the widening of income differentials in response to market forces. These differentials had changed to the relative detriment of workers in the largest state enterprises and to the relative benefit of managers, peasants, the self-employed and workers in cooperatives. In 1972, Kadar, reacting to growing political discontent, came down in favor of the workers, arguing for equality over efficiency, and by 1975-6 the central authorities had regained control over both the average level of money wages and income differentials within the state sector. In essence, the wage control mechanism established a range of permissable increases in average wages and in wage differentiation, using a set of guidelines that established a minimum increase for the lowest wage categories and a maximum increase for other wage categories, beyond which a steeply progressive tax would be levied (see Marrese, 1979). In addition, profit-leveling charges and taxes and new regulations on the division of profits among enterprise funds reduced the role of the profit-sharing fund as a source of financing large differentials between managerial and worker incomes. Available data suggest that over the 1970-75 period, income differentials declined due to the gradual imposition of these measures. For example, in 1970, earnings of top- and middle-level managers were 270 and 164 percent of average earnings in industry, while those of workers were 94 percent of the average. The corresponding figures for 1975 were 234, 128 and 94 percent respectively (Racz, 1977, p. 212).

Breaking the already-weak market links between wages and labor performance, on the one hand, and between profits, enterprise performance and managerial rewards, on the other, resulted in a slowdown of the economic reform mechanism, particularly in the area of prices. This slowdown was aggravated by deteriorating external economic circumstances that began to develop with the 1973–4 OPEC price increase and its effects on world prices and Western demand for Hungarian exports. World price changes led to both a dramatic adjustment of relative prices in favor of raw materials and energy, and a steep increase in the overall prices of Hungarian imports.[6] The potential impact of the overall external price increase on the aggregate price level in Hungary could be and was offset – but not completely – by a gradual revaluation of the forint. The potential domestic impact of changes in external relative prices, however, could not be offset in this way. As it was, the authorities used taxes and subsidies on production and extensive subsidies on consumption goods to shield domestic relative prices from external changes.[7] The extension of these wedges between domestic and foreign prices became central to the government's strategy of insulating the domestic economy from the effects of deteriorating external circumstances. Had domestic relative prices been allowed to adjust to foreign price changes, there would have been significant effects on resource allocation and sectoral and enterprise profitability, with implications for individual job security, income differentiation and real living standards. In certain sectors, prices, profits and wages would have increased – to the extent permissable under the wage control mechanism – relative to those in other sectors. Changes in relative profitability would have implied some industrial adjustment, with the dismissal and transfer of workers in sectors rendered unprofitable by the new price structure. Changes in relative prices would have produced changes in important consumer prices, such as energy-related prices, with consequent implications for both the average level of real consumption, and the differentiation of real consumption levels among different household types. Had these price, profit and income changes been allowed to occur, the market would have determined the distribution of the burden of the real income loss implied by Hungary's terms of trade deterioration. The loss was not insubstantial – Brown and Tardos (1980) estimate that it was equivalent to 5–8 percent of national income in each of the years 1974 to 1977. Hence, it is not surprising that given the magnitude of the burden, the Hungarians were unwilling to allow the market mechanism to determine its distributional consequences.

The decision not to use prices as a distributional mechanism, however, did not free the Hungarians from the difficult task of handling the adjustment problem. As the discussion in this section indicates, a trade imbalance, such as the one which developed in Hungary in response to the slowdown in export demand and the terms-of-trade deterioration, requires some adjustment in Y or A or both, with consequent distributional implications. The initial response of the Hungarians, however, was to shield the domestic economy from the burdens of adjustment by allowing the trade deficit to climb sharply and by increasing the use of foreign credit. This decision shows up clearly in the 1974 and 1975 figures presented in Table 6.1, which indicate that real output, real incomes, real consumption and real investment continued to grow rapidly along with a virtual doubling of the overall trade deficit.[8]

1976 is the first year which shows an attempt by the Hungarians to handle the adjustment problem by slowing the overall growth rate to cut import demand, by cutting investment growth sharply, and by reducing the rate of growth of real per capita consumption. These developments were consistent with the 1976–80 plan that called for a reduction in output growth rates and an even greater reduction in absorption growth rates so as to cut imports and increase goods and services available for exports. Adjustment was to be realized primarily through traditional planning methods – a slowdown in the rate of growth of money wages and a slowdown in the production of goods for domestic investment and consumption purposes. According to plan targets, the rate of growth of investment, although below its 1971–5 level, was to be above that of consumption, implying that a larger proportion of the adjustment burden was to be carried by consumption expenditure. Since prices did not reflect the relative profitability of different types of production, the planned change in the composition and use of output was to be accomplished largely by administrative means. As it turned out, the planners were unable to slow money wage increases, but the rate of open consumer price increases picked up, reducing the purchasing power of wages and forcing consumers to share some of the adjustment burden. Adjustment was, thus, accomplished by a combination of market and planning forces.

The figures for 1977 and 1978 suggest that the retrenchment initiated in 1976 was relatively short-lived. 1977 was certainly an expansion year in which output and absorption grew rapidly, with an investment boom occurring along with rapid increases in real wages and consumption. The general view is that the stimulation of investment led to rapid increases in money wages over which the planners lost control, with consequent inflationary pressures on the markets for consumer goods.[9] 1978 saw slower growth in both output and absorption but still at rates that were higher than those in 1976. The results of the 1977–8 expansion on the trade balance were disastrous. Failure in those years to pursue adjustment policies to cut import requirements for inputs and to free up domestic resources for exports, aggravated by a further deterioration in the terms of trade in 1977, caused the trade deficit to more than double between 1977 and 1978. As a consequence, gross convertible currency debt rose by 35 percent over the same period, and the debt service ratio (in convertible currency) hit 44 percent (Portes, 1980, tables 10, 11).

By 1979, the problems of the external deficit and rising indebtedness forced the Hungarian authorities to introduce measures to adjust the economy to external circumstances. Although the figures for 1979 are still preliminary and incomplete, those available suggest that these measures had their intended effects – output growth fell sharply to the lowest level realized in the 1970s; the rate of growth of investment fell sharply; the rate of inflation reached the highest level reported in an East European economy, with the exception of Yugoslavia, during the postwar period; and scattered evidence suggests that real incomes per capita stagnated and real wages fell by 1 percent. Real incomes and real wages were reduced by the very large price adjustments of July 1979, which raised food prices by 20 percent and prices for fuels and energy by 34 percent. Although the impact of these price increases on incomes was offset to an extent by a system of income compensation payments, the compensation was only partial, about two-thirds of the total impact, and was paid only to certain groups, including workers, students, pensioners and the disabled.

The July 1979 price increases, significant in themselves as a mechanism for distributing some of the adjustment burden to consumption expenditure and worker incomes, are even more important as an indication of a basic decision by the Hungarian authorities to rely more on prices and the market to guide the adjustment process. Traditional planning and direct-control methods, executed in a system of largely inflexible relative prices, had failed to produce the necessary adjustment during the 1974–8 period. The authorities were apparently both unable and unwilling to achieve adjustment by traditional methods, such as controlled reductions in the rate of growth of money wages, in the rate of growth of investment and in imports. Moreover, even when they were partially successful, as in 1976, the coexistence of a large degree of enterprise, worker and consumer discretion and a distorted price structure meant that decentralized decisions were not producing the most efficient allocation of scarce goods and resources. In a situation of sharp limits on the availability of additional resources, growth depends critically on their efficient use. Such is the case in Hungary, where increases in labor resources are not anticipated for demographic reasons, and where increases in capital resources requiring an even greater investment effort are not politically desirable. Hence, future growth prospects depend on eliminating the distortions of the existing system, and the Hungarian leaders made a clear decision in 1979 to try to do so by expanding the economic reform.[10] The alternative, of course, would have been a further reversion to traditional planning methods.

What are the implications of the current economic situation and the leaders' decision for the goals important to workers? First, it seems certain that increases in real wages and real consumption standards will be slowed down over the next few years, probably through a combination of measures, including tighter control over money wages, a slowdown in the production of consumer goods and a redirection of some of them to export markets, and greater upward flexibility of prices at both the consumer and producer levels. By 1980, approximately 55 percent of all consumer prices were categorized as freely determined, up from 45 percent in 1978. Secondly, it seems likely that if the authorities stick to their decision to allow domestic relative prices to adjust to foreign relative prices, then the goals of individual job security will be compromised.[11] Changing domestic relative prices, in tandem with the abolition of the charge on enterprise fixed assets, implies large relative shifts in profitability among enterprises and sectors. These microchanges necessitate industrial adjustment – the movement of labor from less profitable to more profitable enterprises. Full employment under these conditions means the right to some job, not the right to a given job as it has heretofore been interpreted. Interenterprise and intersectoral shifts of labor are particularly needed because Hungary has no available labor reserves, other than reserves of redundant labor currently employed by subsidized firms.[12] To encourage such shifts, Hungary's labor laws have been altered to allow enterprises to dismiss workers somewhat more easily for either production, or market reasons. Easier dismissals, combined with new legislation allowing firms to assign one worker to several part-time jobs, to substitute part-time jobs for full-time ones, and to impose fines on careless or tardy workers, are also part of a strategy to eliminate undisciplined work practices thought to contribute to the labor redundancy problem (see Marrese, 1979, 1980). These new policies in favor of labor transfers and dismissals have been openly supported by the trade union organization, acting in its traditional role as a 'transmission belt' between party and workers.[13]

Finally, recent reforms also imply some compromising in the area of income differentiation. Beginning in 1979, there has been repeated emphasis on the need for greater differentiation to provide market indicators of where labor is needed and most profitably used, and to act as an incentive mechanism for individual workers. Accordingly, the authorities have reduced the wage tax from 35 to 17 percent, thereby broadening the scope for acceptable wage increases in the first economy. So far, however, the authorities have maintained their control over the bands within which skill-specific wage rates must remain. Another indication that the authorities are willing to tolerate a greater degree of income differentiation is suggested by their hope that the legal private sector will absorb some of the workers dismissed by state enterprises. To this effect, tax concessions, rebates and a more conciliatory approach to the legal private sector have marked official encouragement of its role in the economic adjustment process. According to most estimates, the average hourly income in the 'second' economy (encompassing legal, semi-legal and illegal private activity) remains higher than that in the 'first' economy or state sector (see Marrese, 1979, pp. 6–9). Of course, if relative wage differentials increase in this sector, some workers may redirect effort there and away from their 'second' economy, moonlighting activities. If so, the net impact of the new measures on the allocation of labor (measured in terms of both time and effort) between the 'first' and 'second' economies is difficult to predict. Altogether, recent pronouncements on the need for and desirability of greater income-differentiation and a possible expansion of the legal private sector are similar to those that accompanied the 1968 reform. If the past is any guide, actual increases in income differentials can be expected to lead to discontent among industrial workers employed in the 'first' economy.

In short, the greater use of the market mechanism to solve Hungary's adjustment problem implies several years of reduced growth in real living standards, greater labor discipline, a reduction in individual job security and increasing income differentiation. Some workers will gain while others will lose, but viewed from the perspective of workers as a group, the near future will necessitate sacrifices on all major goals, except perhaps the goal of aggregate full employment. Two questions about these future prospects arise. First, will the workers accept these sacrifices as inevitable in

Hungary's circumstances, or will they view them as unfair and unacceptable, with consequent implications for political and social stability? Secondly, even if the workers go along with the anticipated sacrifices, will they be sufficient to solve the adjustment problem if, as anticipated, the country faces a continued deterioration in its terms of trade due to rising energy prices, stagnating supplies from CMEA of raw materials and energy and increased competition and protectionism on the world market?

3   Economic Adjustment and Workers' Welfare in Poland in the 1970s

When viewed from the perspective of the goals important to workers, Poland's economic performance presents a mixed picture over the 1970s, a picture that becomes progressively bleaker over the course of the decade. Certainly, the period from 1971 to 1975, the heyday of Gierek's new economic strategy, was a success in some respects, particularly when compared to the 1960s. For example, money wages increased an average of 9·8 percent a year and real wages an average of 7·2 percent a year, after a period of annual increases at about 1·8 percent between 1961 and 1970.

Table 6.2   *Macroeconomic Indicators in Poland*

	1971-5	1974	1975	1976	1977	1978	1979
Annual Percentage Change Real Net Material Product							
Plan	7·0	9·5	9·8	8·3	5·7	5·4	2·8
Actual	9·8	10·4	9·0	6·8	5·0	2·8	-2·0*
Industrial Output	10·5	12·5	10·9	9·3	6·9	5·8	2·8*
Agricultural Output	3·7	1·6	-2·1	-1·1	1·4	4·2	-1·4*
Consumption†	5·9	4·6	8·7	6·6	3·6	0·7	3·0*
Gross Fixed Capital Formation	18·4	22·5*	14·2	2·2	4·3	1·6	-8·6*
Real Income per Capita	9·6	5·0	8·9	7·2	6·1	6·4	—
Consumer Price Index	2·5	6·8	3·0	4·7	4·9	8·7	6·7*
Money Wages per Employee*	9·8	13·8	11·8	8·8	7·3	6·1	8·6
Real Wages per Employee*	7·2	6·6	8·5	3·9	2·3	-2·7	1·8
Terms of Trade*	1·2	-0·5	3·2	2·0	-2·3	0·0	-3·2
Balance of Trade (million $)	-659	-2168	-2256	-2853	-2353	-2100‡	-1300‡
Balance of Trade with Industrial West (million $)	-1318	-2269	-2746	-3237	-2496	-2195	—
Net Hard Currency Debt to West (million $)*		4120	7381	10680	13532	16972	19590

Sources: Unless otherwise indicated, figures from Portes (1980).
*Figures from Fallenbuchl (1980); 1979, provisional;
†Figures from Alton *et al.,* 1979, table 5;
‡Figures from *Economist,* 16–22 February 1980, p. 87; 1979, provisional.

Indeed, the average real wage increased by approximately 42 percent over the 1971–5 period, far in excess of the planned increase of 18 percent. On the other hand, the very large increases in the real purchasing power of both worker and agricultural households, fostered in part by planned increases in social-welfare payments, in the minimum wage and in the entire wage structure, and in part by the loss of central control over money wage increases, very soon outstripped the ability of the economy to provide equivalent increases in the real volume of household goods and services. Shortages of desired commodities were the result, shortages that were aggravated by the inability of the system to adjust the structure of supply to the structure of demand.

In the second half of the decade, there was a further reduction in the ability of the economy to support real wage increases and matching real increases in goods and services due to the pressures coming from the external sector and to a succession of poor agricultural harvests between 1974 and 1977. Despite a major reorientation of the 1976–80 plan in favor of consumption and away from investment, shortages of consumer goods persisted, necessitating more rapid increases in consumer prices, when politically feasible, and slower increases in real wages. The average official rate of inflation of consumer prices increased from 2·5 percent per year between 1971 and 1975 to 6·1 percent per year between 1976 and 1979, and real wage growth fell to 1·3 percent per day during the later period, sharply down from the earlier 7·2 percent a year. Moreover, official price increases during the later period undoubtedly underestimated the underlying rate of inflation, since several prices, among them the critically important prices of meats and other foods, remained fixed and highly subsidized, after the abortive attempt to raise them to reflect market conditions in 1976. As a consequence, shortages of consumer goods persisted on and off through the end of the decade. One indication of these shortages was the emphasis in the 1979 plan on the need to reduce disequilibrium in the markets for consumer goods. Another was the introduction and expansion of a two-tier system of shops, allowing consumers to buy a broader selection of higher-quality goods at higher prices in so-called 'commercial' shops (currently estimated as several thousand in number). The two-tier system allows for upward price flexibility for those kinds of goods most desired by consumers, while relegating the least desired, lower-quality items to the usual fixed-price categories. Thus, the system provides a mechanism for both open inflation in the prices of some goods, and repressed inflation in the form of fixed prices and deteriorating quality for others. As a consequence of this system, persistent shortages, and the blossoming of illegal transactions at higher than official prices, the actual rate of inflation in Poland in 1979 was estimated to range from 11 to 19 percent a year, with the higher figure considered more likely (*Economist,* 12–18 January 1980, p. 69).

Although the Polish authorities were unable to match increases in purchasing power with real supplies of consumer goods, they were able to continue to maintain conditions of aggregate full employment and individual job security. They were also able to deliver on attempts to reduce the degree of nominal income differentiation in the 'first' economy somewhat by raising the minimum wage, pensions and certain social-welfare payments.[14] And finally, the rapid expansion of output allowed for the continued reduction of labor employed in agriculture by about 0·4 percent a year (1971–5 figure, taken from Kabaj, 1978).

In contrast to Hungary, the adjustment problems that began to overtake Poland rapidly in the early 1970s were not the consequence of a deterioration in the terms of trade. Rather, Poland, as a net exporter of raw materials, actually benefited from changes in world relative prices in 1975 and 1976, years of large increases in Poland's trade imbalance. Undoubtedly, Poland's situation was aggravated by slowdowns in Western demand for some of its exports and the dependence of its growth strategy on imports of capital inputs from the West. The main sources of Poland's problem, however, were internal and stemmed from the pursuit of an overly ambitious development strategy during the 1971–5 period. According to most observers, this strategy was simply unsustainable, leading to simultaneous increases in consumption and investment beyond the wherewithal of domestic resources and spilling over into large trade deficits to fill the gap between domestic absorption and realisable domestic output. In retrospect, it is easy to call this strategy a mistake, but the Polish leaders probably perceived it as a political necessity, combining as it did large increases in investment for modernization, and large increases in consumption to stimulate labor productivity and to ensure political support for the new leadership and its policies.

A gap between domestic absorption and domestic output was foreseen by the Polish authorities as part of this strategy, a gap that was to be reversed once the investment program produced additional output that could be exported to Western markets to repay Western credits. To an extent, deteriorating Western demand for Polish exports after 1973–4 made this reversal more difficult to achieve (see Fallenbuchl, 1980). But the real problem was that the anticipated exportable surplus failed to materialize for internal reasons. First, the rapid expansion of investment was excessive, exceeding the capacity of the construction and engineering industries, necessitating delays, and causing a deterioration in work-manship. The additional output from the investment drive either did not become available when planned, or, when available, frequently lacked the quality characteristics to make it competitive on Western markets. Secondly, the rapid domestic expansion led to larger than anticipated increases in imports and led domestic producers to sell potential exports to domestic users. The domestic market presented an easier alternative to exports which were subject to a greater degree of uncertainty and risk. Nothing in the incentive system for domestic producers encouraged them to shoulder this risk. Rapid growth in consumer demand resulting from the excessively high increases in money wages also encouraged domestic producers to sell at home.

Underlying all of these problems was the decision to insulate domestic prices from changes in world prices. Like the Hungarians, the Poles used a system of taxes and subsidies to shield domestic prices from the effects of changing world prices. At an aggregate level, this system acted much like an exchange-rate adjustment to protect the level of domestic prices from increases in the level of world prices. At a microeconomic level, however, the system meant that changes in relative prices, reflecting new conditions of relative profitability stemming from changing international conditions, did not occur. This, of course, meant that there were no changes in underlying profitability and wage incentives among enterprises and sectors to guide the allocation of production toward export and import substitution activities that might have alleviated the foreign imbalance. Thus, the decision to shield domestic relative prices from changes in world relative prices made the problem of producing the necessary exportable surplus all the more difficult.

In the absence of price signals indicating which goods should be expanded, which contracted, which goods exported, which imported, traditional planning methods were required to solve the absorption problem by direct controls over exports, imports, the level and composition of domestic output, and the level and composition of domestic absorption. But the lesson of the 1970s is that such planning methods do not work very effectively in the Polish economy. As is the case in the other planned economies of Eastern Europe, the planners in Poland cannot easily control aggregate increases in money wages, the level and composition of investment, the level and composition of consumption, and the level and composition of imports and exports by direct means. In Poland, however, these traditional planning problems are aggravated by a lack of strong central control, stemming from a more fundamental lack of political legitimacy and authority. In the absence of political authority and with a distorted price structure, there is nothing in the system to solve the adjustment problem.

The authority of the political leaders was reduced further and their freedom of maneuver in planning further restricted by the workers' strikes of 1976. As a consequence of the need to appease worker discontent, the authorities had to try to solve the absorption problem while preventing politically disastrous declines in the rate of growth of consumption. Consumption was accorded priority over investment, and between 1976 and 1979, the average rate of growth of consumption was higher than that of investment. Despite its priority, consumption growth slipped from an average rate of 5·9 percent per year between 1971 and 1975 to 3·5 percent per year between 1976 and 1979. The primacy of domestic consumption goals over external adjustment in the immediate aftermath of the 1976 strikes is suggested by the fact that, during the second half of 1976, the government cut meat exports by 60 percent and imported 42,000 metric tonnes of meat, followed by another 100,000 tonnes in 1977. Unfortunately, these measures only allowed per capita meat consumption to remain at 1975 levels, while aggravating the problem of external imbalance (CIA, 1978). The growing burden of the policy of maintaining fixed food prices after the 1976 strikes is reflected in the tremendous growth in the volume of food subsidies. According to a recent statement by the Polish Prime Minister, these subsidies now amount to almost 170 billion zloty compared to 7·9 billion in 1970 (*Economist,* 12 January 1980, p. 69).

The authorities hoped to achieve a reduction in the trade imbalance while protecting consumption growth rates by slowing investment and improving efficiency in the production of both investment and consumption goods. But they relied on traditional planning methods to achieve these results, and the methods predictably failed, particularly in promoting the production of goods for export. Fallenbuchl (1980) has a fascinating account of how the planners' emphasis on production for consumption and export purposes in the 1976–80 annual plans led to the production of goods that went to the 'right address' but could not be used for the designated purposes, due to quality, specification, assortment and other problems, by now well known to students of central planning under taut conditions. As a consequence, although some progress was made on the adjustment problem, it was insufficient to reduce the trade deficit to sustainable levels, and by the end of 1979, Poland's net convertible currency debt had risen an estimated 375 percent over its 1974 level (Table 6.2 figures). By the end of 1977, Poland's estimated debt-service ratio (in convertible currency) was 60 percent compared to 44 percent for Hungary, and 31 percent for the six East European members of CMEA (Portes, 1980a, table 11).

By 1979, the external situation was critical, and Poland was forced to negotiate a new loan from a consortium of Western banks in order to meet its debt-servicing and loan-repayment installments during that year. The Western press picked up the fact that to get loan approval, the Poles had to open their books to Western bankers in a way not thought possible in the past. But the pressure to be forthcoming with information was only symbolic of the much greater pressure brought to bear on Poland to take action to reduce its trade imbalance. The pressure became a substitute for domestic political authority. Something had to be done at the risk of possible default in the future. Within the confines of the existing economic systems, the most effective policy measure available was the imposition of drastic administrative restrictions of imports. This policy measure had already been employed in 1977 and 1978, when the rate of growth of real imports (constant prices) had declined to 0·4 and 1·5 percent, respectively, from a 1971–6 level of 14·7 percent per year. In 1979, import controls were tightened even further, and real imports actually declined by 2·5 percent (Fallenbuchl, 1980, table II).

The drastic reduction in imports reverberated throughout the entire economy. Shortages of imported inputs for which there were no readily available domestic substitutes necessitated a slowdown and then an absolute reduction in the level of domestic output as a consequence of the supply multiplier. In 1979, the critical nature of the adjustment problem in Hungary was reflected in the highest rate of open inflation realized in Eastern Europe during the postwar period. In Poland, where there was a greater degree of price control, the manifestation of the crisis occurred in quantity indicators – in particular, in the form of the lowest rate of output growth realized in Poland during the postwar period. Inevitably, the fall in output, exacerbated by a disastrous agricultural harvest, had an impact on various indicators of workers' well-being, such as the rate of growth of real wages, the rate of open inflation, and the extent and severity of shortages on consumer goods markets. By the end of the decade, these developments had increased political and social discontent among the workers as well as among other groups in the population.

What is the prognosis for the economy in general and workers' welfare in particular in Poland in the near future? The main conclusion to be drawn from recent political developments is that the regime plans to rely on traditional methods rather than on a reform of the price and incentive mechanism to achieve the macroeconomic and microeconomic adjustments required to reduce external imbalance. This decision stands in stark contrast to the Hungarian decision to push forward reform. It also runs counter to the almost-uniform opinion of theoretical economists in Poland that the present difficulties cannot be eliminated without some systemic change. But the very crisis that makes such change so important makes its introduction fraught with political and social difficulties. The regime does not have the authority to push through reforms with their potential consequences on prices, income differentials and job security in the present circumstances of macroeconomic disequilibrium and political and social discontent. Yet even without reform, this disequilibrium will necessarily continue to affect the well-being of workers. At the very least, if the planners continue to rely on import controls to reduce the trade deficit, continued slow growth or even reductions in real wages and real consumption can be anticipated, with continuing shortages in certain markets and no improvement in the quality and assortment of goods. Shortages on official markets will most likely encourage the continued development of the 'second' economy, the increasing importance of which is reflected in the flood of letters denouncing black-marketeers in the official press. One policy response to cope with the shortages and 'second' economy pressures, is the introduction of a series of incentive measures (tax concessions, family benefits and better access to materials) to encourage the private craft and service sector. But the most important area of private activity, namely, peasant farming, has not been the beneficiary of the incentive and structural changes necessary to break the agricultural bottleneck in the economy.

If the planners go beyond import controls to reduce the trade deficit and try to adjust the composition of domestic output in favor of certain primary sectors – such as engineering or chemicals – this could affect individual job security, since there is a decreasing number of new entrants into the laborforce and since participation rates are already at maximum levels. Microeconomic adjustment may, thus, require the transfer of labor among enterprises. Full employment is likely to be maintained, but that in itself is not so very much if increasing money wages cannot be exchanged for desired goods and services. Altogether, it seems inevitable that aggregate economic difficulties in Poland over the next few years will necessitate sacrifices in most of the goals of collective or individual importance to workers. This will be so whether the Polish authorities attempt to cope with these difficulties by traditional methods, as currently seems likely, or whether economic pressures force them to experiment with reform.

4   Economic Adjustment and Workers' Welfare in Different Economic Systems: The Hungarian and Polish Cases in Broader Perspective

To better understand the links between various indicators of workers' welfare and deteriorating economic conditions identified in the Hungarian and Polish cases, it is instructive to think about these links in broader terms once again. As the absorption model indicates, a trade imbalance resulting from the interaction of domestic activity levels and external developments requires adjustments in domestic output and absorption levels. How various indicators of workers' welfare are influenced by these adjustments, depends on the policy measures introduced to realize them. Fundamentally the issue is a distributional one: how do workers share in the burden imposed on an individual economy by deteriorating economic circumstances.

The simplest way to pose the distributional question is to consider an economy, like Hungary and many of the material- and energy-dependent economies in both Eastern and Western Europe and throughout the developing world, that suffers a real income loss due to a deterioration in its terms of trade. As a consequence of an external shock over which the domestic authorities have no control, the economy is now worse off in real terms and something in the system must adjust to reflect this deterioration in real economic circumstances. Even in the limiting case where policy measures prop up both domestic output and domestic absorption, and hence real exports and real imports, the country will either lose foreign-exchange reserves and/or increase foreign indebtedness in the amount of the increase in the trade imbalance that occurs as a consequence of relative increases in import prices. In this case, the real national loss will be reflected directly in the decrease in reserves and/or the increase in indebtedness. In other less-extreme cases, this loss will be reflected in changes in the level and composition of exports, imports, domestic output and domestic absorption.

In these intermediate cases, which of these changes actually occur depends on the specific nature of the terms-of-trade deterioration – which prices are actually affected and to what extent – and on the specific institutional features of the economy in question and its policy response. In such cases, nothing very general can be said without more information. Further speculation is possible, however, under the specific conditions of the mid-1970s, when the terms-of-trade deterioration involved an increase in the relative prices of productive inputs.

In market systems (including Yugoslavia for the purposes of this discussion), the relative price change appeared as what economists call a 'supply shock' – an increase in the price of an (imported) intermediate input, energy, that cut into the profitability of production and induced producers to cut back on their output levels and to raise their selling prices to cover their higher costs. Thus, the supply shock tended to generate both higher domestic prices, and lower domestic output levels—in a word, 'stagflation'. The output concentration, in turn, led producers to trim back their labor demand (since labor could not be substituted in the production process for more expensive energy inputs). The cutback in labor demand necessitated a fall in the rate of growth of real wages, if employment levels were to remain unchanged, and if the shares of wages and profits in total value-added were to remain constant. In other words, the supply shock required a slowdown in real wages, if the goal of full employment was to be realized under the new economic conditions. In the absence of such a slowdown, the cutback in labor demand at unchanged conditions of labor supply necessitated a decline in employment levels and an increase in the unemployment rate, indicating disequilibrium in the labor market.

Whether the necessary slowdown in real wages occurred depended, of course, on the institutional characteristics of the country in question. Empirical evidence from Japan and Western Europe for the 1973–6 period suggests that, while real wage growth did decline somewhat, it remained in excess of what was consistent with full employment and constant shares of labor and capital in national income (value-added). The results were an increase in unemployment levels and a decrease in investment rates, reflecting the decline in the share of profits and in the profit rate under the new economic conditions (Sachs, 1980). Moreover, these results were accompanied by an acceleration in aggregate inflation rates, partly as a consequence of higher prices for energy and energy-using output, and partly as a consequence of successive rounds of nominal wage and price increases, reflecting the efforts of wage- and profit-earners to maintain their real income levels. Inflationary pressure emanating from the second of these sources was the manifestation of the struggle to distribute the burden of the real income loss resulting from the terms-of-trade deterioration in the market system. Finally, in addition to the macroeconomic effects of this loss, there were underlying microeconomic effects. Changes in relative prices touched off by changing conditions of demand and supply on individual markets worked to the benefit of workers and property-owners in industries in which real wages and profits increased in either absolute or relative terms, and to the detriment of workers and owners in other industries in which real wages and profits decreased or remained unchanged. These microeconomic changes, in turn, implied changes in wage differentials, profit differentials and the job security of individual workers. Such changes were the mechanism whereby the market redirected labor and capital resources to their most profitable uses under the new set of world and domestic relative prices.

As the above survey suggests, the particular changes in world relative prices that confronted market economies in the 1970s had potential adverse effects on all of the goals identified as important to workers in this chapter. All of these adverse effects were felt to some degree in the advanced market economies of Western Europe, the United States and Japan: the rate of inflation accelerated; output levels declined or output growth rate fell; the rate of growth of real wages declined, though not enough to prevent some reduction in employment and some increase in unemployment; and job security within industries particularly hard-hit by the relative increase in energy prices was eroded.

Theoretically, the strength of the planned economy under the adverse circumstances of the 1970s should have been its ability to avoid the increases in unemployment and inflation caused by the market struggle over the distribution of the burden of adjustment to the real income loss. In a system in which central decisions on this distributional issue can be made, adjusting nominal wage growth to achieve the desired distribution of the burden between wages and profits, or equivalently on the supply side between consumption and investment, the costly tradeoff between unemployment rates and inflation rates that develops in the market system can be avoided. Stagflation is a phenomenon that at least theoretically should be the dubious distinction of market systems in response to supply shocks. This is not to say, however, that planning can dispense with the difficult choices between consumption and investment and the difficult task of reallocating labor and capital among industries in response to changing macroeconomic conditions. Overall, the goals of importance to workers can be insulated from the adverse effects of external conditions in a planned economy, as in a market economy, only if other goals of significance to national economic well-being such as investment rates and the most efficient allocation of resources are sacrificed.

What the experience of the 1970s in Hungary – and in several other East European economies, among them Czechoslovakia and the German Democratic Republic – reveals is that, even in planned economies, it is difficult to amass the political consensus and will to make distributional decisions that will allocate the burden of economic adjustment without necessitating a slowdown in the rate of growth and an increase in the rate of open or repressed inflation – the equivalent of some stagflationary tendencies. Without the ability to cut nominal wage growth to the extent necessary, and to trim domestic consumption and investment demands accordingly, the Hungarians at first avoided the task of adjustment by allowing their trade balance to deteriorate. But, inevitably, the task had to be faced, and when it was as in 1976, and more completely in 1979, output growth declined and the inflation rate picked up, substituting for a slowdown in nominal wage growth to achieve the necessary slowdown in real wages. Once the insulation provided by foreign credit was reduced, Hungarian workers, like the workers in market systems, had to share to some extent and in similar ways in the adjustment burden. From the perspective of the goals important to workers, the only significant difference between the Hungarian experience and the experiences of market economies in Western Europe and the developing world was the greater ability of the planners to use direct controls over supply-side decisions and extensive subsidies to industry to maintain full employment.

The Polish case, of course, differs from the Hungarian one and the case of most of the industrial market economies, in that Poland did not suffer a real income loss from a terms-of-trade deterioration. The difficulties of the Polish economy were by and large the consequence of internal economic difficulties aggravated by external conditions. Both the source of these difficulties, and the failure to devise adequate policy responses to them, reflect the fundamental lack of political will and power of the Polish leadership and the weaknesses of traditional planning methods. At least temporarily, the Polish authorities were able to use external credits to postpone the adjustment policies they seemed unable or unwilling to introduce. By the end of the 1970s, however, postponement was no longer a viable alternative, and strong policy measures halted economic growth, slowed the rate of growth of real wages, and increased open and repressed inflationary pressures. In Poland, as in Hungary, however, the evidence suggests that, contrary to theoretical interpretations of the functioning of the planned economy, adjustment was not free of inflationary consequences, because of the inability of the planners to distribute the burden of adjustment by direct controls over nominal wages and by supply-side adjustments in the rate of growth of consumption and investment. In Poland, as in Hungary and in many industrial market systems, inflationary pressures became a mechanism whereby the distributional consequences of the burden could be worked out by default, in the absence of explicit policy measures to do so. Regardless of the exact distribution that occurred in each of these systems, whether by policy or by the workings of the market, the available evidence in this chapter and elsewhere suggests that all of the goals important to workers were adversely affected by the deteriorating economic circumstances of the 1970s.

5 Economic Adjustment and Workers' Welfare in Eastern Europe: Future Prospects

As the foregoing discussion suggests, the macroeconomic and microeconomic adjustments required to restore external balance in Hungary and Poland have not yet occurred. Until very recently, continued reliance on external financing substituted for domestic economic policy measures to cut imports and/or to expand exports. Only when the magnitude of external indebtedness began to be perceived as a critical problem by both internal policy-makers and external creditors, did this reliance give way to important policy shifts to deal with the trade balance. In Hungary, the policy shifts included a reaffirmation of market principles, a dramatic increase in consumer prices, and a slowdown in the growth rate of both domestic output and domestic absorption. In Poland, the political leaders used traditional planning methods to clamp down on imports of needed capital and material inputs, with disastrous consequences for both domestic output and domestic absorption. In neither case, did the new policy maneuvers eliminate the need for further economic sacrifices in the future, sacrifices that will extend to most of the indicators of workers' well-being discussed in this chapter.

The fundamental unanswered question is whether the Hungarian and Polish leaders have the political will and authority to enforce these sacrifices without inciting widespread political and social discontent. Historical evidence on workers' behavior in Hungary and Poland is consistent with the view that satisfaction with economic performance produces at the very least political apathy and sometimes even active political support for the leadership on the part of workers. Economic progress does not seem to promote widespread worker demands for political liberalization. On the other hand, dissatisfaction with economic progress promotes political and social dissatisfaction that tends to spill over quickly into more radical worker demands for political and workplace liberalization, especially in the form of workers' councils. Although workers are motivated by bread-and-butter issues, when dissatisfied, they tend to become a radical force in support of wide-ranging political and economic reforms. The Hungarian and Polish leaders are, no doubt, wary of the potential political consequences of a workforce radicalized by the economic sacrifices required in the coming years.

When viewed from a broader perspective, the case studies of Hungary and Poland analyzed in this chapter are illustrative of the economic tradeoffs that must be confronted by policy-makers throughout Eastern Europe in the coming years. As a result of deteriorating external conditions interacting with unresolved internal economic weaknesses, the realization of competing economic goals has become more difficult, and economic sacrifices are required. How these sacrifices are distributed among different groups has implications for economic and political stability throughout the region.

A Postscript after the Polish Strikes of August 1980

This chapter was completed before the strikes that developed in Poland in August 1980. None the less, seen from the perspective of the analysis presented here, these strikes were not unexpected. Deteriorating economic conditions necessitated sacrifices on the part of Polish workers, yet the political regime under Gierek appeared to lack the authority to enforce such sacrifices. As in the past, in Poland (and less frequently in the other countries of Eastern Europe), mounting worker discontent culminated in strikes to express worker dissatisfaction with bread-and-butter issues. In this respect, the strikes of 1980 were nothing new. Unlike the earlier strikes, however, the most recent ones continued to spill over into more radical political demands, even after the authorities had promised to respond to the economic complaints of the workers. In short, the strikes of August 1980 seemed to be more than just another episodic outbreak of dissatisfaction over economic issues. In addition to their economic demands, the workers demanded independent unions to represent their interests and a liberalization of political power to ensure that their interest articulation would become a reality.

There are several factors unique to the Polish situation as it evolved during the 1970s that explain why the 1980 strikes encompassed demands for political liberalization. Strong links between Polish workers and groups of intellectuals meant the formation of a more effective political coalition, better able to diffuse information about the strikers' demands and to arouse popular support for them. The intellectuals also provided an ideology for the striking workers, encouraging them to request permanent institutional changes in the system rather than to settle for temporary conciliatory measures in response to immediate economic demands. The existence of the Catholic Church as a popular alternative power center to that of the government also mobilized worker opinion to rally in favor of values and institutions contrary to those espoused by the communist leadership. The enthusiasm and solidarity inspired in the Polish citizenry by the recent visit of the Pope undoubtedly contributed to the workers' willingness to take a determined stand for fundamental change. Finally, the workers in 1980 must have been inspired by the memories of their earlier success in the strikes of 1970 and 1976, which were promptly followed by government accession to worker demands. This earlier success enhanced the confidence of the workers, while correspondingly reducing the confidence of the political authorities in their dealings with them.

If the strikes of 1980 represented something new in their emphasis on significant political reform, they also took place in a new set of economic circumstances that limited the ability of the political authorities to respond adequately even to the narrowly economic demands of the workers. The extremely weak economic situation in Poland meant that the authorities were simply unable to try to bribe the workers into political submission in return for major economic benefits. And the strikes themselves have only worsened the economic situation in the short run, making this strategy all the more impossible to realize. In the precarious economic situation in which Poland now finds itself, perhaps an alternative and reverse strategy must be followed. The political authorities may be forced to continue to accede to worker demands for political representation and liberalization in return for worker sacrifices in the economic arena. Restoring economic growth and external equilibrium in the Polish economy, will require both an improvement in the efficiency of resource use, and the temporary reallocation of resources from domestic consumption and investment to exports. Whether these conditions can be realized, depends to a large extent on the behavior of the workers. Even without additional investment, efficiency can be improved by higher labor productivity, resulting from greater worker effort and improved workplace discipline. But the aggregate constraints on the Polish economy in the short run, require that even if such increases in labor productivity occur, the workers agree to moderate increases in their wages and real living standards so that the resources needed for external balance are available. In short, the strikes of 1980 have not changed the fundamental conclusion of this chapter – namely, that the current situation of the Polish economy will necessitate some sacrifices of the goals of collective or individual importance to workers in the coming few years. Only time will tell, however, whether these strikes have permanently altered the political environment and structure in which such sacrifices will be made. At least to date, it seems that the workers have gained real power to influence both workplace and party decision-making. If the economic crisis is to be resolved, this power must also be used to develop a consensus among workers about a fair distribution of the economic sacrifices required in the near future.

Notes: Chapter 6

The author is appreciative of the helpful research assistance of Leyla Woods, financed by grants from the Committee on Research and the Center for Soviet and East European Studies, the University of California, Berkeley.

1 Openness in international trade is generally measured by comparing the ratio between the value of trade and some estimate of the value of national output. Such ratios are notoriously difficult to estimate for the East European nations, because of price and exchange-rate distortions. Alternative measures of openness, such as measures of per capita imports, suggest that of the CMEA countries, the Soviet Union is the least open and the GDR the most open. For Hungary and Poland, the countries of concern in this paper, this measure of openness reveals Hungary to be more open than Poland (see Fallenbuchl, Neuberger, Tyson, 1977). Estimated trade–national output ratios suggest that Hungary is as open to international trade as many of the smaller economies of Europe.

2 For the purposes of this chapter, 'Western' refers to non-CMEA sources, be they developed nations or developing ones.

3 The general approach in this section is based on the discussion of the macro-economic interconnections between the foreign sector and the domestic sector in an individual market economy found in Portes (1980) and Neuberger, Portes and Tyson (1980).

4 Also in Yugoslavia, where full employment has not been achieved, the full-employment goal is one of job security for the industrial workers, who already have jobs, plus a reasonable rate of growth of new industrial jobs to absorb labor from agriculture and the unemployed. Finally, in Yugoslavia, additional goals related to the realization of self-management rights are also important to workers' well-being.

5 In Hungary, as in the other economies of Eastern Europe, a distinction must be made between the so-called primary or 'first' economy, which encompasses all regulated activity within the state and cooperative sectors of industry and agriculture, and the so-called 'second' economy, which includes all legal private-sector activity, and all semilegal and illegal economic activities. The state exercises direct control over wage differentials only within the 'first' economy.

6 Portes (1980) estimates that foreign price levels facing the East European countries in non-CMEA trade approximately doubled between 1972 and 1976.

7 The magnitude of the subsidies on consumer prices implied by this policy is suggested by the following figures: in 1977, subsidies for meat, milk and cereals were 16, 66 and 26 percent of the respective retail prices, while subsidies for foodstuffs averaged 26 percent. For mass transit, home heating and laundry, the subsidies were 117, 168 and 140 percent, while for gasoline, the subsidy was 38 percent (Marrese, 1980).

8 Indeed, the Brown–Tardos calculations suggest that the trade deficit over the 1974–6 period was approximately equal to the loss from the terms-of-trade deterioration after 1972. In other words, the Hungarians borrowed or used their existing reserves of foreign exchange to offset totally the domestic impact of the terms-of-trade loss over this period.

9 See Szekffy (1978), for a discussion of how investment cycles lead to a loss of control over money wages in the Hungarian economy.

10 The coalition of political forces behind the decision to use the market to solve the absorption problem was strengthened by the recent (1980) dismissal of one-third of the fifteen-member Politburo. The dismissals included known hardliners, who preferred traditional planning methods to the market and who were blamed, along with external circumstances, for Hungary's poor economic performance in 1979.

11 The new 1970 price systems for industry, construction and transportation imply that the ratios of world market prices and the export prices of firms will determine the level and ratio of domestic prices in a more direct manner. In particular, the prices of primary energy and basic materials are to adjust to world market prices under the new system, while the domestic prices of manufacturers are to depend on their export prices. At the beginning of 1980, the price level of industry increased by 6 percent, and the procurement prices of agricultural products by an average of 11 percent.

12 Although no reliable estimates of redundant labor reserves in Hungary exist, almost everyone agrees that such reserves are large and are the consequence of enterprise efforts to store labor as insurance against the risk of not being able to find workers when needed in a situation of aggregate labor shortage. A recent Radio Free Europe report estimated redundant labor to be about 20 percent of the state-sector laborforce (*Radio Free Europe, Hungarian Situation Report*, no. 11, May 1979).

13 This role for the trade unions in the implementation of the new policies is suggested by the fact that the recently appointed deputy secretary-general of the National Trade Union Council is a party functionary with no immediate links to the trade union movement. A similar conclusion is suggested by a recent interview with the secretary-general of the Trade Union Council, who argued that in principle unions do not oppose transfers of labor, and that the right to work does not mean the right to a certain place of work. See *Radio Free Europe, Hungarian Situation Report*, no. 8, April 1979; and no. 16, August 1979.

14 The preliminary effects of policies to reduce nominal income differentials in the 'first' economy are seen in the following figures taken from the 1970–73 period:

	1970	1973
Intelligentsia	150·0	142·4
Routine non-manual	102·8	92·4
Worker	100·0	100·0
Peasant	75·0	94·1

These figures show the index of average pay by occupational categories, where the average pay of a worker in state industry is the index base of 100·00, and where peasants include only workers in state socialist industry (Connor, 1979, p. 231). Given the existence of 'second' economy production and consumption activities, it is impossible to draw conclusions about differentials in real income from information on nominal income differentials.

References: Chapter 6

Alton, Thad, Bass, Elizabeth, Lazarcik, Gregor and Znayenko, Wassyl, *Personal Consumption in Eastern Europe, Selected Years, 1960–1978* (New York: L.W. International Financial Research, 1979).

Brown, Alan, and Tardos, Martin, 'Global stagflation and the Hungarian economy', forthcoming in Egon Neuberger and Laura D'Andrea Tyson, eds, *The Impact of External Economic Disturbances on the Soviet Union and Eastern Europe* (Elmsford, NY: Pergamon Press, 1980).

Central Intelligence Agency, National Foreign Assessment Center, *The Scope of Poland's Economic Dilemma,* July 1978.

Connor, Walter D., *Socialism, Politics and Equality* (New York: Columbia University Press, 1979).

Fallenbuchl, Zbigniew, Neuberger, Egon, and Tyson, Laura, 'East European reactions to international commodity inflation', in Joint Economic Commitee Report, *East European Economies Post Helsinki* (Washington, DC: Government Printing Office, 1977).

Fallenbuchl, Zbigniew, 'The impact of external disturbances on Poland', forthcoming in Egon Neuberger and Laura D'Andrea Tyson, eds, *The Impact of External Economic Disturbances on the Soviet Union and Eastern Europe* (Elmsford, NY: Pergamon Press, 1980).

Fallenbuchl, Zbigniew, 'The Polish economy at the beginning of the 1980s', Joint Economic Committee Report, *Poland, 1980: An East European Economic Country Study* (Washington, DC: Government Printing Office, 1980).

Kabaj, Mieczyslaw, 'Manpower resources and employment in Poland, 1950–1990', *Vienna Institute for Comparative Economic Studies,* report no. 46, November 1978.

Marrese, Michael, 'The evolution of wage regulation in Hungary', Department of Economics Discussion Paper, no. 111, Northwestern University, October 1979.

Marrese, Michael, 'The Hungarian economy: prospects for the 1980s' (unpublished manuscript, February 1980).

Neuberger, Egon, Portes, Richard, and Tyson, Laura, 'The impact of external economic disturbances on the Soviet Union and Eastern Europe: an overview', Joint Economic Committee Report, *East European Economic Assessment. Part 2: Country Studies, 1980* (Washington, DC: Government Printing Office, 1981).

Portes, Richard, 'Hungary: economic performance, policy and prospects', in Joint Economic Committee Report, *East European Economies Post Helsinki* (Washington, DC: Government Printing Office, 1977a).

Portes, Richard, 'The control of inflation: lessons from the East European experience', *Economica,* vol. 44, 1977b, pp. 109–30.

Portes, Richard, 'Effects of the world economic crisis on the East European Economies' (forthcoming, in *The World Economy,* 1980).

Racz, A, 'Incomes of the population and their proportions in Hungary', *Acta Oeconomica,* vol. 19, no. 2, 1977, pp. 203–14.

Sachs, Jeffrey, 'Wages, profits and macroeconomic adjustment in the 1970s: a comparative study', *Brookings Papers on Economic Activity,* no. 1, 1980.

Szekffy, K., 'Relation between wages and productivity in Hungarian industry between 1950 and 1974', *Acta Oeconomica,* vol. 21, no. 1–2, 1978, pp. 73–90.

Wiles, Peter, 'The control of inflation in Hungary', *Economie Appliquée,* vol. 27, 1974, pp. 119–48.

Wolf, Thomas, 'On the adjustment of centrally planned economies to external economic disturbances', paper presented at Conference on East European Integration and East–West Trade, Bloomington, Indiana, USA, 1976 (forthcoming).

7

Poland, 1980: the Working Class under 'Anomic Socialism'

GEORGE KOLANKIEWICZ

'There are boundaries which no one is permitted to cross. They are defined by Poland's conditions of existence.'
E. Gierek
(First Secretary, during August 1980, of the PZPR).

Introduction

By the end of August 1980, after two months of disconcerting and damaging strikes, after the exit from the political arena of almost the whole Polish leadership including the First Secretary of the Polish United Workers' Party (PZPR) and the Prime Minister, after the acceptance of what two weeks earlier had been unmentionable, namely, the Interfactory Strike Committees or MKS and independent trade unions, these boundaries appeared to have been well and truly crossed, if not actually erased. The world had seen the Gdansk shipyard workers take the largely *economic* demands of Warsaw and Lublin workers and transform them into *organizational* demands which could not help but have political implications.

This *qualitative* change can only be explained in terms of the specific heritage of 1970–71 which had remained rooted in the consciousness of the population on the northern seaboard, in Gdansk, Szczecin and Elblag. While the bus and tram drivers of Warsaw may have made incoherent demands for 'workers councils', it was the shipyard workers who, after an apparent agreement on economic issues on 16 August, took up the slogans of the Founding Committee of the Coastal Free Trade Unions and forged them into a concrete set of demands – the Twenty-one Points. The grievances aggregated and expressed in this document were not new, nor were they unknown to the leadership. The official trade union movement had just completed its election campaign at which many of these points had been raised. Now, however, a new urgency was instilled into the negotiations not just because of the infectious· and economically debilitating effects of the occupation strikes, but because the longer the conflict continued, the more questions it would raise. It would draw increasing sections of the population into the debate, and the greater would be the possibility of reaching a point of no return, which would threaten the survival of the system itself. Leaving aside the precipitating factors which are embedded in the unique conditions of Gdansk, its dissident movement and the Polish December, the scope of the strike action, solidaristic or purely opportunistic, can only be explained in terms of the underlying socioeconomic and political factors which had emerged during the last decade in Poland.

A summary of some of the grievances and demands spelled out in Lublin in July, and Gdansk and Szczecin in August, provides an insight and starting-point for such an analysis. The sheer number of postulates, 110 in Lublin, 37 in Szczecin and the more condensed 21 in Gdansk, is just one indicator of the depth of disenchantment within the working class. The major postulates could be subdivided into:

(1) *trade union* demands;
(2) *egalitarian* demands;
(3) *anti-corruption* postulates and demands as to
(4) allocation of *responsibility* both for positive and negative results.

Apart from the demands concerning free trade unions, its basic prerogatives, if not its actual structure, non-victimization and payment for strike period, there were those associated with freedom from censorship, access to the media for religious groups, release of political prisoners, truthful information concerning the situation in the country and the publication of the Helsinki agreement in a more widely accessible format. The egalitarian demands focused on pay increases to compensate for price rises and a control of the latter, index-linked pay, equal family benefits for all groups (the reference here being to the privileged position of the police and army), a better-equipped health service, which was a surprisingly detailed demand, earlier retirement age, equalization of pensions, increases in paid maternity leave to three years, a five-day working week and some such arrangement to compensate for those in mining and the four-brigade system, a rationing if needs be of meat and other goods in short supply, the abolition of 'dual'– or 'triple'-tiered price systems, such as the commercial meat shops, and the abolition of sales of Polish goods in dollar shops (some wanted these shops to be abolished altogether).

The anti-corruption postulates concerned such wide-ranging demands as curbing excessive business trips abroad for managers and bureaucrats, observability of criteria determining the distribution of sought-after goods, such as housing, cars, holidays, etc. They dealt with the 'second' economy, black-market sale of services, particularly health care. Other demands concerning the pruning of the administrative apparatus, abolition of sinecures for incompetent managers, plush official receptions, privileges associated with party membership (which should not influence selection to managerial posts), such as villas, excessive numbers of official cars and other forms of 'high-life', all barely tapped the cumulative feeling of disenchantment with the 'self-enrichment' of sections of the political elite. Finally, there was a felt need that those responsible for the economic crises, of which the population had now been informed, should be held responsible. That truthful information transmission, the rotation of state functions and regard for the opinions of workers, would go some way toward remedying this situation (Wesolowska, 1980, Strike Information Bulletin, 1980, and *Trybuna Ludu,* 2 September 1980).

At the meeting of the 5th Plenum of the Central Committee and the Parliament (Sejm) in early September, most of these demands were granted to take effect immediately, from January 1981 or by 1983 (*Trybuna Ludu,* 2 September 1980, 6 September 1980). As a sign of good intentions a list of 118 articles of foodstuffs, consumer durables and services was published on 5 September and a Trade Union Commission for Control of the Cost of Living named. The latter contained specialists, who were known for their vociferously expressed views on privilege, income inequality, the structure of consumption patterns, etc.

The Legacy of the Polish December

One of the more distinctive demands put by the strikers of Gdansk and Szczecin was for a memorial plaque or monument to be set up at the gates of the Lenin and Warski shipyards to commemorate the dead of 1970. This was to be completed by 17 December 1980 – or ten years after the fateful incidents. The significance of this demand was that it highlighted the source of the astonishingly high level of discipline, solidarity and determination displayed by the enterprises of the northern seaboard. It explains, in part, how the workers of the Polish ports were able to survive the 'sensory deprivation' imposed on them by the government when they were all but cut off from the rest of the country. Most importantly, the collective memory of those days in December 1970, when an as-yet-unknown number of workers and citizens were killed and wounded by units of the security forces after their protest spilled out onto the streets of Gdansk and Szczecin, provided a constant spur, a continuous reminder of the promises made and subsequently broken by the then-incoming communist leader, E. Gierek. These promises were officially translated into the program of the 6th Congress of the PZPR held one year after the riots and included among other things: greater social-welfare benefits, shorter working hours, better housing conditions, increased maternity grants and unpaid leave, a more active role for trade unions (which were to become more democratic); and for workers' self-management, greater supplies of meat and consumer goods, the 'peoples car' or Fiat 126, more-just division of income, improved health services, sanatoria facilities and holidays (*Nowe Drogi*, 1972). While some of these promises were kept, at least in part, a material aspirations explosion, demographic growth rates, and relative deprivation inspired by increased sources of consumption-based differentiation, all served to highlight the areas of failure. For example, the housing deficit (despite the housing or rehousing of one in four of all households in the last ten years) is greater in 1980 than in 1960; it primarily affects young families of whom one-third are working class, and who have been subject to a process of 'pauperization' during the last ten years of inflation (Fikus, 1980). The increased egalitarianism and moral sensitivity as to the distribution of income and goods grew out of a complex of ideological, religious and socioeconomic factors which affected Poland during the 1970s. Suffice to say that sociological research had indicated that existing differentials were seen as too great, unjust and the major source of social tension and conflict – although for different reasons by different social groups (Blachnicki, 1979; Nowak *et al.,* 1974). The vehement rejection of the party as the appropriate opposite number in negotiations, the embracement of Polish nationalism symbolized by the red-and-white flag without its usual red companion (and for a brief period, a 'crowned' white eagle alongside the Lenin shipyard in Gdansk), the portraits of the Pope, John Paul II, are just some phenotypical manifestations of the complex motivations underlying what has been called the most important event in communist history since Kronstadt.

While anti-Soviet sentiments were never publicly voiced, constant reaffirmations of the inviolability of Poland's 'system of international alliances' drew attention to the precipitative causes of the strikes in Lublin and the underlying disgruntlement with Poland's shipbuilding program for the Soviet Union. The expense borne by the Soviet Union's partners in staging the 1980 Olympics was also no small item of conjecture. The actual 'terms of trade' are here less important than the popular conception of Polish-Soviet economic relations.

The post-1970 legacy must include reference to the 1976 workers' riots in Radom and the Ursus strike out of which grew the dissident movements, such as the Workers' Defense Committee—Committee of Social Self-Defense (KOR–KSS), or the Movement for the Defense of Human and Citizens Rights (ROPCIO), and the less well-known organizations, but highly involved for all that, such as Young Poland. The subsequent experience of intensified strike action, generally confined to issues concerning the divisions of premium payments, payments for worktime lost due to lack of raw materials or poor work organization, was an important form of anticipatory socialization into an activity which had as yet no normative structure. The industrial working class found itself in a legal-juridical void, since the communist legal system did not legislate for spontaneous *collective* as opposed to *individual* action. However, other issues such as the gross insensitivity of the reported 1 million zloty banquet at the Gdansk shipyard on 19 August 1979 attended by Gierek (*Robotnik,* no. 38–9) was just one example of the causes which were transforming largely economistic factory-based demands into wider, more searching appraisals of Poland's leadership, both its policies and its personnel. The founding committee of the Coastal Free Trade Unions was set up on the eve of 1 May 1978 (*Robotnik Wybrzeza,* 1978). This was the year in which average real wages *declined* by 2·9 percent and the cost of living had officially risen by 8·7 percent.

Anomic Socialism, or Wages for What?

It seems clear that the economic chaos which characterized the wave of

Table 7.1 *Growth in Productivity and Average Wages in Socialized Industry in 1971–8*

Year	Productivity	Average net nominal wage	Cost of living index	Average real wage	Indicator of productivity growth paid for by growth in average wages	
					Nominal	Real
	Growth in relation to preceding year (%)					
1971	5·7	5·3	-0·2	5·5	0·93	0·96
1972	5·6	4·7	0·0	4·7	0·84	0·84
1973	8·5	9·1	2·6	6·3	1·07	0·74
1974	9·5	14·3	6·8	7·0	1·51	0·14
1975	10·0	13·6	3·0	10·3	1·36	1·03
1976	8·8	9·7	4·7	4·8	1·10	0·55
1977	6·2	7·1	4·9	2·1	1·15	0·34
1978	2·7	5·6	8·7	-2·9	2·07	-1·07

Source: Kabaj (1980).

strikes in July 1980, and the government's readiness to defer to inflationary wage demands was a continuation of the wages 'policy' which had emerged during 1971–5. As Table 7.1 clearly demonstrates there was a deregùlation of the relationship between wage increases and productivity. The government saw fit to raise real wages by 50 percent, average living standards by 75 percent and more damagingly nominal wages by 114 percent during 1971-9 (Krencik, 1980). Wage increases were given 'on account' and were funded by imported technology and credits (which accounts for no small part of the increased productivity noted in Table 7.1), or were accounted for by product substitution and assortment manipulation which statistically raised value-added growth (Zawalski 1980). Average norm fulfillment was 140 percent, in some cases reaching 300 percent, which made a nonsense of the supposedly technical work norms governing the 3 million or so piece workers but already reflected a felt need on the part of the authorities to maintain class peace in the factories. At the same time, 25–30 percent of nominal wage growth was due to central wage regulation, which led to the not illogical conclusion on the part of the working class that wage growth was primarily an act of administrative fiat, rather than an outcome of increased productivity. There was evidently a total lack of respect for the basic wage as it declined in proportion to the variable element composed of various premiums, bonuses, rewards, comprising only 45 percent of miners' take-home pay, 20–23 percent of some highly skilled workers' total pay and about 60 percent for most groups of workers (Kabaj, 1980; Melich, 1978). This worked in the interests of management, who could use premium payments to 'buy-off' strikes, sanction groups of workers, expedite problems of delivery and cooperation with other factories, etc.

The upshot of this was that blue-collar workers came to believe that the quality and the results of their work were unrelated to the rewards or sanctions received. The latter, they felt, was. largely in the gift of management, who could dispose of these rewards as they saw fit (Sarapata, 1979). This represented a *subjective* reflection of the objective decline in productivity. The wages system was discredited and incentives had become 'demoralized'. Consequently, the effort–reward equation was lost in a morass of thirteenth- and fourteenth-month bonuses, various premiums and reward funds which left workers unclear as to what they were being paid for, and obscured the already-dim perceptibn of what constituted legitimate expectations as to the relationship between work and pay. The effect of this can be seen by the two-thirds of workers in a national study, who declared that the majority of their colleagues could work better or much better (Sarapata, 1980). It is not surprising, therefore, that a major demand made by the workers in 1980 was that work done and no other· criteria such as formal qualification, organizational membership, or informal contacts, should be the basis of pay.

As is now evident, the consequences of this deregulation were concealed by the massive import of foreign technology and knowhow. By 1975 every second machine installed in Polish industry was imported and nearly 50 percent of the total means of production had been introduced during the

Table 7.2

	1971	*1973*	*1974*	*1975*	*1976*	*1977*	*1978*
Value of production licences (million zloty)	24,736	52,816	75,914	108,891	121,263	164,187	185,870
Export of production from licences	6,926	20,097	23,584	28,696	33,457	42,477	46,604
Export Productivity (1·2)	28·0	38·1	37·1	26·4	25·5	26·4	25·0

Source: Monkiewicz (1980).

years 1971–5 (Brzost, 1979). As Table 7.2 shows, the effort to pay for this investment by exporting the goods produced under license had by 1978 taken a severe blow. An increasing percentage of these goods were consumed at home either because of increased internal consumer pressure due to inflationary pay awards, or because of the difficulties encountered on foreign markets entering into deep recession.

Other questions have since been asked concerning the logic and rationale behind some of the investments. Why was investment continued despite the decision of the 5th Plenum of the PZPR in 1976 to cut back on capital investment? Could corruption and graft have figured in some of the investment decisions (Wroblewski, 1980)? By 1979, 58 percent of all capital investment had not achieved its scheduled production capacity. This was in part due to poor organization, and labor supply problems, but also in part due to the fact that 60 percent of this capital investment was long term (that is, three years or more) which released considerable earnings power into the population during its construction without producing the necessary goods (Gornicka, 1980). Much of the information as to Poland's foreign indebtedness was nevertheless kept from the population at large and only publicly admitted in the national media on 25 August 1980 in an interview with the new Minister of Finance, as a response to one of the strikers' demands. By then, however, appeals made to the working class 'that we were living beyond our means . . . on credit which had to be repaid' (Urban, 1980) had little effect. Unfortunately, the breakdown in legitimate expectations as to work and pay were further aggravated by the explosion of consumer appetites fueled by the pay increases of 1971–5.

Socialist Consumerism

As is clear from Table 7.3, the growth in the possession of consumer durables during 1971–5 was sufficiently widespread to implant consumer consciousness into most strata of society and particularly into the working class. The youthful demographic structure of the country helped to stimulate demand for other goods, such as furniture, clothing, cosmetics, etc. During the period 1973–6, household budget expenditure on non-foodstuffs goods rose for non-manual-worker households by 12·4 percent per annum and by 17 percent per annum for manual-worker households (Dlugosz, 1980). Yet, nearly 40 percent of manual workers when asked 'Did the living conditions of you and your family generally speaking

Table 7.3   *Annual Sale of Certain Consumer Durables*

	1970 (thousand)	1975 (thousand)	Growth (%)
Washing machines	377	717	190·2
Refrigerators	356	954	268·0
Vacuum cleaners	333	746	224·0
Radios	883	1571	188·8
Televisions	543	920	169·4
Tape recorders	104	527	506·7
Automobiles	47	110	234·0
Motorcycles	90	202	224·4
Bicycles	631	1044	165·5

Source: Mozolowski (1980).

improve during the years 1970–78?', replied that there was either no change, or a deterioration. Furthermore, 64 percent of manual workers (47 percent of intelligentsia) evaluated their family budgets as 'highly strained' (Beskid, 1980). The incongruence of increased consumer-goods provision being associated with a perceived deterioration in living standards can perhaps be explained by a change or elevation in comparative reference group on the part of the working class. Paradoxically, with the formal abolition in 1974 of the manual–non-manual divide in industry, conflict between these two groups may have increased. Greater income differentiation both within, as opposed to between, social categories, declining inter- and intragenerational mobility, higher levels of education, particularly within the ranks of the working class, may have shifted the emphasis from intragroups to intergroup comparisons and, therefore, intensified perceptions of relative deprivation in both the ranks of manual and non-manual workers (Remer, 1980). The increased, although still insufficient, availability of consumer goods, may focus attention on the ability to purchase the same, that is, on income differences, which may in turn lead to a questioning of such inequality. Income as such has been shown to be an increasing source of tension in Polish society, particularly during the late 1970s (Slomczynski, 1977; Wesolowski, 1977). The collision over scarce consumer goods was made even more inevitable by the rapid convergence of manual and non-manual patterns of *material* aspirations. Access to consumer goods, then, became informal and associated with the privilege of position rather than money, the latter being now more generally available. Gradually greater observable consumer inequality came to be associated with an unobservable system of privilege (Komar, 1978).

A socially distorted access to consumer durables was accompanied by equally unacceptable developments in the sphere of services provision in both the state and private sector. Having been given the 'green light' to develop in November of 1976, only the cost of services appeared to increase not the quantity or quality of its provision. The direction of what growth there was favoured such areas as 'automobile' services, which given the nature of car-ownership was not likely to assuage working-class appetites.

Where the private sector did develop, the so-called 'agency' shops and restaurants, and some private craft-based production, the level of earnings achieved by some of these socialist entrepreneurs in what was after all a seller's market, further antagonized the working class. The stereotype of 'private-sector affluence' blurred, for example, rich peasants, tomato growers, venetian-blinds manufacturers, pâtissiers, hairdressers and tailors into one group, the supposed wealth and earnings of which was further evidence to the working class that the interests of the 'worker' were being ignored.

As shortages in consumer durables and subsequently in basic foodstuffs became more apparent, so attention was turned to the stratification of outlets within particular occupations (for example, police and military), within factories and institutions (that is, so-called 'buffets' and canteens which also *sold* foodstuffs) and, in particular, to the party apparat and higher functionaries. Dollar shops and 'commercial-priced' meat shops were the observable example of the subsurface inequality in access to goods in demand. The Agreement signed between the Gdansk strikers and the government commission on 31 August 1980, while denying the existence of privileges for police and party apparat, agreed to exclude home-produced goods, such as sheepskin coats, clothing and food which were in short supply, from the dollar shops (Protokol Porozumienia, 1980).

An important side-effect of the above-mentioned shortages which aggravated workers' perceptions of inequality was the growth in 'colored markets' (Katsenelinboigin, 1978) and of bribery and corruption. It appears that not only was the latter phenomenon spreading, but that in popular opinion, it was gaining increasing acceptability. In fact, almost two-thirds of respondents in one study regarded it as a 'rational' activity given the circumstances (Falkowska, 1980). Here again, key sections of the working class were by the nature of their employment and marketability of services excluded from the circle of barter, exchange-in-kind or exploitation of key positions. While the 'moral' outrage which constantly burst through into workers' demands may in part be seen as a reaction to this exclusion from the 'second' economy, in general it was attacked because it symbolized the broader disintegration of norms governing the activities of personnel as much in management administration, and government as in the services sector.

Technocratic Socialism and its Consequences

References to autocratic and technocratic tendencies among industrial managers were increasingly to be heard during the late 1970s (Bielicki, 1979). By all accounts, managers' attitudes to workers had not significantly altered in the post-1970 period, with 53 percent of workers in one survey noticing insignificant or no change at all during 1971–2 (Jerschina *et al.*, 1973; Widerszpil, 1979). The policy of rapid modernization appeared to provide a *carte-blanche* for managers which was further secured by their party membership. Added to this was the fact that modern managers and administrators have less and less contact with the working class either through social origins, or occupational career paths (Wasilewski, 1978). Educated in Western-style management theory, experienced and adept at coping and indeed exploiting to their own advantage the irrationalities and shortcomings of a centrally planned economy, they nevertheless appeared to ride rough-shod over their employees with an arrogance and insensitivity which could only be explained by the total lack of means for curbing their power. To the injustices and particularism associated with the division of the all-important premiums and bonuses, was added cynical and unrestrained personal corruption. Only this can explain the vehemence of demands for the removal of managers, for a more objective *cadres* policy where incompetence was not rewarded by a similar or better managerial position elsewhere and where party membership was often a necessary and sufficient condition for joining the ranks of the managerial elite regardless of individual worth or qualifications.

Workers blamed their own 'demoralization' and lack of work discipline upon management. Theft, drunkenness, absenteeism and a lack of 'work ethic' happened, because they were permitted to happen by managers whose interests this served, directly or indirectly (Letter, T. Kromer, *Polityka,* 1980). The ineffectiveness of representative bodies such as the Factory Council of the trade union and the Factory Committee of the party stimulated a form of 'retreatism' or internal migration among large sections of the working class, while obviously radicalizing others.

High levels of labor turnover, for example, reaching 100–200 percent per annum in extreme cases were admitted to be 'an effective source of pressure upon management for enforcing work rationalization and improving technical and managerial practices' (Kalinowska, 1979), while management–worker relations were shown to be more important in explaining employee mobility than the often-cited causes of pay and housing (Bugiel, 1977).

A rough calculation showed that, in 1978, approximately one in twelve industrial workers was absent from work, for whatever reason (Rocznik Statystyczny Przemyslu, 1979), particularly in the building industries and in mining. Clearly associated with this high level of absenteeism is the appalling rate of alcoholism, particularly within the working class. In 1977, alcohol consumption was estimated to interfere, in one form or another, with the production activity of 40 percent of workers, and to be the direct cause of 8–15 percent of industrial accidents. There were calculated to be 5 million excessive drinkers in Poland (out of a total population of 35 million), and it was no longer easy to portray this as a result of the 'peasantization of labour' (Lopienska, 1980; Morawski, 1979).

The astonishing level of self-discipline and determination shown by the Gdansk strikers in particular stands in sharp contrast to the picture of indiscipline usually presented when industrial activity is discussed. Even allowing for the unique factors which made Gdansk first the touchstone and then the guardian of the working-class demands, the solidarity and organizational restraint shown by workers elsewhere throughout the country suggest that this was not an isolated incident. The quasi-religious undertones of moral renewal within the working class in particular, and throughout Polish society in general, suggest that the foundation of the free, self-governing trade unions was in part an expression of the working classes' need for a reaffirmation of its self-identity and self-respect. Arguments for creating a 'thin layer of unemployed' as an incentive to work and to work discipline represented a characteristically typical technocratic response which tackled the symptom and not the cause of the problem (*'Twardo donikad', Polityka,* 1978). The working class was the end-recipient of the consequences of mismanagement and poor planning, observed the underbelly of machinations and corruption, witnessed the power of cliques and coteries and yet was powerless to do anything about it. Initially the strike movement had sought to defend the working class against the *consequences* of this managerial and administrative ineptness (for example, *Robotnik,* nos 1, 15, 16, 24) so that shortages of raw materials, of energy, poor planning, etc. should not negatively affect their earnings. Even in this, the official representative organs proved of little value.

In Whose Interests?

The official trade union movement, governed by a Stalinist statute dating back to 1949, comprised twenty-three branch unions, covering all major industrial and service sectors and subordinated to the Central Council of the Trade Unions. At the regional level, there were a further forty-nine councils, some 30,000 factory councils and these in turn split up into 240,000 groups or sections. Over 1·5 million persons were engaged, full-time or part-time, in servicing this bureaucracy. While the trade union interlocked with economic and governmental organs, it was ineffectual and confined itself largely to social–welfare activities within the workplace. It organized recreation and holiday activities, distributed allotments, it was concerned with health and safety, with job security, with work mobilization and work discipline. And yet, despite or perhaps because it was involved in all of these activities, its main function under the Constitution 'to represent the interests and rights of the working people' went by the board. Part of the blame for this was placed on the trade unions' lack of autonomy. Nearly 60 percent of all trade union Factory Council chairmen were party members (Witalec, 1978), which paradoxically discredited by association both one and the other. An alarming generation-gap had emerged between the largely older functionaries (who saw the trade union post largely as a sinecure), whose immediate material and work needs were not as pressing and who had entered into all sorts of 'arrangements' with management (Krall, 1980) and younger workers.

This is not to say that the trade unions were unaware of their shortcomings or the dire need for change. Inflationary pressures on trade union services combined with rapidly growing aspirations for these same services, such as housing, car-purchase allocation and holidays, had already forced the unions to become more democratic and open in their dealings. The 'election' campaign of June 1980 had raised most of the questions which were to be repeated as demands two months later, and had led the leaders of the trade unions to call for greater contacts with government organs while criticizing its own lack of defensive ability in the realm of living standards and prices (Zyci Gospodarcze 1980).

At about the same time, an authoritative article in the party journal pointed to survey results carried out in the late 1970s, wherein the main role of the trade unions was seen as 'representing the interests of *working-class* communities'. The unions were also exhorted to examine unacceptable income differentiation (that is, that which was not worked for), but most importantly, an airing was given to the view that the economic administration might not after all *per se* represent the national interest:

> symptoms exist indicating that in many instances the economic administration at various levels articulates particular interests or have in mind their own group profit (e.g. by setting themselves simplified tasks in order to obtain higher income). (Gilejko, 1980)

The official recognition of the need for a more aggressive role for trade unions had come too late. In a welter of self-criticism and resignations at the 16th plenum of the CRZZ on 26 August 1980 the achievement of 'state' unionism was swept away with all its shortcomings.

The large centralized trade unions had outlived their time. They could no longer even pretend to cope with the increasingly diversified nature and conditions of the working class let alone other socio-occupational groups. The Free Trade Union movement represented:

  (i) the *working-class* need for greater autonomy from and control over the economic administrative apparatus;
 (ii) the need for an organization which could express the sectional interests of an increasingly differentiated working class;
(iii) the need for an organization which would defend the interests of the core working class against other sectors of the socialized and non-socialized economy.

Development and Differentiation

Only 10 percent or so of all workers in Poland had prewar work experience, some 50 percent had spent their youth in the countryside, two-thirds were under 40 years of age, and half of these, less than 24 years old. The experience of the last ten years must, therefore, have had a key role in shaping the attitudes, aspirations and sociopolitical consciousness of large sections of the working class. While the core industrial working class numbers approximately 3·5 million, all those in manual-worker positions total 8 million. Of these, 25 percent have secondary or postsecondary education, generally of a technical, vocational nature, 7 percent have higher education [*sic*] and 20 percent complete elementary vocational education. Again, 60 percent of all workers are of working-class origins with an increasing percentage each year being received from the routine white-collar social category (Zagorski, 1978). The recent slowdown in intergenerational mobility, indicative of the halt in the fundamental postwar transformation of the socio-occupational structure, has tended to harden class boundaries. At the same time, new forms of social mobility, such as that between the highly skilled manual and the engineering-technical strata, have deposited articulate and educated persons into the ranks of the working class (Bielicki, 1979). Furthermore, there is evidence to suggest that while some of these educated recruits may have 'elected' to join the ranks of the working class, in preference to lower-paid white-collar employment, others were there by 'default', either because they could not continue into higher education, or because they could not obtain attractive white-collar jobs (Dziecielska-Machnikowska, 1976). Support for this division of the working class into those there by election and those there by default is provided by female-dominated industries which are particularly 'retentive'. The technological advance of the 1970s has served further to widen the gap between modern and traditional industries, and their associated workforces, between those who gained from the above-mentioned modernization and purchase of foreign technology and those who did not. While textiles had a 78 percent growth in the means of production during 1971–5, the growth in precision tools (290 percent), metal (92 percent), electronics (85 percent), was greater and started from a higher base (W. Brzost, 1979, pp. 109–11). Becoming a manual worker was associated with failing to complete secondary education or gain entry into further education. Furthermore, 75 percent of a sample of women workers wanted their children to become white-collar employees – a tacit rejection of their working-class status (Stronska, 1980). It is possible to see how the organizational discipline, sophistication and confidence shown by the working class in 1980 was fueled by a critical sense of social injustice, of frustrated mobility aspirations and by impatience.

When the meat price rises were officially introduced at the beginning of July 1980, they were in part legitimated (rather belatedly) by the declared need to raise the income of one-parent families (11 percent of households), of multichild families, of pensioners and of the lowest paid, to which end the extra income derived from the price rises would be put. While this did not succeed in stemming the almost-instantaneous wave of strikes which continued throughout July, it did signify the official recognition of the acute inequality which had emerged in Polish society during the 1970s. Approximately 45 percent of three-child families and 77 percent of four-child families, chiefly working class or peasants, fell below the per capita social minimum (Graniewska, 1979). Whereas during 1970–79 nominal wages had increased by an average of over 100 percent, social benefits such as pensions and family supplements grew by only 50 percent. Not surprisingly, Poland was considered to have a differentiation of income similar to, if not greater than, that of Hungary without the excuse of the New Economic Mechanism and a 'socialist market' economy (Zienkowski,

1979). In this context, it should be noted that at least 30 percent of those prices centrally fixed and monitored in 1979 exceeded their permitted limits and further aggravated the effect of officially sponsored price rises. This lack of price discipline was reflected in the demand for trade union control of prices and the cost of living.

Simultaneously, differences in net earnings among manual workers both between and within branches of industry also widened during the 1970s, with the lowest-paid clothing workers receiving on average 46 percent of the highly paid miners' wage. While 60 percent of wages tended to cluster just below the mean, the upper and lower limits were greatly extended. It was argued that it was not the range of inequality, but its unjust and largely incomprehensible bases, which were under attack. Where a qualified doctor earned 85 percent of a chargehand's industrial wage, then the tendency of the former to sell his services legally or illegally for a higher income becomes more understandable, although it does nothing to allay the grievances of workers who then cannot afford this doctor's higher private charges for 'better' more solicitous service (Zagrodzka, 1980).

Inequality within the working class was further accentuated by the disproportion in the factory social funds, which provided subsidized services, such as holidays, sanatoria, canteen facilities, health care and contributed to nursery and crèche provision. Here the amount available per employee per factory varied by as much as 10:1. Those industries which have the lowest-paid workers also have lowest per capita social fund provision, these being largely feminized industries with working mothers, who are unable to afford to take the three years' unpaid maternity leave and yet for whose children there is no room in local nurseries.

Some manual workers have been able to exploit the current shortage of services, personnel or goods, such as bricklayers, hospital ward orderlies, and shop assistants, respectively. It is difficult to assess whether 'second' economy activity serves to diminish or exaggerate income inequalities (for example, professional queuing providing a valuable source of income for old-age pensioners) (Skalski, 1980), but it has served to make the industrial working class more aware of its 'class interest' within the existing socioeconomic formation: 'This is expressed in the universal obligation to work and the principle of distribution according to work' (Gilejko, 1979). This implies an attack upon those sections of society which exploit market conjunctures, the scarcity of desired goods, and in this way undermine what has euphemistically come to be termed the principles of 'social justice'. Workers in key industrial sectors needed an organization or organizations which would represent their interests, and their interests alone in a society which was becoming increasingly more complex, variegated and replete with inequalities of income and lifestyle unimaginable in the stagnant 1960s. The task of the new trade unions will be made all the more difficult given that the blame for subsequent intra-working-class inequalities can be laid at their door.

It is, however, possible to understand how the various measures taken by the authorities in the late 1970s, such as the Committees for Social Control, special taxes on high earnings, measures against speculation in housing, which were all reiterated at the 8th PZPR Congress in February 1980, was a case of 'too little, too late'. Rumours and complaints of the uncontrolled self-aggrandizement of party and state functionaries were heard increasingly often even from within the ranks of the party itself: 'in effect what we have is a gradual process of accumulation of social gratification by a certain group of persons and a deprivation from such on the part of others' (Jankowski, 1980). The much-publicized case of the head of Polish radio and television, who was closely associated with Gierek, was simply the tip of an enormous iceberg.

Whereas egalitarian and 'leveling' demands are never far below the surface and in fact emerged in 1980, in general the call was to make privilege 'observable', rather than abolish it altogether, to lend its sources and justification to scrutiny. It is precisely in the *moral* guardianship of socialist distribution that the party was found wanting. It was not so much what the party failed to achieve after 1970 – the so-called deviation from guidelines of the 6th Congress – but what it permitted to happen, by default or by design, in its stead. This failure can, in part, be explained by the party's attitude to its working-class membership.

The Demystification of Party Membership

The PZPR in all the stages of its activity has maintained a clearly defined model of the social composition of its ranks (Grzybowski, 1977). Whereas up until 1970 it was the quality of the intelligentsia intake which exercised the minds of the recruiting *cadres* and working-class participation was simply a case of an appropriate percentage of the population, after the 'Polish December' the situation altered somewhat.

A policy of 'selective incorporation' was embarked upon and the quality of working-class recruitment was to be raised by focusing upon the 'large industrial' working class, skilled workers and foremen. Key workers, with authority in their shop-floor environment, were to be invited more actively to join the party. The Central Committee and Secretariat of the PZPR would, through its newly adopted policy of 'consultation' and direct tutelage over 164 key enterprises scattered throughout Poland, strengthen its links with the party '*aktyw*'. They, in turn, would be stimulated into working with rank-and-file members, who in their turn, would sound out and transmit the opinions, views and incipient demands of non-party workers.

The outward signs of the new policy were impressive. By 1979, the membership of the PZPR had risen to 3,044,000 compared to 2,319,913 in 1970, and manual workers constituted 46·1 percent of the total (40·3 percent in 1970). It boasted 17 percent of all manual workers in the socialised sector, 18 percent of all skilled workers and 43 percent of all foremen. The average age in 1979 had declined to 40·3 years and that year's intake indicated that 69 percent of all new recruits were under 30 years of age (Ozgo, 1979). Finally 27 percent of all blue-collar members were concentrated in large plants and factories, the 'citadels' of socialism as they were termed.

It was hoped that such a structure of party membership, and a recruitment policy of increased educational qualifications, would not allow a repeat of 1970, when 'some members were passive whilst others consciously supported the demagogues' (*Zycie Partii,* 1971). For a time the practice of 'consultation' appeared to be bearing fruit, and the new work code, trade union legislation, the creation of various social and economic funds, were all discussed with the '*aktyw*' of the key enterprises (Dubinska, 1974). The more-active dissemination of propaganda, schooling in socioeconomic affairs, lectures and conferences for party Factory Committee First Secretaries, regular visits by party dignitaries, were all seen as raising the consciousness and committedness of the lower echelons of the party apparat and the rank-and-file membership.

Almost inevitably, these new practices succumbed to routinization and technocratization. Consultation was transformed into 'informing of decisions', while the party at the factory level, rather than keeping its finger on the pulse of working-class feeling, became increasingly involved with plan-fulfillment, expediting various work disruptions, etc. (*Zagadnienia i Materialy,* 1980). Internal party democracy was sacrificed for the sake of discipline in the face of the burgeoning social and economic crises. Of the latter, the party was given sufficient indication through letters and personal complaints received by its various organs. These expressed concern at income disproportions between the private and socialized sector, complained of managerial autocracy, cliques, waste, etc. The party control Commissions in the period 1976–9 examined one-third of all basic party organizations and dismissed among others 300 managers and directors for 'attitudes incompatible with the title communist' (*Zycie Partii,* 1980). It publicized campaigns against those in the party apparat who used their positions for personal gain (Pawlak, 1979). But these campaigns only served to highlight the ineffectiveness of actions taken.

Another warning sign to the party was the high level of deletions and resignations from the ranks of the party, 50 percent of whom were manual workers (Kolodziejczyk, 1979). The ensuing reversion to a crude chase for working-class membership merely lowered the status of such membership in the eyes of those the party wished to attract, while allowing in those who saw it as a means to less reputable ends.

When the wave of strikes commenced in July 1980, party members and '*aktyw*' were often to the fore in representing the strikers' demands. This practice had emerged during the late 1970s and was based as much upon their presumed personal immunity from subsequent victimization as to the undoubted authority of some party members. At Ursus, in the Szczecin MKS, in the Warsaw bus-depot strike committees, party members were not slow to take action. 'The party is more realistic at its lower levels', was a quote from one such activist.

That the incoming leadership's first task under Stanislaw Kania was seen as restoring party discipline, is not surprising. This will, however, be more difficult and will involve considerable concessions to party democracy. It will entail greater rotation of personnel in leading party organs, the retreat from the almost-compulsory monopoly of certain key organizational positions, such as chairman of the Workers' Self-Management Conference (KSR) in each enterprise or the leadership of local councils (*Polityka,* no. 36, 1980), and even the mutual exclusivity of party office and other official functions. The experience of the last ten years has shown that experiments in 'working-class' incorporation into the party are naïve, if they assume that a 'correct' social composition and statisticial representativity will somehow automatically guarantee party loyalty in times of legitimacy crises.

Organizational Solutions towards a Responsible Society

Apart for the brief experience of workers' councils spontaneously set up in 1956 but emasculated by the Conference of Workers' Self-Management in 1958, the working class has remained bereft of any organization which could specifically represent its interests, economic, social or even political, while remaining free of other organizations or superior organs (Kolankiewicz, 1973). The emergence of Soviet-style production councils to replace even the innocuous workers' councils in the late 1970s was simply a recognition of the *de facto* role performed by the latter within the enterprise. During the early part of the last decade there appeared to be no particular need for such an organization, since real wages growth and consumerism, financed by the 20 billion dollar foreign debt, effectively 'bought-off' any instrumental demands which might be made.

The sharp downturn in the economic climate after 1978 described above witnessed renewed effort on the part of the authorities for an institution which could channel working-class discontent. Some favored the technocratic solution, namely, a more active Conference of Workers' Self-Management tied to a more decentralized industrial enterprise, with greater freedom and responsibilities (Rogowski, 1980). Others argued that such an arrangement did not provide an organizational base for manual workers to develop a common point of view to put to the KSRs, and was therefore inherently undemocratic (*Polityka,* 23 February 1980). The latter saw in a reanimated trade union movement a powerful counterweight to the technocratic forces ensconced within the party itself and a means for reasserting the political primacy of the party as mediator. While the advent of the free, self-managing trade unions overtook this cautious debate, these may yet find themselves in an unenviable position.

Decentralization of economic management and the loosening of the wage fund, will be tied to an increasing emphasis upon productivity. Coupled with the restructuring of industry from investment to consumption, it appears that some form of redundancy and unemployment, however temporary, will have to be made acceptable to the working class. Hints of this, even if by denial, were evident in key speeches in early September 1980 (J. Pinkowski, *Trybuna Ludu,* 5 September 1980). The free trade unions as the only democratically elected organizations have the legitimacy to introduce such measures. Their readiness to do so will depend on such unknown factors as their spheres of competence, ambiguously set out in the strike settlement, their future organizational structure (regional, branch-based, or hierarchical), the fate of the traditional unions and their social-welfare functions and funding and, particularly, on the role of the party in the new unions.

On this last point, the party appears to accept the likelihood of finding its members within the ranks of the free trade unions: '[The] fundamental principle of the Party is to be everywhere where the working-class is to be found' (*Trybuna Ludu,* 5 September 1980). This provides a unique opportunity for combining power with legitimacy, for the *genuine* articulation of working-class interests and their eventual mediation and integration into an increasingly complex socialist society. Above all else, it provides an opportunity for restoring *moral* legitimacy to the basic institution of Polish society and into economic, political and social life.

Conclusion

Whether the free trade unions are institutionalized into Polish society or whether they cease to exist as autonomous entities in the near future, their impact upon working-class consciousness and practice as well as on party policy will be less easily dealt with. For the party, the Polish August demonstrated the following:

(i) The failure of the party's strategies of selective incorporation, namely, that the recruitment or implantation of party '*aktyw*' in key social strata and in key institutions does not of itself guarantee party control during times of legitimacy crises.

(ii) Further it clearly showed that consultative or passive democracy cannot substitute for the *dynamic* aggregation, articulation, mediation and eventual integration of interests. Knowing what the working class think or feel, is not synonymous with the active representation of their interests and needs and the subsequent translation of the latter into *observable* policy outcomes.

(iii) Again it made evident that the party sacrifices political authority when it engages in economic supervision and runs the almost inevitable risk of losing the confidence and loyalty of lower-level '*aktyw*' and rank-and-file members, who find it impossible to represent central party policy when they have no influence upon its formulation. When economic policy fails, the party's political legitimacy is seriously undermined. The vehement rejection of the party as a negotiative partner in August 1980 and the relegitimization of Parliament (Sejm) and civil society is serious because it bypasses the party, ignores it and seeks to make it irrelevant. Many of the causes for this brusque treatment are to be found in economic promises made and promises broken.

(iv) The four-step communication belt between party center –'*aktyw*'–rank-and-file member–non-party employee, has been shown to have become routinized at the first three stages and the fourth stage was taken for granted. Institutional guarantees involving mandatory rotation and recall can be one of the means for avoiding the repeated 'goal displacement' and information distortion within the party.

For its part, we saw the emergence of nascent interests within the working class. Perhaps the most important demand underlying the enormous variety and volume of specific demands was for the introduction of wide-ranging *accountability* in all spheres of social, economic and political life. Allied to this was the call for *observability* and *transparency* in the social relations, for example, governing distribution and interest representation.

The retreat of censorship would allow economic as well as political life to become more open and forestall the social pathologies of corruption, cliques, economic irrationality, excessive and unwarranted privilege, etc. made so manifest in the late 1970s. This, in its turn, would lay the foundation for the restoration of the work ethic or the input–reward equation, which almost disappeared in a welter of managerial particularism and administrative incompetence.

A confident working class which has regained its collective self-respect should be treated as an asset and not as a threat by the communist leadership. The emergence of free, self-governing trade unions was of immense *symbolic* value, and their future organizational structure and role will be evaluated as less important than what they signified in lessons of the future relationship between the working class and the party in socialist society. The growth of working-class consciousness is now becoming more apparent in its outlines. The question is whether, after two lessons in 1970 and 1980, leadership, ideologists and party have recognized those elements which do not sit easily with their preconceptions. The later the lesson is learned, the tougher will each subsequent examination become.

Notes: Chapter 7

The author is grateful to the British Academy who sponsored an exchange visit to the Polish Academy of Sciences, Warsaw, in the summer of 1980. Further thanks have to be extended to the Fuller Bequest Research Fund of the Department of Sociology, University of Essex, for its assistance in financing complementary research visits.

References: Chapter 7

Beskid, L., '*Potrzeby ludnosci w swietle badan spolecznych*', *Nowe Drogi*, no. 6, 1980.
Bielicki, W., and Widerszpil, S., '*Z problematyki przemian spolecznych w Polsce Ludowej*', *Nowe Drogi*, no. 7, 1979.
Bielicki, W., '*Robotnicy ze srednim wyksztalceniem, nowa kategoria klasy robotniczej*', *Przeglad Zwiazkowy*, no. 4, 1979.

Blachnicki, B., *Pracownicy Przemyslu Wobec Egalitaryzmu* (Wroclaw: Ossolineum, 1979).

Brzost, W., *Importowany Postep Techniczny a Rozwoj Gospodarczy Polski* (Warsaw: PWN, 1979).

Bugiel, J., *'Psychospoleczne przyczyny plynnosci zalogi w kopalni miedzi'* in J. Bugiel, ed., *Procesy Adaptacji i Stabilizacji Zalogi Kopalni Miedzi* (Wroclaw: Ossolineum 1977).

Dlugosz, Z., *'W uslugach-bez zmian', Zycie Gospodarcze*, 15 June 1980.

Dubinska, B., *'Zdaniem sekretarzy komitetow zakladowych PZPR', Zycie Partii*, no. 1, 1974.

Dziecielska-Machnikowska, S., *'Co sadza o swojej pracy robotnicy ze srednim wyksztalceniem', Przeglad Zwiazkosy*, no. 6, 1976.

Falkowska, W., *'Kto lubi lapownikow?', Polityka*, 7 June 1980.

Fikus, D., *'Mloda Rodzina', Polityka*, 30 August 1980.

Gilejko, L., *'Postawy spoleczno-polityczne klasy robotniczej i ich unwarunkowania'*, in A. Wajda, ed., *Klasa Robotnicza w Spoleczenstwie Socjalistycznym* (Warsaw: KiW, 1979), p. 282.

Gilejko, L., *'Zwiazki zawodowe wobec aktualnych zadan', Nowe Drogi*, no. 7, 1980, p. 73.

Gornicka, T., *'Co robic z inwestycjami?', Zycie Gospodarcze*, 24 August 1980.

Graniewska, D., *'Rodziny wielodzietne wymagaja wszechstronnej spolecznej uwagi', Przeglad Zwiazkosy*, no. 7-8, 1979.

Grzybowski, L., *'Partia i klasa robotnicza: 1948-75', Zeszyty Naukowe WSNS, KC PZPR*, no. 3, 1977, p. 68.

Jankowski, A., *'Z zagadnien sprawiedliwosci spolecznej', Nowe Drogi*, no. 8, 1980.

Jerschina, J., *et al, Zycie Partii*, no. 4, 1973, p. 18.

Kabaj, M., *'Efektywnosc wzrostu plac', Nowe Drogi*, no. 2, 1980.

Kalinowska, J., *'Ocena wykonywanej pracy iwarunkow pracy a stabilnosc pracownika', Praca i Zabezpieczenie Spoleczne*, no. 4, 1979, p. 50.

Katsenelinboigin, A., 'Studies in Soviet economic planning', *International Journal of Politics*, 1978, ch. 7.

Kolankiewicz, G., 'The Polish industrial working class', in D. Lane and G. Kolankiewicz, eds, *Social Groups in Polish Society* (London: Macmillan, 1973).

Kolodziejczyk, T., *'Skreslenie-problem niepokojacy', Zycie Partii*, no. 8, 1979.

Komar, K., *'Kiesien i przywileje', Gazeta Robotnicza*, 11 December 1978.

Krall, H., *'Delegaci', Polityka*, 6 September 1980.

Krencik, W., *'Za parawanem plac', Zycie Gospodarcze*, 26 April 1980.

Kromer, T., *'Moja praca, moja godnosc'* (letter), *Polityka*, 30 August 1980.

Lopiensk, B., *'Na dostawce', Kultura*, no. 31, 1980.

Melich, A., *Problemy plac w Polsce* (Warsaw: Instytut Wydawniczy CRZZ, 1978).

Monkiewicz, J., *'Licencje', Zycie Gospodarcze*, 20 April 1980.

Morawski, J., *'Alkoholizm w zakladzie pracy', Praca i Zabezpieczenie Spoleczne*, no. 2, 1979, pp. 32-6.

Mozolowski, A., Ushigi i Rzemioslo: Uwagi i Propozycje (Warsaw: Krajowa Agencja Wydawnicza, 1980) p. 37.

Nowak, S., *et al., Ciaglosc i Zmiana Tradycji Kulturowych* (Warsaw, 1974), mimeo.

Ozgo, A., *'Rozwoj szeregow Partii', Zycie Partii*, no. 11, 1979.

Pawlak, A., *'Kontrola warunkiem sprawnego kierowania', Zycie Partii*, no. 3, 1979.

'*Protokol Porozumienia zawartego przez Komisje Rzadowa i Miedzyzakladowy Komitet Strajkowy*', *Trybuna Ludu*, 2 September 1980.

Remer, T., *Niektore Aspekty Psychologiczne Struktury i Ruchliwosci Spolecznej* (Wroclaw: Ossolineum, 1980).

Rogowski, W., '*Zasada wspoldecydowania*', *Polityka*, 5 January 1980.

Rocznik Statystyczny Przemyslu (Warsaw: GUS, 1979). pp. 200-201.

Sarapata, A., '*Dobra praca podstawa nagrod i awansow*', *Nowe Drogi*, no. 7, 1979.

Sarapata, A., '*Morale pracy – blaski i cienie*', *Nowe Drogi*, no. 6, 1980.

Skalski, E., '*Fuchy i Chaltury*', *Polityka*, 15 March 1980.

Slomczynski, K., and Wesolowski, W., '*Przemiany struktury spolecznej i jej potocznej percepcji*', Paper V, *Ogolnopolski zjazd socjologiczny w Krakowie, 1977*.

Stronska, A., '*Okolica kobiet*', *Polityka*, 19 April 1980.

'*Twardo donikad*', anonymous article and subsequent discussion, *Polityka*, 30 September 1978.

Urban, J., '*Zycie na wlasny rachunek*', *Polityka*, 26 August 1980.

'*VI Zjazd PZPR*', *Nowe Drogi*, no. 1, 1972.

Wasilewski, J., '*Spoleczne mechanizmy selekcji na wysze stanowiska kierownicze*', *Studia Socjologiczne*, no. 2, 1978.

Wesolowska, M., '*Teraz jestesmy w przyspieszieniu*', *Polityka*, 30 August 1980.

Witalec, A., '*Organizacja partyjna pomocnikiem i inspiratorem zwiazkowe go dzialania*', *Przeglad Zwiazkowy*, no. 12, 1978.

Wroblewski, A. K., '*Buty dla zony*', *Polityka-Eksport-Import* (IOO), 8 August 1980.

Zagadnienia i Materialy, no. 12, June 1980.

Zagorski, K., *Rozwoj Struktura i Ruchliwosc Spoleczna* (Warsaw: PWN, 1978), p. 133.

Zagrodzka, D., '*Za parawanem sredniej*', *Polityka*, 30 August 1980.

Zawalski, A., '*Umowa czy plan?*', *Polityka*, 5 January 1980.

Zienkowski, L., '*Nasze dochody i co o nich myslimy*', *Polityka*, 23-9 December 1979.

8 Workers and Power

WALTER D. CONNOR

Introduction

Marxism placed the worker – its sole creator of material value – at the center of its analysis and calls to action. Born of the industrial revolution and capitalism, dispossessed of all but the labor power that was his to sell, no longer (as his peasant forebear) woven into the more intimate servant–master relationship with its overlay of traditional obligations and reciprocities, but confronting impersonal 'capital' in uneven contractual relationships, the worker was the exploited of the present, the revolutionary of the future. That future, achieved, would see proletarian triumph through an exercise of power ('dictatorship') by the working class, against exploiting classes (the bourgeoisie) but in favor of *all* men's 'true' interests; so evident that, after a transition period, the problems of power, control, the segmentation of man's life between work and other roles, would all dissolve in the construction of a new society.

History has played both Marxists and workers false. Marxism has yielded 'workers' states' – as yet no communist societies – not in the states where capitalism had run its course and done its historic work, but where it had hardly begun. It became the ruling ideology, with various national adaptations and distortions, not where large proletariats had been concentrated, but over societies where peasantry dominated – first Russia, then the states of Eastern Europe. Rather than basing itself on the industrial civilization laid down by capitalism, Marxist rule faced the task of creating a socialist variant of that civilization on an underdeveloped base.

The results, diverse as they run from East Berlin to Vladivostok, look little like any nineteenth-century design. No aspect of these societies, save propagandists' rhetoric, approaches the utopian. Power is radically concentrated in leaderships which, in addition to traditional instruments of political control, hold the economic fate of individuals in their hands through far-reaching state ownership and centralized management of productive resources. In none do living standards equal those of the countries of developed capitalism – among the latter those very states where Marxist expectations predicted the revolution would first come. In none does the diversity and liveliness of cultural and occupational expression rival the advanced societies of the West, much less resemble that arcadia where a man might practise a craft, farm and criticize all in the same day.

All this means that 'workers' are still a distinct group in Marxist socialist societies – takers rather than givers of order, specialized in their work functions, performing these distinct from other aspects of their lives. Lacking workers, socialism created them through industrialization – and created workers of a sort not readily distinguishable, for many purposes, from their counterparts under capitalism. These workers 'fit' in a system of stratification – the patterned, unequal distribution of material goods, power and prestige, and opportunities to achieve these – advantaged compared to some groups, disadvantaged *vis-à-vis* others. Exalted as the leading class by regimes still tied to nineteenth-century rhetoric, they are, along with the vast majority in socialist society, among the *led*.

Thus, the problem of *power* reasserts itself in the situation of the socialist-industrial class. Power is neither equally distributed among all (and hence not 'power' at all), nor is it all in the hands of the workers after thirty-five years of socialism in Eastern Europe. It is a multifaceted problem, involving the sorts of resources workers possess to assert power *versus* other groups, the regime, or both; the liabilities and weaknesses of the workers as a power group, and the institutional–ideological constraints of the systems they inhabit. The assertion of working-class power, directly and indirectly, has a history as well, combining success and failure, which we will review later. Finally, the present state of worker 'consciousness', assertiveness, and degree of cooperation with other forces need be assessed to project possibilities for the future.

The present chapter attempts to do all this, in a general way. Much of what follows is summary – specificity in single-country situations has been sacrificed in an attempt to isolate and discuss some general themes. Much is also speculative, not lending itself easily to documentation – hence, a relative paucity of reference. It is offered, in a serious way, as an *introductory* look at workers as a power group in socialist societies, since other chapters in this book deal in much greater depth with both individual issues and distinct national patterns.

Power Potential and Resources

Save in Czechoslovakia and the German Democratic Republic (GDR), the leaderships in East European socialist states faced, at their inception, a deficit of workers – the group supposedly providing a natural support base for socialist politics and policies. Inheritors of under- and semi-developed economies disrupted by war, they sought to establish rule over societies where the peasantry's demographic weight ranged from preponderant (Poland and Hungary) to overwhelming (the Balkan states). Stabilizing that rule to a certain degree, with significant Soviet aid and control, they set about the task of transforming societies in the image of their regimes – the creation of workers to inhabit and justify a 'workers' state'.

They succeeded. Throughout Eastern Europe today, the workers constitute the largest 'class' or stratum – outnumbering the peasantry and white-collar groups and, in some state, amounting to a majority of the population. This numerical predominance of the blue-collar industrial workforce bespeaks both success and failure in socialist economic performances. The successful mounting of industrialization strategies in the late 1940s–early 1960s drew off the underemployed surplus from agrarian labor pools, added them, frequently at high social cost, to the burgeoning urban factory laborforces, *and* generated professional and administrative *cadres* of greatly increased size through the recruitment of ambitious adults and youth from worker and peasant backgrounds. Failure, however, is registered in the fact that no socialist state economy has yet passed through the 'second industrial revolution', or the move to a postindustrial society, wherein more than half of the laborforce produces *neither* finished goods, nor crops, but renders services: a society wherein the tertiary sector is dominant.

Faulting the socialist regimes on this point may be unfair, since it is not clear that they have aimed at such an outcome, but not entirely so. References to the scientific-technical revolution, the various theories of 'developed socialism' in futurological rhetoric indicate *some* end-point not yet arrived at. The socialist economies have proven poor at the substitution of capital for labor, of technological and management resources for capital, and slow to adapt to the challenge of increasing materials costs, decreasing laborforce growth rates, etc. All this contributes to the situation wherein workers make up the largest social stratum; one less mechanized and skilled, all in all, than its counterparts in Western Europe and North America, but larger *versus* the society as a whole.

Thus, a prime power resource of workers is that of their absolute and relative *numbers*. Whether this potential is actualized is not at all a simply-answered question in polities where no institutions provide for the regular and legitimate exercise of workers' 'class power'. But it is well to contemplate certain aspects of·the matter of numerical strength. First, it makes workers the largest 'consituency' group in relation to general regime policies; for good or ill, workers (and their families) make up a majority or near-majority of all persons affected by particular policies. *Not* one group among several ('workers, peasants, socialist intelligentsia . . .') groups, the workers are, from some viewpoints, *the* society, or as close to it as any group is likely to approach.

Secondly, whatever the differences in social perception and expectations formed among the different social strata, working-class size guarantees that any views peculiar to, but adequately diffused among, this class become major elements in the political psychology of regime–society relations. 'What the workers think' *en gros* assumes an importance beyond what 'the intelligentsia' think in certain ways. Any development of a combative 'class consciousness' among workers, expressed finally in organizational forms which facilitate their ability to negotiate with the state, would be profoundly consequential. On the other hand, a fundamentally apolitical, 'economistic' orientation on workers' part – a failure of class consciousness to develop – is also a social fact of political importance.

Beyond *numbers,* the *location* and *function* of the working class or stratum in the society and economy confer upon it several potential strengths. The day to day functioning of industrial societies depends on an immensely complex set of interactions, exchanges, activity patterns predictable and persistent – and 'workers', broadly conceived as including not only manuals in industrial production, but also those in energy production and distribution, transportation, waste removal, etc., stand at a number of the most critical points in the pattern. True, they are not potentially 'independent' of the economy to the degree that peasants – direct producers of the means of subsistence – may be regarded so (although the dependence of today's peasants in socialist states on many items *from* the market places some limit on their ability, even *in extremis,* to withdraw). But compared to the intelligentsia and many administrative *cadres,* a 'withdrawal of services' on the part of workers will be felt by the whole society much more readily. Universities, schools, publishing houses, even a broad range of government offices, might close with only moderate immediate effects on the daily life of citizens – in the West as in the East. But *all* depend on the operation of human and goods transport, the flow of electricity when a switch is turned, the removal of garbage, in a direct and everyday way. The potential, then, of large-scale strikes and disruptions by workers is immense. It has been actualized, to degrees moderate compared to the logical extremes it might reach, in Poland (1956, 1970, 1976) most frequently, and less so in other states. It has led to more *response* from regimes than has intellectual dissent, measured by reallocative decisions, changes in leadership composition, etc. But, as yet, it has left the *design* of regimes unchanged. This points to some of the *limits* on working-class power and the exercise thereof to be considered in a later section.

Workers' relatively high degree of concentration – the ecology of the medium-to-large-size factory, mine, etc. – amplifies the likely simultaneity of actions and responses, and provides a possibility of spontaneous organization greater than office work or agricultural labor typically afford. This is an old point, well-appreciated by the Marxist propagandists and organizers of the past who found proletarians so 'reachable' in the large, bureaucratically-managed factories which succeeded the smaller-scale, often family-owned and managed workshops of earlier stages of industrialization. The factory, the shipyard, the mine – a physical property which is also the locus of complex activities involving large numbers of persons – offers a base for rapid diffusion of rumors, complaints, reactions, an audience for those who will at critical times speak out uninvited. This is the workers' natural habitat.

Finally, the element of myth is a critical potential asset in the inventory of working-class power. What one analyst (Staniszkis, 1979) has called the 'legitimacy myth' of socialist regimes – that they draw their mandate, legitimacy and support from the working class, whose interests they articulate and advance – makes working-class perceptions of the rough 'justice' or effectiveness of the system extremely salient for those regimes, however they may seek to control the behaviour and manipulate the perceptions. From no quarter are regimes so vulnerable to populist appeals to their own professed ideals as from those who can conceivably be seen as representative of, or at least rising from, 'the workers'. The countervailing realities of the workers' real place in the system of social, economic and political rewards – hardly a leading one – do not matter here. True, such a background is disadvantaging with respect to access to higher education at the most elite universities and institutions. True, there is less of the regime rhetorical populism (epitomized perhaps by the Novotny period in Czechoslovakia) which castigated the instability and ingratitude of intellectuals, and on occasion the recalcitrance and truculence of peasants, while extolling proletarian virtue. But the elements of charade have *not* been acknowledged as such: no regime has yet *declared* that its critical, legitimating support lies domestically in its intelligentsia and managers, or its peasants, or in any other stratum save the working class. None can without abandoning the ossified and confining set of symbols and catch-phrases they have grown so used to. And to do so would be taken as something serious indeed by workers who, while aware that materially and in power terms they do not lead, are not by that reason likely to take any forced move out of symbolic center-stage with equanimity.

Workers' Liabilities: Limits on Power

Many entries can be made in the debit side of the ledger of workers' political power – some of these the mirror-images of some of their elements of power potential, others factors that in a more direct way inhibit their development of effective power.

Large *numbers,* diffusion across the landscape of cities and factories, and across various social boundaries within the working class (skilled, semiskilled, unskilled categories, as well as divisions by industrial branch) all *complicate* any possibility of effective worker organization – especially in a hostile political environment. Intelligentsia organizational capacities are limited enough, yet much greater than those yet manifested by workers: hence, the smaller numbers and freer communication of the former play a role. And, while regimes such as Poland's seem to have settled, grudgingly, for a certain amount of unofficial but permanent self-organization on the part of the intellectuals, they have typically cracked down harshly on any sign of working-class attempts at self-organization.

Weakness also stems from a relative lack of ideological and conceptual resources. Working-class movements have not, in the past, elaborated their *own* ideologies to give meaning and shape to their activity – they have received or adopted them, generally from upper-class 'defectors', or intellectual allies. Given the degree of control socialist regimes exercise over intelligentsia-worker contacts, passing on a new ideology to the workers will be difficult. It may indeed be, as a recent provocative analysis argues (Konrad and Szelenyi, 1979) that only 'traitors' to the class interests of an intelligentsia which enjoys many rewards under socialism will make such an effort.

A further complication is that socialist workers live in systems whose ideology decrees that workers themselves are the leading or ruling class. This 'myth' constrains the regime in some sense, but it also constrains the workers. Workers' riots are serious, and taken so by the regimes, but the myth which 'helps to attain momentary success' by riots 'creates difficulties in developing protracted, lasting action by the workers: it is very difficult to fight for something that nominally exists', in the words of one Polish analyst (Staniszkis, 1979, p. 168). Similarly, the conceptual–psychological problems of developing a sustained opposition against a regime which claims to base itself on the class in question, has tended to leave 'class consciousness' at a rather simple level:

> this class consciousness does not go beyond the level of a primitive 'us and them' distinction. This kind of distinction, because of its non-differentiated character, can only be used to orient social behaviors among the interest relations of the groups concerned in the workplace and the living area, where all that is needed to decide who belongs to 'us' and who belongs to 'them' is to interpret the typical activities and material symbols (clothes, etc.). On a broader scale, this turns out to be an empty interpretative framework without practical con-sequences in any situation other than the extremely rare cases of mass riots, which are quickly crushed. In order to reach a point where there is solidarity and extensive co-operation, in order to realise an overall social programme, the classes need to institute their own political and economic organizations. But in Soviet-type society, none of the social classes is in a position to organize itself. (Rakovski, 1978, p. 47)

To these liabilities can be added the relative lack of information at workers' disposal about issues that affect them – their dependence, in a real sense, on a regime's willingness to 'share the facts' with them. This is rarely manifested except in those times of crisis when, accommodating some worker demands with concessions, a leader may point to grim economic information dictating the need for workers to limit the scope of their further demands, 'understand' the delicate situation of a leadership placed between popular demands and Soviet concerns, and go back to work. East European workers live in a world of economic mystification, flooded with information about inflation and unemployment in market economies (as well as high income-tax rates) in the West, but less knowledgeable about their *own* situations. Few understand the tradeoff of shortages for inflation, few realize the extremely high (and regressive) reabsorption of purchasing power through the hidden 'turnover tax'. Few, in sum, understand how the system taxes its subjects, taxes away what it has 'given'.

The exigencies of working-class life, finally, impose somewhat restricted frames of reference and time on workers as participants in politics. Given the presocialist political cultures of most of Eastern Europe, and the experience in the thirty-five years since World War II, it is not patronizing to note that workers have shown less concern with the intelligentsia's agenda of dissent – civil liberties, freedom to travel, to publish, etc – than with bread-and-butter issues. Material grievances can be, and have been, accommodated by regimes, often swiftly, when disorder arose – 'cooling' the situation until the next crisis. These episodic material concessions, however, limit workers' motivation to settle into the long fight, the protracted struggle, and help give worker protest its own episodic, short-lived quality. While most intelligentsia have been 'bought off" by a combination of job security and material rewards, the *dissident* intelligentsia's demands are not subject to easy accommodation, nor so time-bounded that concessions offered would automatically lead to a moderation or cessation of political activity.

Thus, working-class liabilities are considerable. They would weigh heavily in an *open* political system; they do so all the more in systems whose design excludes spontaneous participation, and whose leaders are committed to maximizing control and monopolizing effective political power. The range of tolerance-to-repression is a wide one in Eastern Europe. Yugoslavia's 'openness' is unique, as are its economic and political designs. Poland and Hungary are 'liberal' – the former more through the sheer difficulty of maintaining control over the feisty mix of church, mass nationalism and an eternally belligerent intelligentsia than through any regime leanings; the latter because Kadar's deft political and economic management is complemented by a popular response, which itself has showed consciousness of the utility of moderation. Czechoslovakia remains repressive, its regime designed to contain the elements of a political culture incompatible with state socialism, and prevent even at high cost the repeat of the 1968 experience. Romania and Bulgaria also cluster at the repressive end of the continuum. But for all the differences, it should be noted that 'liberalism' perceived in any of these states is defined by the negative reference point of the Soviet Union. All are illiberal, repressive by any West European standard, and thus in all any independent assertion of power by workers is a matter of uphill struggle, a fight where challengers to the current order are likely to be overmatched.

Action Direct and Indirect

How has the balance between workers' resources and liabilities been struck in action? The answer – general as it must be given space-constraints here and the more than thirty-year period of worker socialist regime relations – has two aspects: first, touching those actions emerging from and remaining essentially of the workers, and secondly, referring to those actions where workers have operated in concert with other groups (primarily the intelligentsia).

Direct worker action has ranged from the smallish in scale – many of these remaining largely unknown outside the country or area of their occurrence – to the 'high points' of their involvement in Berlin (1953), Plzen, Poznan (1956), Budapest (1956), the Polish outbreaks of 1970 and 1976, and the Jiu Valley miners' strike in Romania in 1977. Many of these have involved spontaneous protests on economic issues. 'Speedups' via an upward-ratcheting of work norms threatened real incomes of workers, or changes in the price structure of everyday consumption items jeopardized living standards. Reactions to these, in turn, have ranged from factory sitdown strikes to street riots, from swift, episodic and almost-wholly unorganized actions to those more lengthy, wherein committee structures have emerged to negotiate with leaders local and national.

Not *all,* however, have been simply economic in their base – some of the worker militancy in Poland in 1956, for example, and also in Hungary in the same year, emerged and simultaneously took on a political character only as they became linked to *national* agendas against Soviet domination. In the 'reform' of Czechoslovakia of 1968, worker support – moderate in the early period of the reform movement, since the economic package of the reformers seemed to threaten as much as it promised workers in the economic sphere – only took on the character of politicized direct action after the Soviet invasion. Indeed, instances of worker–intelligentsia coordination (as opposed to parallel anti-regime action) seem in general to have arisen in response to real or threatened Soviet intervention to restore a 'balance' in favor of unpopular regimes destabilized by social forces beyond their control (Connor, 1980, pp. 5–6, 17).

The history of worker action also encompasses important elements of change in the composition of the industrial blue-collar world and the underlying nature of regime–worker understanding of their mutual relationship. The early postwar periods – those of coalition or 'popular front' governments in most states and policies of economic reconstruction – saw the survivors of the old prewar working class making up the new. In Czechoslovakia, this amounted to a large, experienced proletariat used to 'politics' in a competitive sense — though heavily under communist influence. In Hungary and Poland, much smaller old proletariats, heavily affected by the war, re-emerged. The Balkans, of course, boasted little by way of a recognizable working class or stratum at all.

This situation changed rapidly, as the industrialization drives inundated the surviving 'core' of seasoned industrial workers with a massive inflow of new factory recruits from the peasantry – recruits whose level of political consciousness, whose attitudes toward the new industrial environment, and whose traditional modes of relating to authority (patron–client relations and bribery) little disposed them toward political action of a 'classic' proletarian sort. Whatever political intelligence and capacity for action survived among the experienced workers was overcome by the readiness of regimes to resort to coercion during the period of rapid industrialization, and by the peasant influx – a 'labor draft', cushioned from the general fall of living standards in this period of high investment rates and beggarly distribution by their move from the uncertain countryside to the better rewards of working life in the factories, and to the urban world hitherto seemingly closed to them (Connor, 1977).

Thus, tendencies toward worker rebellion underwent some moderation. The new working *mass,* albeit heavily pressured in the earlier 1950s, was *not* a working *class* – it had been assembled too swiftly, from the 'wrong' components, to coalesce into a conscious, interest-seeking collectivity against managers, bogus trade union bosses, and the regime at large. The outbursts of the early 1950s left little or no organizational heritage. Suppressed and defused in various ways in the GDR, Czechoslovakia and Poland, they were also easier to contain because the mass social mobility which saw peasants enter the working class also saw many ambitious workers and their sons, who might have provided leadership for their class in a different situation, co-opted into the white-collar managerial-administrative world – and ready to use the rhetoric of the 'workers'·state' against the workers.

However, East Europe's working strata have been, since the late 1950s or early 1960s, moving away from this pattern. The new workers of today are fewer, year by year, since the peasant labor pool is largely exhausted and in any case declining rates of industrial growth demand smaller increments to the working class. Those new workers are, increasingly, sons (and daughters) of workers. Hereditary recruitment has become more common as mobility out of the working class has slowed, with the stabilization of the status advantages of socialist elites and their inheritance by their offspring. Over the long term, then, the trend is toward a more hereditary working class, wherein the young cannot look toward solving status problems on an individual basis through mobility – as many did in the past – but instead face the prospect of achieving satisfactory rewards *as* workers: the beginning, at least, of 'class consciousness', and politically important in so far as it translates itself into action.

This changing working class, whose composition departs with each year further from the 'yesterday's peasants' image familiar to analysts in and out of Eastern Europe, is also a partner of sorts in a 'social contract' agreed upon in various states at different times, still valid in those countries where it has been reached, but subject to increasing strain in the years to come. Its terms are specifiable at a rather general level. The 'people', but workers most specifically, will forswear political challenge and organized expression of discontent, will work (regularly if not always well), and generally remain quiet. The regime, in turn, undertakes to avoid broad-scale terror or coercion in everyday administration, and promises to provide (and to take credit for) moderate but steady increases in the living standard, secure employment, and to shield workers from the psychological status consequences of a too-evidently differentiated reward system which would underline the disadvantages of this 'leading class'.

It was not always in effect. It has been broken on the regime's side, from time to time, by the 'drift' of central investment policies. It has barely been reached in some states. Still, it is a critical element in worker–regime relations, and to its fate are tied the probabilities of direct worker action in the 1980s.

Without distorting history too much, one can probably find the social contract first in Czechoslovakia – where Novotny's rule fell harshly indeed on intellectuals and 'nationalists', 'cosmopolitans', etc., but where workers were exalted rhetorically and compensated economically by Eastern Europe's most egalitarian economy. The large working class benefited from this, and the early date of the contract was facilitated by a well-developed economy which allowed the regime to 'make good' on its side of the bargain.

Poland and Hungary – cases of 'medium underdevelopment', with initially small working classes – showed a different pattern. In the former, the 'contract' dates, really, from the latter period of the Gomulka honeymoon after the Polish October of 1956 – perhaps 1958 – when it became clearer which concessions of the immediate postcrisis period would remain, and which (active workers' councils in the factories, for example) would be gradually dismantled by the regime. In Hungary, Nagy's post-Stalin New Course offered a broad contract, victimized by the byplay of Kremlin and Budapest politics in the 1953–6 period. The 1956 débâcle eliminated all hope of a renegotiation until 1961, when Kadar implied the broad terms of the one which remains in force today with the statement 'he who is not against us, is with us'.

In the Balkans, Yugoslavia's contract remains unique – so unique that its pattern and terms deserve a separate consideration we must forgo here. In historically underdeveloped Bulgaria and Romania, but especially in the latter, it is not clear that one has, in the sense of the earlier discussion, yet been 'negotiated'. Bulgaria remains quiescent, accepting its rather profitable 'market-garden' role within CMEA (as it did once before in the Ottoman Empire), orthodox politically and close culturally to the Soviet Union. But in Romania, alone among the states considered here, the rhetoric of sacrifice today for the benefit of one's children and grandchildren, long abandoned elsewhere, remains. In place of the 'social contract' in conventional terms, Ceausescu has imposed stern discipline, short rations and a personality cult, but compensated the population by offering the psychic rewards of a strident nationalism and 'independence' from the Soviet Union. In its formation, the Romanian working class is perhaps a phase behind the Polish and Hungarian, heavier in ex-peasants, and thus not yet as acclimated to the sorts of demands its counterparts elsewhere express. But the Jiu Valley events of 1977 – among a relatively well-paid group of workers – signal for perhaps the first time that Ceausescu's formula is losing its potency, that economic demands are moving toward center-stage.

The social contract, of course, represents a *secularization* of the legitimacy claims of the East European socialist regimes – but does not insulate regime–worker relations from strains of two sorts. The first is the 'cyclical' character of compromise between 'doctrinal' growth goals and consumption pressure in the socialist economies, most manifest, in the estimation of one analyst (Mieczkowski, 1978), in Poland. The Soviet-style 'heavy metal' bias of socialist economic planning, and consequent favoring of reinvestment over consumption, generates low living standards and dissatisfaction. Disorder results, and (the first time) 'social contracts' are offered, grudgingly, in crisis situations. Amelioration of wages and consumer goods stabilizes the situation, economic activity picks up; more absolute funds may even become available for reinvestment, but represents a declining *percentage* of national income. The state looks with concern at such figures, and, reassured by evident stability, turns the screw toward depression of consumption and increase in investment, since it still regards 'personal consumption as a *cost* of growth rather than the ultimate goal of growth' (Zielinski, 1973, pp. 43, 40). This violates the contract, leading to worker reaction – as in Poland in 1970 and 1976 – especially when changes in price and subsidy mechanisms represent the visible leading-edge of a change in economic course. As long as the strong doctrinal reservations remain, in most East European states, to treating consumption as the ultimate rationale of production, the cyclical strain on the social contract will recur as well.

The other strain – of a different sort, and not one to detain us here – is connected with regime moves, 'pushed' by generally pessimistic economic diagnosis, toward market-type reforms. Though of generally less than a wholesale or consistent sort, such reform programs have demanded profitability at the factory level, more efficient work, a closer tying of reward to performance and output at the individual level – all of which threaten what workers see as valuable elements of the social contract. The costs come in the short term; the rewards (of a more productive, affluent economy with more to distribute) are located in the more remote future. Violent worker reaction has not followed the announcement of reform *programs,* which rarely seem to reach reality in anything like original form (whereas price increases are provocative, simple announcements). But coolness toward these economic designs is a characteristic reaction, as noted above in the case of Czech workers in 1968; in this sense, workers can exercise a certain considerable 'braking' influence on the process of introducing even benign alterations in the social contract.

Maintenance of the social contract will grow even harder for regimes in the 1980s. The economic slack available in earlier years when manpower and capital could be treated as plentiful, and Soviet-supplied energy was cheap, is gone. The future is bleak – as is the present, in a Poland where 1979 recorded -2·0 percent growth. Poland is not unique. Rising energy costs, unfavorable alterations in terms of trade and other factors expose Eastern Europeans not only to stagnating consumption and shortages – familiar enough from a decade ago – but also to the new and unsettling experience of inflation. It will be surprising indeed if the next decade does not see instances, with whatever outcome, of workers directly protesting regime 'non-compliance' with contractual terms it can no longer meet, but is unwilling to revise with respect to the demand that workers forswear organized protest.

Direct action, however, does not exhaust the manifestations of workers' power. Indeed, the whole texture of socialist industrial life reveals the sort of power constantly exercised by the workers in a non-direct way – not so much to improve conditions, as to guarantee that they do not worsen.

In an unorganized but rather unanimous way, workers have limited their 'contribution' to the state-owned economy by a slow rhythm of work – one among the causes of low labor productivity in the socialist economies. At the factory level, disagreement over the social contract's concrete terms arises when managers – truly men in the middle – attempt occasionally to speed up work in response to downward pressures. Workers respond to the threat by further absenteeism, simulating compliance through 'faster' work which produces an excess of reject goods, and other forms of sabotage and withholding of effort (see Haraszti, 1978).

In many industries, workers' low in-factory effort and productivity reflects a husbanding of energy for work outside the state sector. The worker who 'moonlights' in the service–repair sector of the 'second' economy contributes to the economy, but at the same time asserts a certain amount of power: that conferred by his particular skill or access to materials/facilities which allows him to operate in the *market* as well as in the non-market state sector of the economy. It may well be that on the whole workers *are* dependent on the insulation statist-planned economies provide them *from* the disciplines and uncertainties of the market – and are thus unlikely allies for reformers whose aim is further efficiency and differentiation of reward via marketization (Bauman, 1974). But this in no way precludes a rational, opportunistic participation at the same time in an illegal but tolerated labor market, where the ability to charge what one's skills will command generates the higher return per hour of work. Workers' 'market position' differs here depending on branch of industry and function – some are better placed than others, having a specialty of the assembly–repair sort that allows the development of maintenance skills saleable to those with broken plumbing or appliances, and access to necessary spare parts. But a huge number, in one fashion or another, find a way to participate, insuring themselves against complete state-sector control. The power workers assert here has several components: their own 'marketability', the demand for various 'second' economy services by a population ill-served by the state sector, and the state's recognition of its own inefficiency in the service area and unwillingness to use sufficient coercion to bring this economic activity under control.

A related but distinct element of worker–regime relations is the victimization of enterprises via theft. The rather massive 'inventory shrinkage' in factories is attributable partially to goods being rechanneled as raw material into the shadow service sector, and partially to simple theft for use or resale. In either case, the practice is common, the workers' attitude toward such activity tolerant. The quantum of repression necessary to prevent such theft is evidently too high – since the practice is so massive and involves a group whose morale must be kept above a critical minimum – to be seriously contemplated.

Theft of this sort is hardly an articulate political statement, but it does reflect political and economic costs the state incurs through a combination of political dogma and practice. Sole or near-sole proprietors of the national wealth, socialist regimes have made themselves ready victims of those who have no other source to steal from, and who can rationalize their behaviour ('He who steals not from the state, steals from his family'; 'They pretend to pay us, and we pretend to work') in a populist fashion, with a touch of redistributive rhetoric. The gap between real status and idealized status as 'leading class', the politicization of welfare issues when the state is governor, sole employer, and welfare agency all in one, and the appeal of redistribution from an impersonal, distant employer/controller ('What belongs to the state, belongs to no one'), all promote such behaviour among workers. The state, facing the problem of numbers, discipline and morale, can do little to decisively alter it.

Prospects for Power: the Future

Some of the present patterns – especially the more 'apolitical' forms of action just described – will clearly persist into the indefinite future. More organized, politicized varieties of protest face less certain prospects.

Independent, organized action is, thus far, in its infancy. 'Free trade unions', established in Poland and Romania, are a striking form of such activity. These are, of course, 'mass organizations' only in potential – at the present phase, they represent the only sort of organizational initiative which workers have taken. Their nature – recognizing the existence of inherent conflict between socialist workers and socialist 'owners' – is itself important as an element of demystification of the nature of worker–regime economic and political relations. There is, no doubt, something 'utopian' about the formation of interest-articulating organizations, according to a free-society model, where regimes exclude such bodies as *de facto* unnecessary, and therefore subversive. Trade unions faced a long struggle toward legitimacy in Western market systems as well, a fact not to be underestimated – but the dissident free unionists in Eastern Europe operate under political game rules aimed against *all* unofficial organization, and in an environment which *provides* trade unions of a non-independent sort, presented as serving the workers' legitimate interests.

Repression has been decisive and harsh against worker activists. In Poland, Kazimierz Switon and others have been tried on various *criminal* charges, intimidated in extrajudicial ways, and generally faced a different response than many dissident intellectuals whose recurrent forty-seven half-hour confinements have become regular parts of their lives. This is espcially true of trade union activities, but in general workers who get a 'ringleader' label in the context of militant action are high-probability candidates for stern measures. In Romania, concessions were granted the Jiu Valley miners, but a surgical repression of those identified by the regime as 'organizers' followed. The probability of similar action has no doubt helped limit any positive workers' response to the Charter 7.7 group in Czechoslovakia.

None of this at all precludes further outbursts of worker militancy touched off by discrete events – the most typical scenario of protest. But evidence thus far strongly suggests that episodic uprising and violence is 'manageable', and does *not* readily convert itself into more stable organizational forms suited to long-run struggle. The most striking fact emerging in a thirty-five-year review of workers' political activity in Eastern Europe, even allowing for the massive coercive resources of the regime, is how little organized activity there has been.

If workers acting alone have accomplished little of a lasting sort, what are the prospects for collaboration between this most numerous and potentially powerful group, and the better-organized dissident intelligentsia, whose activity has been less episodic? One may make optimistic projections, and construct a future view of sustained worker activism with intelligentsia guidance and support, though not control. But in doing this, one assumes away a number of problems important enough to make such projections extremely questionable.

A large gap still separates the concerns and perspectives of workers and intelligentsia. Not even the initiatives of the KOR in Poland in the period immediately after the 1976 events – so different from the do-nothing, faintly contemptuous attitude of the intelligentsia in the wake of the 1970 crisis – have generated a sufficient worker–intelligentsia bridge to sustain any large-scale working-class organization or commitment. The intelligentsia is inclined to take a long-term perspective, to analyze, to seek inter-relationships, to place reform in a broad context of political and economic measures. Their day to day 'bread-and-butter' concerns are, obviously, of a less pressing nature than those of the workers, and their relations to *power* are more ambiguous. The workers' very real, and at any given point primarily *economic* concerns, do not in general find expression in questions about the linkage of economic problems to the nature of the political system. Hence, the economic reform proposals with which workers have come to connect reformist intelligentsia have often been unattractive to workers. The combination of political liberalization and, typically, greater industrial discipline and differentiation of reward does not seem a 'necessary' one to workers (1) not ready to connect their economic grievances to the political *system* (as opposed to the perceived performance of individual leaders), and (2) likely to perceive the burdens of the 'short-run' early reform period as falling particularly upon *them*.

Thus, while recognition of the legitimacy of workers' economic grievances as ground for political action, and endorsement of trade union action as a fitting response (as opposed to earlier concentration on 'workers' council' schemes) says something positive about the widening political and ideological perspectives of the intelligentsia, it has not been sufficient to build a worker–intelligentsia coalition, *nor* to set into motion self-sustaining organizational activity among the workers: either of which would provide possibilities of converting workers' potential power into real ability to exert pressure on regime decisions and activity.

To leave the matter here, though, would be to ignore two longer-term factors, mentioned earlier, whose operations may conduce to greater worker power, or (equally significant) diminution of regime power.

First, the continuing trend toward a hereditization of the working class draws attention to the changing perspectives with which workers must view regime performance. To expect a mass of ex-peasants in factories and construction sites to act as a *class,* is to expect too much. The large number of recent arrivals from the countryside, *and* the upward exit of many experienced workers to administrative work, kept the working population fluid. These factors no longer operate on the scale of the past, and the increasing working-class inheritance rate guarantees that more and more workers will view their rewards and demands from the perspective of urbanites used to factory life. The working *stratum* can, slowly, become a 'class', and with this, become more demanding and hard to satisfy. Such a process of conversion is a long-term one; classes are not made overnight. The process described here, the product of declining mobility rates, is not completed – in some limited measure, regime policies *can* retard it. Analytically, we may be posing questions about the (lack of) workers' political action too soon.

But, secondly, it is not too soon to note that Eastern Europe's grim economic prospects raise the specter of regimes' declining powers to honor their side of the 'social contract' with the workers. The multiple woes of the overcentralization critically affect the ability of these economies to respond to the new problems of soaring energy costs, labor shortage and mounting hard-currency debt. 'Designed' to run on a diet of cheap energy, plentiful resources, abundant labor supply in a context of isolation from the cyclical swings of Western and world markets, they now live in a world less favorable in the supply of factors of production, and are more enmeshed in relationships with Western economies.

Eastern Europeans have long known shortages – but have, overall, seen significant increases in their living standards over the past decades. Expectations have risen (though *not* in a revolutionary manner), and, though the shortages now affect less critical items, they are still present. Some of the more affluent life enjoyed in the better-developed East European states emerged with the general process of economic growth out of poverty, and political adjustments made in favor of consumption. More recently, a good deal has depended upon imports of Western plant and finished goods. The debt incurred is large, the prospects for continuing imports at anything like the levels of the early mid-1970s quite remote for controlling *consumption* is once again a central problem, from the viewpoint of economic planners and regime leaders – this new countertrend promises rough times ahead, as heavy price subsidies are reduced on various items to redirect and restrict the habits socialist consumers have developed over the last ten to fifteen years.

What socialist workers face in the future, may well be the volatile and quite unfamiliar *combination* of shortages *and* inflation, as low-growth economies retrench. There will be, of course, attempts to 'cushion' these effects, especially for the blue-collar stratum. But it will be difficult to find the maneuvering room to do much cushioning. Food, fuel, clothing all grow more expensive – a price rise or cutoff of *luxury* items generally not consumed by workers will not suffice to assure that average workers' wages will buy a satisfactory share of life's necessities. Not all the socialist economies have these problems at the same level of intensity; not all populations have a history of reaction similar, say, to that of the Poles. But it is clear that the regimes face increasing difficulties in honoring their guarantees to the population. From this may come, in the 1980s, hitherto undreamt-of levels of unrest, exacerbating problems of internal political stability. Whether growing class consciousness and the economic weakness of regimes will deal workers more political power, what organizational forms (if any) that power may assume, and what the consequences will be for the regimes and their Soviet guarantor, are perhaps the most important questions the East European states will face in the next decade.

Notes: Chapter 8

The opinions and conclusions expressed in this chapter are the author's, and not expressions of US government policy or positions.

References: Chapter 8

Bauman, Zygmunt, 'Officialdom and class: bases of inequality in socialist society', in *The Social Analysis of Class Structure* (London: Tavistock, 1974), pp. 129–48.

Connor, Walter D., 'Social change and stability in Eastern Europe', *Problems of Communism,* vol. 26, no. 6, 1977, pp. 16–32.

Connor, Walter D., 'Dissent in Eastern Europe: a new coalition?', *Problems of Communism,* vol. 29, no. 1, 1980, pp. 1–17.

Haraszti, Miklos, *A Worker in a Worker's State* (New York: Universe, 1978).

Konrad, George, and Szelenyi, Ivan, *The Intellectuals on the Road to Class Power* (New York: Harcourt, Brace, Jovanovich, 1979).

Mieczkowski, Bogdan, 'The relationship between changes in consumption and politics in Poland', *Soviet Studies,* vol. 30, no. 2, 1978, pp. 262–9.

Rakovski, Mark (pseudon.), *Towards an East European Marxism* (New York: St Martin's Press, 1978).

Staniszkis, Jadwiga, 'On some contradictions of socialist society: the case of Poland', *Soviet Studies,* vol. 31, no. 2, 1979, pp. 167–87.

Zielinski, Janusz G., *Economic Reforms in Polish Industry* (London: Oxford University Press, 1973).

9 Observations on Strikes, Riots and Other Disturbances

J. M. MONTIAS

Introduction

This chapter was written before the Polish workers' strikes of July and August 1980, which forced the government to make substantive concessions on wages and working conditions, trade union representation and human rights. No part of the chapter has been revised in the light of these recent events. Most of the tentative observations that follow, based on newspaper reports, relate the events to points made in the article.

(1) The strikes were again triggered off by the government's decision to raise meat prices (through the transparent device of supplying meat in large measure to 'commercial shops' selling at higher prices).

(2) The authorities repeatedly attempted to divide the workers by offering special concessions (on working conditions and food supplies) to limited groups. This strategy was defeated by the rapid spread of information throughout the country which prompted workers in factories or regions that had not received concessions to demand matching advantages. By the partial concessions that it made, the government revealed its weakness and encouraged the spread of strikes.

(3) In Lublin, where transportation workers struck in mid-July, strikers' demands included a rise in hourly wages to compensate for the price increases, a fourfold increase in family allowance to match the allowances given to members of the police, the security and armed forces, and the closing of the 'special' (restricted-access) butcher shops (*Le Figaro,* 17 July 1980). These demands, as in 1970–71 and 1976, reflected the workers' angry opposition to politically rooted inequalities. About the same time, workers in Lublin began to negotiate for trade union autonomy. This marked the usual progression from economic to sociopolitical demands. This progression continued after the strikes broke out in the shipyards of Szczecin and Gdansk when trade union autonomy became a major subject of negotiations with the Warsaw authorities.

(4) The railroad conductors' strike of mid-July marked the first time that an important work stoppage had gone beyond an industrial factory, a mine, or a construction site. The spread of strikes to many towns and to industries where they had not occurred in the past, suggests that the risks of

forming a coalition had diminished. Almost any group of workers could now organize themselves to press for their claims. An estimated 347 factories, employing 150,000 workers, participated in the strikes in mid-August, and some 300,000 in the last days before the settlement in Gdansk. The strikes in the mining districts of southern and western Poland, which began at the end of August and were settled on 2 September, took in about 250,000 workers in thirty-one mines and twenty-seven related industries.

(5) Workers voiced their demands in the relative sanctuary of factories and other workplaces, avoiding street demonstrations which might have resulted in uncontrolled violence (as they did in all previous upheavals). By maintaining strict order, by disavowing any intent of subverting the socialist order or the ultimate authority of the party, and by applying graduated rather than brusque or sudden pressure, the strikers denied the government any pretext (or motive) for resorting to force. They also reduced the risk of Soviet intervention.

(6) As in 1970–71, communication among workers in plants of the same city and among cities was essential for the instigation and the spread of strikes. The KOR played a major role in disseminating information throughout the country about the workers' demands. The KOR-gathered information was also relayed to the country via Radio Free Europe, which retained its credibility by the moderate tone and objectivity of its broadcasts. In mid-August the government tried to put a stop to the dissemination of news about the strikes in Szczecin and Gdansk by cutting off telephone communications with the rest of the country. A few days before the settlement of the strike, under heavy pressure from the workers, the government finally restored communications with the Baltic coast.

(7) There was no major split in the party leadership as there had been in 1956 and, to a lesser extent, in 1970. However, the pressure of events flushed out major differences among influential members holding divergent attitudes on economic reforms, the advisability of resorting to force, and the possibility of breaking the party's monopoly of power in the domain of labor relations. These personal divergences made it possible for Gierek to introduce personnel changes in the government without serious damage to party unity. No faction developed, as far as we know at present, which either urged the Soviets to intervene or covertly supported the workers against the government.

(8) The KOR was remarkably successful in establishing links with the workers, who, in turn, applied pressure on the government to release members of the group who had been arrested in the second week of August. Even though links between workers and intellectuals are still fragile, definite progress toward a rapprochement – if not an alliance – has been made, which will undercut any attempts at reimposing the party's exclusive domination over socioeconomic and intellectual life.

(9) The question in everyone's mind now is whether the government will be able to emasculate the agreement signed on 31 August by whittling away at its individual provisions. While authorities may try to fudge on certain concessions – that 'the media will be open to varied opinions' or that censorship will be limited to the protection of 'defense, economic and

diplomatic secrets' – the new freedom to engage in independent self-governing union activity is likely to give the organized workers an instrument for maintaining this and other gains. For, as long as the workers can freely communicate with each other, across ministerial jurisdictions and regional boundaries, in the framework of an organization of their own making, the costs of mounting a coalition to strike, in case the government rescinded its promises, will presumably be much reduced compared to similar efforts in the past. The threat of such a strike must surely put a restraint on the ability of the party to withdraw its concessions. On the other hand, the right to communicate freely within the organization cannot be abolished without a major struggle. This time around, in my view, the government has run out of moves. Short of Soviet intervention, which does not appear to be an attractive option either for the Kremlin, or for the Polish party leaders, in the foreseeable future, I do not see how the *status quo ante* can be restored. Some of the strikers' hard-won gains will surely endure.

September 1980

1   A Framework for Analyzing Disturbances

Significant disturbances in communist countries happen only rarely. The sample that we have available to analyze their incidence is so small, and the number of possible explanatory variables so large, that statistical analyses cannot fruitfully be applied to ascertain the relative importance of various causative factors. We must rather be content to isolate plausible connections, to develop simple conjectures relating observed conditions and their presumed effects, mindful that these propositions cannot be rigorously tested at the present time.

The disturbances that make up our small sample are these: Pilsen (Czechoslovakia), June 1953; Berlin, June 1953; Poznan (Poland), June 1956; Budapest, October 1956; Novocherkassk (Soviet Union), June 1961; Warsaw, March 1968; Szczecin–Lodz (Poland), December 1970–January 1971; Radom–Ursus (Poland), June 1976; Jiu Valley (Romania), August 1977. Out of these nine major disturbances, all but two – Budapest (1956) and Warsaw (1968) – had their origin in economically motivated work stoppages.

The explanatory variables that are discussed to a varying extent in this chapter may conveniently be divided into two sets. The first set is intended to capture the proximate causes of disturbances and why they spread or failed to spread; the second focuses on the response of the authorities. The first set includes: (1) economic policies or unanticipated outcomes of policies giving rise to grievances (currency reform, increases in retail prices, revision of labor productivity norms, conscription of workers to work on weekends and holidays, food shortages); (2) violations of governmental promises other than those pertaining to prices and norms (failure to pay promised overtime and bonuses; failure to honor the promise that individuals responsible for a disturbance will not be prosecuted); (3)

possibilities of forming effective coalitions to voice grievances (type of workplace, facilities available to strikers or rioters for diffusing information, cohesiveness of groups). Among the explanatory variables in the second set may be listed: (1) political conditions in the ruling party (divided or solidary leadership, sympathy or antipathy of individual party members for the aspirations of strikers or other dissatisfied groups); (2) the attitude of Soviet leaders to a disturbance which may affect Soviet strategic interest; (3) constraints on the government's use of force to re-establish order (pressure or absence of other loci of power such as a church hierarchy commanding the loyalty of a substantial fraction of the population; a free or a collectivized peasantry; a reliable or an unreliable army).

One way to articulate the relations among these variables is to model the interaction among participants as a game played by two sets of players: (1) individuals, dissatisfied with governmental or party policies, intent on bringing about peaceful or forcible change favorable to their interests, and (2) power-holders wishing to maintain orderly communist rule. Each set of individuals has strategies available to it. Dissatisfied individuals, for instance, may strike or not strike to bring about the improvement they desire. Power-holders may choose to repress a strike by force, extend concessions, or do both, to varying extents. If we look at the power relations between the two sets of individuals as a game in 'extensive form' – a series of moves and countermoves – then it becomes important to understand how the history of previous moves may affect the bargaining situation at later moves. Thus, a country's historical record of rebellions and upheavals, sometimes going back 100 years or more, will affect the choice of strategies open to the power-holders.

In the next two sections of the chapter, observations, most of them based on anecdotal evidence, on the strikes and riots that have occurred in communist countries since the death of Stalin are very loosely organized and discussed in the general framework presented in this first section. Section 2 concentrates on the economic variables that motivate dissenters, Section 3 on the problem of forming effective coalitions under conditions where the power-holders have a monopoly of information media.

2   Economic Conditions and Political Disturbances

Because so many variables interact to produce a single observable action, any attempt to place the entire burden of causation on any one variable is likely to fail. Take, for example, the relation between changes in living standards in Eastern Europe and the incidence of strikes and riots. The statistical correlation between the two, if other political variables cannot be held constant, may easily yield a sign opposite to that which common sense would lead us to expect. There were no riots in the early 1950s when real wages were falling throughout most of Eastern Europe. They began to crop up, starting in 1953, when consumption rose in the wake of the New Course (East Berlin and Pilsen in June 1953; Poznan in June 1956). True, the Szczecin events of late 1970 and early 1971 followed upon a period of four or five years of stagnating or possibly even declining real wages. But then again, the Radom–Ursus strikes and riots of June 1976 came about after five years of unprecedented improvements. Clearly, a more detailed, disaggregated analysis is in order, if we wish to isolate the critical factors associated with these popular disturbances and begin to understand how certain conjunctions of these factors may start a conflagaration.

The fact that no meaningful statistical correlation can be found between changes in average real wages and the incidence of strikes and riots should not lead us to underestimate the importance of popular dissatisfaction with living standards as a basic moving force in the complex sociopolitical process that sometimes eventuates in a riot. We need only read the detailed accounts of any riot in Eastern Europe or the Soviet Union to persuade us that dissatisfaction with economic conditions is the prime force behind the popular defiance of governmental authority. Strictly political demands come only after a revolt has gained momentum. One reason for the salience of economic demands is that they are safer for dissatisfied elements in the population to articulate without immediate repression than political ones. Another is that the workers who initiate the strikes that in many cases trigger off popular riots are particularly sensitive to any deterioration in their living standards (and tend to react to such deterioration far more emotionally than they would to the suppression of a newspaper or to the arrest of dissidents, assuming these political events ever came to their attention).

Workers and the population at large, for good and valid reasons, hold the party and the government responsible for changes in the level of consumer goods prices. The nature of the bureaucratic economic system is such that these prices tend to stay more or less at the same level for several years until the authorities find themselves compelled to alter them, at which time discontinuous jumps are often unavoidable, given the pursuit of the government's economic goals. (The alternative would be to scale down investments and increase imports of consumer goods at the expense of producer goods – a price that the leadership is not usually willing to pay.) Work norms are left unchanged for several years. As a result of the introduction of labor saving machinery, they get to be overfulfilled by wide margins. When the authorities finally tighten them up, workers are likely to suffer a sudden loss in their take-home pay. The discontinuous nature of these changes concentrates and sharpens discontent, which may then erupt in the form of strikes and riots in the period immediately following the announcement of an increase in prices or the revision of work norms. Whether or not discontent spills over into riots, depends on a number of social and political factors which will now be surveyed.

As was noted above, every move in the game pitting power-holders against dissatisfied elements in the population (who are likely to make up a majority) is affected by the consciousness in the minds of both sets of players of the history of previous moves. In Eastern Europe, the historical sequence begins at least as early as the Hungarian revolution of 1848 and the Polish revolts of 1830 and 1863. It also comprises the Warsaw uprising of 1944.[1] The memory of each such event – its success or its failure – affects the consciousness of participants in a contemporary situation, even though the cases and circumstances of the earlier event may be very different from one more recent. In Poland, both the potential rioters and the government know that many uprisings have occurred in the past and that their repression is costly and difficult and may be hazardous to the political survival of those who must see to it that they are put down. The relative success of the January 1971 strike in Szczecin, which forced the rescinding of the price increases decreed in December 1970, gave workers greater confidence in their potential power and simultaneously lowered the regime's confidence in its ability to take measures inimical to workers' interests. Czechoslovakia (with the anti-German uprising of 1944 and the Pilsen revolt of 1953) and perhaps even Romania (with the Great Peasant Revolt of 1907) have some history of political resistance. Though less flamboyant than Poland's, this tradition probably plays a role in their rulers' calculations. Bulgaria has no history of major uprisings to encourage those who might take arms against their political oppressors. But the consciousness factor cuts both ways. The government also knows that, after a revolt has been neatly and quickly repressed and its instigators severely punished, it may be many years before people gather up the courage to mount a new challenge. The government's promises regarding the redress of the iniquities that led to previous disturbances, and the degree of fulfillment of these promises, are also factors in the dynamic interaction between the governing and the governed that makes each new event a function of all preceding ones.

A riot, of course, represents only one of several possible outcomes of the interaction process that has just been mentioned. It may be headed off or at least rapidly contained by measures of appeasement, reforms, or even a show of party unity and force. A crucial variable here is the effect of economic problems, particularly of plan failures, on the cohesiveness of the ruling party. In 1960–61, the economy of Czechoslovakia underwent a rapid deterioration, manifested chiefly in a balance-of-payments crisis and a catastrophic decline in investment. The party was split by dissension over the causes of the slowdown, some functionaries being of the opinion that it was due to persistent overcentralization (despite the tentative reforms initiated in 1958–9), others arguing that discipline had slackened and the party was losing the reins of control over the economy. There were no riots, perhaps mainly by reason of the decision to shield the population from the effects of the recession, but also because the gradual opening up of public discussion over the causes of the country's economic difficulties gave promise of real reforms that allayed discontent in the population.

Yet, dissension in the party need not produce a period of liberalization-cum-reforms. When dissension is (weakly) repressed from the top, as at the end of the Gomulka period in Poland in the late 1960s, and meaningful reforms are blocked, intraparty feuding may actually create a climate favorable to riots, especially if some faction, like the Moczar group in Poland at the time, believes it is to its advantage to provoke them. The situation in Poland and Hungary in the summer of 1956 was marked by fundamental disunity in the party, which, given the degree of popular dissatisfaction with economic and political conditions and the inability of the divided leadership to launch serious reforms or even to placate the population with any improvements in its levels of living, could only result in a dramatic confrontation. In both countries, important changes in leadership occurred at the end of the summer that basically altered the situation. (The Poles allowed themselves to be taken in by Gomulka's *'équipe de rechange'*, which turned out to be more similar to the team that it replaced than most people had anticipated, while in Hungary the political changes were sufficiently profound to provoke a Soviet invasion.)

The 1976 events in Poland marked the only major popular disturbance in postwar Eastern Europe that coincided neither with a split in the party, nor provoked one. It was also more brutally repressed than most. Once the price increases were rescinded (or, more precisely, once the proposal to increase prices was withdrawn), the party leaders felt no need to make any concession of a political or of an economic nature. There was no faction vying for power within the Polish party that was in a position to court popularity by pressing the placatory measures within the leadership.

A closer look at what actually happened in a few instances where the interaction process between rulers and ruled actually resulted in strikes, riots, or both, may be instructive. I shall focus on five major disorders of clearly economic origin: Pilsen, 1953; Poznan, 1956; Novocherkassk, 1961; Szczecin–Lodz, December 1970–January 1971; and Radom–Ursus, 1976. The first of these began as a workers' protest against a currency reform which in effect confiscated a large part of the population's cash holdings. This upheaval climaxed in the occupation of the town hall of Pilsen by the insurgents, who, for a few days, ran the town.[2] The second disorder (Poznan, 1956) began with a dispute concerning overtime wages, but quickly turned into a violent expression of dissatisfaction over living conditions. The last three disorders were directly provoked by announcements of impending or actual increases in food prices. The Poznan, Novocherkassk and Radom affairs got started in metal-processing factories;[3] the Szczecin strike was staged in the vast shipyards of the city. Shipyards resemble metal-processing factories in that they make lavish use of skilled and semiskilled workers, who, unlike the workers in a more or less automated steel mill or fertilizer plant, control the pace of their own operation.

Before dwelling on these instances, three types of work situations should be cited in passing, which do *not* seem to be conducive to defiance of authority. It is remarkable, first of all, that no peasant revolts have occurred in Eastern Europe despite a history of *jacqueries* in the precommunist past. True, collectivization has not been introduced in Poland, which has the longest and most persistent tradition of popular uprisings, and farming there remains chiefly in private hands. But if such riots were to occur at all in the countryside, one would have expected them to take place during the collectization period of 1959–62 in the rest of Europe, when the peasants were under the greatest pressure. Peasants' resistance, if it has occurred at all, has been passive rather than active, possibly because of the logistic problems of bringing together large numbers of dissatisfied individuals. Secondly, unskilled workers, with the exception of the rather special case of the East Berlin revolt of 1953 which began on construction sites, have not been conspicuous in starting strike movements, perhaps because they are newcomers to a workers' culture, lack any sort of trade union history and feel their new-won workers' status is too precarious to risk a confrontation with the authorities[4]. There is apparently some sociological evidence collected in Poland – so far unpublished – suggesting that unskilled workers are more prone to violence than skilled workers. They may be among the first to go out in the street and join disorderly crowds attacking public buildings, but they do not seem to play a major role in organizing the strike actions that trigger off the subsequent disorders. Finally, almost all recorded cases of strikes occurred in factories dominated by men.[5] Women may protest against higher prices or about shortages, as they did in Poland in early 1975 and in Bucharest in the fall of that year (when meat disappeared from butchers' shops), but their uncoordinated, spontaneous actions do not present the authorities with the serious problems that the strikes of skilled and semiskilled male workers do.

It is remarkable that people do not rise against the authorities in the Soviet Union or in Eastern Europe when food shortages develop but rather when the government introduces price increases designed to 'ration by the purse', that is, to eliminate shortages by forcing consumers to restrict their purchases to the amounts they can afford at these higher prices. This is curious because, as economists have long been taught, rationing by the price system, by cutting down on waste and on the time lost in queuing, may leave consumers better off than if the same amount of sausage or ham had been formally or informally rationed. One reason why workers may be more upset by price increases than by (equivalent) shortages, is that they sense that they personally are more adversely affected by the former than by the latter. In general, rationing benefits the poorer classes of the population as compared with rationing by the purse. However, the incomes of semiskilled and skilled workers, who have been so conspicuous in East European strikes, are close enough to the average that they would not be much worse off in one case than in the other. Another more persuasive reason may be that nationwide price increases (or, for that matter, the general tightening of work norms) are seen as a violation of an overt or tacit social contract between the ruling party, which is supposed to represent the working class, and the workers. (Price reductions on less important items of consumption, instead of mitigating the impact of price increases, are sometimes seen as a mockery, especially if they compensate only to a small extent the increases in the prices of items consumers consider to be essential, including, of course, meat.) The poor timing of price increases may be an additional irritant, as in the case of the price increases decreed just before Christmas of 1970, which were particularly resented by the great majority of Poles who were preparing to celebrate their Christmas holiday.

General price increases cannot be blamed, as shortages can be, on local deficiencies or temporary difficulties. They result from a conscious political act which the workers regard as disloyal, espcially when a public promise has been made by government authorities that no such price increases would take place (as after the January 1971 strikes in Szczecin and Lodz). The sensitiveness of the population to overt inflation may also be heightened by the official propaganda which harps so much on the disastrous effects of inflation in the West and attempts to make political capital (and to derive some measure of legitimacy) from the alleged stability of consumer goods prices in socialist countries.

Other instances are known where the violation of promises triggered off riots. Thus, just prior to the currency reform 1–2 June 1953 in Czechoslovakia, the workers in Pilsen had been assured by party authorities that the currency was 'firm'.[6] The work stoppage began shortly after the announcement of the 'reform' was made.

Workers' demands other than the rescinding of the price increases were put forward by the strikers in 1962 in Novocherkassk and in Poland in 1970–71 and 1976. Some of the most insistent complaints were directed at the manipulation of workers by party authorities behind a façade of trade unionism and labor participation in decision-making. In Novocherkassk, an emulation campaign designed to increase productivity and lower labor costs apparently irritated workers in the large metal-processing factories where the campaign took place shortly before the riots.[7] In Szczecin in January 1971, similarly, a 'voluntary' drive to make up for time lost in the December strike by Sunday labor, which was falsely publicized by the official press as a workers' initiative, played an important contributory role in provoking the second strike on the Polish littoral. The transcript of the strikers' meeting with Edward Gierek of 24 January shows that workers' delegates placed an extraordinary weight on this point, demanding – and eventually obtaining – a retraction on the part of the local press of the false information given out about the allegedly spontaneous character of this action. Another point in common in the Soviet and Polish disturbance of 1962 and 1970 was the workers' dissatisfaction with 'their' trade unions, which were powerless in staying the hand of management bent on increasing productivity at any cost.[8]

The Strike Committee of the largest shipyards in Szczecin headed its list of demands with a simultaneous call for the resignation of the shipyards' trade union committee 'which never came out in the defense of the workers' and for the creation of independent unions 'subordinate to the working class'.[9] The rescinding of the price rise of December 1970, incidentally, was only the second demand on this particular list. Finally, a complaint that transpires through all the accounts of workers' strikes, although it does not always appear in the lists of specific demands addressed to the party authorities, is that the management and the auxiliary bureaucracy that administer production plants and shipyards are inflated in numbers, paid too much in relation to workers, and receive disproportionate benefits in the form of vacations, sick leaves and other privileges.[10] One workers'. representative at the Szczecin shipyards put this issue in ideological terms, claiming that the authorities by creating different working conditions for blue-collar workers and for white-collar employees and management, were artificially segregating people into classes. 'Isn't this class differentiation made from above? Is a white-collar worker different from me?' he asked. [11]

Even though some of the striking workers' demands in 1971 bordered on the political – especially in so far as they dealt with the privileges of the elite – they were not construed as such by the strike representative who claimed, as the twenty-first and last point on their list, that they were eschewing demonstrations of a political or anti-governmental character and that their demands were 'exclusively economic'. [12] However that may be, it is evident both from the formal complaints and from the points formally raised at meetings with officials, that justice and human dignity – including the right to have a say in working conditions and in other pertinent matters – are issues that are virtually as basic to the interests of Polish workers as prices, wages and working hours.

3   The Formation of Coalitions

An issue that came up at the Szczecin shipyards' meeting of 24 January 1971 with Poland's top leaders deserves attention for what it reveals about the problems of organizing a strike action in a situation where strikes, if not technically illegal, are thought to be illegal by the majority of the population and are at the very least discouraged by the government. [13] The problem lies in coordinating plans and lists of demands among thousands of workers employed in different workshops and departments, often spread over a considerable area, when management possesses a monopoly of intercoms, loudspeakers and all other means of communication. A demand voiced by the chairman of the workers' committee was that the committee should have exclusive use of the yard's radio network to get in touch with the crews. On this point, the workers' representative went on to say:

It is our will, the will of the workers of the shipyard as a whole – we must have a microphone. What is involved is information, which must be in our hands, objective information, correct information. [14]

The lack of means of communication isolates shops, crews and working parties from each other and makes it far harder, given the controls on unauthorized personnel movement from one part of the shipyard, factory, or mine, to get in touch with one another, to reach the consensus to launch and to formulate the demands for a strike. The difficulty of transmitting more or less subversive information may throw light on a point raised earlier in this chapter. In a steel mill, an automated chemical factory, a petroleum refinery, or a conveyor belt-driven assembly plant, workers often cannot leave their jobs without jeopardizing the entire operation of the factory. There is far more danger of a plantwide breakdown, which may be termed 'sabotage' by the authorities, in case workers gather together to talk over their problems, than in a labor-paced metal-fabricating factory, a coal mine, or a shipyard, where many workers may take a break from their jobs without seriously affecting the rate of production of the factory as a whole. (If they work on an individually controlled machine or at a mine face, they may make up later the shortfall in their output.) It may then be easier to exchange the information required to mount a strike operation in the latter situation than in the former. This observation on past disturbances gives rise to the conjecture that strikes and other defiant actions are likely to arise in large, labor-intensive and labor-paced enterprises where coalitions can be formed without excessive risk.

The problem of communication has also a wider aspect. Given the government's policy of isolating localities where strikes or other disturbances occur and of preventing the rest of the population from hearing about them, how can strikers make known their demands to the nation at large? It is remarkable that several disturbances in Poland have gotten started in places and under circumstances where it was relatively easy to diffuse the news about these developments *urbis et orbis*. The Poznan events of June 1956 began during the International Fair, at which there were present thousands of Polish and foreign visitors, who could bring out the news about the riots. Word about the Szczecin and Gdansk strikes of 1970 spread quickly, both at home and abroad, carried by sailors and other travelers, who normally move in and out of these littoral cities. Events in Radom and Ursus provide even better evidence of the strikers' concern for diffusing the news about their actions as quickly and widely as possible. Without any apparent prior coordination, the strikers in both places hit upon the idea of interrupting railroad traffic in the vicinity of the factories which they had occupied in order to signal their action to the rest of the nation.

Another demand of the Strike Committee in the Szczecin shipyards with significant ramifications was that members of the Committee should be guaranteed personal safety, presumably from arrest or harassment by the police or by other shipyard authorities responsive to governmental orders. A similar demand was put forward by the striking miners in the Jiu Valley in August 1977. In the Romanian case, Ceausescu promised the miners that there would be no retribution and then reneged on his promise, ordering thousands of dismissals and a number of arrests. Thus, workers' attempts to organize strikes are met by intimidation on the part of the authorities, who are able to discourage any but the most resolute instigators.

Notwithstanding the potential for intimidation on the part of the authorities, workers are in a better position to organize actions in opposition to their rulers than other groups of the population. First, it is ideologically awkward for a workers' party to bar strikes as illegal. Secondly, there is loss of legitimacy whenever a party ruling in the name of the workers is obliged to repress a strike. (It is much easier for a party spokesman to qualify other types of civil disobedience as hooliganism than an orderly strike by workers.) Thirdly, repression of a strike by force when the workers occupy production sites, as has usually been the case in Poland, may cause serious damage to machinery and plant with adverse effect on future output. It is often wiser, therefore, for the authorities to negotiate with strikers than to resort to force. For these reasons, if there is any institution in communist countries which has some of the earmarks of a sanctuary – like the church in the Middle Ages or the university in certain Latin American countries – it is surely the factory or mine.[15]

Spontaneous movements of protest often develop a momentum which carries their participants beyond the bounds of safety. They may get their start in the comparable safety of the factory, but they quickly spill over in the street where they can be more conveniently repressed. It may seem like a good idea at the time to burn down party headquarters, to free political prisoners, or to attack the Ministry of Interior; but it also brings into action violent repression by political armed forces, which do not take very long to restore order. The regime is then in a position to take judicial action against participants – whether active or passive – who are alleged to have violated 'socialist legality', as strikers normally cannot be said to have done. Thus, strikes may be more effective in giving effect to workers' demands if they can be self-contained.

In Poland, the country where the constellation of the forces of power (including the Catholic Church) is such that disturbances are most frequent and most likely to occur in the future, the creation of the Committee for the Defense of Workers (KOR) in September 1976 has widened the strategic options available to protesters in their opposition to the authorities. First, KOR now makes it possible for news about strikes and riots to spread far more quickly than before, a matter that must be of great concern to the government intent on isolating these incidents.[16] Secondly, the committee, using students and other mobile elements in the population to make contact with the workers, can quickly alert strikers to their rights and, thus, harden their will to resist the blandishments of the authorities until their demands have been met. Thirdly, KOR is the first effective link between the workers and the intellectuals. The government and the party may now be simultaneously confronted by the demands of both groups and may find it a good deal more difficult to resist them. Finally, KOR may gradually supply the workers with the elements of an ideology – a set of symbols to which they can relate and with the aid of which they can integrate their experience. This ideology is essentially patriotic, legalistic, socialist and democratic. With its emphasis on legalism, KOR may enable workers to formulate more abstract system-related demands, which would offer strikers and other instigators of disturbances better guarantees of permanent gains (for example, legal guarantees to protect them against reprisals, in contrast to *ad hoc* petitions for safeguards which, when granted, can be withdrawn at the discretion of the authorities). The Catholic Church, which has shifted its ideological ground in recent years from indiscriminate anti-communism to more-nuanced and sophisticated anti-totalitarianism, is now more willing to enter into coalitions with socialists and even with democratically inclined communists in order to support workers' demands than in the past. The new solidarity between the working class and other influential elements in the population, including the Catholic Church, may turn strikes into instruments capable of applying graduated pressure against regime authorities and of extracting fundamental and permanent concessions, perhaps with less danger to the delicate, limited autonomy of Poland under Soviet aegis than the wild outbursts of violence that erupted in the past.

Conclusions

To sum up, very briefly. Poor economic conditions, at least as perceived by workers, have in the past motivated strikes and other protest actions in Poland, and, more rarely, elsewhere. Most of the disturbances were triggered off by perceived violations of promises made by the authorities regarding the conditions of workers (price increases, revision of work norms, confiscatory currency reform). Protest actions frequently got their start in factories and other worksites employing many skilled and semiskilled workers, where the pace of the production process enabled crews to meet to exchange information and voice their complaints. The chances of occurrence of such strikes is much greater if the country has a past history of successful civil protests: if the government is not determined to repress the strike immediately and at any cost (as it would have throughout the communist bloc in the Stalinist period, or as it would in today's Albania), and if the regime is unwilling to make prompt concessions or reforms aimed at pacifying potential insurgents (as is likely to occur in situations where the party is divided). While the primary demands made by strikers are economic, secondary demands regarding workers' participation and representation play an important subsidiary role in the interaction between the authorities and the strikers. Abstract 'system demands' – such as the institution of full-fledged parliamentarianism or the restoration of capitalism – have so far been conspicuous by their absence. Nevertheless, the violent attacks on the headquarters of party, police and other regime institutions that develop in the wake of strikes are a clear expression of wider popular dissatisfaction with the regime than those normally voiced by strikers' representatives, who are perhaps more conscious of the need for prudence and discretion to achieve lasting results.

Notes: Chapter 9

I am indebted to Jan Gross for valuable comments on an earlier draft of this chapter.

1 In the Soviet Union also local traditions of defiance of authority may play a role in the incidence of uprisings. Perhaps the most important postwar riots occurred in Novocherkassk, which was founded in 1805 as the capital of the Don Cossak region and served as the capital of the ephemeral anti-bolshevik Don state during the Civil War period (Albert Boiter, 'When the kettle boils over', *Problems of Communism,* vol. 13, January–February 1964, p. 36). On the relevance of historical rebellions for contemporary Poland, see various articles in *Robotnik* (a 'non-censored' Polish publication), especially no. 20, 30 August 1978, p. 2.

2 Otto Ulc, 'Pilsen: the unknown revolt', *Problems of Communism,* vol. 14, May–June 1965, pp. 46–9.

3 On the Novocherkassk riots, see Albert Boiter, op. cit., pp. 33–43. The best account of the Szczecin strike is contained in *Rewolta Szczecinska i jej znaczenie* (Paris: Instytut Literacki, 1971).

4 According to a *Trybuna Ludu* article of 30 January 1976, managers in the

construction and foundry industry actually prefer unskilled, new immigrants to the city as workers, because they are harder working and less demanding.

5 In February 1971, textile factories with a majority of female employees struck in Lodz. By this time, of course, the ground had been prepared by the December strikes in the shipyards, and the risk that the strikers incurred was probably a good deal smaller than what it had been for those who had initiated the wave of strikes.

6 Ulc, op. cit., pp. 46–7.

7 Boiter, op. cit., p. 37.

8 *Dokumenty: Rewolta Szczecinska*, op. cit., pp. 26, 46; and Boiter, op. cit., p. 37. An anonymous referee for this paper pointed out that complaints about trade unions are 'legal', whereas attacks on the party are considered *de facto* illegal. Hence, some workers may lash out against the trade unions as a proxy for the party apparatus whose actions and policies they are really incensed about.

9 *Dokumenty*, p. 196. At the meeting of the Central Committee of Trade Unions which took place a month later, the delegates of the trade unions of the shipyards laid the blame for this state of affairs on the central economic administration which ignored their demands on behalf of the workers (ibid., pp. 238–46).

10 A fairly typical complaint about the excessive salaries of ministries and directors was expressed by the delegates of Section W-2 of Szczecin shipyards at the meeting with Gierek (*Dokumenty*, p. 82). Demand 13 of the Strike Committee stated that the earnings of the employees of the party and government apparatus should be limited to the average earnings in industry. Demand 14 called for the elimination of the differentials existing between the (privileged) prices charged in (reserved-access) shops of the army and security police and the prices generally prevailing in the country. During the 1976 disturbances in Radom and elsewhere, representatives of the administration were frequently asked why they earned so much more than workers (see, for example, the eye-witness account of the strikes in Radom and Gdansk in *Liberation*, reprinted in *Aneks*, July 1976, pp. 28, 32).

11 *Dokumenty*, p. 103.

12 ibid., p. 197.

13 Several representatives of Strike Committees at the Szczecin meeting of 24 January 1971 seemed unsure whether strikes were or were not illegal, although some of them asserted they were within the law (*inter alia*, ibid., p. 132). The authorities present were careful not to answer the question in unambiguous terms.

14 *Dokumenty*, p. 129.

15 The authorities often have other means beside force to induce strikers to resume work. In a mine at Jastrzeb (Poland), a work stoppage occurred in June 1978 to protest against mandatory twelve-hour shifts on Saturdays. Management stopped all conveyorbelts and the means of transportation that would have enabled the miners to ride back from their workplace to a central elevator shaft. Nevertheless, 80 percent of the miners were said to have made their way to the surface by walking a kilometer or two to the shaft (*Robotnik*, no. 18, 25 June 1978).

16 Thus, it was the KOR which reported a strike that occurred in the summer of 1977 at a light-bulb factory at Podjamice near Lodz. The strikers, incidentally, were successful in compelling the government to restore some bonuses of which they have been deprived (*International Herald Tribune*, 10–11 September 1977).

10 Poland: Workers and Politics

JAN B. DE WEYDENTHAL

Introduction

The main concern of this chapter is the relation between the workers and the political system in contemporary Poland.[1] This concern was prompted by recent manifestations of a successful workers' dissent against the implementation of government policies which would adversely affect their immediate socioeconomic interests. This development provided a sharp contrast to earlier conditions, when the workers found themselves locked into an institutionalized pattern of governmental controls, and when the traditionally egalitarian appeal of the socialist social order appeared to preclude any large-scale politicization of industrial conflicts.

In search of an explanation for this development, perhaps the obvious approach would be to investigate the changing elements of the socioeconomic situation: the changes in the composition and characteristics of the worker population and the sudden fluctuations in economic conditions. This chapter acknowledges the significance of those factors. In addition, however, it draws attention to some important elements of the Polish political situation: the emergence of workers as a distinct, albeit unorganized, political force and the inability of institutionalized leadership groups to integrate the workers into the existing pattern of systematic operations. If these processes were to remain unchanged, the persistent threat of social disruptions could undermine the effectiveness of government operations.

The central proposition presented here is that, although industrial conflicts in Poland tend to generate from economic scarcity and deprivation, it is the structural characteristics of the political system and its *modus operandi* which have provided a crucial factor in fashioning the patterns of the workers' dissent. The form and extent of industrial conflicts, it is argued, appear to have become increasingly perceived by the workers as resulting from the functioning of political structures and the methods of political controls. Their dissent is not seen here as an attempt at revolutionary change which would bring about a fundamental transformation of the system. It is, however, more than a desperate reaction to specific decisions or events. Rather, it is an effort, grounded in occupational solidarity, to influence – directly or indirectly – the direction of policy-making over the issues which affect worker interests.

For purposes of analysis, this investigation uses a conceptual framework suggested by Samuel P. Huntington (1968, 1971). Within this framework, the emphasis was put on the relationship between political participation and political institutionalization as the main determinants of systemic stability. Huntington argues that, in order to maintain an effective government, it is necessary to develop adaptable political institutions capable of channeling and responding to social demands. If the flow of social demands, which lead to the intensification of political participation, outstrips political institutionalization, dissent spreads and systemic decay sets in.

When trying to apply this framework to contemporary Polish politics, the problem is to identify the alterations in political participation that cause modifications in the types of governmental responses to social demands. The discussion focuses on the choices which have to be made by political leadership. An account of political response to workers' demands indicates evolutionary trends within the Polish system.

Workers and Politics: the Institutional Framework

Industrial conflicts in socialist Poland have a history as old as the system itself. To a large extent, they reflected the disruptive consequences of rapid social changes resulting from the processes of massive industrialization through which the country has gone during the last thirty years or so. Usually, those conflicts had a rather amorphous character which made generalizations very difficult. Only in recent years have they shown some signs of being replaced by a new form of collective action, with political overtones and concerned with general aspects of national economic policies.

Widespread manifestations of industrial unrest, which frequently took the form of strikes, were relatively common during 1945–8, the formative years of communist rule. With the gradual establishment of a firm system of political control, the frequency and scope of those upheavals rapidly declined. It was not until June 1956 that a major worker revolt rocked the political system. It generated from specific economic grievances voiced by workers against local management decisions at a large machinery plant in the city of Poznan, but grew to a series of mass demonstrations after the protesting workers were attacked by police units. Following two days of unrestrained violence, the revolt was finally suppressed with the use of a considerable military force. Although the workers' grievances were not immediately satisfied, the brutality of repressive reaction provided a catalyst for a larger movement toward social reforms which eventually led to a comprehensive change in the composition of the leadership and an introduction of new socioeconomic policies. In subsequent years, scattered strikes took place in industrial plants throughout the country. They were, however, easily contained by the government through a series of temporary and localized measures of appeasement.

The principal obstacle to the politicization of workers' protests seems to have come not from the efficacy of suppression, however, but from the government's ability to win the support and participation of workers in its centrally directed program of industrialization. The main source of its appeal was in offering both a comprehensive strategy, and an institutional framework, for attainment of a basically egalitarian social transformation. The widespread acceptance of this objective made the occasional outbursts of workers' dissatisfaction with current material conditions appear like politically marginal incidents related to limited economic and social problems in isolated factories.

A crucial institutional feature of Poland's sociopolitical system has been the dominant role played by the Polish United Workers' Party (PUWP) in all aspects of decision-making activities. Its systemic essence has been the party's self-asserted leadership in goal definition and the setting of directions for society at large. The main practical consequence of this assertion has been the intolerance of any social and political organizations which could compete with the party. Although this has not precluded the very existence of such organizations, it has put them outside the main arena of policy-making and restricted them to essentially supportive functions.

Within this general conceptual framework, the PUWP's relation toward the workers has been characterized by the insistence on their complete subordination to party policies as well as the claim that those policies represent the best interests of the working population. The roots of this claim go back to the Leninist concept of a revolutionary party acting as a *sui generis* vanguard of the proletariat and a custodian of its historical destiny. Its contemporary expression led to a more instrumental orientation in which a centrally planned program of socioeconomic evolution has been sought through the party-directed coordination of all organized worker activities.

Foremost among the worker organizations have been the trade unions. Their history goes back to the nineteenth century, and by the end of the 1930s, the number of established unions reached about 300 with more than 1,000,000 members within their ranks. During the pre-World War II period the unions maintained a record of high militancy and achieved a considerable degree of political influence (Mond, 1972).

Following the consolidation of communist power, the political importance of the unions declined considerably. The number of national unions was trimmed to thirty-six by 1948 and further reduced to twenty-three in the mid-1970s. Their internal organization and activities became subjected to a centrally directed process of unification and strict regimentation. In accordance with the governmental decrees of 1949 and 1958, each national union formed a hierarchical structure within which the local branches (enterprise councils) were completely subordinated to the directives issued from above. The delegates from each union elected the Central Council of Trade Unions which served as a policy-setting organ for the entire movement.

The legally defined scope of trade union activities at the local level has ranged from the supervision of the work safety standards to the administration of social programs, such as health services and recreational benefits. At the national level, the Central Council of Trade Unions has had the right to participate, with an advisory voice, in the formulation of government policies related to economic planning and setting of wages and financial bonuses for different categories of employees. Their most important task, however, has been to secure the cooperation of workers with management in the joint efforts to fulfill the economic plans (Lopatka, 1962; Ostrowski, 1970). To this effect, the unions have had the responsibility of preventing production slowdowns and work stoppages and of acting as organs of arbitration in disciplinary conflicts between the workers and the management.

The second institution empowered to represent the occupational interests of workers has been the workers' councils. They sprang to life in 1956 as a result of a spontaneous movement of dissatisfaction with the lack of effectiveness of the unions' performance and a growing determination to increase direct worker participation in the management of individual factories and enterprises. The councils received their official recognition in November of that year as elective organs of worker self-government, separate from any other organizations and endowed with extensive powers, including the initiation and/or approval of personnel changes at the management level, participation in factory management, as well as access to the formulation of local production plans (Kolankiewicz, 1973).

Their autonomy and prerogatives were severely limited, however, by the formation in December 1958 of the Conference of Workers' Self-Government, an institution created by a governmental decree to act as a main organ of collective decision-making at the enterprise level. It united the representatives of the workers' councils, the trade union and the local party organization, as well as other social and professional groups within a single body with economic and production functions rather than a mandate to defend the interests of the employees. This development effectively arrested the expansion of workers' participation in factory management which had been previously exercised through the workers' councils alone. The councils themselves became only one organ among many operating within the conference. Their authority as a representative organization of the workers declined rapidly and the deciding influence within the conference shifted toward the union and party delegates (Owieczko, 1966, 1967).

This end of a rather short-lived experiment in worker autonomous representation only underscored the party's determination to maintain a close supervision over organized worker activities. Its continuing success in coordinating their actions resulted from the party's ability to control the institutional resources of workers' organizations as well as from the widespread penetration of their leadership groups by the loyal party members.[2] In those conditions, the impact of party decisions on workers' institutions has been of critical importance as was the conformity of their leaders to the party line. Their principal task has been to secure the participation of workers in the fulfillment of party policies. The function of formulating the direction and the pace of socioeconomic evolution has been the exclusive domain of the party itself.

In as much as this insistence on institutional, party-centered cohesion has helped to maintain systemic stability, it has also created a fertile ground for serious political difficulties. These difficulties originate essentially from two sources. The first lies in the functional incompatibility between the centralistic institutional framework and the changing objectives of governmental activities. Formed with an explicitly stated goal of a radical social transformation, the institutional framework has become an obstacle rather than an instrument of an effective implementation of stabilizing efforts. The second source of difficulties comes from the growing social and economic differentiation within the population. The persistently unequal patterns of allocation of social rewards, despite the traditional systemic commitment to egalitarianism, have threatened to build up social tensions and disillusionment.

The communist seizure of power in the wake of World War II heralded a series of social changes which promised to benefit greatly the proletarian segment of the Polish population. The expropriation of landed estates and large industrial property altered the traditional balance of social advantages, thus laying down the foundations for a lasting restructuring of society. To be sure, there remained large areas of inequality, most obviously those related to income differentials between the blue- and white-collar workers. Their political impact, however, was moderated by the uniform extension of social benefits, such as the national health service and social security to all groups of employees, as well as a significant expansion of manual workers' upward mobility into administrative, managerial and similar white-collar occupations (Najduchowska, 1963). Furthermore, the adoption of full-employment policies provided the guarantee of economic survival in the conditions of prevailing economic scarcity.

This initial impetus toward social leveling appears to have been partially arrested, or even reversed, since the mid-1950s. The policy of promoting manual workers to white-collar occupations was abandoned and professional as well as educational criteria adopted as the main factors in personnel recruitment (Najduchowska, 1969). Similarly, although the wage levels of manual workers were raised in relation to clerical and lower administrative employees, the real income differentials between the workers and the management increased substantially (Zagorski, 1970).

To some extent, this weakening of egalitarian tendencies came about as a result of larger political changes. Set in motion by a general movement of de-Stalinization, those changes centered on a shift away from the primary reliance on administrative controls in promoting social change and toward an attempt to secure a degree of systemic stability through accommodation to the traditional social values. On a more specific level, they signaled an evolving trend toward more pragmatic and technologically oriented solutions in social policies coupled with a measure of disregard for earlier revolutionary commitments.

Within the party, the levers of power were being gradually taken over by new professional elites. Preoccupied with the problems of efficiency and productivity rather than ideology, they pushed for a development of a new pattern in the systemic relationships in which highly trained personnel would play a crucial role in policy formulation. Once started, this process produced serious sociopolitical consequences. The rapidly unfolding functional division of labor led to the emergence of a kind of social boundary between the specialized elites commanding access to the avenues of policy-making and the working masses which were left on the 'outside' (de Weydenthal, 1978). This development, in turn, has given rise to the undercurrent of resentment from the workers who, lacking the skills and the organization which give bargaining power in policy-making, found themselves threatened by the erosion of egalitarianism. In these conditions, any attempt at institutionalizing the existing inequalities was likely to produce a general sharpening of political consciousness of the workers themselves.

The Politicization of Discontent

Until the end of the 1960s, the party leadership was hesitant to introduce any drastic changes in its social orientation lest a faulty move could reinforce the latent tensions. The first steps toward the implementation of a comprehensive reform of the existing socioeconomic situation, which marked a decisive departure from the principles of egalitarianism and an adoption of economic criteria in deciding the issues of social policies, were taken in the years 1969–70.

To a large extent, the impetus toward economic reforms was generated by the growing need to streamline the working of Poland's economy, and in particular to eliminate some of the inefficiencies resulting from the centralized system of planning. The inefficiencies, as well as the numerous attempts to combat them in the past, have been amply documented by Polish and Western economic analysts and there is no need to discuss them here. Suffice it to say that a mounting concern over production waste, technological backwardness and costly overemployment encouraged by a highly bureaucratized planning machinery brought about in the late 1960s the realization of an urgent need for a drastic overhaul of the entire strategy of economic development.

This sense of urgency was further compounded by several political considerations, among which the drive to unite diverse elements of the party around the central leadership appears to have been the most important. Having gone through a severe political turmoil in 1968, the party emerged torn by internal dissension and factional strife. The effectiveness of its central leadership, and in particular the authority of the then First Secretary Wladyslaw Gomulka were seriously undermined (de Weydenthal, 1978). To regain the lost ground, Gomulka seemed to have become determined to expand efforts at furthering a program of economic reorganization through which the role of the central organs would be considerably reinforced.

The decision to reform the industrial wage system, adopted by the PUWP Central Committee in May 1970, signaled the first important operational measure in the program of economic innovation. Its essential feature was a shift from strict plan guidelines toward productivity indices as the key determinants of wage increases. The reform envisaged the imposition of a stable basic wage structure, to be changed every five years with the introduction of large-scale economic plans, and the creation of separate bonus funds for white- and blue-collar industrial employees. The white-collar bonus fund was to be made up from savings gained by lowering the costs of production and was conceived as a direct financial incentive for the managerial and technical staffs to stimulate efficiency in their enterprises. Any increases in the workers' compensation were to be correlated with those of the white-collar employees, hence they were to depend on satisfactory fulfillment of production targets by the management, with additional funds made available as a result of the decrease in actual blue-collar employment.

The acceptance of the reform, which was to be implemented in January 1971, created obvious implications for society at large. Its main principle, that is, an assertion that efficiency and productivity were to be the major determinants of rewards pointed to still-greater reinforcement of the existing inequalities which were now given a permanent character. By stressing the intensification of managerial effectiveness as the prime objective of its developmental strategy, the party seemed to have embraced an essentially technocratic approach to economic and social problems. The most significant consequence of this development was a departure from the traditional insistence on full employment. The new approach, which had envisaged the creation of a pool of about 500,000 unemployed workers by the end of 1975 (Krol, 1971), aimed at forcing greater productivity through the use of threat of unemployment as an incentive for better and more efficient work.

Despite its explicitly anti-labor overtones, the adoption of the reform did not produce any immediate adverse reactions from the workers themselves. It seems fair to assume, however, that this apparent absence of workers' opposition was due to the continuing importance of institutional constraints upon the policy-making process rather than to the willing acceptance of the new program. The participation in policy formulation was restricted to a small group of top party officials and their advisers. The workers' organizations were kept at the level of passive supporters and the working masses were simply ignored. This only contributed to the growing isolation of the party top leadership from the workers, whose anxieties at the prospects of unemployment and economic scarcity gradually crystalized around specific events, finding in them a convenient rallying-point.

The event that brought those tensions into the open was an announcement, on 12 December 1970, of a government decision to immediately impose a 15–30 percent increase in the price of food and fuels. Endorsed two days later by the PUWP Central Committee Plenum as both a remedy to the shortage of meat and grain resulting from the consecutive years of bad harvests, and as an instrument to impose the change in consumption patterns from foodstuffs to manufactured goods, it triggered an outburst of workers' protests. The government attempt to suppress the protesters by force set off a chain reaction of demonstrations and strikes which provoked a wholesale change in the composition of the party and government leadership, forced a gradual repeal of the reform program and culminated, on 15 February 1971, with a revocation of the food price increases.

The events of those two months have sometimes been considered, by Polish as well as Western observers, as providing a turning-point in the evolution of Polish politics. While it will remain for future historians to assess the lasting validity of this judgment, there is little doubt that the course of the crisis demonstrated several important changes from the earlier manifestations of workers' unrest.

The crisis developed through two separate stages in which the pattern of governmental intervention was the key determinant of the form and the intensity of social strife. The first stage was characterized by mass street demonstrations, rebellious turmoil and violent confrontations between the workers and the police supported by military units. Its main battlefields were the industrial centers of northern Poland, and particularly the coastal city of Gdansk, where a spontaneous manifestation of workers' despair turned into a riot when confronted with repeated governmental attempts to disperse the crowds. The brutality of repressive reactions provoked a wave of protests in other coastal cities – and quickly spread to other industrial cities throughout the country (Zamorski, 1971). The abortive governmental attempt to impose a nationwide state of emergency on 18 December 1970 – the first action of this kind in the history of People's Poland – created a clear danger of provoking a generalized revolt. Confronted with such a possibility, the party leadership persuaded Wladyslaw Gomulka to resign from the PUWP Secretariat. He was replaced, on 20 December, by Edward Gierek. In a few weeks following this event, almost all Gomulka's associates departed from the leading party posts.

While these personnel changes provided a partial release of existing tensions, they did not bring to an end the movement of workers' discontent. On the contrary, it seems that the political changes decided under the conditions of growing social restlessness, produced by the long-existing strains in public life, might have only triggered a powerful workers' movement which developed a momentum of its own and created a source of political influence upon the established hierarchy of power. Gomulka's dismissal and the subsequent criticism of his former associates by the new leaders seems to have appeared to the workers as an explicit recognition of the failure of the entire program of economic change and as a symbolic rejection of authoritarian methods in dealing with social protests. For once, the popular agitation seemed to them to produce an immediate political result. This gave the workers a new determination to press for a comprehensive reversal of all those decisions which they considered as detrimental to their interests. The change in political conditions led to a change in workers' tactics. The street demonstrations and violent confrontations with the police gave way to a series of occupation strikes. This stage of the protest movement ended only after 15 February, when the food prices were rolled back to the pre-December levels.

In as much as the failure to arrest the expansion of workers' dissent through the use of force stands out as the most important consequence of the 1970-71 crisis, several other factors made it a rather novel phenomenon in the Polish political experience. Perhaps the most significant was the extent of participation in collective activities and the social characteristics of the protesters. The earlier outbursts of workers' discontent took place within the confines of isolated factories or in a single city at best. They tended to reflect narrowly defined economic interests of specific groups of industrial employees. The 1970-71 protests became a truly national event. Although the greatest intensity of initial demonstrations concentrated in the northern region of Poland, the wave of protests spread quickly to other industrial centers. There is every reason to believe that within a week or so after the announcement of the price increases there was no large city, nor important industry, left unaffected by work stoppages, protest meetings, or other form of manifestation of workers' discontent.

The full personal and social dynamics of this movement will probably never be adequately described, due to the existing political circumstances. All available sources agree, however, that the protesters were not a tiny minority of chronic law offenders, nor were they highly distinct in terms of occupational characteristics or political preferences. Rather, the protests involved a large group which was generally representative of the worker population as a whole. Their leaders included a considerable percentage of rank-and-file party and trade union activists, who found themselves at odds with the centrally imposed program of economic changes (Wiatr, 1971; Seidler, 1971).

Another aspect of the changing patterns of participation was an active attempt to self-organize the flow of collective protest activities. In contrast to the earlier manifestations of discontent, when the workers' response was a spontaneous and often fatalistic show of despair, the 1970-71 movement developed political overtones in the sense that emerging group consciousness pervaded this particular form of proletarian self-mobilization. These trends were particularly noticeable in the shipbuilding industry of Gdansk and Szczecin, two large coastal cities, where the workers set up permanent democratically elected Strike Committees. They promptly established channels of communication with other factories throughout the country and successfully conducted direct negotiations with top party and government officials (Instytut Literacki, 1971). There were numerous indications that this movement toward occupational self-representation could gather a national momentum. Already some of the local party and union organizations either lost, or were in the process of losing, ground in several industrial centers (Furchel, 1971).

The growth of social consciousness and organizational effectiveness made a decisive contribution to intensifying the workers' aspirations to achieve their goals. Of course, the economic issues, in particular the demand for revocation of the food price increases, occupied the most important place here. In time, however, these pressures for change expanded to include an implicit criticism of the political system. Among the most striking elements of this process, were growing calls for independent and truly representative workers' organizations, for punishment of the officials judged responsible for repressive actions, and for a reform of administrative procedures with regard to protest demonstrations.

This process of politicization of workers' demands was deeply influenced by the essential ambiguity of the party and government responses to the protest movement. For the new party leaders, Gomulka's departure was a long-awaited culmination of factional struggles for which the workers' unrest might have merely provided a convenient stimulus. While critical of Gomulka's operational tactics, they had never been opposed to the principle of centrally imposed economic programs of change as exemplified by his policies. Once in power, they were determined to carry them out, while accepting certain appeasement-oriented measures, such as an immediate distribution of allowances to low-income families and a promise to revise some of the more rigid stipulations of the impending wage system (de Weydenthal, 1978). Faced, however, with the continuing workers' unrest, the party gradually yielded to the workers' demands. The most important concession was a revocation, on 25 January 1971, of the wage system and a return to the policy of full employment. This was combined with further increases in subsidies for the lowest-paid employees and the extension of the retirement programs. Finally, on 15 February, confronted with the prospect of a new strike in the textile industry, the government decided to rescind the food prices, but only after announcing that this change was made possible by an injection of financial help from the Soviet Union (Gamarnikow, 1972).

The fulfillment of its economic goals was, without a doubt, the most obvious success of the 1970–71 protest movement. To emphasize the economic measures alone, however, would distort its potential long-range significance. The crucial political issue which developed through the evolution of the protest movement was that it made a decisive contribution to consolidating occupational solidarity and group consciousness. In the most remarkable absence of the visible involvement – either existing or emerging – of other social groups in the workers' protests, they united broadly representative segments of the specific socioeconomic class of the urban community capable of expressing their social and economic dilemmas. The impact of this development on the political system was drastic in .that it promised to make future workers' demands more politically militant and more oriented toward their specific needs.

The Patterns of Political Response

To contain the threat of further political dislocations, the party developed a wide-ranging strategy of stabilization. Its crucial feature was a centrally coordinated effort to promote economic growth and modernization. The main emphasis was put on a rapid increase in mass consumption with an expanded program of imports and foreign credits as the primary source of domestic development. The intended consequence of this effort was to produce a firm basis for industrial expansion, and improvement in the standard of living, both considered as the key determinants of a successful restoration of political stability (Fallenbuchl, 1973). Implicit in this strategy of stabilization through economic advancement, however, was the return of forms of government more in consonance with the systemic traditions of political and institutional centralism.

With regard to the workers, this strategy developed a two-pronged action: first, the adoption of new policies aimed at an improvement in real wages and working conditions with a view to regaining the workers' support for the party and its leadership; secondly, the restoration of party political control over workers' activities and validation of its special role as the main spokesman for proletarian interests.

During the next few years, the new strategy produced impressive economic results. By the end of 1975, the gross national product increased by 59 percent over 1970 and industrial employment rose 14·8 percent, with the rate of industrial production going up by 44·3 percent. Aided by the imposition of the freeze on food prices until the end of 1974, real wages in 1975 were up by 40·9 percent over 1970 for an average growth rate of 8 percent per annum, a major change from the average of 1·9 percent during the whole previous decade. There was no doubt about the rise in the standard of living, and the growing investments – 147·3 percent in capital goods and 75·3 percent in consumer industries since 1970 – reinforced expectations for further progress (GUS, 1976).

The workers greatly benefited from the economic expansion. The industrial boom provided new jobs, brought higher income and created the foundations for an emerging feeling of material security. Furthermore, several measures were taken to improve the conditions of work in industrial enterprises. The most important was the introduction of a new comprehensive labor legislation, the Labor Code, which came into effect in January 1975. Its major provisions included the abolition of any differentiation between white-collar employees and manual workers with regard to their respective rights and obligations of employment, the expansion of benefits for working women, and the codification of rules related to employment contracts, work discipline and termination procedures.

At the same time, considerable effort was made to reconsolidate the party's hegemony over the workers' participation in the process of social and economic policy-making. Opposition to any demands for greater political autonomy of the workers' groups was remarkable in its thoroughness. Although the strike committees of early 1971 were dissolved following the change in conditions which had provided the basis for their emergence, the government promptly moved to undermine the popularity of the former strike activists and to sever their links with production crews. The measures taken against them included dismissals from shop-floor jobs through transfer to other duties, co-option into established agencies of workers' representation with a view to political resocialization and, in some cases, direct political persecution (Sulik, 1976).

The right to strike itself, while not explicitly denied, was never officially acknowledged. This only reflected a long-standing and frequently repeated assertion that in the Polish system 'there are no and cannot be any antagonistic conflicts between the workers' organizations and the economic and state administration' (Kruczek, 1972, 1976).

Neither was there a change in the systemic role of trade unions and self-management conferences. Despite numerous demands for the expansion of their responsibilities and power, voiced by various advocates of institutional reforms in the wake of the 1970–71 strikes (CRZZ, 1972), the government not only failed to heed those calls, but in fact augmented the prerogatives of various agencies representing state interests. Thus, a new government body was created in 1972, the Ministry of Labor, Wages and Social Affairs, with an explicit task of controlling all matters pertaining to employment, wages, work organization and working conditions. At the factory level, several measures were taken to increase the powers of plant managers with regard to work discipline and personnel matters. The government decree of 1972 expanded managerial prerogatives related to decisions regulating wage increases, employment needs and internal work organization. This was further reinforced in the 1975 Labor Code, which put the manager in charge of enforcing work discipline, including the unilateral right to impose fines on insubordinate employees and the authority to terminate their employment for disciplinary reasons.

To a large extent, these restrictive measures were rooted in the exigencies of economic and organizational efficiency; the net political effect, however, was a decline in workers' institutionalized participation in political and industrial policy-making. The function of trade unions and self-management conferences remained restricted to cooperation with the appropriate state bodies in preparing and implementing labor legislation. The effective control over the flow of political and organizational activities became firmly re-established in the hands of the party and government officials.

Yet, the party did more than successfully resist any pressure for an autonomous workers' access to policy inputs. While assenting to the economic demands of all social groups, it also developed a vigorous campaign to ensure popular support for its long-range sociopolitical programs in the hope of solidifying positive attitudes into a more durable commitment to the system. This was combined with a deliberate attempt to forge and expand direct links between the central party leadership and the workers.

Perhaps the most significant were the efforts at ideological mobilization aimed at greater involvement of workers in the fulfillment of economic plans. They included an expansion of party educational activities at factory level designed to inculcate the workers with its socioeconomic objectives, a massive dissemination of slogans propagating the values of good and efficient work, and an introduction of a system of moral rewards for productive achievements. To coordinate those efforts, the PUWP Central Committee undertook a direct supervision of the party work at almost 200 of the largest industrial establishments.

Another important innovation was the practice of periodic meetings between the top party leaders and the workers in large industrial plants. They were to provide a specific forum for a continuing process of popular consultations which would help the leaders in the formulation of social and economic policies.

In so far as these measures were designed to calm social tensions and prevent political disruptions, they were successful in imposing a new political stability endowed with a considerable degree of popular support. At the same time, however, they were not free of certain ideological and political ambiguities. In particular, by veering toward a more realistic perception of societal needs, the party appeared to discard some elements of its traditional egalitarian outlook and to embrace some clearly pragmatic notions. The crucial point here seemed to be not so much an outright rejection of egalitarian principles, but rather an attempt to recast them in terms of current developmental needs. Similarly, the systemic function of popular consultations, aside of their public-relations appeal, remained undefined. Their main impact seemed to be in weakening the prerogatives of the established workers' organizations while preventing the emergence of others.

This emphasis on centrally coordinated economic development illustrated a major effort at securing lasting systemic stabilization but within a framework of traditional institutions and structures. Its social acceptance, however, remained clearly dependent on the government's success in maintaining a reasonably high level of economic performance.

The Threat of Fragmentation

Signs of serious economic problems emerged in the mid-1970s. They included sharp increases in the cost of energy carrying resources – the price of imported fuel went up in 1974 alone by about 80 percent in comparison with the previous year – a perceptible decline in exports, and a general slowdown in industrial activity. At the same time shortages of food and consumer products appeared as the volume of imported goods declined and domestic production proved insufficient to satisfy public demand.

To some extent the emergence of these problems was prompted by Poland's reliance on imports, largely financed by foreign credits, for stimulating domestic expansion. A deteriorating international economic situation, resulting from the worldwide oil crisis, seriously affected the government's ability to continue its program of development. It restricted Poland's export capacity while imposing limitations on imports and, therefore, on consumption at home. These problems were greatly intensified by domestic mismanagement and operational inefficiency. Long-standing management shortcomings were only further magnified by the developmental boom in the early 1970s, producing widespread overinvestment, overemployment and an inflationary growth in wages. This was, of course, simply a consequence of the leadership's strategy of stabilization, the main purpose of which had always been to preserve and strengthen the existing institutionalized framework of power, rather than to introduce innovation and facilitate economic adaptability. Under the worsening economic conditions, however, the continuation of that strategy was bound to produce social tension and, eventually, undermine the stabilizing efforts themselves.

The government's approach to dealing with the economic problems suggested its relatively small appreciation of the potential implications of the social discontent for political stability. No attempt was made to introduce general adjustments into social and economic policies and operations. Instead, the economic difficulties were discounted by political leaders as essentially temporary. As such they were to be dealt with primarily through administrative means, regardless of possible public resentment at such measures.

Illustrative of that attitude was a sudden government announcement on 24 June 1976 of drastic food price increases, ranging from 50 percent for butter to a 69 percent average for meat and 100 percent for sugar. While that decision might have appeared economically justifiable since growing world inflation and shortages of consumer products at home had created strong pressures for some form of domestic price changes, the magnitude of the increases must have come as a shock for the population. Equally shocking must have been the manner in which the price changes were intróduced. No attempt was made to inform the public about the impending changes and the need to prepare for them. Instead, they were arbitrarily imposed for immediate implementation. The entire operation was reminiscent of the earlier attempt at price regulation in December 1970. As then, the decision was taken by a small group of top political leaders and their advisers, while the public was simply ignored.

Just as it had done in 1970, the government action provoked an immediate outburst of public discontent. Its most important element was again a massive protest by industrial workers. Within a few hours of the announcement of the price increases, there were strikes throughout the country. The protests were basically peaceful; only in a few communities in central Poland were there instances of vandalism and looting. But it was clear that if the price decisions were to remain unchanged the workers' protest would effectively paralyze the economy. It was that potential threat of a nationwide strike, with political repercussions possibly even exceeding those of 1970, that forced an immediate reversal of the government decision. On 25 June, less than twenty-four hours after the original announcement had been made, the food price increases were rescinded.

In many respects the June 1976 workers' protest against the government's price decision could be seen as politically even more important than the rebellion of 1970–71. Its major significance was in the fact that the protest repeated the earlier workers' success in preventing the implementation of government economic policies. This, more than anything else, exposed the vulnerability of the system to social pressures, thus undermining the effectiveness of government operations. The immediate effect of this development was the expansion of political activism by other social groups, coupled with growing demands for official acceptance of some form of political pluralism. Furthermore, the workers' success in forcing a reversal of government policy seriously impeded economic decision-making and influenced the general policy orientation of the leadership (de Weydenthal, 1979a).

The development of broad political activism was directly related to the basic ambiguity of the leadership's responses to the workers' protest. During the months following the revocation of the food price increases, official promises were frequently made to hold popular consultations, particularly with the workers, before any economic policies were decided upon. Neither the scope, nor the actual form, of this process was clearly defined, however, and the practical implementation of this consultation process has remained clouded in uncertainty. At the same time, immediately after the social tension had calmed down the government began a series of punitive measures against selected groups of workers from those factories in which incidents of violence had taken place. Several hundred workers were arrested, many lost their jobs, and an undetermined number of persons were sentenced in numerous trials lasting throughout the summer and fall of 1976.

Those repressive actions provoked widespread criticism around the country. This was indicated by a series of letters and petitions, addressed to the authorities, demanding investigations of police brutality in the treatment of the workers. They included complaints from workers' groups, letters of protest from intellectuals, and appeals by students and teachers. Concurrently the Catholic Church began to issue, in the form of sermons and pastoral letters, protests against government methods of dealing with the workers. Gradually, in the face of government disregard of these protests, public criticism extended beyond specific appeals for leniency and led to the development of a movement of active opposition to what was considered the official policy of repression.

Among the numerous separate dissident groups which have emerged on the Polish political scene during the last four years or so, perhaps the most important has been the Committee for the Defense of the Workers (KOR). It was set up in September 1976 by a small group of prominent intellectuals with the aim of providing legal and financial help to the families of imprisoned workers and of campaigning for their release. Its goal and its activities received a significant degree of popular support, both at home and abroad. Especially important was KOR's ability to collect funds to aid needy workers, and throughout 1977 several hundred workers' families were provided with the necessary financial and medical help from those funds.

KOR's activities did not cease when a government amnesty freed all the arrested workers in July 1977. On the contrary, the release of the workers might have appeared to the dissidents as an indication of their growing strength. In September 1977 KOR changed its name to the Social Self-Defense Committee–KOR (KSS–KOR), and established itself as an autonomous, openly operating body for the defense of human rights. Moreover, largely as a result of KOR's success, new opposition groups began to appear (Bromke, 1978). They included the Movement for the Defense of Human and Civil Rights (ROPCO), a Polish chapter of Amnesty International, several student and youth groups, and many others. While their immediate goals and interests might have differed, and even contradicted one another, they appear to have shared a common denominator in the rejection of state control over areas of their concern.

The main proponents of these trends have been intellectuals and students, but the movement gradually expanded to include various groups of workers as well. In the fall of 1977 a small unofficial trade union group was established in central Poland. Subsequently, similar groups emerged in the mining region in the south as well as in the ports on the coast (RFER, 1979). Their activities largely revolved around the publication and distribution of an unofficial periodical, *Robotnik* (The Worker), printed with the help of KSS–KOR in several thousand copies every two weeks or so. In September 1979 *Robotnik* published a 'Charter of Workers' Rights', which constituted an outline of regulations with respect to wages, work safety and workers' rights, as well as an appeal for broader movement toward proletarian self-organization (RFER, 1979b).

The government's response to political activism has been ambiguous: mostly antagonistic, but also tolerant. In order to contain the spread of opposition groups, the authorities have continually used restrictive measures ranging from press and institutional harassment to police intimidation and the detention of individual dissidents. Particularly harsh measures have been directed against the most active members of the unofficial trade unions. Some of them were forced to emigrate, while others were periodically arrested and intimidated. During 1979–80, several worker activists were tried on rather dubious criminal charges and sentenced to prison terms.

At the same time, there has been no indication of any official determination to permanently destroy the basis of the dissident organizations. No decisive actions have been taken by the authorities to stop the publication of dissident literature and, even if some of the publishers and writers were periodically harassed, these journals and books have been largely ignored. The government has occasionally tried to extend some gestures of reconciliation toward its opponents, particularly those from among the working communities. This was indicated, above all, by the release of imprisoned workers in 1977. In addition, there have been constant efforts made to recruit workers into the party and to project the party's policies as being essentially oriented to supporting the interests of the working class.

There are, perhaps, several possible explanations for the government's relative tolerance toward domestic opposition. These would include the potentially restraining impact of international public opinion – there have been many interventions by Western intellectuals and human rights organizations on behalf of the dissidents – as well as a formal obligation, arising from the provisions of the Helsinki Declaration on Security and

Cooperation in Europe, for the government to respect basic civil liberties. But it appears that the crucial element that has stayed the hand of the authorities is their determination to preserve social peace in the country. After experiencing two major political setbacks, prompted by social protests in 1970 and 1976, the leadership has clearly been hesitant to introduce openly any major political changes lest a faulty move provoke a new outburst of dissatisfaction.

Nowhere has this concern over possible social resistance been more obvious than in the crucial area of consumer prices, especially those for food and food products. Despite the rapidly deteriorating economic conditions, food prices have been artificially maintained at 1975 levels. This was made possible only through a massive program of government subsidies which, for meat and meat products alone, increased from 12·3 billion zloty in 1971 to a staggering figure of 91·4 billion zloty in 1979. To make matters even worse, the supply of food and other consumer products on the market has steadily declined over the years as the cumulative effects of deteriorating domestic production, due both to bad harvests and administrative mismanagement, and the mounting cost of imports made it increasingly difficult to satisfy public demand.

The general impact of this situation on other sectors of the economy has been serious, in that it tied up funds which could have been used for other services, complicated planning, and forced the government to seek new foreign credits for larger imports of grain and other products. To neutralize somewhat those economically adverse developments in 1977 the government set up a network of special so-called 'commercial shops', which sell food, primarily meat products, at premium prices, usually double the official price or even more. It is estimated that by the end of 1979 the number of such shops had reached about 500, which is a fivefold increase over 1977, and that they handled about 18 percent of all meat sales on the market (Kowalik, 1980).

Irrespective of purely economic considerations, however, the main significance of the consumer price issue has always been political rather than economic. The government has long exercised a tactic of widespread, but hidden, price increases by putting different labels on the same products, changing packaging, etc. Yet these increases have been largely unofficial, none of them was announced, and all have been indirect. This, more than anything else, has emphasized the caution with which the authorities treated the problem of economic change, limiting it to only those aspects that might be more acceptable to the population. The most obvious consequence of this approach, however, has been mounting public dissatisfaction with the leadership's performance. If nothing else, it has served as a reminder of the government's vulnerability to social pressure and has greatly contributed to a perceptible weakening of its authority.

Underlying this aspect of the political situation has been an apparently growing conviction – frequently voiced by the dissidents, but also increasingly accepted within some segments of the cultural and economic establishment – that the government is incapable of solving the current problems by itself.[3] This, in turn, has given rise to an increasingly manifest undercurrent of demands for a potential reconstitution of different elements of power within the system and for an explicit acceptance of political pluralism. These demands, largely relating to current problems and difficulties, none the less implied the threat of a fragmentation of the political system, a fragmentation which could eventually endanger the dominant position of the party itself.

It was this prospect of a potential political fragmentation of the system, coupled with the realization that any further delay in official response could only breed its deeper decay, that brought the government to action. On 1 July 1980, the authorities introduced a new, and official, increase in meat prices. The decision was preceded by a long propaganda campaign of press articles and statements by political leaders. It followed a formal proclamation by the authorities of their general policy of economic austerity, a policy adopted by the party congress in February 1980 to be gradually implemented by a new government installed by that congress. The decision itself was presented as part of a comprehensive package of internal economic changes aimed at improving efficiency and increasing productivity.

These preparatory measures notwithstanding, the manner in which the decision was announced, its meager economic scope, and the logistics of its implementation, have all testified to the continuing apprehension of the authorities about social reactions. The announcement was made belatedly, on 2 July, a day after the price increase had been implemented. It took the form of a radio and television interview with a minor government official. Its main point was that, as of 1 July, the 'commercial' shops network had increased its share of meat sales by some 2 percent in comparison with the 1979 levels. It meant that the price for some categories of meat – primarily beef, bacon, some poultry and canned meat – would go up by about 40–60 percent on average (RFER, 1980). Furthermore, it was subsequently announced that the new sales system would be introduced gradually in different parts of the country. The eventual profits from the change, which would amount to a mére 2 billion zloty in 1980, would be used to improve the lot of the lowest-earning groups in the population.

The motivation behind the government's decision to change the system of meat sales and, therefore, to increase the price of meat was clearly political rather than economic. Its main significance was to establish, in the minds of the public as well as among the government itself, the feeling that the government had both the right, and the ability, to issue decisions which would be obeyed by all. This was fully confirmed by the relatively minor economic importance of the measure. In this context, it is sufficient to note that the recent increase involved only 2 percent of the available meat, while earlier shifts in sales of meat and meat products away from ordinary and to 'commercial' shops amounted to 8 percent in 1978 and 10 percent in 1979. The crucial difference here, however, was that while the earlier changes had been 'unofficial', the recent one was openly, even if belatedly, announced to the entire country.

Yet, whereas there had been no public protests against the earlier unofficial measures, the announcement of the meat price increase once again prompted a series of workers' protests. Almost immediately following the implementation of the price changes there were strikes in factories throughout the country. These protests were uniformly peaceful and, in contrast to the previous instances of workers' unrest, involved not so much a rejection of the official policy as demands for additional compensation which would neutralize the impact of price changes on the workers' budgets. It was officially admitted by government spokesmen that some form of negotiations between the workers and the management started immediately after the first outbreaks of the protests. Reportedly, the settlements reached in the first few days following the price change oscillated around a 10 per cent increase in wages and/or some changes in work norms which would allow for a comparable increase in benefits.[4]

The immediate results of the operation appeared to have been beneficial for the government. To the degree that its intention had been to affirm its capacity to make difficult decisions and to stick by them in the face of social protests, it certainly gained a degree of self-confidence. Indicative of that attitude was a comment made by a government official to a Western press correspondent: 'The precedent has now been set for further price increases, and that is important' (Reuter, 1980). By the same token, it is worthwhile noting that the economic price for this authority-building exercise, a price calculated in terms of promises given to and obligations undertaken with respect to the workers, would probably exceed the very gains derived from the meat price increases. Yet, there was little doubt that such a price had been anticipated, as the rapidity with which the bargaining between the workers and the management started seemed to have indicated, and the potential political benefits for the government clearly over-rode any concerns over economic losses.

However, the long-term effects of this development, even if difficult to predict at this stage, could be less favorable for the government and the system over which it presides. Some difficulties could arise from the very tactics which the government used to assure the implementation of the decision. The most obvious problem revolved around the gradualist manner in which the decision had been introduced separately in different parts of the country. In as much as that tactic had been employed to prevent any form of a nationwide and simultaneous protest, it also opened the way for a protracted process of new protests and new negotiations. Indeed, it should have been clear to government officials that the bargaining precedent set in one factory would be used by other workers elsewhere to obtain the same results. As if to confirm the validity of that assertion, the work stoppages and negotiations extended for some time after the decision had been implemented.

An additional factor which could complicate the position of the government was the official, but largely abortive, efforts to halt the workers' demands. This was pointedly illustrated by Gierek's (Gierek, 1980) statement made on 9 July, soon after the first series of negotiations with the workers had been completed. Speaking to a special meeting of top political and social activists, the party first secretary proclaimed, without the slightest mention of the negotiations themselves, that 'any broader increases in salaries' would not be accepted. Predictably, the statement, which was subsequently followed by similar press commentaries, had no effect upon the workers; factory negotiations continued unabated. This indicated, if nothing else, that the relative consolidation of the government's authority achieved through the implementation of the price increase might rapidly and irrevocably deteriorate.

Even more important for the future of the political system could be the possible evolution of a more-pronounced syndicalist orientation among the workers themselves. It was difficult to conceive that the experience of the negotiations, so reminiscent of Western-style collective bargaining between unions and management, could be forgotten by the workers and not used again in the future. In this sense, the 1980 situation differed from the earlier instances of worker–government confrontations. The successful preventive actions of the workers in 1971 and 1976 served to instill a sense of power into the working communities. They did not, however, contribute to the emergence of an organized workers' representation capable and prepared to deal with the authorities. The experience of the 1980 negotiating sessions and the workers' success in gaining concessions from officialdom could lead to specific future efforts to translate this power into a more tangible regulation of relations between workers and management. Furthermore, to the degree that the management serves as a representative of the state, this relationship could also affect the working of the government itself.

The possible result of that development could be a more pronounced fragmentation of the political system in which the positions of the government and specific social groups, especially the workers, but also other sociopolitical formations, such as dissidents, for example, would become more autonomously defined. In this context, it is certainly important to note that the workers' actions with respect to their demands for higher wages and benefits received significant support from the dissident organizations. In particular, the members of the Social Self-Defense Committee–KOR served as the principal source of information about the worker–management negotiations for the Western press and the country. There was no doubt that they were helped in this task by the workers themselves. This, more than anything else, could lead to some form of closer cooperation between the workers and the dissidents in the future. In light of all these developments, it is possible even to speculate that the apparently successful government effort to strengthen its own position might still turn out to be the measure which prompted a major, but unexpected, evolution in Polish politics and within the Polish system of rule.

Notes: Chapter 10

This is an updated version of an article that appeared in *East European Quarterly*, vol. 13, no. 1, 1979, pp. 95–119.

1 This chapter is based, in part, on sections of my earlier work (de Weydenthal, 1979b).
2 As a rule, senior trade union leaders have been recruited from among the members of the party Central Committee. Similarly, party secretaries at the factory level have belonged to the Conferences of Workers' Self-Management on an *ex officio* basis.
3 Two recently issued unofficial documents, reflecting the views of many Polish intellectuals and social activists, illustrate the depth of this conviction. One of the documents, released in mid-1979, presented a strongly critical assessment of the sociopolitical situation in Poland. The other, prepared at the beginning of 1980, contained an outline for the reform of Poland's political system. Both were edited by a group of former members of the now-defunct discussion club, Experience and the Future (DiP). Many of them belong to the party. The documents were submitted to the party authorities before their public release.
4 Day by day information on the workers' strikes as well as reports on their negotiations with the management were provided by Western press agencies from Warsaw.

References: Chapter 10

Bromke, A., 'The opposition in Poland', *Problems of Communism,* September–October 1978, pp. 37–51.

CRZZ, Main Council of Trade Unions, *Propositions* (Warsaw: CRZZ, 1972).

Fallenbuchl, Z. M., 'The strategy of development and Gierek's economic manoeuvre', *Canadian Slavonic Papers,* vol. XV, Spring-Summer 1973, pp. 52–70.

Furchel, A., Article in *Polityka* (Warsaw), 13 February 1971.

Gamarnikow, M., 'Poland under Gierek: a new economic approach', *Problems of Communism,* September-October 1972, pp. 20–30.

Gierek, E., Speech on 9 July 1980.

GUS, Main Statistical Office, *The Small Statistical Yearbook 1976* (Warsaw: GUS, 1976).

Huntington, S. P., *Political Order in Changing Societies* (New Haven, Cn.: Yale University Press, 1968).

Huntington, S. P., 'The change to change: modernization, development, and politics', *Comparative Politics,* vol. II, no. 3, 1971, pp. 314–15.

Instytut Literacki, *Rewolta Szczecinska i jej znaczenie* (Paris: Institut Literaire, 1971).

Kolankiewicz, G., 'The Polish industrial manual working class', D. Lane and G. Kolankiewicz, eds, *Social Groups in Polish Society* (New York: Columbia University Press, 1973), pp. 103–18.

Kowalik, A., Interview in *Zycie Warszawy* (Warsaw), 12–13 January 1980.

Krol, H., Article in *Trybuna Ludu* (Warsaw), 15 February 1971.

Kruczek, W., Speech on 13 November 1972.

Kruczek, W., Speech on 6 December 1976.

Lopatka, A., *Panstwo socjalistyczne a swiazki zawodowe* (Poznan: Wydawnictwo Paznanskie, 1962).

Mond, G. H., 'Pologne', in *Le Syndicalisme en Europe de l'Est* (Paris: La Documentation Française, 29 September 1972), pp. 46–68.

Najduchowska, Z., 'Occupational advancement of workers', *Studia Socjologiczne,* no. 3, 1963, pp. 115–36.

Najduchowska, Z., 'Occupational careers of the managers', *'Studia Socjologiczne,* no. 3, 1969, pp. 253–69.

Ostrowski, K., *Rola zwiazkow zawodowych w polskim systemie politycznym* (Wroclaw: PAN, 1970).

Owieczko, A., 'Activities and structure of workers' self-management as viewed by the workers', *Studia Socjologiczne,* no. 3/22, 1966, pp. 65–99.

Owieczko, A., 'Workers' self-management in an industrial enterprise and the employees', *Studia Socjologiczno-Polityczne,* no. 22, 1967, pp. 13–50.

Reuter, Press Agency dispatch, 5 July 1980.

RFER, *Radio Free Europe Research. Polish Situation,* Report/23, 30 October 1979a, item 2.

RFER, *Radio Free Europe Research. Charter of workers' rights.* Background Report/200 (Poland), 20 September 1976b.

RFER, *Radio Free Europe Research. Polish Situation,* Report/14, 9 July 1980, item 1.

Seidler, B., Article in *Zycie Literackie* (Cracow), 21 February 1971.

Sulik, B., 'Workers', in *Kultura* (Paris), October 1976, pp. 65–77.

de Weydenthal, J. B., *The Communists of Poland* (Stanford, Ca.: Hoover Institution Press, 1978).

de Weydenthal, J. B., *Poland; Communism Adrift. The Washington Papers,* vol. 7, no. 72 (Beverly Hills, Ca., and London: Sage Publications, 1979a).

de Weydenthal, J. B., 'The workers' dilemma of Polish politics: a case study', *East European Quarterly,* vol. XIII, no. 1, 1979b, pp. 95–119.

Wiatr, J. 'Lessons for the political system', *Polish Perspectives,* November 1971, pp. 6–15.

Zagorski, K., 'The socioeconomic status of the workers and the intelligentsia', in W. Wesolowski, ed., *Struktura i dynamika spoleczenstwa polskiego.* (Warsaw: PWN. 1970), esp. pp. 155–6.

Zamorski, K., 'The chronology of events', in *Poznan – 1956 – Grudzien 1970* (Paris: Institut Litteraire, 1971), pp. 20–37.

11 Czechoslovakia: a 'Prolétariat Embourgeoisé'?

JIRI VALENTA

Introduction

The feeling of estrangement (*'Entfremdung'*) attributed to the worker by Karl Marx has not been abolished (*'aufgehebon'*) in Eastern Europe.[1] In most of these countries, working-class participation is limited, ironically, to the mode of production and consumption which Marx attributed to workers in the classic capitalist system. Strict control over worker participation in public life is especially marked in Czechoslovakia, because of pronounced inequalities in the allocation of authority and power.

What potential is there for worker assertiveness in light of this alienation? Are workers in Eastern Europe developing 'class consciousness'? Is the East European environment producing a class-oriented, 'more politicized' working class, capable of establishing 'linkages of an enduring sort' with 'the more articulate intellectuals' (Connor, 1980)? The primary argument of this chapter is that the development of class consciousness on the part of the workers has thus far been noticeable in very few East European countries, perhaps only Poland. In Czechoslovakia particularly, worker assertiveness has been effectively stifled by skilfull policies of the ruling elite.

The following questions will serve as guidelines in this inquiry: Who are the workers? What motivates them and how are they organized? Have there been significant workers' revolts in Czechoslovakia and what factors have provoked them? What were the attitudes of the workers toward the experiment with pluralist communism of 1968, known as the Prague Spring? Do the workers possess revolutionary potential? Are the workers capable of building a coalition with the intellectuals? What have been the regime's policies for coping with potential threats of worker militancy? What outlook is there for worker opposition to the regime?

'Nostalgic' and 'Penitent' Workers

Czechoslovakia professes to be a workers' state run by the working class. The extent to which this is true can be understood, if one differentiates among 'nostalgic' workers, 'penitent' workers and 'authentic' workers. Many of those who rule the Eastern European countries are so-called 'nostalgic' workers – old party *cadres* who were recruited from their positions as industrial workers into the bureaucratic stratum. They have not served as genuine workers for many years, sometimes a few decades. Yet, nostalgically they continue to perceive themselves as representatives of the working class, in essence the very workers. Belonging among the ranks of the 'nostalgic' workers are the thousands of officials in the various ruling bureaucracies: members of the party apparatus, officials supervising the areas of economics, security, ideology, defense and culture, and 'worker' directors in individual enterprises (Klokočka, 1979). In Czechoslovakia 'nostalgic' workers have served even in the party presidiums and as the ministers of government. Important among them for twenty years, was the son of a bricklayer and one-time mechanic, former President and First Secretary of the Communist Party of Czechoslovakia (CPCZ), Antonín Novotný.

The 'nostalgic' workers in the ruling elite are responsible for cultivating the image of heroic class struggle, the revolutionary tradition of the working class, and the workers' mandate. Although they remember willingly the glorious days of their worker and revolutionary activities, they are unwilling to assume their former jobs as laborers. This was uniquely demonstrated, in 1968, during the Prague Spring in Czechoslovakia, when many 'nostalgic' workers who had not yet reached retirement age (and so were unable to retire with high pensions) were forced by public pressure to face the prospect of resignation and resume their former activities as 'authentic' workers (Binar, 1979). It is no wonder many of these 'nostalgics', upon facing the prospect of again becoming genuine workers, asked their 'nostalgic class brothers' in the Soviet Politburo for 'fraternal assistance' in halting the peaceful revolution (Valenta, 1979).

Another category of worker in Czechoslovakia is the one who has been relegated to this position as a form of punishment – the 'penitent' worker. These workers, the victims of demotions and purges, were originally politicians, officials in the various bureaucracies, technical intelligentsia, writers and students. They became workers involuntarily because of retribution for various 'anti-state', 'anti-party', or other 'deviationist' activities. Obviously, the 'penitent' workers are not the most satisfied group of citizens in Eastern Europe. This has been particularly true in the case of Czechoslovakia, where some 500,000 former members of the party (many of them former officials) who were purged or resigned during the process of 'normalization' in 1969–71 are referred to by Jiří Pelikán as the 'Party of the Expelled' (Pelikán, 1973). Thousands of them have since become genuine workers and, in some cases, genuine dissidents. Indeed, they are the most outspoken members of the opposition. This should not come as a surprise since the 'penitent' workers are viewed by the ruling elites as class enemies of the people, a distinction once applied to former capitalists. Thus, the Czechoslovak workers' underground paper *Pokrok (Progress),* which in the early 1970s circulated in various large industrial enterprises in Prague, was published by 'penitent' workers. During the same period these workers also distributed leaflets which they signed 'Workers, legally elected functionaries of the CPCZ' (Pelikán, 1973, pp. 160–63). Many of the signatories who signed the famous Charter 77 Manifesto, although nominally workers, were also former members of the intelligentsia and students (Hájek and Nižnanský, 1978).

'Authentic' Workers: Economic, Social and Political Potential

The real subject of our inquiry is the 'authentic' worker. A typical skilled worker in Czechoslovakia, which is one of the most advanced, industrialized countries in Eastern Europe, comes from a second- or third-generation worker family more than from an upwardly mobile peasant background. (Only in East Germany and Czechoslovakia did industrial laborers outnumber the peasants prior to the communist takeover.) He is usually high-school educated and urbane. His parents and grandparents were probably also workers with strong socialist leanings – either social democrats, national socialists, or communists. These characteristics are particularly true of workers in the more advanced Czech lands.

The 'authentic' worker in Czechoslovakia has not reached his political, social, or economic potential. Unlike the 'nostalgic' worker, he has never tasted power and probably never will. Marx's early notion about the total liberation of the worker and the abolition of the state has not become a reality in Czechoslovakia or elsewhere. It is true that the Czechoslovak regime guarantees social security: the right of each worker to exercise his skills in a job, medical insurance and a pension. It has tried to satisfy the workers' basic economic needs while keeping the price level of basic commodities from rising. The degree of social security guaranteed the workers' families (wives and children) has been very substantial, certainly much greater than in many other countries of the world. The regime also offers educational opportunities to authentic workers and their children. (These benefits do not accrue to 'penitent' workers and their children, thousands of whom have been denied the right to pursue graduate education.) However, access to better jobs and housing, graduate education, and travel to Western countries, are privileges enjoyed only by the party's ruling elite – 'nostalgic' workers and some privileged 'authentic' workers. 'Authentic' workers are faced with a number of serious socioeconomic problems: general disregard for workers' safety and hygiene, poor working conditions, shortages of consumer goods, corruption and extremely crowded living conditions. The existence of special shops (*Tuzex*), which sell important goods from Western countries to privileged citizens with foreign currencies, but which are not readily available to 'authentic' workers, widens the social differences.

The political potential of the East European worker remains even more unfulfilled than his social and economic potential. For more than thirty years, the worker has been lauded as the creator, the ruler and the pillar of the political regimes in Eastern Europe. Yet the reality, recognized even by some Marxist theoreticians, is that in most of Eastern Europe the workers have traditionally played only a very passive role in public life and politics.

Despite their official rhetoric and ideological slogans about having the 'highest level of democracy in history', the Czechoslovak regime has actually pursued a deliberate policy of depoliticization of the working class. The ruling elite possesses an absolute monopoly of political power. As a result, the workers do not enjoy any of the traditional democratic rights – freedom of expression and information, the right to leave the country, religious freedom, and most importantly, the right to strike – which have been the patrimony of the worker in democratic societies of the West. This is not new to the worker in such Balkan countries as Romania and Bulgaria, which have had no significant democratic experience. It is, however, completely demoralizing for workers in countries with democratic traditions, such as Czechoslovakia.

The Czechoslovak workers are not permited to strike or involve themselves in any way in debates on a national scale involving wages, rates, or output norms. The workers are only permitted to express their opinion about the work in their factories, particularly the economic plan, production and social insurance. There is a kind of unspoken agreement between the ruling elite and the workers. In this agreement, the ruling bureaucracy promises that it will secure a citizen the fruits of a consumer society and refrain from involvement in his private life. In return, the worker promises that he will not become involved in politics – the profession of the ruling elite ('Bohemicus', 1980). The regime's policies are aimed at raising the social and economic status of the authentic workers – the *embourgeoisement* of the proletariat – and at exalting their social respectability. By assuring them of a continuously higher standard of living, the regime strives to dull the workers' senses to the political conditions and any notion of class consciousness. Chancellor Bismarck would have called these measures policies of 'sugar and the whips'; Nikita Khrushchev, an advanced version of 'goulash socialism'; and Herbert Marcuse, the 'consolidated consumer society'.

Trade Unions: the Workers' Agents?

In Czechoslovakia, a majority of the workers in all branches of the national economy are organized in trade unions. The workers are not only permitted, but encouraged and, occasionally, even forced to belong. The trade unions in Czechoslovakia – the Revolutionary Trade Union (*Revoluční odborové hnutí*) (ROH) – differ from their counterparts in the Western democracies in several important respects. First, their structure is similar to that of the communist party in that they are organized according to the Leninist model of democratic centralism. It is a pyramidal organization in which decisions made at the highest level of the pyramid (the presidium of the unions) are binding for the lower levels. Initiative from subordinate elements can occur only within the limits set by the decision-making center.

The function of the trade unions in Czechoslovakia is, like the structure, also very different from that of the trade unions in the West. According to

Leninist theory, the trade unions are only 'transmission belts' in the one-party system and do not have any real power of independent action. This means that the trade unions' function is to transmit the commands and instructions of the communist party to the workers. In this capacity, the trade unions only play a significant role' (with varying degrees of responsibility) in the administration of social insurance, vacations, education, recreation and culture. Yet, they do not protect the workers' basic rights, such as the right to strike. The trade unions' primary function, as defined in the labor code of Czechoslovakia, is to reinforce and fulfill national economic policy goals. Thus, according to Czechoslovak labor laws, the trade unions are supposed to mobilize the entire working class and the intelligentsia to fulfill the economic plan and to promote a high level of socialist work morale and the rapid growth of labor productivity. Politically, the role of the trade union is to reinforce the political monopoly of the communist party (Moravec, 1970).

Worker Militancy in Czechoslovakia

Whereas, in Poland, there have been numerous workers' revolts, in Czechoslovakia there has been only one significant workers' revolt which took place on 1–2 June 1953 in the city of Pilsen, which has the highest concentration of industry in Bohemia. It was initiated by the highly skilled workers of the famous Škoda-Enterprise who, having considerable savings, are often described as a 'workers' aristocracy'. The motivation for this revolt was the workers' dissatisfaction and anger with the regime's economic policies of heavy industrialization at the expense of light industry, which caused the workers' standard of living to decline to the pre-war level. The specific cause was the unexpected May 1953 Currency Reform Act, whereby the workers lost their savings and their standard of living was further lowered. The revolt, prompted primarily by economic grievances, was conditioned by the systemic frustration which set in when the population began to expect improvements in the social, economic and political circumstances which were not forthcoming. The workers' revolt in Pilsen, like the revolt in East Berlin one month later, did not occur during a time of despair, but rather when the society was expecting conditions to rapidly improve. It occurred shortly after Stalin's and Czechoslovak President Klement Gottwald's deaths, when the workers' expectations regarding the liberal economic policies of the 'new course' hinted by Gottwald's successor, President Antonín Zápotocký, who promised at least some redistribution of the resources to the consumer sector, were at their peak. Instead, the Czechoslovak regime sharply reversed the trend toward salutary development for one of greater economic austerity. When these unrealistic expectations were suddenly followed by economic disaster in the form of monetary reform, many workers lost their savings, and their great discontent and indignation were followed by revolt (Ulc, 1965, pp. 46–9).

The revolt in Pilsen was an emotional outpouring. The workers had no coherent demands or political program, no leadership and no organization. Although general dissatisfaction with bureaucratic communism was evident in certain demands of a political nature which were expressed in unison with the prevailing economic demands, they were spontaneous and naïve. A classic example is the popular workers' slogan heard at that time which recalled Pilsen's liberation eight years earlier (1945) by US troops: 'We shall have fun again; the boys from the USA will return [*Bude zase hej, přijdou hoši z USA*]' (Ulc, 1965, p. 47). The rebels, instead of organizing themselves after initial successes, succumbed to a brief euphoric state before being suppressed by security forces. During this state of euphoria, the workers destroyed such sites and symbols of the communist regime as banners, special party posters and pictures of leaders and propaganda kiosks. They also exercised violence against the secret police and party members wearing party emblems on their coats.[2] This spontaneous revolt caught the communist authorities unsuspecting and unprepared, at least for a period of time, to cope effectively with the situation. In Pilsen, the regime was unable to contain the revolt with local police forces and had to call on special units of the Interior Guard (*Vnitřní stráž*), a branch of the Ministry of the Interior.

Another important element of the workers' revolt in Czechoslovakia in 1953 concerns the attitude and reactions of segments of the intelligentsia, who (by and large) did not join the rebellious workers. Segments of the intelligentsia, including members of the technical intelligentsia, feared the loss of their jobs and being relegated to worker positions. Moreover, the intelligentsia had become demoralized in Czechoslovakia by massive emigration to the West. In Pilsen, economic measures only reinforced the opposition of many of the workers against the regime. Thus, only the workers were sufficiently motivated to act. To paraphrase Marx, they had nothing to lose by violence except their shackles.

The Workers and Pluralistic Communism: Prague Spring

The workers' attitudes and their behavior during the peaceful revolution in Czechoslovakia in 1968-9 is one of the few subjects related to the workers in Eastern Europe which has been studied in depth. Indeed, several writers – H. Gordon Skilling, Alex Pravda, and others – have examined the subject extensively. Their findings demonstrate that, for a long time, certainly until the Soviet invasion on 20 August 1968, the workers had viewed the pluralistic communist reform being carried out by the politicians with the advocation and support of economists, journalists, writers and students in a passive manner and, in many cases, with mistrust (Skilling, 1976, pp. 579-85; and Pravda, 1973). The workers have always been suspicious of the intellectuals, and have feared the latter's 'hegemony'. Thus, the ruling 'nostalgics' in Novotný's regime were able quite successfully to indoctrinate the workers with suspicion regarding the 'petty bourgeois, unstable' intellectuals. More importantly, the workers have always been concerned more with their economic and social rights than with political freedom. The authentic workers felt that the 'nostalgic' workers in the ruling elite and their so-called 'worker' polices had at least provided them for twenty years, as Skilling points out, with '"social security", assuring them both employment and a minimum and stable standard of living, and affording certain sectors of the working class a privileged position' (Skilling, 1976, p. 580). Moreover, there has existed a certain subtle, unspoken affinity between the 'nostalgic' and 'authentic' workers in Czechoslovakia. Widespread among the 'authentic' workers is a certain degree of sympathy for the unpolished, not too well-educated 'nostalgic' workers in the Czechoslovak ruling elite. This writer, for example, witnessed a discussion in 1966 among a group of Czechoslovak workers and students following the speech of President Novotný, who had a habit of ending his speeches with various pacifying promises such as, 'There will be meat [*Maso bude*]'. When the students objected to Novotný as being 'primitive [*blbec*]', one of the workers replied, 'Yes, perhaps primitive, but one of us [*Možná blbec ale náš*]'.[3]

This frame of mind was one of the reasons why the reformers had difficulty, in 1968, in making the workers understand the connection between political and economic rights. Although a large number of small stoppages and strikes occurred, until the invasion the workers for the most part remained an apathetic majority, courted by reformists (whose ranks also included a few 'nostalgic' workers) and anti-reformists (many of them 'nostalgic' workers) alike in the Czechoslovak leadership. The former tried to assure them that the reforms would in the long run bring them economic benefits, while the latter, most of them fearful of losing their jobs, denounced the reforms and in the name of socialism 'defended' the interests of the 'authentic' workers threatened by 'anti-socialist extremists' among the intelligentsia.

The Invasion and the Changing Role of the Unions: Working People's Councils

Included in Dubček's unique experiment, was the intent to encourage and enhance the role of the trade unions, and later to establish institutions which would facilitate more active participation of the workers in economic and political life – the Working People's Councils. Thus, the Action Program of the CPCz, published in April 1968, viewed the function of the trade unions as needing to be changed. A special conference of delegates from the union organizations confirmed this objective in the same month. Although the organization of the trade unions still remained centralized, and although the unions continued to be run primarily by 'nostalgic' workers, such as new chairman and old *apparatchik* K. Poláček, they nevertheless began to implement Dubček's program of democratic communism. Thus, the trade unions were gradually being transformed from 'transmission belts' into more-autonomous organizations geared more to defending and protecting the interests of the working class. Although striking was viewed as a last-resort protest measure and wildcat strikes were completely ruled out, strikes were not forbidden when issues such as wages were concerned. The new trade union leadership drafted a program which even included the creation of a strike fund (Golan, 1973). Moreover, strikes even occurred. In spring 1968, at the Dukla Mine in Ostrava a workers' strike was instrumental in bringing about the dismissal of the manager and the election, by workers themselves, of a new director. This was not an isolated incident. The workers and the Czechoslovak trade unions, however, began to play a truly active and autonomous role only after the Soviet invasion. The invasion created a feeling of patriotism and prepared unusual conditions for the temporary establishment of new linkages between intellectuals and workers against the invaders and their fifth column. Thus, in December 1968 the most powerful trade organization – the Metal Workers' Union – threw its weight behind the reformers and their program. In March 1968, the Seventh Congress of the Trade Unions adopted the reform program, despite growing anti-reformist pressures. The Metal Workers' Union remained restive until the summer of 1969, encouraging a slowdown in production in defiance of Gustav Husáks's new regime.

It is not possible, in this chapter, to deal in depth with the complex issue of the Working People's Council. In short, they were institutions created in 1968–9 to give workers a greater voice in management. In Czechoslovakia, the idea of worker participation in management has had a long tradition. There have existed workers' councils of various forms as early as the 1920s, and again in 1945-7. These organizations provided an historical precedent for the Working People's Councils of 1968–9 which, although a highly discussed topic, were never actually accepted as a general model for workers' participation in management. The concept was neither fully developed, nor completely implemented. Until the Soviet invasion, the reformers had pushed for the establishment of the councils, whereas the apathetic majority of workers showed only a little interest. Both before and after the invasion, workers were reluctant to become directly involved or participate actively. Instead, they chose to have the technical intelligentsia represent for the most part their interests. However, the Soviet invasion stimulated greater interest on the part of the workers in the debate on the councils. When the idea finally caught on, some Working People's Councils were formed, albeit still with a small minority of authentic workers, from the fall of 1968 until Dubček's demotion in April 1969. In this period, the councils became symbols of new worker participation in the reform movement. With the polarization of the political scene in Czechoslovakia, in the spring of 1969, there were increasing signs of the development of an unusual coalition of reform intellectuals, students and workers, many of whom now gave political support to general reforms. Before the coalition could become active, it was overtaken by events – the threat of a second Soviet invasion in April 1969, the subsequent fall of Dubček and the counter-revolution of 'nostalgic' workers. The trade unions resumed gradually their previous mission and the Working People's Councils were eliminated.[4]

The Workers' Revolutionary Potential

What lessons can be drawn and what prognosis can be made about potential worker militancy in the light of the revolt in Czechoslovakia in 1953, and worker participation in the final stage of the Czechoslovak peaceful revolution of 1968? The Czechoslovak experience suggests that under certain conditions worker alienation can become so pronounced as to prompt the workers to resort to slowdowns in production, strikes, political unrest and even violent revolts. Because of the workers' revolutionary potential of which the ruling elite in industrial East European countries have become well aware, there exists a hidden antagonism between the ruling bureaucracy and the workers. This antagonism has been particularly acute when worker militancy has intensified latent conflicts among various factions of the bureaucracies, the best example being the workers' revolt and power struggle that led to the overthrow of the Polish leader, W. Gomulka, in 1970. The workers can play an important role in conflicts among the various groups in the leadership. This was demonstrated in Czechoslovakia after the Soviet invasion of 1968, when large sectors of the working class began to support the reformers in Dubček's regime and to coalesce with the reform-oriented intellectuals.

Why are the workers' attitudes and behavior taken so seriously, more seriously, for example, than the dissent of students and intellectuals? The most important reason is quite simple. The ruling elite, particularly the 'nostalgic' workers, realize that their role could not continue permanently against the will of a militant working class. The ruling elite have tended to demoralize, banish or even jail dissenting segments of the intelligentsia. They have also dealt successfully with the peasants, who have never presented a serious challenge to the communist regimes. As history illustrates, however, they have had more difficulty coping with the workers. Authoritarian regimes can survive for decades without a contemporary literature, impressionist painting, surrealist sculptures, 'new wave' film art, new theatre forms, objective historiography, modern sociology and psychology, etc. They can forbid their citizens to partake of the fruits of Western and even their own native cultures. These restrictions were commonplace throughout Eastern Europe during the Stalin era and in Czechoslovakia to some degree in the 1970s. The ruling elites can rule without all but the technical intelligentsia, but they cannot survive without the workers. Workers' revolts, such as the one in Pilsen in 1953, may lead to large-scale systemic disruption and weaken the system. Thus, the ruling elite is restrained from outright oppression of the working class which provides the economic basis for the East European social structure. 'The proletariat', Marx hypothesized, 'cannot stir, cannot raise itself up without the entire super-incumbent strata of official society being sprung into the air' (Marx, 1962, p. 21). The use of military force to suppress the workers' strikes and revolts is not an optimal solution, since it can lead to yet other revolts and further violent oppression, which in turn can stimulate a larger national revolt with possible changes in the leadership, as happened in Poland in 1970. It is difficult to severely punish a large number of workers for revolting. The East European regimes will undertake such punishment if it is deemed necessary, but then only as a limited and final measure. It is much easier to punish 'authentic' intellectuals than 'authentic' workers. The workers have little to lose. Giving up a hammer for a shovel is not the same as giving up a pad and pencil for a shovel.

The workers' profession is unique. In all modern industrial societies, the majority of workers are organized in large industrial groups and have a massive audience in the big cities. Unlike the solitary intellectual and the peasant isolated in his rural environment, the worker functions under conditions in which the authorities cannot keep a close watch on his activities. Communication and the dissemination of information are much easier in the industrial environment than among the peasants and the intellectuals. These features can facilitate strikes and revolts (*Svědectví*, 1976, pp. 599–603).

In spite of this revolutionary potential, the attempt at revolt in Czechoslovakia in 1953 failed. This was partly because it occurred only in one large industrial city, and partly because the revolt was not supported by other social classes – mainly the intelligentsia. The workers in Pilsen, like the workers in Berlin in 1953 and in Poland in 1970, acted alone and not within a broad coalition of social classes including the intelligentsia and peasants. The workers' actions in the Pilsen revolt were motivated by economic issues, political freedom (the main concern of the intelligentsia) being of only secondary importance to them. This is one of the most important reasons why they were not joined by the intellectuals. In contrast, the peaceful revolution in Czechoslovakia, in 1968, was for a long time the sole undertaking of intellectuals. The primary concern was political freedom, while the basic economic issues such as wages and social security, which are usually the workers' concern, remained secondary. It is no wonder most of the workers did not join the coalition until after the trauma of the Soviet invasion which aroused the passion of patriotism. The Czechoslovak experience confirms that the fulfillment of the workers' revolutionary potential presupposes an uncompromising struggle against the ruling elite, the existence of a coherent revolutionary program, and leadership. Most indispensable in any worker attempt to challenge the ruling elite, is the workers' alliance with revolutionary intellectuals.

The Policies of the Ruling Elite

In the view of this writer, the ruling elites in Eastern Europe have understood for a long time that the forming of an assertive worker–intelligentsia coalition must be prevented to ensure the stability of their regimes. This was particularly true of Novotný's regime which dealt harshly with intellectuals while exalting the workers ideologically and awarding them with guarantees of social security. After the impact of the workers' revolts in Pilsen and East Berlin, and the revolutionary year of 1956, the 'nostalgic' workers in Novotný's regime had also begun to implement a new strategy of '*divide et impera*'. Their objective was to drive a wedge between the workers and the intellectuals, and to prevent the building of a hostile anti-regime coalition. By artificially cultivating a permanent conflict among the various social groups, the Czechoslovak regime was able to maintain its societal hegemony while presiding as broker over the conflicting groups. The Czechoslovak Marxist philosopher, Karel Kosík, described the strategy of the ruling elite in Czechoslovakia as follows:

The conflict between the workers and the intelligentsia, which the ruling bureaucracy has been provoking constantly since 1956, was not only artificially created, but was also an artificial conflict. The real meaning of the conflict was that it incited one group, the workers, against another, the intelligentsia. It was also an attack on the wisdom, the critical thinking, the judgement, in short on the intelligence of one class of society, the workers. It was aimed chiefly at them. The meaning of the conflict will become quite clear when we understand that together with this campaign against the intelligentsia, against reason and judgement, there was a revival of primitive instincts: anti-semitism, mass psychosis and so on. As a result, a dark alliance of superstition, prejudice and resentment was being secretly and sometimes even publicly organized against the possible alliance between reason and intelligence. (*Literárni listy*, 25 April 1968)

The strategy of playing the classes against one another was also employed by the anti-reformists in the Czechoslovak leadership during the Prague Spring.

Since the revolt of 1953, the regime has also adopted more flexible economic policies. After the demise of the Prague Spring, the new Husák regime initiated a period of 'normalization' which meant a return to a centralized system of management and an end to economic reform, accompanied by regular increases in the wages of industrial workers. The regime also made a new effort to effect a dichotomy between the workers and the intellectuals. These trends were reinforced under the impact of the 1970 workers' revolt in Poland which toppled Gomulka from power. The experience of the Prague Spring of 1968, and the Polish experience of 1970, contributed to convincing the Czechoslovak leadership that it should refrain in the future from further experiments with economic reforms, even though they be of a limited scope, and place added emphasis on social stability and discipline, but also on a good standard of living for the workers, even at the price of slower economic growth. Thus, the Czechoslovak regime again turned to policies designed to promote the continuous embourgeoisement of the proletariat. In the last decade, this policy has for the most part been effective. It brought about increased discipline by amending the labor code in 1971. At the same time, it tried to satisfy the economic and social needs of the workers. The overall level of investment in industry was reduced so that special emphasis could be placed on preserving 'social security', keeping the price level of commodities down, providing regular increases in wages, and improving the overall quality of life, in particular by supplying somewhat better consumer goods and housing. The complex and advanced economic system of Czechoslovakia experienced very serious dislocations in the 1950s, and stagnation if not recession in the early 1960s, but performed rather well in the 1970s. There has been sustained quantitative improvement in economic production. Overall economic success, conditioned by steady economic growth from 1967 and continuing through 1978, cannot be denied. In comparison with the early 1950s, Czechoslovak workers have a fairly decent standard of living. This is due in part to a high agricultural yield, which has made feeding the population less of a problem than in the past. However, the overall economic situation is still destabilized by persistent shortages and undermined by a pervasive and powerful 'second market', and by widespread cynicism and corruption, one can venture moral decay (Kusin, 1978; Ulc, 1979). The overall result of the regime's policies of embourgeoisement, is that the workers in Czechoslovakia have not rebelled in any major way against the regime, nor played an important role in any significant form of dissent in the 1970s. The regime has even had some success in its drive for increasing worker recruitment into the party in the 1970s. Dissent associated with Charter 77 comprises a very small minority (roughly 1,000–1,500 signatories as of 1979). Many of those who signed the Charter as workers were 'penitent' workers and former politicians of Dubček's era.[5]

Outlook for the Future

Although there is a hidden conflict between the ruling class and the workers in Czechoslovakia, and the workers possess a revolutionary potential for overtaking their rulers, successful worker revolutions have not taken place. There can be no successful workers' revolt without the support of the intellectuals, and no revolutionary attempt of the intellectuals can succeed without the workers' support. The prospects for building such a coalition of workers and intelligentsia in Czechoslovakia are generally not very promising in the 1980s. The Czechoslovak regime has successfully pursued strategies for driving a wedge between the intelligentsia and the workers. Moreover, with their policies of embourgeoisement, the ruling elite has succeeded in appeasing significant sectors of the working class and has isolated the intelligentsia. It remains to be seen, however, whether the Czechoslovak regime will be equally successful in the 1980s. With the energy crisis and worldwide recession, there are growing signs that Eastern Europe may be again approaching a period during which a reduction in the standard of living of the workers may be unavoidable. The outlook for worsening economic conditions in Czechoslovakia may serve as a catalyst for worker dissatisfaction. This dissatisfaction could then be exacerbated by the tension between the aging 'nostalgic' workers and the new, better-educated *cadres* coming from the universities.

The prospects for building a worker–intellectual coalition in Czechoslovakia, however, are not very good, certainly not in the foreseeable future. This contrasts with the unique situation in Poland where a worker–intellectual coalition has been in the making since 1976. In Poland, as in other East European countries, however, external factors impose limits on the development of such coalitions on a national level. The most relevant factor is the Soviet response. The Soviet use of military force in East Germany, Hungary and Czechoslovakia, and the recent invasion of Afghanistan, indicate the immense degree of Soviet sensitivity about political instability in neighbouring countries and its potential effects on the Soviet Union. This is so now and will probably continue to be so for a long time to come. However, the Soviet Union abstained from intervening militarily in Poland in 1956 and 1970. In 1956, Soviets were aware that the Polish workers, particularly in Warsaw, were armed and willing to resist. Also, in 1970, the workers' willingness to fight the regime's security forces undoubtedly played an important role in the Soviet decision.

One can only speculate as to whether significant workers' unrest will occur in Czechoslovakia in the 1980s and as to how the Soviet leaders might respond. If history serves as a guide, one could conclude that the prospects for increasing workers' militancy and the building of an intellectual and workers' coalition in Czechoslovakia are not very good. Only in 1953, and only in one city, did the workers of Czechoslovakia rise up to defend their interests, and this uprising has already been almost entirely forgotten. This history stands in sharp contrast to that of Poland, where three times in the last decade (1970, 1976, 1980), the workers, acting as genuine revolutionaries, forced the regime into political and economic compromises by virtue of their strikes in factories across the country. Because of its successful policies of embourgeoisement, particularly in the last decade, the Czechoslovak regime has been able to avoid such a confrontation. Can the Czechoslovak regime, in the face of a deteriorating worldwide economic situation, continue to maintain the proletariat's bourgeois status? The high cost of energy, the high currency debt, the ever-present but more-severe shortages, and the new experience with inflation (unavoidable high increases in the prices of consumer goods and a reduction in price subsidies), are problems that have become even greater in 1979–80. Will the serious deterioration of the overall economic situation and inevitable social and economic sacrifices overtake the regime in Czechoslovakia? How will they affect political, social and economic equilibrium? How could the workers respond to the violation of their unspoken agreement with the regime? Will the Czechoslovak leaders be able to meet this challenge and enforce the necessary sacrifices without inciting the workers? The Polish situation, at the onset of the 1980s, is not unique. Was the July 1980 national wave of strikes following a government increase in the price of meat another typical example of exceptional assertiveness of the Polish proletariat, or a symptom of a more-profound and pervasive economic crisis to come? In the 1970s, most experts came to believe that there is '*nichts neues in Osten*', particularly in Czechoslovakia. This may not be necessarily true in the 1980s.

Notes: Chapter 11

1 Because the role of the workers in Eastern Europe has been a neglected subject, I have been able to consult only a few studies in preparation of this essay. At the same time, however, I am fortunate to have been able to draw on my own, albeit limited, experience as a worker during several brief intervals, in the 1960s, in Czechoslovakia, and on interviews conducted with various personnel from Czechoslovakia including workers. I am also indebted for their comments to Professors Jan Triska, Charles Gati and Alex Pravda.
2 I have relied here on the recollections of workers, some of whom were participants and witnesses of the revolt in 1953, and whom I encountered in 1963–4 as an employee of the Škoda factory in Pilsen (Plzeň).
3 From personal recollections, Prague, 1966.
4 Here also I benefited from interviews with former Czechoslovak trade union officials living in the West.
5 Personal interviews.

References: Chapter 11

Binar, I., *'Kdyby dělník u nás vladnul', Listy* (Rome), vol. 9, no. 2, 1979, pp. 1–5.
'Bohemicus' (anonymous writer living in Prague), *Listy,* vol. 9, no. 1, 1979, pp. 6–9.
Connor, W. D., 'Dissent in Eastern Europe: a new condition?', *Problems of Communism,* vol. 29, no. 1, 1980, pp. 1–17.
Golan, G., *Reform Rule in Czechoslovakia. The Dubcek Era, 1968–1969* (Cambridge: Cambridge University Press, 1973), pp. 60–66.
Hajek, J., and Nižnansky, N., 'Czechoslovak dissent: sources and aims', *Radio Free Europe, Background Report,* no. 143, 29 June 1978, p. 7.
Klokočka, V., 'The ideological and social foundations of power in the system of "real socialism"' (Working Study No. 1, of research project), Z. Mlynar, ed., *The Experience of the Prague Spring 1968* (March 1979, p. 12).
Kosik, K., 'Our present crisis', *Literarni listy,* 25 April 1968.
Kovanda, K., 'Works councils in Czechoslovakia, 1945–47', *Soviet Studies,* vol. 29, no. 2, 1977, pp. 255–69.
Kusin, V., *Political Grouping in the Czechoslovak Reform Movement* (London: Macmillan, 1972).
Kusin, V., *From Dubček to Charter 77. A Study of 'Normalization' in Czechoslovakia, 1968–1978* (New York: St Martin's Press, 1978).
Marx, K., 'Manifesto of the Communist Party, 1948', in A. Wittney, ed., *The Communist Blueprint for the Future* (New York: Dutton, 1962), pp. 3–44.
Moravec, P., 'Trade unions in Eastern Europe', in George Schöpflin, ed., *The Soviet Union and Eastern Europe. A Handbook* (New York: Praeger, 1970), pp. 331–5.
Pelikán, J., *Socialist Opposition in Eastern Europe. The Czechoslovak Example* (New York: St Martin's Press, 1973), p. 40.
'Polska lekce', Svědectví (Paris), vol. 13, no. 52, 1979, pp. 599–603.
Pravda, A., 'Some aspects of the Czechoslovak economic reform and the working class in 1968', *Soviet Studies,* vol. 24, no. 1, 1973, pp. 102–24.
Pravda, A., 'What about the workers?', in A. Oxley, A. Pravda and A. Ritchie, eds, *Czechoslovakia. The Party and the People* (New York: St Martin's Press, 1973), pp. 149–218.

Skilling, G. H., *Czechoslovakia's Interrupted Revolution* (Princeton, NJ. Princeton University Press, 1976).

Triska, J., 'Soviet–East European relations', in R. Wesson, ed., *The Soviet Union: Looking to the 1980s* (Stanford, Ca.: Hoover Institution Press, 1980), pp. 45–64.

Ulc, O., 'Pilsen: the unknown revolt', *Problems of Communism,* vol. 14, no. 3, 1965, pp. 46–9.

Ulc, O., 'One decade of post-invasion Czechoslovakia', *Survey,* vol. 24, no. 3, 1979, pp. 201–13.

Valenta, J., *Soviet Intervention in Czechoslovakia, 1968: Anatomy of a Decision* (Baltimore, Ma.: Johns Hopkins University Press, 1979).

12 Hungary: the Lumpenproletarianization of the Working Class

Ivan Volgyes

Introduction

There are very few topics that are as unwelcome in the depoliticized Hungarian polity as the topic of workers' power and the concept of the working class. Indeed, if one were to have to list the acts of the party to stifle dissent in that country since the end of the abortive 1956 revolution, one would list almost exclusively those acts of repression that were aimed against groups that questioned the role of the working class in socialist societies, in general, and in Hungary, specifically. Hence, the Lukacs–Hegedus group, the intellectual circles associated with the Konrad–Szelenyi circle or the younger worker intellectuals associated with Haraszti and his comrades were all questioning the role of the working class in Eastern Europe and in Hungary, and as such their crime was greater than merely engaging in an intellectual debate: they attempted to forge an alliance between the workers and the intellectuals, and their questioning and organizational attempt challenged the theoretical bases of legitimacy in communist systems.

In the country under our scrutiny in this chapter, the question of the role, power and achievements of the working class are issues central to the very bases of regime existence. Paradoxically, while the regime theoretically rules in the name of an amorphous working class, in reality the elite does just about everything to stifle interest aggregation and power articulation by the social class in whose name they rule. In fact, the contention of this chapter is that the working class among all other classes existing in contemporary Hungary – and by extension in most communist states – is the most dispossessed of power and most vulnerable in the defense of their own interests. The working class in the neighboring capitalist states of Europe is better off in wealth, most social benefits and general economic well-being than under the communist systems; that much is clear to anyone examining the distribution of welfare in Europe as a whole. But the fact that *politically* the workers in Western Europe are more powerful than their Eastern neighbors – ranging from true power at the ballot box to the applicable concept of *Mitbestimmung* in practice – is a reality that, though well-known to specialists, must be constantly hammered home for the general and concerned public. This chapter, then, will discuss the role and limitations of the power of the working class and different national policies aimed at controlling workers' dissent and assertiveness.

The Working Class

There can be no doubt that theoretically the working class is the most important part of society; the constitution of Hungary states that in Hungary the 'working class is the leading class of society' and its power is firmly embedded in all public documents. Notwithstanding these facts, the definition of the working class is not as simple as the Constitutions would have us believe. The major cause of the confusion stems from the fact that the definition of the 'working class' has constantly shifted with the postscriptive, tortuous justifications of power used by the communist elites that have passed for ideology throughout the last six decades in the Soviet Union and the last thirty some years in Hungary.

Throughout those years, it has been one of the most obfuscated definitions, and the theoretical impossibility of defining the 'working class' in other than exclusionary bases – for instance, those who have nothing to sell except their labor – has left communist and non-communist theoreticians baffled. The Marxist attitudes of admiration for the class and contempt for the individual, followed faithfully by the implementers of Marxism-Leninism, moreover, left the working class in theoretical limbo, and posed a serious definitional problem for the regimes that came to power in Eastern Europe after World War II.

Before coming to power in 1948, the Hungarian communists attempted to use broad inclusive definitions, terms like the 'working people' or 'working class' were used interchangeably. By 1949, however, the 'working class' (*munkasok, munkasosztaly*) as a phrase began to be utilized almost exclusively for those who came from the industrial working class themselves, or who have been forcibly removed and chosen from the working class for positions of power (Rakosi, 1950). Although *some*, but not all, agrarian proletars were included in the concept of the working class, the exclusionary nature of the definition began to be clear; the only exception was, of course, the exalted party elite.

Throughout the 1950s, it was this restrictive phraseology that was applied by the elite. By the mid-1960s, however, Janos Kadar and the Hungarian leadership embarked on broadening the basis of the legitimacy of his own position and that of his party. Aside from the reform policies that later were to be introduced and implemented under the collective term of the New Economic Mechanism (NEM) and were designed to enhance his economic bases of support, Kadar also began to broaden the concept of socialist democracy and in the process opened up the concept of the working class. His policy of forming an 'alliance' with the entire 'working people' (*dolgozo nep*) removed the working class from its sacrosanct ideological position of unquestioned ideological supremacy over the other non-antagonistic classes of the working peasants and working intellectuals.

And although the revised Constitution of 1972 states unequivocally that 'In the Hungarian People's Republic the leading class of society is the working class', immediately the qualification appears that the working class 'employs the power [to rule] together with the cooperative peasantry, with the intelligentsia and with the other working strata of society' (*A Magyar Népköztársaság Alkotmánya,* 1974).

In reality this meant that the number of people who could claim to belong to the 'working class' has grown to include all those who were engaged in physical labor or were the managers of such laborers in the primary, secondary and the tertiary sectors as well (Blaskovits, 1968). Such broad definitions by 1966 included 61 percent of the population, and this figure has remained relatively unchanged throughout the last decade and a half: in 1980 it was 59 percent (Blaskovits, 1964, p. 14; MSzMP, vol. XII, 1980, p. 21).

It would be incorrect to state that the working class did not object to this 'watering down' process; indeed, during 1972–4 a group of party leaders known as the 'workers' opposition' made a major effort to restrict the use of the term. The opposition group drew emotional solace from the traditional attitudes of worker superiority that the working class and especially some of the elements of the trade union leadership saw eroding. They drew intellectual solace from the sociologists' well-founded claim that the working class in Hungary was losing its power, its influence to the elite, to the party, to the technocrats and to the ancient enemy, the peasants (*Szociologia,* I, 1972). It was all true, of course; the working class was losing its influence. As Hungary sought a more 'rational' system of economic management, the influence of the workers *was* diminishing *vis-à-vis* other segments of a rapidly modernizing community. The 1972–4 attack against the technocratically oriented leadership, although temporarily successful, was the last hurrah of the workers' opposition. Although the trade unions were given greater say than in other communist states in the directors' councils of the factories, including the right to veto legislation affecting the trade union membership and the institution of trade union stewards (*Magyar Kozlony,* 13 May 1967; Gáspár, 1968), these rights were not enforced, and the rights of the working class became whittled down – so much so that they are again similar to those of other working classes in the region. In the end, the opposition's failure to re-ensconce working-class influence in the decision-making apparat through permanent institutionalization left only anti-systemic activities open for organized workers. Indeed, the working class since then has been defined away ever so gently, merged with other concepts and became resurrected as a phrase to be used only on ceremonial occasions celebrating the ensconced rule of entrenched rational bureaucracies. The process of 'defining away' the concept of the working class – at best elusive and at worst meaningless – has been an observable phenomenon and leaves the observers – and the leadership of communist Hungary – only with a vague notion of the parameters of the term: the working class.

The Working Class and Political Activity

Attempts to describe the working class of course are politically motivated acts, especially in polities where radically different political processes are at work. The definition of a 'worker' – both as a productive unit and as a part of a class – is a task that depends frequently on categorical bias and is little different, as a task, in Western or Eastern societies. The polity under examination, however, has evidenced such enormous growth in both the absolute number of industrial workers, and manual laborers, that a 'semantic exercise' at this stage seems to be unwarranted.

The development and modernization of Hungary has been dramatic and a clear proof of the successes of the regime in industrializing Hungary. The number of industrial laborers grew by leaps and bounds (see Table 12.1). As the industrialization drive has continued and as collectivization–industrialization policies have tapped hitherto underutilized manpower, the rapid process of increasing the number of workers has proceeded unabated.

It should be noted, however, that the process of industrialization has *not* been concomitant with the process of urbanization. Unlike in Western Europe where the two processes of industrialization and urbanization have been generally coterminous, in Eastern Europe they have been somewhat disparate. Industrialization has run in Hungary dramatically ahead of urbanization; creating urban residences that could be regarded as adequate has been far more difficult than bringing people into the industrial workforce. An industrial worker in Hungary is not necessarily an urban laborer; rather, he is an individual who is likely to possess ties to rurality.

The data presented in the table show that the number of industrial workers in Hungary in 1945 was 648,000. Most of these were urban residents, presumably possessing some class consciousness and worker *élan*.

Table 12.1 *Industrial Workers in Hungary for Selected Years*

1910	500,000
1930	660,000
1938	770,000
1945	648,000
1950	910,000
1959	1,400,000
1960	1,710,000
1970	1,710,000
1972	1,740,000
1977	2,070,000

Needless to say, we are aware of the difficulty defining class consciousness and worker *élan*. Though criticism of these terms can easily be made, it is clear that attributes of class consciousness can easily be observed. In work attitudes and efficiency, production-oriented mentality, and in performance, the Hungarian industrial workers were close to or equivalents of their Western European counterparts. This working class, moreover, has always been quite active politically: the prewar votes for the fascists, the working-class demonstrations of the 1930s, the high rate of participation in trade unions, are ample evidences of these attributes (Ranki, 1980; Nagy-Talavera, 1979; Lacko,1966). Such political activities, indicative of the vaguely defined class consciousness, continued after the war throughout the period of the struggle for power as is demonstrated in the working-class vote pattern in Budapest (Ranki, 1980). Of the nearly 650,000 workers following World War II, some 200,000 or around one-third of the total number of 'old workers' have been tapped by the party in the following few years for party and state offices; usually the best, most skilled, most 'class-conscious' workers have been recruited for positions of 'power' and left their industrial workplaces. Consequently, between 1945 and 1977 roughly 1,600,000 new entrants made it into the ranks of the working class from other walks of life. Of these people, no more than 50,000 individuals came from sectors other than agriculture; the vast majority came from the land, driven out by the successive waves of collectivization, industrialization and the neglect of the primary sector (*Mezögazdasági Adattar,* 1966).

It is instructive to note the group from which most new workers came to industrial occupation. Due to the lack of major land reforms in the post-World War I years, and the inadequacy of the post-World War II land reforms, it can be estimated that nearly 60 percent of the new entrants had left the land to which they had no *property* ties; for instance, these were people who were formally landless agricultural proletars, or people who had such a small amount of land that they were forced to work on the estates of other, more successful peasants or large landowners (Markus, 1980). It is imperative to mention this, because these new entrants had possessed none of the characteristics of the class-conscious working class. Most of the new workers possessed a mentality that aimed at maximizing their income with the least amount of effort, at undertaking minimal amounts of labor for the common goal, of reserving their efforts for reaping maximum benefits for themselves. They did not prize efficiency and productivity; they prized only ensuring their existence and advancement at all costs. In short, in Hungary, one has witnessed a 'watering down' of the working class, the *lumpenproletarianization* of the working class as a whole.

The term lumpenproletarianization, of course, carries too many negative connotations to stand alone. Unlike Marx, who identified the lumpenproletariat only in negative terms, reference is made here to this group as one which works only for its own interests, for its own betterment and which is not interested in political power. It is a class without an identification, a 'name', or *'Bewusstein'* of its own, whose only goal is the maximization of its own economic interests at all costs, including its merciless self-exploitations.

Accordingly, the new class – in sharp contradistinction to the New Class heralded by Milovan Djilas in his much-acclaimed study – was in reality a sharply divided conglomeration of separate and disparate groups. The old workers. who remained in the ranks of the working class, possessed values regarding work and power the new workers did not share; the old working class felt, especially at the beginning, that the new regime was of them, for them and, indeed, by them. Many of their former coworkers were in positions of power, and the benefits accrued to them – ranging from wages higher than in the villages and in other sectors to guarantees of social benefits not available in the countryside – filled them with pride. Though originally there have been plenty of fascists among them and strong fascist influences remained observable, the workers of yore remained a tightly knit group with a *Bewusstein* common to their stratum (Szelenyi, 1979; Kemeny, 1978). These workers were proud of the activities of the communist regime; they supported its collectivization drive, its ruthless industrialization. They backed its internationalism, its atheism and its fanaticism as much as they backed its anti-peasant and anti-bourgeois bias. And by backing the regime, they felt they were going to be not merely its mainstays, but also its beneficiaries as well.

The new workers were vastly different. Chased out by history from their village existence into jobs that paid better than the jobs in the rural sphere, they came to the cities – but most were not integrated into the fabric of urban industrial societies. They commuted on 'black trains' on weekends, retained their residences in the village, drank too much; 'howling with boredom in the December night'; unskilled, untrained and alienated, they possessed different attitudes than their coworkers (Fabian, 1977; Laszlo-Bencsik, 1973). They wanted to get by with as little work as possible, steal as much as they could, drink as much as was allowed and 'rip whitey off' – whitey, of course, being the state, the workers' state, their own state – wherever possible (Haraszti, 1978). Their background was strongly religious, and they considered the old workers as backers of the communists – and, hence, blamed them for the collectivization that herded their families into the much-hated collective farms. And they considered the old workers as communists or communist sympathizers as well as pro-Russian – and that went ever so sharply against their own native nationalism. In short, the new working class slowly *lumpenproletarianized* the working class, as a whole, leaving only a small minority that possessed the old worker *élan* (Gondos, 1968).

It would be tempting to leave this analysis dangling and suggest that the cleavage is merely one between the 'old' and the 'new' working class. The reality, however, has been much more complex. Other factors have come into play as well, such as the workers' skill-level, the locus of his residence, or his possession of a 'convertible' skill.

The question of skilled *versus* unskilled laborers suggests wide divergences affecting work attitudes. Far more skilled workers are permanent urban residents, possessing urban apartments, than unskilled workers; attitudes toward work are only marginally different among these groups. Absenteeism, alcoholism, loafing are about on the same levels. Regarding political activity, there is, to be sure, a larger involvement of skilled than unskilled workers, but the differences once again are quite marginal.

The locus of residence also affects the cleavage. Indeed, commuters are more frequently absent when urgent agrarian tasks are to be accomplished on the household plot, when a house must be brought under roof; they are more tired, and alcoholic rates are somewhat higher among the commuters than among permanent urban residents living in the proximity of their workplace. It is true that political activity is also considerably lower among the commuters; they participate less in social-educational activities than the urban residents (Siklos, 1976). Even though the differences are significant in some instances, in the view of this author they are merely dependent variables contributing to increased differentiation caused by the possession of convertible or non-convertible skills.

Such a *lumpenproletarianization* has had severe implications for the Hungarian regime. It has succeeded in creating a working class, but it is not a class on which the regime can rely to fight *for* the advances of communist society. The new working class possesses few characteristics that are desirable as the bases for reliant political activity. With nearly a million working-class commuters, allegiance to a workplace, to a factory, or indeed to a profession or a class, is hard to come by (Gelleri, 1977). Among the peasant workers occupying hovels, dormitories or cheap, rented rooms with filthy rented beds, the only allegiance is to *a* workplace – any workplace – that can provide the maximum benefit and allows the individual the greatest opportunity to earn additional income from the 'second' economy (Lencses, 1978).

Political activity of the working class only seems to be at an acceptable level. Superficially, working-class representation shows that in 1980, 62·4 percent of the party was composed of individuals who have come from the 'working class', and 52·6 percent of the party members are occupied as workers; for example, physical laborers or those directly involved in productive work. If we disaccumulate from the latter figure around 13 percent agricultural laborers (collective and state farm members and employees), only 39·6 percent of the party members can be said to be 'real' workers (MSzMP, vol. XII, 1980, p. 9).

Outwardly, therefore, *organized* and party-controlled political activity seems to reflect the predominant weight of the working class as a whole. Such political activity, however, as emphasized above, refers only to organized political activity controlled by the party. In Hungary, the general process of depoliticization has made political participation non-compulsive; a symbolic support function in times of prosperity. Since, however, the economic-based legitimacy of the regime has run into significant troubles in the economic stagnation prevalent in the country at the beginning of the 1980s, party members have been expected to 're-engage' themselves and actively assist the party in convincing the population that the party's policy remains 'correct'. The party's problem is that it is caught between the devil and the deep-blue-sea. On the one hand, it desperately needs to restructure the country's industrial base by eliminating industries that are unprofitable. It needs to fire workers where unprofitable work is being done and employ them where they are really needed. It needs to enforce labor discipline and get an honest hour's work for an honest hour's wage. It needs to allocate benefits on the basis of need – and there are so many people whose needs are legitimate.

It is in these areas where the regime runs into the greatest problems. The fear of unemployment – whether real or imagined, whether hidden in the guise of restructuring or masked as the redeployment of labor – has been fanned as an ill imaginable only in capitalist societies. Now, at the beginning of the 1980s, the state needs to end overemployment, but the workers oppose it tooth and nail (Asperjan, 1980). In Gyor, where Ede Horvath, the former Stalkhanovite worker and current iron-handed manager of the Raba Wagon Factory, actually fired some 300 workers, near-riot conditions existed. Even though he guaranteed jobs elsewhere to those fired, only the presence of the police prevented the outbreak of major violence.

Economic restructuring, the current drop in the standard of living, and the efforts of the state to enforce labor discipline have also caused major dislocations in Csepel Island and its huge steel complexes. Workers' unrest during the summer of 1979 was widespread, work stoppages frequent, and Kadar himself had to go out to Csepel to talk to the workers and try to mollify them. How severely he misjudged the mood of the workers, is indicated by the fact that work stoppages actually increased after his speech in the complex. Similar work stoppages and hidden strikes have continued to exist at major construction firms throughout the country during 1978–80 (Hethy and Mako, 1978; Hethy, 1978; Nemeth, 1979).

At the root of many problems, of course, lies the major complaint of the workers that they receive a pittance for their work. It is, indeed, true that the average hourly wage of 17–20 forints (less than $1) is dismally low. In reality, these low wages are the only means whereby the state is capable of maintaining an economic existence at all; the exploitation of labor for the accumulation of profit is characteristic of the *modus operandi* of state capitalism. But in Hungary the disparity between the low wages paid by the state and its subsidiaries, on the one hand, and the wages paid in the 'second' economy, on the other, are enormous; on the free market, before, during or after work hours, with state machinery or without, legally or semilegally, the price of labor is at least five times that given in the socialist sector. And since in Hungary at least 50 percent of the laborforce – especially those with convertible skills – are engaged in the 'second' economy, efforts to restrict earning from this sector, or efforts, conversely, to force greater labor for the socialist sector, are bound to create tension and stress (Gabor and Galasi, 1978; Pusztai, 1980; Kolosi, 1980a). The reality of secondary distribution – as the official term so gently calls this phenomenon – is too entrenched to be disturbed without major dislocations the regime can ill-afford to cause. But the beneficiaries of the secondary distribution are *not* the class-conscious workers of the traditional working class: the lathe operators of Csepel, the smelters of Diosgyor, or the miners of the Mecsek. Their hard and arduous labor is non-convertible, and most of them are permanently settled as urban residents with minimal extra-earning opportunities. They are the ones who are hurt by the inflation, by the higher prices and by the greater economic difficulties. As they look around, it is they who see the 'other working class' getting rich and taking every opportunity to sell their labor for a good price on the free, or secondary, market.

Intraclass tensions have begun to come to the surface between the two strata of the working class. The 'class-conscious working class' with roots in the city, with stakes in a particular place and a particular job, agitate for equality of incomes and for an egalitarianism that perhaps never existed and presses the regime to fulfill its promise of making *them* the real rulers. They feel their position is threatened and eroded by the economic management of the state, on the one hand, and by the new entrants who possess none of the attributes of the 'old' working class, on the other. The 'new workers' – with their rootless, get rich, get drunk, mind-your-own business mentality – are not about to struggle for political power; that is not a struggle for which their poor peasant roots had prepared them (Markus, 1980). They want no share of political power – they just want to be left alone and make a comfortable living ripping off the system wherever they can. Paradoxically, however, the regime must rely on this new *lumpenproletariat* for support against the class-conscious workers: its very political passivity is the guarantee that the working class as a whole cannot act as a class, which allows the regime to break down instances of 'workers' opposition'.

Conclusion

It is clear that communist societies have always been able to deal with dissent and dissenters; repression or co-option, as implied above, are traditional tools, and they have been well practiced by the rulers of communist states in Eastern Europe. The existence of independent interest aggregation and articulation by the working class in Hungary, however, is clearly a troublesome question for the regime. Emerging from the cocoon of 'transmission belts of the party', the restless working class is striking at the very heart of the theoretical bases of the system; the people in whose name the party rules begin to complain against the party's rule.

Simply put, their complaint aims at the regime itself. As the working class looks around in Europe as a whole, they realize that their lot in *all* areas of human existence is far worse than that of their fellow workers' elsewhere. With a guaranteed income available in France, the type of unemployment compensations available in Scandinavia, with '*Mitbestimmung*' slowly in practice in many places in Western Europe, the working class in Hungary recognizes that the workers have very little to lose except their chains.

Moreover, they also recognize that after thirty-five years in existence the regimes in Eastern Europe have run out of ideas of renewal and change (Schopflin, 1980). Stagnating or declining rates of growth, real decreases in the level of living, are always causes of major dislocation. Houses planned and begun that cannot be finished stand as mute testimony of the regime unable to deliver upon its promises. As the regime's promise of modernization dwindles, or is restricted to paper gains, the *raison d'être* for communist rule also fades and only the bayonets remain as the ultimate mainstay of rule.

Does all this mean, then, that a revolution is imminent among the workers? Not very likely. The popular proverb regarding the futility of spraying in the eastern wind seems to be accepted by Hungarians as a *modus operandi* for their behavior. But a second reason for the non-existence of a revolutionary situation among the workers lies in the success of the regime in the *lumpenproletarianization* of the working class. The stakes offered and given to the not-very-class-conscious workers – in the bakshish and thievery-based 'second' economy and in the process of secondary distribution in privatized Hungary – make it likely that the lumpenproletariat will support the system (Markus, 1980, p. 33). Not communism, not the regime, but the system – the system that gave them an opportunity to exist and to reap rewards far in excess of their contribution to the nation, and to avenge the 'true' working class whom they still blame for dispossessing them of their heritage, of their traditional nationalism, and of their 'mythical' lands.

References: Chapter 12

Asperjan, György, *'Járdát épitünk'* ('We're making a sidewalk'), *Elet és Irodalom,* 2 February 1980, p. 3.

Berend, Ivan T., and Ranki, György, *Magyarország gyáripara az imperializmus elsö világháboru elötti idoszakában, 1900–1914 (The Manufacturing Industries of Hungary in the pre-World War I period of imperialism, 1900–1914)* (Budapest: Közgazdasági és Jogi Könyvkiado, 1955); *Kozép-kelet-Europa gazdasági fejlödése a 19.–20. században (Economic Development of East Central Europe in the Nineteenth and Twentieth Centuries)* (Budapest: Közgazdasági és Jogi Könyvkiado, 1969).

Blaskovits, Janos, *A munkásosztály fogalmárol (Concerning the Concept of the Working Class)* (Budapest: Kossuth, 1968), p. 15.

Erdelyi, Sandor, *'A másodlagos elosztásrol'* ('Concerning the secondary distribution'), *Valoság,* no. 12, 1979, pp. 38–52.

Fabian, Katalin, *A Makoldi család (The Makoldi Family)* (Budapest: Szépirodalmi, 1977).

Ferge, Zsuzsa, *Társadalmunk rétegezödése (The Stratification of Our Society)* (Budapest: Közgazdasági és Jogi Könyvkiado, 1973).

Gabor, Istvan R., *'A második gazdasàg'* ('The second economy'), *Valoság,* no. 1, 1979, pp. 22–37.

Gabor, Istvan R., and Galasi, Peter, *'A másodlagos gazdaság: a szocializmusbeli magánszféra néhány gazdaság-szociologiai kérdése'* ('The second economy: some economi-sociological questions of the private sector in socialism'), *Szociologia,* no. 6, 1978, pp. 329–44.

Gaspar, Sandor, *A magyar szakszeryezetek szerepe a szocializmus épitésében (The Role of the Trade Unions of Hungary in the Construction of Socialism)* (Budapest: Táncsics, 1968).

Gelleri, Peter, *A vándorló munkások (The Commuting Workers)* (Budapest: Akadémiai kiado, 1977).

Gondos, Ernö, *Jonás és a cet Obudán (Jonah and the Whale in Obuda)* (Budapest: Magvetö, 1968).

Haraszti, Miklos, *Darabbér (Piecework)* (samizdat): in English: *A Worker in a Workers' State* (New York: Universe, 1978).

Hegedüs, Andras, *A szocialista társadalom strukturájarol (Concerning the Structure of Socialist Society)* (Budapest: Akadémiai kiado, 1971).

Hethy, Lajos, *'Bérvita az épitkezésen'* ('Wage dispute at the construction site'), *Valoság,* no. 1, 1978, pp. 76–88.

Hethy, Lajos, and Mako, Csaba, *Munkamagatartások és gazdasagi szervezet (Labor Behavior and Economic Organization)* (Budapest: Akadémiai kiado, 1972); and *Munkások, érdekek, érdekegyeztetés (Workers, Interests, Interest Balancing)* (Budapest: Gondolat, 1978).

Kemeny, Istvan, *'La Chaine dans une Usine Hongroise',* Actes de la Recherche en *Sciences Socialies,* no. 6, 1978, pp. 62–77.

Kenedi, Janos, *'Tied az ország, ·magadnak épited'* ('The Country is Yours, You Build it for Yourself') (unpublished samizdat, 1979).

Kolosi, Tamas, *'A "mellékes" nem mellékes'* ('The "secondary" [income] is not secondary'), *Élet és Irodalom,* 29 March 1980a, p. 5.

Kolosi, Tamas, *'Uj tendenciák a társadalmi szerkezet fejlödésében'* ('New tendencies in the development of social structure'), *Valoság,* no. 3, 1980b, pp. 38–50.

'A Központi Bizottság Állásfoglalása' ('The stand [taken] by the Central Committee'), *Társadalmi Szemle,* no. 10, 1972, pp. 26–39.

Lacko, Miklos, *Nvilasok, nemzetiszocialisták* (Arrowcross Members and National Socialists) (Budapest: Kossuth, 1966).

Laszlo-Bencsik, Sandor. *Történelem, alulnézerben (History – Viewed from Below)* (Budapest: Szepirodalmi, 1973).

Lencses, Ferenc, *'Az ingázásrol'* ('Concerning commuting'), *Valoság,* no. 12, 1978, pp. 89–97.

A magyar forradalmi munkásmozgalom története (The History of the Hungarian Revolutionary Labor Movement) (Budapest: Kossuth, 1966).

Magyar Közlöny (Hungarian Digest), 13 May 1967, and 27 December 1977.

A Magyar Népköztársaság Alkotmánya (The Constitution of the Hungarian People's Republic) (Budapest: Kossuth, 1974).

A Magyar Szocialista Munkáspárt XII. kongresszusa (The 12th Congress of the Hungarian Socialist Workers' Party) (Budapest: Kossuth, 1980).

Markus, Istvan, *'Az ismeretlen föszereplö – a szegényparasztság'* ('The unknown primary actor – the poor peasantry'), *Valoság,* no. 4, 1980, pp. 13–39.

Mezögazdasági Adattár (Compendium of Agricultural Data) (Budapest: Statisztikai Hivatal, 1966).

Mezögazdaságunk a szocialista átszervezés idején (Our Agriculture at the Time of Socialist Reorganization) (Budapest: Statisztikai kiado, 1963).

Nagy-Talavera, Miklos, *The Green Shirts and the Others: A History of Fascism in Hungary and Rumania* (Stanford, Ca.: Hoover Institute, 1979).

Nemeth, György, *'Teljesitmény és érdek'* ('Productivity and interest'), *Valoság,* no. 10, 1979, pp. 86–94.

Pusztai, Éva, *'Lehangolt csodavárás'* ('Dejected expectation of miracles'), *Élet és Irodalom,* 1 March 1980, p. 16.

Rakosi, Matyas, *Válogatott beszédek és cikkek (Selected Speeches and Articles)* (Budapest: Szikra, 1950).

Ranki, Gyorgy, 'Hungarian fascism', in *Who were the Fascists?* (Bergen: Universitat Verlagt, 1980).

Rupp, Kalman, *'Munkások a melléküzemekben'* ('Workers in the secondary industries')* (Budapest: samizdat, 1976).

Rupp, Kalman, 'Private entrepreneurs and the communist political machine' (paper presented at Research Conference on the Second Economy, Washington, DC, USA, 1980).

Schopflin, George, 'Why cracks are widening in Eastern Europe', *The Times,* 12 February, 1980.

Siklos, Laszlo, *Picasso a gyárban (Picasso in the Factory)* (Budapest: Kozmosz, 1976).

Statisztikai Evkönyv (Statistical Yearbook) (Budapest: Statisztikai kiado, selected years).

Szelenyi, Ivan, *Az uj munkásosztály (The New Working Class)* (Paris: Magyar Füzetek, 1979).

Vegh, Antal, *Erdöháton, Nyiren (In the Forest, in Nyir County)* (Budapest: Szepirodalmi, 1972).

Volgyes, Ivan, 'The private economy of socialist Hungary', in Ivan Volgyes, ed., *Social Deviance in Eastern Europe* (Boulder, Co.: Westview, 1978), pp. 65–88.

13 Romania: Participatory Dynamics in 'Developed Socialism'

DANIEL NELSON

1 Issues

Karl Marx's argument for collective control of the means of production (Marx, 1972, p. 94) is inherent to the rhetoric by which communist parties seek legitimacy. Particularly where communist parties rule in nation states with a significant stratum of industrial labor, as in Eastern Europe, the Marxist call for redistributing economic power (by which he meant political power) is a core tenet for rationalizing party dictatorship. Simply put, communist parties take and hold the reins of government assuring that political power will pass, through the party, into the hands of the working masses, usually seen to include not only industrial labor, but all wage-earners. As interpreted by Lenin, the development of socialism should bring workers into the 'functions of control and accounting' (Lenin, 1943). In developed socialism, therefore, the integration of the masses in the organization and management of production and 'the direct participation of all who work in taking decisions regarding economic and social development' are regarded as *de facto* (Nichita and Neagu, 1977, p. 235; Ceterchi, 1974). In short, workers are to fill 'participant roles' (Almond and Powell, 1978) in developed socialism; they are, collectively, to exercise decision-making authority in the economy and, implicit to a Marxist, the polity as well.

This chapter has both descriptive and analytical purposes related to the foregoing observations. At the outset, we will seek to describe quantitative and qualitative dimensions of participatory behavior among workers (for the most part, industrial labor) in Romania–a communist party state which has, since 1965, referred to itself as 'socialist'.[1] Following earlier studies of participation, we will exclude those whose *career* it is to be engaged in mass organizations, the party or the state in communist countries (Huntington and Nelson, 1976).

The third and fourth parts of the discussion are devoted to analytical issues: first, the impact of workers' participatory behaviour and attitudes on communist governments, their stability and political change and, secondly, the significance of findings regarding such behavior and attitudes for comparative hypotheses about political participation. The first of these issues brings us beyond the microcosm of factories and other places of employment since, in socialist states, workplace behavior is not only relevant to politics but *is* a locus of political life. That the party in Romania and other socialist systems recognizes such an equation, is evident by the great amount of *cadres'* time and party funds devoted to both creating channels for workers' participatory behavior, and to assuring that there is a semblance of enthusiasm for such activities. The success or failure of structures and processes for worker involvement is, therefore, a political 'stake' invested by the party – an investment it *must* make not simply because of its Marxist heritage, but also because the economic plan it pursues requires higher worker productivity. Ultimately, the issue at hand for communist systems is one of power. Do workers fill participant as opposed to subject roles, thereby sharing political power? Do workers have influence in making public policy as opposed to performing roles of symbolic involvement?[2] And, if workers *do* influence public policy, thus acting in participant roles to some degree, what proportion of such influence falls within the bounds of their officially sanctioned authority? Such questions, for the moment left unanswered, are foci for this chapter's third section.

Finally, we will turn to the relationship between workers' participation in a communist party state and broader, comparative hypotheses. A widespread expectation, so prevalent that it is stated as a given rather than in hypothesis form, is that 'citizenship roles' in authoritarian political systems are 'confined to the political output processes' (Almond and Powell, 1978, p. 37). This chapter suggests reasons to doubt such an expectation, and we shall offer some alternative hypotheses about citizenship roles in authoritarian politics maintained by communist parties. Hypotheses regarding the relationships between and among development, political participation and socioeconomic equality will also be considered. The pursuit of socioeconomic development and the ideological commitment to equality are twin tasks of communist governments which cannot be divorced from citizen involvement, particularly the participatory behavior of workers upon whom the developmental goals depend and for whom communist parties ostensibly strive to attain equality. Within that stratum of the population, then, relationships among these variables should be more strongly evident if, indeed, they are to be found at all.

2   The Quantity of Workers' Participation

There is little purpose to operationalizing 'participation' in a communist state through statistics regarding trade union membership; such membership is inherent to being employed and the number of benefits, in any case, contigent upon being nominally associated with the trade union make membership mandatory. It is not much more beneficial to use party or Young Communist League membership as an indicator of participation, since the category of 'workers' as reported for both the PCR and UTC (Partidul Comunist Roman and Uniunea Tineretului Comunist) cannot be assumed accurate. Local organs, in reporting the backgrounds of their membership, are not necessarily uniform in defining the term 'worker', nor are individuals uniform in emphasizing certain aspects of their life for party-membership purposes. To know, therefore, that trade unions in Romania encompass the vast majority of the workforce, says little about workers' participatory behavior. It is, moreover, difficult to judge whether or not the party's claim of 52 percent workers within its membership is at all close to an accurate reflection of industrial labor in political activity (*Era Socialista*, 1979, p. 1).

Since 1971, the Romanian Communist Party has promoted Workers' Councils (Consiliilor Oamenilor Municii COM) as the key mechanism through which the participation of industrial labor in the making and implementing of decisions was to be effected.[3] Party leader Ceausescu had raised, as early as December 1967, the need for some form of collective management to resolve the multiple problems of economic life, to eliminate arbitrary decision-making and to bring the experience of specialists, *cadres* and working masses into management (Ceausescu, 1968). By 1971, the intraparty debates had run their course and the Political Executive Committee's (that is, Politburo equivalent) decision, soon announced at a Central Committee plenum, was then enacted by the Grand National Assembly.

Workers' Councils, however, received little attention until 1977. In these first six years of their existence, the operation of Workers' Councils was given only occasional propaganda emphasis. In early 1978, a strong push for Workers' Councils was reinstituted, making them the cornerstone of a campaign denoted by the word *'autoconducerea'* – 'self-management'. It is a reasonable presumption that such renewed concern for the COM system had some relationship to 1977 labor strife among miners in the Jiu Valley, and strong sociological evidence building over the early mid-1970s that dissatisfaction at the workplace was correlated with high rates of job turnover (instability of the workforce), and had a negative impact on productivity.

Varying from nine to twenty-five members according to the enterprise's number of employees, Workers' Councils in Romania involved over 153,000 workers and management *cadres* only two years after their inception. As originally conceived, however, the majority of each council was composed of non-elected members, primarily those occupying the highest management, technical and political positions in a factory or enterprise. Those 'elected' by workers at a general assembly of the enterprise to be their 'representatives' in the council constituted but a minority of the council. Only eight of a nineteen-member COM at the Bucharest central post office were 'elected', for example, in the 1976–7 period, of whom three were foremen (production department chiefs), one was an engineer, one a national post office official, and only *three* could be labeled as manual workers – two technicians and one postman (Popa-Micsan, 1977, p. 45). Eight of the nineteen were *de jure* members from the highest party and managerial positions – director, assistant directors, chief accountant, party secretary, chief of quality and technical control, president of the trade union and Young Communist League secretary. Three 'nominated' members (nominated by the party leadership of the enterprise) filled out the Workers' Council. All three were chiefs of administrative departments.

With such a minor presence in the principal mechanism for their self-management, it is not surprising that workers play a small role in most of COM discussions and debates. Sessions are, indeed, dominated by *de jure* ('*mebrii de drept*') members or the several individuals present as nominated members. In the example cited above, an analysis for fifteen meetings (once per month) suggested that elected members spoke for only 18 percent of the time (Popa-Micsan, 1977, p. 45). The three people one might label as 'manual labor' spoke for a combined total of 2·1 percent of the council's sessions over the same fifteen months, an aggregate less than any single *de jure* or nominated member except for the UTC secretary. An earlier research effort reinforced the above finding. For all of 1972 and the first half of 1973, COM members in the 'elected' category were asked how often they spoke at Workers' Council meetings. Ninety-five of the 215 respondents said that, over eighteen months, they had spoken fewer than five times. Since a median COM had eighteen members in 1972–3, speaking fewer than five times over a year and a half in a small group, suggests a reluctance or inability to speak out – that is, every third meeting one elected COM member might speak. A more interesting question that was not asked might have inquired who spoke at *every* meeting and for what proportion at the time (Petrescu, 1977).

One such example does not allow us to make nationwide generalizations. Corroboration can, however, be inferred from other fragmentary evidence. Of his experience in a Workers' Council in a Bucharest electronics factory, the chief quality control engineer (a *de jure* member of the council) told this researcher:

> I am often unsure why we meet at all. Surely the few workers' representatives present know what will transpire, and I am quite aware of the messages that will be conveyed. They are, in fact, symbolic gatherings at which we say what is required of us, and listen to the factory director repeat our enterprise's planned production targets, the need for economies in material, etc. If these meetings serve a purpose, I think it is to see one another face to face . . . I haven't participated in decisions of significance for the factory *at the workers' council*. (Oral communication, 1979; emphasis added)

Manual labor seems to be cognizant that Workers' Councils have little power and offer little opportunity to them. Notwithstanding constant reminders via signs in factories, newsletters and verbal communication by party *cadres*, few workers devote their attention to the councils or their activities. It is noteworthy that one-fourth to one-third of 215 workers sampled from machine-construction and chemical-refining industries were unable to identify by name *any* of their 'elected' representatives on their respective councils, and about two-thirds knew either none, or only a few

(Petrescu, p. 56). Moreover, almost half of workers on COM said fewer than ten workers from the enterprise during a six month period had sought their help in their capacity as council member (Petrescu, p. 79).

General Assemblies (*adunarile generale*) in each enterprise, of which the Workers' Councils are *de facto* executive committees, have 'a special role in affirming workers' self-management', through which the working masses participate directly in the socioeconomic management activities, in debating and resolving problems related to filling the production plan, and exercising control as leading organs (Nichita and Neagu, 1977, p. 241). Meeting twice a year, General Assemblies of the enterprise bring together all employees – over 5,000,000 at such assemblies held at the beginning of 1977, for example. As reported by Romanian government sources, past 360,000 expressions of opinion (no definition is offered of such a term) were made at those early 1977 sessions, while about 180,000 proposals were formulated to better the work program . . . the construction, the planning and research of socialist production units. Presumably, the proposals are those made in written form or presented as floor motions (Nichita and Neagu, p. 241). These statistics imply rather significant quantities of participatory behavior.

A 1975 survey, however, suggested that participation at General Assemblies of the enterprise varied with political identity, that is, if a worker was a party or Young Communist League member beyond the mandatory trade union affiliation. Since only 15 percent of factory workers might be party members and an additional 15 percent in the UTC, it is instructive to see the disproportionate share of certain kinds of behavior performed by party–UTC members[4] (see Table 13.1). Only 'preparing for the session' necessarily implies an action with some initiative, in so far as that phrase suggests assigning roles and tasks to others while determining the session's agenda. Almost one-fifth of the party members stated that they had behaved in this way, while somewhat more than one-twentieth of workers with only trade union background gave such a response. These data, then, put a different light on undifferentiated statistics about worker

Table 13.1   *Participation at General Assemblies of the Enterprise by Political Identity (N=610)*

Activity	Party (%)	Political ID Young Communist (%)	Trade Union Only (%)
I prepared for the assembly session	18·9	9·2	4·4
I filled a role at the session	28·1	31·8	21·4
I accomplished a task for the session	46·4	30·8	26·6
I was only present	6·6	28·2	47·6

Source: Mariana Sirbu, *'Integrarea în Muncă si Participarea Politică în Procesul Dezvoltării Constiinte Socialiste',* in Constantin Potînga and Vasile Popescu, eds, *Constiinta Socialistă si Participare Socială* (Bucharest: Editura Academiei, 1977), p. 42.

participation at General Assemblies. It may be true that millions attend the assemblies, hundreds of thousands speak and tens of thousands of proposals are made. Party members, however, dominate these forms of participatory behavior, while others perform functions assigned by *cadres*.

Sections of an enterprise (which can be a particular shop, assembly unit, or office) hold 'production meetings' before general assemblies. In these smaller gatherings, workers are to air proposals, grievances and complaints relevant to their immediate workplace. Management attends, usually in the person of the plant director or assistant director. Whereas the General Assembly of the enterprise appears to have many *pro forma* aspects to it, the production meetings evoke more generalized participatory behavior; topics more germane to daily conditions and tasks are raised. A national sample in the early 1970s of 6,236 workers from three sectors of Romanian industry (see Table 13.2) found that one-third to two-fifths of industrial

Table 13.2 *Participation in Production Meetings by Young Workers*

	Industry		
Behaviour	Machine	Chemical	Textile
Made proposals	1233 (39%)	510 (32·7%)	534 (35·2%)
Do not make proposals	1927 (61%)	1051 (67·3%)	981 (64·8%)
Totals	3160	1561	1515

Source: Ovidiu Badina, '*Participarea Tinerilor la Procesful de Realizare a Unor Inventii, Inovatii si Rationalizari*' in Ovidiu Bădina and Cătalin Mamali, eds, *Tineret Industrial* (Bucharest: Editura Academiei, 1973), p. 123.

labor aged 30 years or younger 'made proposals' at production meetings – a category which lacks specificity in the report of this research but which, one can presume, involves a workers' assessment as to whether or not he 'speaks up' at such sessions. Quantitatively, then, there is considerable participatory behavior among Romanian workers in the sense of trade union membership, attendance at General Assemblies, and at the lowest level of production meetings. But party *cadres* dominate general assemblies of the enterprise and discussion in Workers' Councils, constituting a majority of the council membership in any case.

3 Qualitative Aspects of Worker Participation

Romanian workers are not without opinions about channels for their participation, as well as assessments of their own efficacy. From a mid-1970s survey of workers in two major Bucharest industrial plants (the chemical factory 'Grivita Rosie' and the Intreprinderea de Utilaj Chimic), for example, only 38 percent of employees thought their participation was a regular part of decision-making processes (Cornescu, 1977, p. 214). Moreover, between 23·3 and 38·9 percent of those sampled declared that they were neither informed about the main problems of the enterprise before decisions by their representatives in Workers' Councils or in

General Assemblies, nor after such decisions (Cornescu, p. 214). Approximately 18·5–20 percent of the workers thought their opinions were considered, while foremen more frequently said their opinions were considered.

It is difficult to compare such findings with Western or American experiences. To be sure, assembly-line workers at General Motors might not see themselves as part of decision processes either. Yet, there is no effort to promote the rhetoric of self-management, nor is the party system explicitly tied to interests of the proletariat. Also, while participation at any single American union local may not be high, the strength of the union *vis-à-vis* management may be seen nationally or can be witnessed during strikes. In communist systems, however, there is no national voice for workers except one sanctioned by the party; workers must, in fact, rely upon their local interaction for the resolution of workplace grievances. Were even a large minority to sense a lack of efficacy at the local level, the nationwide result could seriously impair the legitimacy of party-provided channels for participation. Indeed, other data suggest that even among those who *do* participate, there is widespread acknowledgement that workers have little effect on policy. Asked about their participation in production meetings, only one-third of surveyed workers replied that they had made proposals at these sessions. But, of that one-third who *do* make proposals at production meetings, a mean (across different industries) of about 40 percent thought their proposals would be ineffectual. In other words, a sizable part of the minority of workers who do more than attend production meetings are dubious about the value of their participation (see Table 13.3).

This sense of minimal efficacy may also be responsible for the

Table 13.3   *Sense of Efficacy among Workers who make Proposals at Production Meetings*

		Industry	
Evaluation	Machine	Chemical	Textile
Proposals have an Effect	699 (59·8%)	307 (60·3%)	353 (66·1%)
Proposals have no Effect	533 (43·2%)	202 (39·7%)	181 (33·9%)
Totals	1232	509	534

Source: Ovidiu Badina, 'Participarea Tinerilor la Procesul de Realizare a Unor Inventii, Inovatii si Rationazari', in Ovidiu Bădina and Cătalin Mamali, eds, *Tineret Industrial* (Bucharest: Editura Academiei, 1973), p. 124.

small proportion of foremen who would bring matters of 'excessive bureaucracy' to the attention of supervisors (only 6–7 percent). Over half of women in such posts (53·5 percent) and a fourth (23·4 percent) of men with such factory jobs offered no response to this kind of questionnaire item, which may have some significance as well in terms of the liberty with which employees think they can respond. Even among that stratum above workers, then, the responsiveness of managerial elites and party *cadres* to complaints of inefficiency and unfairness is doubted.

Concern or cynicism about their efficacy exacerbated the dissatisfaction among Romanian workers regarding material rewards. A smaller proportion of workers than any other category of employment (only 5·12 percent of a national sample) are motivated at their job by creating something of 'social value'. Other categories such as engineers, administrators, etc. scored higher (Dan-Spinoiu, 1974, pp. 94–5). Material rewards dominate workers' motivation and are first among the points leading to their dissatisfaction. Female workers, for whom family identity and the role of wife remain vital, nevertheless rank material rewards most often (46·15 percent in one survey) (Dan-Spinoiu, p. 176) as a motivation in their on-the-job performance. It (pay and related incentives) and personal requests such as transfers and promotions are most often the topics brought up at COM sessions (Popa-Micsan, 1977, p. 451). Dissatisfaction with salaries seems to vary with age, being most acute in the 40–60-year-old categories, reaching 60·7 percent among 40–44-year-olds (Sirbu, 1977, p. 37). Across three principal industries, young workers nevertheless place pay as the chief factor likely to create dissatisfaction more than difficulty of promotion, working conditions, lack of free time and other circumstances (Weintraub, 1973, p. 104).

More generally, workers rank their primary life duties or obligations as familial or interpersonal, not in terms of their professional or citizen roles (Dan-Spinoiu 1974, p. 107). The organization of work, implicitly the party's organization, is not regarded as satisfactory either, since tasks are distributed in a 'bureaucratic' way such that there is 'too much or too little demand on one's capabilities, thereby not permitting an optimal development of one's capacities' (Dan-Spinoiu, p. 124).

Young workers (under 30), although less concerned about pay, have the poorest self-image of any age category, regarding themselves as inferior to others (Dan-Spinoiu, p. 167). Other research, ironically conducted in the Jiu Valley, has found young people without advanced education to be those least likely to intervene when witnessing 'hooliganism' (Preda and Vida, 1975, p. 324). Such a category, of course, is largely coextensive with industrial labor in that part of Romania. Thus far, some findings can be summarised:

(1) Romanian workers are almost always trade union members, and about one-fourth to one-third are party or Young Communist League members, depending on the enterprise.
(2) Workers attend regularly production meetings in their section or shop plus General Assemblies of the enterprise and vote, in uncontested elections, for a few of the Workers' Council members, the exact number varying with the council size, which depends upon the number of employees.
(3) Workers' participation at such sessions tends to be perfunctory, with the agenda, tasks and roles assigned by party *cadres.*
(4) Workers' Councils are not primarily composed of workers, nor do workers who are 'elected' members contribute to debates or discussions.

(5) Elected members of Workers' Councils (COM) are not widely known or consulted by enterprise laborers.
(6) Appeals to superiors are not frequently made to correct inefficiences or arbitrary decisions.
(7) Material rewards motivate workers and personal, not societal, concerns hold their attention.
(8) Young workers exhibit the most alienated attitudes.

4   Communist Governments and Workers' Participation

Most of the foregoing conclusions will startle no student of communist politics. But we need to consider an issue of sizable importance which is not widely pursued – namely, what is the systemic impact of such quantitative and qualitative assessments of workers' participatory behavior on communist governments?

Put succinctly, the impact has been enormous. Because dissatisfaction coexisted with an alienation from party-approved participatory roles, Romania's government has been required to mount an immense propaganda campaign of 'self-management' after the December 1977 National Party Conference. Use of the word 'required' is purposeful, since the sudden decisions to place more emphasis on Workers' Councils cannot be viewed as part of a previous long-term plan. Between that 1977 conference and March 1978, media, scholars and mass organizations prepared Romania for the coming campaign by pointing to the need for new measures to better manage and plan the economy. The March 1978 Plenum of the Central Committee announced that *'autoconducerea'* and *'autogestiunii'* ('self-management' and 'self-accounting') would be, henceforth, key principles guiding the country's path toward a multilaterally developed society. The economic and financial autonomy of industrial units were to be effected through the leadership of each enterprise's COM. Each COM was, moreover, 'democratized' by expanding the number of elected members. Simultaneously, the president of each COM was united with the office of party secretary of the enterprise; previously, the enterprise director had functioned as president of the Workers' Council.

In other words, the party's leadership seems to have responded not only to the immediate threat of renewed miners' violence, but also to widespread disaffection among workers readily discernible to party leaders through sociological research (as cited earlier) and/or productivity data (Traistaru, 1974; Cresin, 1973). The measures taken appear to be aimed at diminishing the rationale for further anti-regime sentiment and reinforcing party' oversight of participatory channels.

Linking the self-management campaign of 1978-9 with the rejection of party-approved participatory channels, must be intuitive for we have no decisive leadership statements to that effect or attitudinal data for central elites. An interview with a member of Romania's Political Executive Committee in the summer of 1978 suggested that top leaders did not reject linking these events, although both emphasized that Workers' Councils had existed for a number of years. A *judet* party first secretary and Political Executive Committee member was asked if the hypothesis linking *'autoconducerea'* to a direct party response to worker dissatisfaction had validity:

> Such an interpretation would not be accurate since workers' councils and the structures of self-management are not new. But we are concerned, of course, that workers have the means by which to effect democracy at the enterprises, to involve themselves in the decision-making at that level. We hope that productivity will continue to rise, or rise more rapidly, *as workers sense their interests are served.* Some people will always be unhappy – nothing will satisfy them. But for most, workers' councils and general assemblies in enterprises are important, *and their effect will be continued improvement in efficiency and economy of materials.* (Oral communication, July 1978)

This national leader appears to be saying that the negative economic impact (low productivity, waste) of workers' alienation from party-approved channels for their participation were recognized and had to be counteracted. The newly reformed COM, as a structural embodiment of self-management, was, then, linked by the leadership to the resolution of urgent *political* difficulties – namely, negative attitudes toward party-approved participatory mechanisms in the midst of general workplace dissatisfaction. The party tried, quite consciously, to identify itself with workers' autonomy and the material interests which motivate that class. The rubric of self-management, the expansion of each COM to include more elected members, and the self-accounting (*'autogestiunii'*) of each enterprise were all part of a broad effort to counteract alarming signals from opinion surveys, productivity figures, rumor and 1977 violence from Lupeni, Petrosani and the mines of the Jiu Valley.

If such an interpretation is accurate, then, the party has demonstrated the limits of its flexibility and has implied dilemmas for Romania's future. Moreover, we might be able to anticipate some of the problems faced by ruling communist parties in states elsewhere in which development and modernization play such a pre-eminent policy role. Having failed to maintain its alleged identity with interests of working people, and faced with the apathy or antipathy of industrial labor toward party-approved means of workplace governance, the Romanian regime has been forced to take a risk by adopting the rhetoric of self-management. No Leninist party can, however, submit itself to a diminution of democratic centralism, that is, the absolute subordination of lower units to higher authorities, because it would then admit to a diversity of interests and needs allegedly diminishing under party rule. The limits Ceausescu must defend are those of any Leninist organization; how to speak the language of self-management and create the institutions for its nominal operation without decentralizing authority, is his dilemma.

Ceausescu's problem is exacerbated by relationships among developmental policies, workers' participatory expectations and 'democratic centralism' – relationships crucial not only in Romania, but in any centrally planned economy ruled by one Leninist party. To pursue development and modernization is the *sine qua non* of legitimacy for many political systems, and for that reason, as well as to establish the societal bases of a Marxist polity, communist parties also push for these socioeconomic advances. Particularly in Marxist states, modernization and development cannot be separated from an emphasis on the interests of that stratum which must bear the greatest burden. To expect a greater voice in workplace affairs and increasing material rewards, are logical correlates of developmental policies in the eyes of the working class. In order to assure worker cooperation and productivity for the achievement of party-decreed plans, industrial labor cannot be as dissatisfied with their material rewards or as indifferent to participatory mechanisms provided by the party as data reveal had become the case in Romania. But to relinquish decisions within the factory to non-*cadres*, or to provide enterprises with autonomy in budgetary matters, suggests that the ultimate subordination of lower levels to higher authority (democratic centralism) is being weakened.

Over time, it may well be that Leninist parties can resist the extension of rhetoric to actuality – that self-management and Workers' Councils will remain symbolic activities with no impact on public policy or conditions in factories. Nevertheless, ruling communist parties will have to *manage* their relationship with the working class, never being confident in the willing obedience or productivity of industrial labor. Whether in the Jiu Valley, Poznan and Radom or Shanghai, evidence is quite clear that communist regimes cannot be sanguine about workers in a workers' state. If national leaders must speak the language of self-management to pacify industrial labor, the question will not long remain moot as to whether or not participatory expectations have been heightened or blunted by such rhetoric. Long before the Jiu Valley or '*autoconducerea*', it was evident that workers and party had different expectations for Workers' Councils. Workers in the COM structure were indicating that the degree to which information is shared by management is the key to the participation of workers, while people in *cadre* posts argued that a 'collective spirit' was the key to encouraging worker participation (Petrescu, 1977, p. 46). While recent Romanian history does not exhibit a strong tradition of worker unrest, unlike Poland by contrast, it is clear to miners and other key sectors of industrial labor that their collective action in a strike or protest can rapidly bring the attention of the country's leaders to grievances.

In conversations during the summer of 1978 in the Jiu Valley, that is, the year after strikes there brought Ceausescu and the Romanian army to the area, I recorded some of the responses to questions I asked of workers in chance encounters at numerous snack bars (the Romanian word for these small restaurants, where liquor is served, is '*bufet*'). Although I was unable to talk with many miners, my effort was to discuss their work in general and, when possible, to bring up the topic of strikes. Of those who were willing to discuss this sensitive and sometimes bitter issue, sixteen said that they would be willing to strike again, while only two said they would not, two others being unsure. A dozen others were not willing to talk about this matter – at least with a foreigner. Of those who indicated a willingness to use the weapon of a strike again, almost all of them (fourteen) qualified their answers with phrases such as, 'If the party leaders don't respond . . .' or 'If we are treated unfairly again . . .'

These personal encounters serve not as data, but as one kind of impression to be gained from conversations; it would seem that there is sentiment favoring strikes as a potential weapon were the need to arise. Having 'drawn blood' in 1977, the miners are cognizant of their strength. Do they now expect that their opinions will be sought, their needs will be conveyed, and their grievances resolved with regularity? In the same series of conversations cited above, I sought to ask whether or not the party would do more for miners now (that is, after the strikes). I categorized their responses as follows:

Will the Party do More for Miners Now?

	Yes	No	Don't Know
Miners N=20	10	7	3
*Others N=27	16	4	7

*All non-mining occupations.

Since these answers are not the product of a sample, the numbers might well not reflect the Jiu Valley population's opinions; there were only two women among those with whom I spoke, for example, and I have excluded people from both occupational categories who would not talk about such issues. Yet, most visitors would not miss the lack of rapport between government and miners. If all miners are not, in fact, of the opinion that strikes will lead to more beneficial attention from the party, it could be because they doubt the efficacy of a strike and/or the party's responsiveness. At the least, it appears that those who struck (the miners) are less sure about the benevolent response of the party. These are, however, the same people who seem to be willing to strike again. That one cannot generalize from such conversations should not prevent us from noting that a sizeable number of people in an area where violent strikes have taken place do not reject the possibility of additional work stoppages even when they are not certain of such action's efficacy.

Although the Romanian Communist Party is confronted by no Committee for the Defense of Workers as in Poland (and the abortive attempt to form an independent workers' union in Romania has faded under government pressure), there is nevertheless unmistakable tension between the party and industrial labor. The stratum for whom the party is to rule is (1) generally dissatisfied with pay and workplace conditions; (2) has little enthusiasm for or confidence in the mechanisms for involvement established by the party; (3) in some industries, such as mining, may be increasingly cognizant that its interests will be served only by confronting the party. We can be confident in such findings roughly in that order, with the latter point most subject to doubt. So severe have these indications become that the Romanian Communist party acted in late 1977 and early 1978 to effect the massive self-management campaign cited earlier.

All of this does not suggest a new-found responsiveness or liberalization in Romania. More accurately, the 1977-80 period has witnessed the continued efforts to offer rhetoric in lieu of decentralization. Only within the confines of democratic centralism, will workers' self-management be allowed. While the party program mentions the principle of democratic centralism in the same breath as 'autonomy and initiative of . . . economic enterprises and other social units', it does so only by emphasizing that such autonomy falls within the scope of 'unitary leadership of socio-economic life' (Romanian Communist Party, 1975, p. 119).

Having trumpeted *'autoconducerea'*, the party is now (late 1979-early 1980) busy limiting its application, being careful to draw the lines beyond which no Workers' Council or enterprise assembly can step. In the unlikely event that some workers would hope to turn such sessions into tests of the party's strength at local levels, none will be able to claim ignorance of the primacy of unitary leadership and the central plan. Whether through its theoretical organ, daily press, factory sessions, or Ceausescu's visits to enterprises, the limits of autonomy were being stressed by early 1979 – if, indeed, anyone had forgotten. Ceausescu's warnings at the '23 August' enterprise in Bucharest on 15 February 1979 are a case in point. Criticizing the outmoded techniques and slow implementation of new designs for motors, compressors and so on, the party leader noted that he had the impression that there was too much satisfaction with results from current production technology and that there was insufficient innovation to transforming the production line. Turning to the political organization in the enterprise, Ceausescu twice referred to the trade unions and youth organization as under the party's leadership, which 'together with Workers' Councils' must deal with problems more efficiently. Ceausescu also took care to mention the need for better political educational efforts in the enterprise to encourage participation in the general assembly of the factory. Meanwhile, articles on 'Democratic centralism and workers' self-management' began to appear emphasizing the hierarchies beneath which Workers' Councils must operate in 'harmony', most notably in *Era Socialista,* the Party's theoretical monthly.

Thus, the RCP is confronted by a thorny problem with the class for whom it allegedly rules. Other communist states are not likely to avoid completely the same difficulty. Developmental plans required great sacrifice by workers while dramatically raising expectations, both material and political. Seeing the clear signs of discontent, a program of self-management was reinvigorated, the limits of which must now be explained to avoid another cycle of antagonism. There is, however, no guarantee that a largely rhetorical policy of self-management will placate workers in Romania or in other systems ruled by Leninist parties (for example, Poland).

5   Comparative Issues

Two issues were raised in the introduction regarding relationships between workers' participation in a communist state and broader, comparative hypotheses. First, citizenship roles – in this case, that portion of the citizenry within industrial labor – are expected to be confined to 'output' processes in communist states. The second has to do with hypotheses linking development, political participation and socioeconomic equality.

There is strong evidence to doubt the first of these hypotheses in Romania and, quite likely, other communist states as well. It is true, of course, that the policy-formulation ('input') phase offers fewer opportunities for the articulation of interests, and that a national organization by which workers might aggregate their grievances is lacking (official trade unions playing no independent role). Moreover, the case of industrial labor (*vis-à-vis* other occupational categories in communist systems) has unique aspects, given that Marxist parties are to rule in the interests of working people, thereby creating an onus from which communist leaders cannot easily escape. But there are clear indications that this stratum of people within communist states does not silently wait for public policies, only then to react with efforts to find intermediaries, that is, ways to 'beat the system'. By contrast, the experience of the East European states suggests that workers are cognizant that their interests are not well served by the party, and that an alternative of confrontation cannot be ruled out.

Western observers will be led to doubt the 'input' role of industrial labor, since trade unions offer no outlets for grievances and because organizations to counter the party-provided channels are not always present. But we need not wait for the establishment of an underground newsletter, hear rumors of party crackdowns, or read appeals for dissident labor leaders, to know of policy influence during the formulation phase. Such influence is, in fact, omnipresent. In Poland, the Gierek regime might be shortened primarily because of its inability to respond to the economic disaster which looms – and fear of worker violence plays a major role in that immobilism. This chapter sought to explain the influence workers have had in bringing the Romanian Communist Party to the point of taking a necessary risk by inaugurating a campaign of self-management at the enterprise level.

Ironically, communist parties have themselves created a situation in which industrial labor has an omnipresent role in policy-formulation. In part because of their Marxist heritage, and in part due to goals of modernization and development, the party has stressed with persistence 'the political importance of increased production as an indication of individual political activism and as a contribution toward supremely important national goals' (Townsend, 1969). Such a description, written by James Townsend referring to China, is no less true of Romania. Whether in Asia or Europe, the performance of daily work, workplace participation and the attitudes which motivate both work and participation, are incessantly political in the eyes of communist parties. In such circumstances, workplace behavior constitutes an ongoing plebiscite, with a permanent place in the formulation phase of public policy. This is surely not the participant role Lenin foresaw for workers in developed socialism, but neither should we dismiss industrial labor as insignificant in defining policy alternatives, advocating those closest to their material interests and personal concerns.

Finally, we must consider relationships among development, political participation and socioeconomic equality. It is fair to say that a consensus exists among comparativists regarding the link between socioeconomic changes vaguely labeled development and modernization, and demands for participation and distributive equality. Taking liberally from many works (Deutsch, 1961; Huntington, 1968), this consensus suggests that when a government pursues policies designed to increase the capacity and complexity of society and economy, a correlate will be an increase in the volume and intensity of demands made upon it by individual citizens and groups. This increase of demands for participation in policy-making or specific policies to distribute wealth can endanger a political system's stability. In other words, the very 'development' of a political system – its stability and institutionalization – can be threatened in the wake of policies designed to bring socioeconomic change.

The kinds of data and historical experience available by which we can test such an hypothesis offer convincing evidence to Western scholars.[5] For a political party with origins in a doctrine calling for the entry of the common man into politics, and which has rationalized its seizure of power and dictatorship by an alleged goal to build a classless society devoid of economically based inequalities, the scenerio posed above is doubtless unnerving. Postrevolutionary, stable and institutionalized socialism under a communist party can, it would seem, be achieved only by denying the fundamental tenets of such a system's legitimacy – mass participation and equality. Were participatory momentum and material demands from a key stratum such as workers to be translated into true self-management and distributive equality, the party's hold on workplace governance would be compromised seriously, its ability to centrally plan would be constrained, and investments in such arenas as heavy industry would have to be curtailed. Sensing these dangers, communist parties offer the rhetoric and structures for *'autoconducerea'* or *'autogestiunii'* while limiting the application of such principles within the narrow confines of democratic centralism.

But workers see the limits on their participation and understand differences between their material interests and party goals. Therefore, the party's 'solutions' to the destabilizing impact of socioeconomic change may exacerbate the instability. Developed socialism as found in European communist states, thus, embodies a dialectic of its own making – where socioeconomic policies foster increased demands which cannot be met but which, when not ameliorated, encourage further demands. Developed socialism in communist Europe, in effect, endangers its own stability and institutionalization by trying to become more 'developed'.

Although this characterization is broad, and cannot account for the many country-specific variations, there seems little question that ruling communist parties must engage in ongoing conflict-management. Of the ironies to be found in such a statement, perhaps the most poignant is that the occupational category for which Marx originally spoke has often been among the most vehement in confrontations with communist parties. Developed socialism in communist Europe has meant the rise of conflict between the proletariat and its erstwhile vanguard.

Notes: Chapter 13

This chapter is to be published as an article in a forthcoming issue of *Soviet Studies*.
1 Romania's 1965 Constitution promulgated that change, thereby making the country the Socialist Republic of Romania, not the People's Republic of Romania, while the party became the Romanian Communist Party *vis-à-vis* the Romanian Workers' Party.
2 Almond and Powell (1978, pp. 122–3) use the phrase 'roles of symbolic involvement' with implicit reference to communist states, although they do not employ the word communist, referring instead to 'penetrative, mobilizational, one-party states' – of which communist states constitute, one must assume, the primary component. Their mention of symbolic roles is coupled with examples such as casting a vote for the single party's candidates, participating in parades and other political events, and vast youth recreation programs.
3 The formal establishment of, and powers for, Workers' Councils are detailed in *'Legea Nr. 11/1971 cu privire la organizarea si conducerea unitatilor socialiste de stat'*.
4 There are some exceptions. The giant '23 August' electrotechnical enterprise in Bucharest has 17,000 workers, of whom 5,000 are in the party – or about 29 percent. It is, however, a showplace, where party leader Ceausescu often delivers lengthy addresses to workers.
5 Huntington and Nelson in their work *No Easy Choice* (1976) discuss much of the available evidence. See in particular, chapters 1 and 2. They point out, however, that the relationship is not linear in so far as development does not always promote participation, because of political and organizational factors independent of socioeconomic change, and other variables; see their chapter 3.

References: Chapter 13

Almond, G., and Powell, G. B., *Comparative Politics: System, Process and Policy* (Boston, Ma.: Little, Brown, 1978), p. 112.
Ceausescu, N., *'Cuvintare la Conferinta Nationala a Partidului, Decembrie, 1967'*, in N. Ceausescu, ed., *Romania pe Drumul Desavirsirii Constructiei Socialiste*, Vol. II (Bucharest: Editura Politica, 1968), pp. 540–41.
Ceausescu, N., *Scinteia*, 15 February 1979.
Ceterchi, I., *Democratia Socialista* (Bucharest: Editura Politica, 1974).
Cornescu, V. I., *Productivitatea Muncii si Factorul Uman* (Bucharest: Editura Politica, 1977).
Cresin, R., *'Aspecte Privind Mobilitatea si Fluctuatia Profesionala a Tinerilor'*, in O. Badina and C. Mamali, eds, *Tineret Industrial: Dinamica Integrarii Socioprofesionale* (Bucharest: Editura Academiei, 1973), pp. 27–44.

Dan-Spinoiu, G., *Factori Obiectivi si Subiectivi in Integrarea Profesionala a Femeii* (Bucharest: Editura Academiei, 1974).

Deutsch, K., 'Social mobilization and political development', *American Political Science Review,* vol. 55, no. 3, September 1961, pp. 493–513.

Era Socialista, vol. LIX, no. 7, 5 April, 1979, pp. 8–12.

Huntington, S. P., *Political Order in Changing Societies* (New Haven, Ct.: Yale University Press, 1968).

Huntington, S. P., and Nelson, J. M., *No Easy Choice: Political Participation in Developing Countries* (Cambridge, Ma.: Harvard University Press, 1976), pp. 4–7.

Lenin, V. I., *Selected Works,* Vol. VII (New York: International Publishers, 1943), p. 48.

Marx, K., *Bazele Criticii Economiei Politice,* Vol. 1 (Bucharest: Editura Politica, 1972), p. 94.

Mitran, I., *'Centralismul Democratic si Autoconducerea Muncitoreasca, Era Socialista,* vol. LIX, no. 7, 5 April, pp. 8–12.

Nichita V., and Neagu, M., *'Participarea Oamenilor Muncii la Conducerea Unitatilor Socialiste',* in Academia de Stiinte Sociale si Politice, *Perfectionarea Statului-Dezvoltarea Democratiei Socialiste* (Bucharest: Editura Politica, 1977), pp. 221–50.

Oral Communication, February 1979.

Petrescu, I., *Psihosociologia Conducerii Colective a Intreprinderii Industriale* (Cralova: Scrisul Romanesc, 1977), p. 98.

Popa-Micsan F., *'"Informatie-Participare" si "Responsabilitate-Decizie" in Activitatea Consiliilor Oamenilor Muncii", Vutorul Social,* vol. 6, no. 3, pp. 446–53.

Popescu, M., *Conducere, Participare, Constiinta* (Bucharest: Editura Academiei, 1973).

Preda, M., and Vida, I., *'Inferente ale Eticului, Politicului si Juridicului la Nivelul Constiintei Individuale', Viitorul Social,* vol. 4, no. 2, pp. 322–30.

Romanian Communist Party, *Programul P.C.R. de Faurire a Societatii Socialiste Multilateral Dezvoltate si Inaintare a Romaniei Spre Comunism* (Bucharest: Editura Politica, 1975).

Sirbu, M., *'Integrarea in Munca si Participarea Politica in Procesul Dezvoltarii Constiinte Socialiste',* in C. Potinga and V. Popescu, eds, *Constiinta Socialista si Participare Sociala* (Bucharest: Editura Academiei, 1977), pp. 33–50.

Townsend, J., *Political Participation in Communist China* (Berkeley, Ca.: University of California Press, 1969), p. 7.

Traistaru, E., *'Factorii Economici si Psihosociali at Stabilitatii Fortei de Munca in Intreprinderile Industriale', Viitorul Social,* vol. 4, no. 2, 1974, pp. 375–85.

Weintraub, Z., *'Indicatori Motivationali ai Integrarii Professionale',* in O. Badina and C. Mamali, eds, *Tineret Industrial: Dinamica Integrarii Socioprofesionale* (Bucharest: Editura Academiei, 1973), pp. 99–117.

14 Yugoslav Exceptionalism

BOGDAN DENITCH

Introduction

An increasingly intransigent problem facing the bureaucratic state socialist regimes of Eastern Europe is one of rising worker assertiveness. This problem gives every indication of being exacerbated as time goes on and as the industrial working class of these East European societies increasingly becomes composed of second-generation industrial workers born and socialized in the new industrial cities. There are several general background factors which make workers' assertiveness a peculiarly sensitive issue not easily subject to bureaucratic manipulation, or direct repression.

To begin with, the generally poor performance of the East European societies with stagnant growth, particularly in the consumer sectors, contrasts ever-more sharply with the realities of West European societies, realities which become more and more difficult to filter out through censorship or isolation. In terms of information, the old Iron Curtain of the Cold War years has become porous, and the standards of living of the East European workers are, albeit unrealistically, compared with the standard of living of the West European blue-collar workers. The successful performance of the regime in providing relatively full employment, and the relatively extensive welfare state are taken for granted as a right rather than accepted as a major asset and concession.

Secondly, the very high upward social mobility characteristic of the early years of the consolidation of state socialist regimes is now stagnating. This mobility was, of course, the product of several converging forces: the elimination of the old ruling strata, the large number of administrative posts opened up in centralized economies which required rapid promotion to be filled, the massive new educational system open to groups hitherto excluded for practical purposes and, above all, the rapid influx from the countryside into industrial life. The most significant move for most Eastern Europeans was from the status of a peasant to the status of an industrial worker. And that leap into the twentieth, or perhaps more appropriately stated, the late nineteenth century, was an enormous step upwards for most of the population affected. However, in this mobility, former industrial workers were generally favored in the next step upwards into the technical and lower managerial strata because of the ideological biases of the regime, a procedure simplified by the relative smallness of the industrial working classes and, with the exception of Czechoslovakia and Yugoslavia, the scarcity of pre-World War II communist party members who would have had claims for such posts. Clearly, this rate of mobility will not be duplicated again, and the present career patterns are far more to the more normal routine advancement through education and faithful time service in the bureaucracies. This will simultaneously age the elites and create a layer of 'deserving' office-holders, whose rapid removal from the path of advancement can no longer be expected.

The saturation of the educational system can be resolved in two ways: either by setting quotas, or by creating an increasing mass of unemployable aspirants for white-collar posts. The quotas, in turn, offer two equally unpleasant alternatives: either quotas based on 'ability', which favor the present middle classes and the reproduction of the present elite in the second generation, thus reinforcing the growing class cleavages, or quotas favoring children of industrial workers, imposing a downward mobility on segments of the middle class and professional strata, sharply increasing their discontent. In any case, the massive open educational system, one of the prouder creations of the regime, now poses long-range policy problems.

Thirdly, no matter what political apathy and cynicism may prevail, the official values of the regimes are a standing incitement to trouble. A regime basing its legitimacy on the power, if not the dictatorship, of the working class, and a regime which spreads the classics of Marxist literature through its educational and propaganda work, is bound to face sharp, persistent and spontaneous tests of the reality *versus* the stated norms. But less fancily, the official ideology makes claims on behalf of the industrial workers which the day to day reality contradicts. This is exacerbated in the East European states outside of Yugoslavia by the absence of any substantial worker participation in the management of the economy, even on the microlevel of the enterprise, and by the absence of legitimate institutions which can funnel non-system-challenging worker demands into political arenas where they can be resolved. The enterprise party groups and the trade unions are clearly viewed by the workers as a part of 'them' rather than 'us', and therefore cannot mediate conflicts which arise in the form of wildcat strikes, massive absenteeism, occasional riots and regime challenges. Because there are no formal legitimate outlets for workers' discontent, grievances which would be resolved through strikes or representation of worker demands turn almost axiomatically into a challenge of the trade union, the party and the political leadership of these countries.

Lastly, the restrictions on emigration exacerbate the potential for conflict, and simultaneously increase the burden of unproductive workers on the economy, thus lowering the general standard of living and productivity, make more difficult economic reforms which would resolve this dilemma, and fail to provide a safety-valve for malcontents.

One could add two other dimensions which are general for East European societies, again excluding Yugoslavia. First, the monolithic centralized character of those states provides for very little give and local initiative in attempting to head off problems, and hence problems rapidly escalate from low-scale, local conflicts to ones which involve the central state itself. Secondly, the absence of relatively open debate about economic policy makes it difficult to generate such proposals regarding worker discontent that are not automatically seen as a challenge to the party itself. The party, by claiming a monopoly of economic decision-making as well as a monopoly of political power, thereby becomes the target of all disputes, including narrowly economic ones which could have been limited to a single plant.

Regime: Workers' and Intellectuals' Discontent

Working-class discontent probably represents the Achilles' heel of state socialist regimes. Further, the more generalized collective wisdom of Western analysts, focusing either on the discontent of the peasantry, or of the intellectuals, has missed the mark. Eastern Europe, to be sure, has had a major problem in agricultural production, but at no point since the consolidation of these regimes has the peasantry as such presented a regime challenge. There are many reasons for this: the dispersal of the peasantry, the absence of political institutions which mobilize it and, quite possibly, again with the exception of Yugoslavia, the absence of arms. Where these factors are not present, as in Yugoslavia in the period of 1949-51, the peasants were able to stop abortive attempts at collectivization and win what amounted to a standoff with the regime.

In the case of the intellectuals, the phenomenon is far more complex, but some generalizations can be made. A substantial part of the intelligentsia in Eastern Europe has quite simply been co-opted, that is, bought off with relatively higher privileges and security and the recognition of status resembling the status of the middle classes in the prerevolutionary period. Another smaller part has been silenced through repression; still another has removed itself through emigration – it has been notoriosly easier for intellectuals to emigrate than for other strata; and the remainder have by and large been marginalized into reservations such as the universities and academies, where a certain degree of genteel dissent is from time to time tolerated. The combination of the carrot and stick seems to have worked somewhat, and when it does not work, the political police and the army have proven willing to take whatever measures are necessary. It might be interesting to contrast this with the repeated hesitation of the East European regimes to use the regular armed forces or police in dealing with worker disturbances. Similarities of class background and the latent legitimacy of workers' demands makes them a formidable opponent.

Yugoslav Exceptionalism: Safety-valves and System Maintenance

The Yugoslav sociopolitical situation contrasts sharply with most of the general points made above about the East European state socialist systems. Even the points of similarity are deceptive in that they hide additional points of contrast. Thus, while it is true that the Yugoslav state and society is dominated by a single-party, the Yugoslav party differs in a number of significant ways from the other East European parties. This is not to argue that the Yugoslav party is more pluralist or permissive necessarily, but simply that the party has far more effective moral and political authority in maintaining social cohesion and defending its policy goals. Thus, the League of Communists of Yugoslavia is seen both by its friends and enemies as a *barrier* to Russian domination and as a defender of national independence, in contrast with the East European parties (except Albania and perhaps Romania). This means that the party or League is far more capable of mobilizing patriotic sentiment and getting across an acceptance of its legitimate right to rule.

Further, while the League of Communists insists on its dominant role in society, it has consistently and continually narrowed the spheres of activities in which the party takes the primary responsibility. It has voluntarily withdrawn the party monopoly from most of the arenas of culture, day to day economic decision-making, management of the enterprise and a considerable section of the academic and intellectual debate on long-range social and economic alternatives before the country. Therefore, the Yugoslav party can claim far less direct responsibility for the day to day economic conditions of the country, and does not have its prestige at stake in conflicts between management and workers in individual enterprises or even between workers and the local political community. The consequence of this policy has been the evolution of the right to strike in Yugoslavia, from a phenomenon which was barely tolerated to one which existed in a gray zone between legality and illegality and, finally, to the present when strikes are not illegal and occur with sufficient frequency to be the subject of several book-length studies and numerous articles.

By emphasizing the role of the market within the limited construct of a *socialist* market economy, the Yugoslavs have introduced an external factor in setting prices and wages which, to a great extent, has managed to depoliticize these questions or, at least, reduce them to issues which do not involve regime challenge. The wages within an enterprise, after all, are on the macrolevel, set by the general performance of that enterprise within the economy. While this performance can indeed be affected by political decisions – favorable taxation or loans, restrictions on competing imports, direct subsidies in certain cases – it is generally accepted that there is some link between the performance of the enterprise and the wages it pays. Within the enterprise, however, the Workers' Councils and their subgroups (BOAL: basic units of associated labor) have an almost complete autonomy in setting the wage differentials, a situation which does indeed cause conflicts, but conflicts between BOALs or different groups of workers or even the blue-collar manuals *versus* the white-collars or even the white-collar employees *versus* the management, but almost never between the enterprise and the state or the enterprise and the party. Thus, it is a Yugoslav phenomenon that, in a strike, the placards interspersed with those making the specific demands include the pictures of Marshal Tito, while on the other side calls to abide by the norms of self-managing socialism. The party is then put in a position of urging the two sides to settle, but is happily out of the line of fire.

One of the points used by critics of the Yugoslav regime, is the presence of a large, somewhat rotating mass of Yugoslav workers abroad. The figure has ranged between 600,000 and slightly over 1 million in a given year, and includes both workers who have permanently emigrated to countries to which Yugoslavs traditionally emigrate (Australia, the United States, Latin America) and the far larger mass of guest workers in Western Europe, mainly in West Germany. There are a number of political and social questions attached to the problem of immigrant workers, but for the purpose of this chapter, three aspects should be stressed: (1) it has certainly provided a safety-valve for almost two decades for those Yugoslavs moving in from the agricultural sector into industry for whom not enough jobs were being generated. The overwhelming majority of Yugoslav workers, working as guest workers, are persons never previously employed in the Yugoslav industries. (2) The returning workers often come back with crafts and skills which make them more valuable to the Yugoslav economy than the raw agricultural labor which was exported and, in any case, while abroad, their remittances amounting to somewhat over \$2 billion in 1979, are a useful factor not only in the general balance of trade, but also increase the standard of living of the communities from which they come. (3) This emigration has, to a limited extent, also been a safety-valve for potential opponents of the regime or, for that matter, of socialism itself, greatly simplifying the situation at home. Travel as a safety-valve has a number of dimensions, and one could add that over 5 million Yugoslavs traveled abroad as tourists last year. This, at the very least, shows the confidence of the regime, unmatched anywhere in Eastern Europe, that travel would not be simply the mechanism for an accelerated brain-drain and drain of skilled workers. Quite simply, most Yugoslavs, the overwhelming majority, in fact, return. The ability to travel, however, militates against the somewhat claustrophic feeling which the existence of Berlin walls imposes on the East European states.

In addition, several institutional factors should be considered. The federal nature of the state, with wide autonomy for the six republics and two provinces, acts to compartmentalize disputes and, while satisfying most demands for cultural and ethnic autonomy, also provides for a limited institutional pluralism within the single-party system. Many Yugoslav observers have noted that it is more correct to speak of Yugoslavia having *eight* Leagues of Communists rather than to describe it as a one-party system. The existence of eight regional parties means, among other things, that a certain diversity in economic and social policies is present within the party. The divergent views often become views carried by republic or provincial parties in a dispute with the federation or with other local parties. To be more specific, there are extensive differences in economic and social policies pursued by the League of Communists in Slovenia, which is highly industrialized and has a standard of living roughly similar to that of southern Austria or northern Italy, and the economic policies of the parties of Macedonia and Bosnia, which have the characteristics of developing republics with a greater emphasis on the role and initiative of the League and considerably more centralism in the administration of the economy. Different republics have divergent policies on the extent to which the private sector can function in services or small-scale manufacturing, the degree of egalitarianism imposed on the wage structures, and the permissiveness of political debate. Therefore, the federal or, rather, confederal nature of Yugoslavia acts as a conflict-diffusing factor.

Institutional Pluralism

In addition to the institutional pluralism created by the growing autonomy of the republic and provincial parties, the Yugoslavs have lately adopted the general political line, pushed by Eduard Kardelj, which has stressed the need for divergent institutions to aggregate legitimate conflicts in a socialist society. More simply stated, Kardelj assumed that sharp divergences of views and conflicts would continue to exist in a socialist self-managing society, not merely as hangovers of old presocialist values or because of the 'false consciousness' of some of the participants in the conflicts, but because there would be legitimately divergent interests which require systemic mediation and representation; he presumed differences as basic as those between agricultural and industrial needs, between various sectors of industry, between the blue-collar workers and management, between the peasants and the townspeople. Therefore, in the past several years, the trade unions have been encouraged to play a far more autonomous and active role than is the case in Eastern Europe, to go beyond the conception of unions as a transmission-belt for the party, and to act as the lobby for the interests of blue-collar workers. They do so, both through legislation which they propose and by defending individual workers against violations of Yugoslav labor legislation, or violations of individual worker rights by workers' councils themselves.

This role of the unions is now still in a developing stage, and it cannot be reasonably stated that the unions have become 'us' rather than 'them' in Yugoslavia. However, they are at the very least a mediating institution increasingly subject and sensitive to pressure from below. The developments within the workers' councils themselves, however, have evolved to a point where the councils or BOALs act as a major shock-absorber in the society. The groundrules are relatively simple and are based on legislation-mandating domination by the blue-collar workers of the workers' council – the law requires that two-thirds be blue-collar workers – and by instituting a fairly rigid system of rotation which spreads quite widely the experience of participation in at least some aspect of worker management through something close to a majority of industrial workers in Yugoslavia.

Yet the balance-sheet of the performance of the councils is not at all clear. Wide varieties exist, but certain generalizations can be made. An increasing proportion of Yugoslav managers fail to be re-elected when their mandate expires, and the councils dominated by skilled workers appear to do a great deal of day to day decision-making within Yugoslav industry. The operation of councils in industries involving less skilled labor – textile and construction, for example – is far spottier, and Workers' Councils institutions, such as hospitals and universities, operate within budgetary limitations which are externally imposed. Nevertheless, accessible instruments for grievances do exist in Yugoslavia to an extent simply not duplicated in any East European country and in many West European countries, and the weight of industrial workers within the system has been increasing more or less steadily since the late 1960s. This is a consequence of two facts: the greater numbers who are literate and skilled in the working class in Yugoslavia, and also the impact of prolonged regime politicization emphasizing the uniqueness of the Yugoslav model as being precisely self-management itself.

Shifting Alliances

There is, however, an additional reason why the political and social weight of the Yugoslav industrial workers has tended to increase in the society. As Yugoslav self-management evolved in the early 1960s, the party flirted with the technical intelligentsia and the new managerial strata as its 'natural' allies. It did so for a number of reasons, not the least of which was the fact that in its early stages, self-management emphasized rather heavily *plant autonomy* from the centralized plan, rather than *workers' prerogatives within the collective*. Thus, in what was viewed by many Western observers as the 'golden years' of Yugoslav self-management (1958–68), a great deal of autonomy in decision-making was taken on by the plant managers and the technocratic elites within industry; consequently, the wage differentials began to spread. However, from 1968 to 1971, the party confronted a number of challenges, both from humanist intelligentsia in the universities and from traditional nationalists who, in the case of Croatia, consciously sought to ally themselves to the managerial and technocratic strata. At its peak, Croatian nationalism was able to draw on a significant section of the university intellectuals and some of the economists and managers of their republic. They failed miserably, however, in attempts to get support from industrial workers in the major Croat cities when they tried to bring out a political strike.

The lesson the party *cadres* drew was quite simple – that the real natural allies of the regime are the industrial workers rather than the technocratic elites and that, therefore, it was necessary to tilt sharply in that direction. The consequence was a drive toward greater egalitarianism, combined with a restructuring of the workers' councils in such a way as to give the worker collectives far more authority over the work process, the wage distribution and the overall policy of the enterprise. It is hard to say how lasting an effect these reforms will have, but a number of studies conducted throughout the 1970s suggest that a very substantial section of the Yugoslav industrial working class accepts, by and large, the norms of socialist self-management. And in so far as it criticizes self-management, it does so *within* the framework of that system by pointing to the contrast between the day to day practices and the claims.

What Yugoslav Studies of Workers Show

Numerous Yugoslav sociologists have carried out studies of workers' attitudes and beliefs, particularly in reference to socialism, self-management and egalitarianism. The best come from the universities of Ljubljana and Zagreb where, under the guidance of Professor Rudi Supek, a whole generation of Yugoslav social scientists has developed. Most of the materials are, of course, in Serbo-Croatian or Slovenian, with two notable exceptions which are accessible to the English-language readers. The first is a series of six volumes, *Participation and Self-Management,* published in 1972 by the University of Zagreb Press, mostly in English with a few essays in French; the other is a reader on *Self-Governing Socialism,* in two volumes, edited by Branko Horvat, Mihailo Markovic and Rudi Supek (White Plains, NY: International Arts and Sciences Press). The second volume reports several of the Yugoslav studies and, for the reader who wishes to delve further, the chapters by Supek, Jerovek and Rus should be particularly helpful.

Even more accessible are the tables available in my book, *Legitimation of a Revolution* (New Haven, Ct.: Yale University Press, 1976), particularly those on Self-Management and Socialism (p. 163), on the Power Structure within Enterprises (p. 164), on Degree of Dissatisfaction Elimination of Workers' Councils Would Cause (p. 165), on Beneficiaries of Self-Management (p. 167), and especially the reports on the studies of Ivan Siber in Zagreb which are summarized in the tables on pp. 177, 169.

To summarize very briefly what these studies seem to show. First, the overwhelming majority of Yugoslav respondents over time, that is, in studies repeated in 1967, 1968 and 1969, agreed that self-management was the *essential* element of socialism and disagreed that socialism could exist without self-management. Approximately one-third of the population in these general surveys gave no opinion. More significant from the point of view of the regime, the findings show that the *younger* the respondents, the *higher* the value placed on self-management and, also, that the blue-collar workers are more attached to self-management than the other strata.

Secondly, if one were to break down the industries in three general types – handicraft, mechanized or automated—the degree of attachment of both individual workers and Workers' Councils' members, rises sharply with the level of complexity of the industry in support of self-management.

Table 14.1 Attitudes toward Self-Management among Six Subgroups of Yugoslav Society, 1969

	University Students (%)	Secondary School Students (%)	Students at Industrial Workers' Schools (%)	Young Workers (%)	Older Workers (%)	General Control Sample of Adults (%)
1 Self-management is the proper direction for the development of our society	58·2	67·0	60·8	53·6	51·1	38·3
2 Our society is not sufficiently mature for self-management	21·4	17·0	16·7	25·0	20·7	20·1
3 Self-management, when combined with a *market economy*, is unacceptable for our society	7·5	7·0	8·3	10·7	14·1	12·8
4 A multiparty system is more democratic than self-management	3·0	3·0	4·2	1·2	3·3	13·4
5 Self-management is acceptable but without the leading role of the League of Communists	10·0	6·0	10·0	9·5	10·9	15·4

Source: Ivan Siber, 'Idejna orientacija mladih', Politicka Misao vol. 6, no. 4, 1969 p. 44.

Yugoslav industry as a whole is generally moving from the handicraft toward the automated stage, and that is a positive prognosis for the regime.

Thirdly, in general surveys of public opinion undertaken in 1972 in Croatia – the point at which considerable nationalist dissatisfaction was recorded – the general respondents identified production workers as the category which gained the most from self-management, compared to other strata, and generally chose by a plurality of 43 percent the definition of self-management which was most 'workerist', that is, 'management of the means of production by the working class'.

The Siber study, undertaken during the period of the so-called Croatian Spring (1969), contrasted the views of six subgroups of Yugoslav society towards self-management and other political alternatives. Table 14.1 (table 41 in Siber's study) is significant enough to deserve reproduction in full, and requires some comment. Clearly, all of the five subgroups contrast sharply in political views with the general control sample of adults. While only a minority of the adults, 38·3 percent, regard self-management as the best direction for the development of Yugoslavia, substantial majorities of all other subgroups do so. Even more interesting are the other alternatives posited; one could reasonably consider alternatives 2 and 3 to represent a more centralist, traditionalist view of what is appropriate for a socialist society or, rather, a view more like that of the dominant strata in other East European countries. In particular, response 3, 'Self-management, when combined with a *market economy* is unacceptable for our society', has low support across the board and is highest, as could have been expected, among old workers and in the general population sample. That over 30 percent of the respondents in at least three categories gave a combination of these two responses is indicative of the validity of the study, since both of these responses are *unacceptable* to the regime.

Even more interesting are responses 4 and 5, which one could regard as 'left' critiques of self-management. Response 4, being bourgeois democratic – 'A multiparty system is more democratic than self-management' – does not get more than 4·2 percent from any subgroup but does get 13·4 percent of the general sample. The more radical response under 5 – 'Self-management is acceptable but without the leading role of the League of Communists' – draws a reasonably respectable 10 percent from most of the groups.

One could reasonably conclude that the pro-self-management point of view is appropriately measured by combining responses 1 and 5 – or the pro- and the anti-party sentiment which is pro-self-management – and thus an overwhelming majority of close to 70 percent within the subgroups that represent the present and future workers of Yugoslav society appear to be pro-self-management.

This, by no means, means that the degree of *anomie* and alienation in the work process has necessarily been lower. On the contrary, comparative studies conducted by American, French and Yugoslav sociologists show that the level of 'bitching' in Yugoslav enterprises is high rather than low; yet this is a consequence of the very high level of expectation that Yugoslav workers have raised by self-management as an ideology. What is significant is that these complaints, whether against the workers' councils or the industrial hierarchy of the individual enterprise, can be and often are taken care of by strikes, work stoppages, moves to recall the Workers' Council or the director. Most such actions tend to be successful.

A large number of studies have been published in Yugoslavia about the strikes and other conflicts within self-management. That alone shows that the League does not regard such actions as a threat to the social order or even to itself. In the early stage of Yugoslav strikes, when they were neither legal, nor illegal, there were for the first ten years – from 1960 to 1970 – on the basis of incomplete statistics, no less than 2,500 strikes or work stoppages involving roughly 120,000 workers. Most of these strikes lasted for a day or less, and most of them have resulted in victories of the strikers. By 1971, Yugoslav industrial sociologists and political theorists dealing with industrial problems moved to a consensus that strikes must 'become an integral and legitimate aspect of self-managing socialism', that is, that 'so long as wage labor existed, there is no reason why there shouldn't be strikes'. In the studies of some twenty enterprises, undertaken in 1972 by Anton Ravnic, two facts came out rather clearly: that while only 11·4 percent of the workers in successful enterprises which had strikes cited wages as the main reason, over 30 percent of the workers in unsuccessful enterprises used that as the explanation; the other reasons most often cited were inadequate information, incompetence of individuals (managers), insufficient responsibility (on the part of the Workers' Council itself), inadequate organization of work and, finally, laziness and undiscipline. These seem not too terribly different from causes of wildcats in other industries.

A second study, however, showed that at that point, at least, while *workers* ranked low wages as the most important single reason for strikes, with bad relations between workers and managers as the second most important reason, the *managers* rated inadequate information as the most important reason and inadequate discipline as the second most important reason. That seems to be a reasonably logical difference of views. Interestingly enough, however, the members of the Workers' Council gave an entirely different reason from either the workers, or the managers: it was bad management. Whatever else these admittedly sketchy studies show, it seems that those industrial managers in whose enterprises there are strikes have reason to be concerned. For if poor management is the central reason for internal conflicts in the enterprise, the councils will more likely than not pick on the managers as scapegoats.

In the late 1970s, the number of strikes has gone up notably, and the percentage of workers giving the internal distribution of wages as the cause has gone up as well. Yugoslav strikes have developed increasingly into straightforward wage conflicts which either appear as internal conflicts within the enterprise between subgroups of workers, or as conflicts between workers and the managers. In the present situation, the organs of the state and the League of Communists act either as mediators or remove themselves completely from the immediate conflict. This means that their role is rarely brought into the solution of the strikes, although quite clearly strikes do have an impact on macroeconomic and social policies, since they make more difficult the imposition of austerity or wage freeze. Nevertheless, it seems reasonable to conclude that worker unrest in Yugoslavia is neither regime-threatening, nor a focus for anti-party organization and dissidence. However, there are potentially serious problems which Yugoslav industry and the Yugoslav workers face in the short-range future.

Even with fully indexed wages and benefits, an inflationary rate in the twenty-fifth percentile range places a burden on all the collectives and weakens their competitive position on the European and world markets. Given the relatively high level of expectation that Yugoslav workers have, a prolonged period of wage stagnation can place major strains on the whole social and political system.

The safety-valve which external emigration has provided for decades is now all but closed, and a greater rate of absorption and job generation and, therefore, capital investment will probably be required in the new period. This may, in turn, be exacerbated by a rate of return of immigrant workers higher than the ability of the economy to absorb. All of these pressures will be directed against the more successful enterprises in order to attempt to extract greater tax revenues for general social welfare than they have been accustomed to paying. This can then generate conflicts between the more successful enterprises and the political system, or between the more-developed regions and the less-developed ones. However, the very large number of persons involved in the institutions of self-management and local self-government have so diffused decision-making in Yugoslav society that, short of a cataclysmic breakdown, it is hard to see how these challenges can develop into a confrontation between the industrial working class or major sections of it and the formal political and party system of Yugoslavia.

In conclusion

In summarizing the Yugoslav case, a number of questions come up which were not dealt with in any detail. These questions are speculative in nature, and the most one can hope for is to make well-educated guesses – founded, hopefully, on a detailed analysis of the existing Yugoslav society. One question that is often raised has to do with the differences which arise between the various regions in Yugoslavia and the impact of these differences on worker unrest. This issue has serious potential for trouble, because the regions in Yugoslavia coincide with ethnically diverse republics and, therefore, economic differences can be transformed into national questions which are, by their very nature, more explosive and less subject to mediation. To counterweight this problem, the Yugoslavs have engaged in a sustained policy of industrialization, particularly in the Kosovo region inhabited by Albanians and in the less-developed republics of Bosnia-Herzogovina and Macedonia. The success has varied, with Macedonia probably being the best case.

However, one generalization needs to be understood here. The industries built in the less-developed regions tend to be very modern and have certain advantages in terms of access to raw materials over the more traditionally industrialized regions in Yugoslavia. Secondly, and more to the point, there are two ways one can look at income differences in Yugoslavia. One would be to look at the income per capita which would show a range of roughly 1:6 between Kosovo and Slovenia – an intolerably high ratio. This figure is explained in good part by two factors: the first is that much of the private peasantry reports next-to-no income, which is an artefact of statistics and of Yugoslav tax legislation. The second is that the demographics of the two regions are completely different and, while Slovenia has a birthrate characteristic of Central Europe, the Kosovo birthrate resembles that of Algeria. Thus, the majority of the population is under 15 years and not in the work contingent at all.

Table 14.2   *Income Distribution in Yugoslavia, by Republic, 1971*

	Income per Employed Person (index: Yugoslavia = 100)*	Income Range: Unskilled Worker– College Educated†
Yugoslavia	100	100–259
Bosnia-Herzegovina	95	100–294
Montenegro	88	100–254
Croatia	109	100–243
Macedonia	82	100–287
Slovenia	114	100–258
Serbia	94	100–258
Vojvodina	96	100–260
Kosovo	82	100–315

Source: Adapted from *Statisticki godisnjak Yugoslavije, 1972.*
*The ratio of the lowest to the highest republic average is 1:1·4
†If the average income of unskilled workers in the lowest-paid area is set at 100, the average income of the college-educated in the highest-paid area is 380.

This is illustrated by the figures on income differences which are more relevant to the attitudes of the industrial workers, that is, income per employed person. These figures are shown in Table 14.2 (see *Legitimation of a Revolution,* table 48), and they show a far smaller and more normal range of differences. By this index, the Slovenians are only 14 percent over the Yugoslav average, and the workers in Kosovo only 18 percent under the Yugoslav average, a difference that is more than made up for in the lower relative costs in Kosovo. Thus, the life of an industrial worker in Kosovo is more like that of an industrial worker in Slovenia, than it resembles the life of the peasants who are outside of the modern economy. Since the ratio of peasants to industrial workers is continually declining, it is significant that the dynamic growing sector of the Yugoslav economy is more egalitarian and, therefore, likely to produce stability and cohesion.

Another dimension that is often mentioned in Yugoslavia is the role of the immigrant workers. Clearly, the ability of the regime to export unemployment permitted the use of resources in more rational ways in the

1960s and early 1970s than would have otherwise been the case. By so doing, the Yugoslav economy was not overburdened by vast masses of unproductive workers and employees. That, in turn, has made the industrial scene in Yugoslavia more like that of Western Europe than of the East European states. Further, the fact that the Yugoslav party leadership appears not to be worried about the possible disruption caused by returning workers, with their tales of life in the West, is an indicator of stability or at least the perception of stability in the system. With the downturn in the general world and European economy, however, while existing guest workers have not been sent back in large numbers, new ones are not being recruited at anything resembling the pace of the 1960s.

A massive return of immigrant workers could have serious consequences: it would deprive the Yugoslav economy of close to $3 billion a year of worker remittances from abroad; it would place major burdens on the existing enterprises to create new workplaces; and it would burden the social welfare system probably beyond the point of tolerance. However, counterbalancing this possibility are two factors which mitigate this threat. The first, of course, is the far smaller rural population contingent entering the workplace in this decade and, therefore, the more manageable pressures which it sets up. The second is that the Yugoslav economy has developed labor shortages throughout the northern tier of industrialized republics, and Slovenia, northern Croatia and Vojvodina already have a negative emigration rate. Or, put in plain language, they are absorbing more workers returning from abroad than the number of workers leaving.

One more general consequence, however, is an increasing shift of the working population across republic lines to the point where 10 percent of the workforce of Slovenia now is from other republics. This process will not only lead to a less homogeneous ethnic workforce – a desirable process, in my opinion – but will make the enterprise and consequently the Workers' Councils even more significant in the lives of individual workers. This is because the Workers' Council in a self-managed economy acts as a social and political mediator for the new workers in the civil society. It is the Workers' Council, after all, which provides housing, social benefits, childcare centers in many cases, and a whole string of benefits within the Yugoslav welfare state. This will make the internal issues within the Workers' Councils even more salient to the individual worker's life than they have been in the past and, consequently, *the industrial arena in Yugoslavia is to a greater extent than in any other East European country also the sociopolitical arena.*

The regime responses to the last decade of development appear to be moving in the direction of institutionalizing more trade union autonomy, on the one hand, while attempting to develop a formal code for strikes, on the other. The greater autonomy of the unions is manifested particularly in the political arena where they act as a fairly coherent pressure group for the overall interests of blue-collar workers and in favor of a self-managing socialism with a minimum of technocratic and managerial prerogative.

The legalization of strikes, however, is a different story. The debate on this issue is based on the assumption that if strikes are formalized, there will be fewer of them. Most Yugoslav strikes, after all, are wildcats which last a day or less. By requiring that due notice be given and a cooling off period is proposed, a distinction will be made presumably between legal strikes and wildcats. Therefore, the moves toward the legalization or formalization of strike activity in Yugoslavia are directed against spontaneous upheaval in a systematic, well-thought-through strategy of channeling these upheavals into the kind of stable 'normal' industrial tests of strength which are less disruptive and more controlled by the unions and the units of production within the economy.

The process described here lies in the future and is typical of the pragmatic and skilled strategy of the party in Yugoslavia in avoiding direct confrontation with popular forces and pressures whenever possibe by channeling these into relatively harmless arenas subject to bargaining and compromise. The Yugoslav case, therefore, stands in sharp contrast with the far grimmer confrontational scene in the rest of Eastern Europe.

15 Workers' Assertiveness and Soviet Policy Choices

JAN F. TRISKA

Introduction

The transition to developed socialism in Soviet-dominated Eastern Europe – Poland, East Germany, Czechoslovakia, Hungary, Romania and Bulgaria – has not been accompanied by corresponding changes in political, economic and social structures. The contradiction between the promised socialist egalitarianism and the actual social inequality, which favors the communist bureaucracy and the technical intelligentsia and militates against the proletariat, has not been resolved. Social mobility, which had kept this disparity within bounds, is on the decline.

Today, social discrimination in Eastern Europe is increasingly based on yield, skill and knowledge. The working class tends to be frozen in place. Workers' children do not compete easily for educational advantages, and their chances of moving up socially are limited. The circle appears to be closed. The working class is searching, therefore, for means of action to have its voice heard. Without changes in social policies and institutions, the communist party elites may find it increasingly difficult to maintain social and political tranquility.

The final decision, however, is not East European, but Soviet. The Soviet Union, the regional overseer, insists that East European communists emulate the Soviet model of building socialism, not in its entirety, as Stalin insisted, but enough to preserve the delegated power monopoly of the East European communist elites intact within the Soviet-type political economy. This built-in Soviet insistence and the Soviet conservative, cautious, distrustful view of political change in Eastern Europe limits the Soviet policy choices. Soviet leaders prefer a safe, slow, politically insured social development to an even remotely risky social experimentation; they still rate loyalty over performance and security over efficiency. It remains to be seen whether this policy stance will be as adequate in the future as it was in the past to cope with the progressive alienation felt by the majority of workers in Eastern Europe.

This chapter is based on the assumption, well tested in the past, that Soviet-controlled Eastern Europe, a geopolitical creature of the Soviet Union, depends on Soviet power for its political existence and that the respective East European communist elites depend on the Soviet elite to stay in power. This assumed generalization should not, however, overshadow the fact that national diversity, built-in and growing, exists in different degrees in the individual communist party states. Eastern Europe may be integrated militarily, but it is diverse politically, and some of the countries are searching for economic and social innovations and realignments. Hungary, with its relatively liberal economic policy, and Poland, with its lively and influential public opinion, are the leading contenders in this respect. Together with the unorthodox foreign policy of Romania, these countries suggest strategies that others in Eastern Europe may wish to emulate. This divergence complicates the Soviet control of Eastern Europe, but it is important to keep in mind when we analyze Soviet policy choices in Eastern Europe with regard to the growing assertiveness of workers.

Developed Socialism and Social Inequality

In the early period of socialism in Eastern Europe, the nationalization of industry and expropriation of land was an important step toward social equality. Between 1949 and 1953, industrial production in Eastern Europe rose by over 100 percent. After that, however, disturbing signs appeared. There were shortages – of provisions, raw materials, labor and capital. The tempo of industrialization had been too rapid for the countries' resources. Heavy industry had grown at the expense of light and consumer industry, and agriculture stagnated. The standard of living fell drastically, and production rapidly declined. In Czechoslovakia and East Germany, the workers rebelled. As a consequence, a new trend had been set in motion in Eastern Europe, a development which was to affect profoundly the workers' sense of social belonging.

In connection with de-Stalinization, a re-evaluation of the Stalinist economic system was initiated. The gradual, cautious, partial replacement of administrative controls in the early 1960s by concepts including economic rationality and efficiency and a relatively greater economic responsibility for managers signaled, however, also an attack on socialist egalitarianism. The Stalinist social leveling meant equality, and sometimes even superiority, for skilled and semiskilled workers over white-collar clerks, technicians and professional people. The introduction of material incentives, wage differentiation according to contribution to production, a system of bonuses, standardization of work norms, and other rewards for performance, favored the white-collar staff, especially those in the managerial jobs, over workers.

And when, in addition, the ruling elites tried to limit consumption by allowing relatively fluid prices, especially for basic food items, the workers revolted. Their sense of social equality was deeply offended. They did not mind shortages as long as they were universal; but they deeply resented shortages which, via price hikes, affected primarily the poorer level of society, the workers.

In the Stalinist period the party elites alone ruled. In the more complex period of developing socialism, however, the elites needed specialized knowledge and sophisticated skills. As a consequence economic reformers and other technical intelligentsia began to infiltrate the party bureaucracy. The workers had no such leverage, nothing that would legitimate their interests; they possessed only their labor. And there was plenty of them, thanks to the massive mobilization of peasants into the working class.

How workers have fared in the period of developed socialism, is described by Gyorgy Konrad and Ivan Szelenyi. They depict the workers as hapless victims of a class struggle in which the working class has not a chance: the ruling class, the elite which claims to represent the workers and rule on their behalf, has the monopoly of power. It cannot permit the development of workers' organizations into potential rival centers. Eagerly supported and assisted by economic reformers and technical intelligentsia, the ruling elite has vested its interest in making

> the percentage of the national income which is drawn into the state budget . . . as large as possible. The bigger the budget [the greater the potential for development and growth] . . . and the greater the power of the officials who administer it.

Anything that would reduce that percentage, like genuine collective bargaining, for example, must be eliminated. For this reason the sale of labor must not be free, but controlled, there must be no open labor market, and the price of labor must be kept as low as possible (Konrad and Szelenyi, 1979).

The workers fear that their social contract has been broken. In over thirty years, they have not received what they had bargained for. Having thought that socialism stood for the end of their exploitation, now they want a market place where they can sell collectively to the highest bidder. They want basic material comforts – higher wages, better food, better housing, more and better consumer goods, good public and communal services and adequate social welfare. After decades of austerity, they are restive. They are beginning to realize that the socialist economy may not be able to deliver their expectations or to cope with their needs. Have the proletarians, 'the leading detachment', been misled? Are the party bureaucrats and the technological intelligentsia the real beneficiaries of the socialist order? In answer, the workers revert to class equality, oppose the merit system the technocrats have built into the economic reforms, and maintain leisure on the job – and so the economy goes down.

Konrad and Szelenyi argue that, for the sake of economic development,

> the technocracy must accept the legitimate articulation of workers' interests, even though they now conflict at times with its own interests and may do so systematically in the more remote future – up to and including worker self-management and the right to organize to defend their interests, *even if such organizations may develop into rival power centers.* (Konrad and Szelenyi, 1979, p. 232; emphasis added).

I disagree. The question is not whether the technocrats would support and accept the development, but whether the party elites would. This is the issue. Workers' organizations may develop into autonomous power centers. Not even Yugoslavia has such centers; even there each individual self-management council is essentially on its own.

To the workers a classless society is attractive, because it is a society where they are no longer inferior. A class society, on the other hand, means to them a built-in class conflict between themselves and the other social strata. The interests of these social sets appear to them incompatible and antagonistic. The party officials are, therefore, compelled to argue that

the workers have not yet completely identified themselves with the principles of wage and income differentiation based on performance. To the majority, egalitarianism is more attractive, however unjust it may be. We must take more effective steps against egalitarianism to safeguard just differentiation. (Sandor Gaspar, Secretary-General of Hungarian Trade Unions, in Robinson, 1971, p. 22)

After all,

socialism is a society of equality and not of egalitarianism. Socialist equality does not mean the equal distribution of goods, but rather that the elimination of class disparities must guarantee everyone equal opportunity to succeed. (Foldes, *Tarsadalmi Szemle,* October 1970)

With the partial exception of Czechoslovakia, socioeconomic inequality in Eastern Europe has been growing, not diminishing (Connor, 1979; Wiles, 1975). Since there are more blue-collar workers than any other single class, it would be prohibitively expensive to raise their standard of living above the acceptable minimum. For this reason they are awarded selectively, not according to their productivity, but according to their loyalty. And this is why they demand a more equitable, less discriminatory, less upper-class-based social system and greater social equality among all social classes.

Workers' Organizations

In his article on workers in Polish politics, Jan B. de Weydenthal argues that 'it is the structural characteristics of the political system', rather than 'economic scarcity and deprivation', which is the real motivating force behind workers' assertiveness. While the strikes, demonstrations and riots are triggered by particular economic hardship – a sudden raise in food prices, higher work norms, lower wages, etc. – the workers' dissent is more than just 'a desperate reaction to specific decisions or events'. While the workers are not revolting against the system *qua system,* they are trying to rearrange the system to the extent that their interests could be articulated, channeled and institutionalized. Just as Samuel Huntington argues that adaptable political institutions capable to channel and respond to social demands are the mainstay of an effective government (while decay sets in if intensified citizen participation outstrips political institutionalization) (1968, pp. 53–5; 1971, pp. 314–15), so de Weydenthal maintains that what is needed in Poland, and in Eastern Europe generally, are 'effective mechanisms which would allow the governments to adopt their policies as new situations are encountered'. 'Tension management', which accommodates immediate workers' demands, 'provides a temporary appeasement', but not the needed change in the political system. The danger is that this sort of a governmental strategy not only 'threatens to exacerbate rather than solve the problems of political and social development', but could produce a stagnation and decay of the system (1979, pp. 96–7). This is a good argument. In the past the government appeasement policy has worked. It may or may not work in the future. The question is, could the governments play it safe, listen to Huntington and de Weydenthal, and permit workers' participation in their political systems on an institutionalized basis?

Workers, in spite of their exalted 'leading role' in socialist countries, which includes the ownership of the means of production, do not participate even in decisions affecting their own factory and their relationship to it. ('We do not have the right to discuss whether the plan is too high or too low, only how best to carry it out', they complain) (Ramet, 1980). Workers have no representation, no real organizations of their own. The trade unions to which all workers (and all management) must belong by law are corporative organizations responsible to the party, not to the workers. This is why workers during riots and strikes form their own organizations: they want institutions which would represent their grievances and their demands before the forum of the party.

Socialist ruling elites cling to the dogma of consensus. They would permit workers to form organizations which articulate, represent and defend their own interests, if it would not mean denying the legitimacy of the party. After all, the communist party is the vanguard of the working class, the advanced detachment of the main body: the rule of the party means the rule of the workers, because the workers exercise power through their own tool, the party.

It would not be easy to return from Lenin to Marx. But that is what it would take, some critics argue, to return from a party of professional socialist revolutionaries, who claim to represent the workers and act on their behalf, to direct class rule and self-organization by the workers themselves. And that would mean to return from Lenin's *What Is To Be Done* to Marx and Engels's *Address to the Communist League.* (Leon Trotsky indeed warned that Lenin's party would 'substitute itself for the working class', acting 'not as a vanguard of the proletariat but the political organization of the bureaucracy' (Lomax, 1976, p. 196). In the meantime, the party elites consider themselves to be the only representatives of the workers without whom the working class could not exist. If

workers act against their own interest . . . then the duty of the Party is to represent their real interest . . . If the wish of the masses does not coincide with progress, then [the leaders] must lead the masses in another direction. (Janos Kadar, in Lomax, 1976, p. 196)

Workers, the Ruling Elites and the Soviet Union

In Eastern Europe, then, the socialist economies are maturing, social mobility is declining, and the population is becoming aged, urbanized and stratified. A trend toward a less flexibile social structure is setting in. Workers, the political mainstay of the socialist governments, are growing restless. They feel threatened by the sustained emphasis on the economic rationality, efficiency and productivity of developed socialism, which they feel violates their tacit, long-standing agreement with their governments on the expectation of leisure on the job in exchange for labor peace in the factory (Vanous, 1978). After over three decades, such an understanding may be difficult to replace. Indeed, the growing assertiveness of workers shows a widespread degree of dissatisfaction unusual among the formerly docile East European working class. If the growing gap between workers' expectations and socioeconomic reality gets much wider, negative social attitudes toward the political systems may, indeed, reach crisis proportions as they have in Poland.

The Soviet perception of East European socioeconomic pressures and tensions is relatively distorted. Soviet leaders did not fully understand the Poznan workers' riots in 1956; misunderstood at first the Hungarian uprising in 1956; and even admittedly misperceived the Czechoslovak Spring in 1968. (After the Soviet occupation of Czechoslovakia, Brezhnev was reported to have said that 'it would have been more favorable to wait until an open counterrevolution broke out in Czechoslovakia, with all its consequences, and only to interfere afterwards' (Valenta, 1979, p. 139).) This is not really the Soviet leaders' fault. They keep well-informed on East European developments, and they do know what is going on. But the Soviet Union is a different world from Eastern Europe, economically, socially, culturally and politically. East European countries may differ a great deal among themselves, but they do differ even more from the Soviet Union. Their party bureaucracies are less firmly established, less autonomous and less pressure-resistant than the strong Soviet party bureaucracy (and the technical intelligentsia and economic reformers are more successful than in the Soviet union); memories of different types of political rule, often more efficient, are still alive in Eastern Europe. The longing to rejoin the West, at least in some ways, is widespread and considerable; and while changes in the Soviet Union influence its East European neighbors, changes in Eastern Europe have almost no impact on the Soviet Union. For this reason, demands for socioeconomic changes in Eastern Europe are greater and more numerous, workers are more assertive, strike, and demonstrate there more often (as far as we know), and East European party elites tend to be more responsive to such outbursts. Workers' assertiveness in Eastern Europe tends to produce strains in East

European–Soviet relations. Both parties to these strains worry about the consequences. The Soviet leaders tend to urge appeasement, and tend to give economic assistance in the end (as they did after the East German riots in 1953, after the Poznan demonstrations and the Polish October in 1956, after the Hungarian revolution in 1956, after the suppressed Czechoslovak Spring in 1968, after the 1970–71 Polish riots, after the 1976 Polish demonstrations and after the 1980 Polish strikes). They want to lower tension and restore social order and political stability, even if they do not appreciate fully the socioeconomic causes.

Over the years, East European party elites have demonstrated that they are, in fact, adequate at coping with sudden exigencies such as the workers' uprisings. They have been helped by the fact – repeatedly stressed – that if they should lose control, the Russians would come in force as the *ultima ratio* of socialist order. (As Edward Gierek put it in March, 1971, 'If the Government lost control, this would have meant Soviet intervention' (Fejto, 1971).) And material assistance from the Soviet Union has been significant in that it has been there to bail out the pressed governments when they needed it most.

Still, the workers' riots have created an additional problem for the party elites to worry about. They are becoming more frequent, there is a growing worker occupational solidarity behind them, there are invariable attempts to create workers' own organizations, and the workers do make political demands. They called for free elections in Pilsen and in East Berlin in 1953; for Workers' Councils and democracy in the factory in Poznan in 1956; for Workers' Councils to introduce 'real socialism' in Budapest in 1956; for democratic socialism under Dubček in Czechoslovakia in 1968; for the representation of workers' interests in Poland in 1970 and again in 1976 and in 1980; and for workers' solidarity against the government's oppression in Romania in 1977. A restless working class can spell political danger more than revisionist intelligentsia and dissident intellectuals. After the December 1970 Polish riots, there were wage hikes, lowered prices, improved housing and trade union shakeups in East Germany, Hungary, Romania, Bulgaria and even the Soviet Union: there, the consumer industry received sudden and unexpectedly larger credits as well (Fejto, p. 34).

The rulers' ideological response to workers' assertiveness, on the other hand, has not been successful. It has consisted primarily of mobilization of workers to make them work more and better, educational activities in factories to socialize workers into the plant and production objectives, moral incentives to achieve greater output, and periodic meetings with top party leaders to make workers understand the leaders' concerns, problems and objectives (de Weydenthal, 1979, p. 109).

Over the years, the bargaining areas between the Soviet and East European leaders have been growing, the scope of permissible domestic change not subject to Soviet veto has been increasing, and the price of power for East European leaders has gone down – not much, to be sure, but enough to suggest that the original goal of regional integration has been quietly substituted for limited (and closely watched) national diversity. The

Soviets no longer treat each East European country alike. They do differentiate among them and tend to judge each case on its own merit. They may tolerate more independence in foreign policy as long as there is conformity at home as in the case of Romania; they may tolerate domestic social vibrations and even waves as long as foreign policy is safe, as in the case of Poland. ('Friendship and alliance with the Soviet Union and other countries of the socialist commonwealth are guarantees of Poland's independence', said Edward Gierek at the 8th Polish CP Congress on 15 February 1980, *International Herald Tribune,* 16 February 1980, p. 1). They may tolerate, given appropriate political guarantees, experimentation with the national economy, as in the case of Hungary; and they may award loyalty by generous economic assistance as in the case of Czechoslovakia. The limits of domestic autonomy consist of two Soviet conditions which must be met: (1) the national leaders must be trusted in Moscow, and (2) the local communist parties must be in full control. The trust is necessary but not sufficient; if party leaders are not in control, others must be found (with advance Soviet approval) to do the job. Otherwise, Soviet peaceful intervention might become violent. And this is well understood in Eastern Europe.

With the growing restiveness of workers and under the pressure of dissenting intellectuals, the East European party elites' staying in office depends no longer on the Soviet leaders alone, but also on their own ability to rule at home. The somewhat less-demanding Soviets are easily matched by the more-demanding social groups at home. The sustained balancing of the two constituents of their power grows heavy for East European leaders. Dubček tried the balancing act and failed. So did Gomulka, Ulbricht and Gierek. Kadar is moderately succeeding. Ceausescu has been successfully exploring new horizons and venturing, carefully, into new territory. Husak, like Honecker, has opted for the easy way out, bribing the workers (in part with Soviet economic assistance).

The successful balancing of the two interests, domestic and foreign, may easily constitute the test of the future in Eastern Europe. Soviet leaders have been facing for a long time the fact that stability and order in Eastern Europe depend on their leadership.

Soviet Policy Choices

The Soviet leaders want social and political order in the area, undisturbed performance, no systemic change. Modernization and development is welcome as long as it is safe – as long as it takes place within an established institutional setting. Economic reforms 'within socialist safeguards', that is, under the direction of party bureaucrats, are welcome in spite of the growing assertiveness of the working class. The increasing social stratification and class differentiation in Eastern Europe is viewed in Moscow as an unfortunate but necessary cost of progress in developed socialist societies (Brezhnev, 1978). An autonomous, institutionalized defense of workers' interests is not. It would threaten the parties' monopoly of power.

East Europe's proverbial instability is thus not only systemic and structural, but political and social as well. A regional hegemony must act as a stabilizing influence, not the other way around. The Soviet Union has had an over-thirty-year-long learning experience in Eastern Europe. It will almost certainly be called upon to display in the future what it has learned in the past.

Workers' demonstrations in Eastern Europe have served as a learning mechanism for both the workers and the governments over time as well as over space. Although successful, the strikes were costly. Demonstrating workers were severely repressed in Czechoslovakia in 1953 (in Pilsen, Ostrava, Prague, and other cities); in East Berlin and the industrial cities in East Germany in 1953, many workers were arrested, tried, and some were executed; in Poznan in the 1956 worker riots, over 300 workers were arrested, some 300 were wounded, and 54 were reported killed; hundreds of rioting workers were wounded and some were killed in the December 1970 Polish strikes; in the 1977 Romanian miners' riots and demonstrations, miners were arrested, fired from jobs, and/or removed to other parts of Romania; and even in the 1976 Polish riots, several hundred workers were arrested and tried, some were sentenced and many lost their jobs.

It would appear that, short of the institutionalization of workers' participation in the political process, one of the workers' options to reach benefits while cutting costs would consist of avoiding violence while refusing to work. Organized, disciplined, purposeful, peaceful work stoppage in plants and factories – rather than riots, demonstrations and violence in the streets – would seem to be a better strategy. Effectively withholding productive work from the political system, is the only power the workers possess (de Weydenthal, 1979, p. 111). Still, given the almost absolute lack of a communication network among the workers and the complex and stratified laws on sabotage in the workplace, this alternative may be difficult to apply without any degree of permanent organization. The noise of violence has the important function of rallying the workers around the flag of worker solidarity in far-away places. Workers' organizations, therefore, are a 'must'.

And, indeed, developed socialism, said to be the product of the scientific-technological revolution, requires the 'active enlistment of the proletariat in participation in governmental affairs and in socio-political activities' (Chekharin and Kerimov, 1973). The socialist model of development stipulates that socialist socioeconomic equality leads to political stability and participation, both of which depend on each other, which in turn leads to socioeconomic development (Triska, 1977, p. 148). (With decreasing socioeconomic equality, however, stability and participation decrease, which in turn leads to socioeconomic decay. The socialist model of development is either doomed or does not work any longer.)

The ruling elites do perceive the political participation of their citizens as an important input in their political processes as well as an essential instrumentality of political development (Kozlov, 1962). The developed socialist society does require processes and institutions that set goals and choose means to respond to and to solve social issues (Friedgut, 1979).

Political decisions need to absorb citizen views; an advanced socialist society can ignore and disregard this problem only to its peril. In fact, 'this need . . . is much greater in socialist countries, where it is a question of vital importance for political life as a whole' (Pasic, 1968).

On the other hand, effective independent trade unions would almost certainly challenge the party's monopoly of power. True, political stability and social order in Eastern Europe does depend on the institutionalization of political change. But only such institutionalization will guarantee stability and order which is based on free choice. If political change in Eastern Europe is induced by the Soviet Union, the regional power, or if it is but a response to a change in that power, then the element of choice is missing. This line of reasoning suggests the hypothesis that the more limited the choice, the more unstable the political systems and the region as a whole. Forced institutionalization depends on whimsical choice, disturbs social order and destabilizes the polity. As David Apter put it (1973, p. 6), 'choices are illusory if people are victimized by them or afraid to utilize them, and dangerous if they are manifestly incapable of directing them'.

Just as pseudochoice organizations become persistent system-destabilizers, so adaptable organizations based on free choice and capable to channel and respond to social demands, as Samuel Huntington argues, are a mainstay of stable and orderly government (1971, pp. 314–15). But can the communist party, which, according to Huntington, is the guarantor of stability and order in socialist states afford a free choice organization of the working class? Would not organizations based on the workers' choice become in themselves destabilizing elements with challenges to social order, in a region which itself is not based on free choice?

I discussed this issue with East European social scientists. Their response was universally negative. They maintained that this would be dangerous. The socialist societies in Eastern Europe, they argued, are closed. They are kept together by force, today as in the past. If force were suddenly removed, they would fly apart. Institutionalized participation of workers in the political process would mean political pluralism, which, as in Hungary in 1956 or in Czechoslovakia in 1968, would release forces which would destroy the Soviet type of socialism. The genie had better be kept in the bottle. They said they would rather be safe than either orderly, balanced, or efficient. Pluralism and democracy? Perhaps, in the long run. But not now and not soon. 'The main thing', added Adam Schaff, the Polish philosopher,

> is that we do know the nature of the tradeoff. This *is* our choice, believe it or not, given the conditions, trends and developments in which we live. It is a calculated, rational choice. Who has free choice anyway?

(These interviews were conducted in Vienna in the winter of 1980.)

Soviet leaders have sought accommodation in Eastern Europe when possible but applied force when necessary. In the original takeover period, they had a plethora of means which Stalin used very effectively, namely, brutal force, fear, isolation, stern authority, as well as persuasion. The post-Stalin leaders did not have that richness of tools. Their 'conflict management' has been adequate, but barely so. They applied force in two cases, in Hungary in 1956 and in Czechoslovakia in 1968. But force has not been used against a major power like China, a distant enemy like Albania, a country with a reputation for partisan fighting like Yugoslavia, or even an unruly, cocky little Stalinist neighbor like Romania.

Under Stalin, there was no formal Soviet intervention needed. Stalin simply eliminated those East European leaders whom he preceived as conceivably opposing his hegemony and replaced them with leaders he trusted. Stalin's successors have kept busy attempting to arrest the emerging, and growing, conditions of pluralism in Eastern Europe. In the main, they tried to contain the pressures emanating from within the area by developing increasingly close economic bonds with East European governments (thus relying on economic determinism repudiated by their own ideologues long ago) (Dudinski, 1978; CMEA, 1979).

Over the years, *Soviet economic assistance* has become a necessary and, if adequate, sufficient prop of the East European governments. In the post-Stalin period, but especially since 1968, Soviet leaders have appeared more sensitive to sociopolitical consequences of declines in welfare in Eastern Europe. They have pumped in funds to help East European leaders satisfy workers' demands in order to maintain social tranquility. Soviet-financed 'buyoffs' may have been temporary but they have, temporarily, appeased socioeconomic dissatisfaction and have, temporarily, solved the East European leaders' major political problems.

Soviet leaders have learned that economic hardships in Eastern Europe tend to lead to social unrest and political turmoil which may have to be put down by force. In a region such as Eastern Europe, tumults and disturbances tend to be contagious. Armed interventions are costly and a last resort, not to be taken lightly. They do not contribute to social stability. And they can be avoided by prudent policies based on sensible relations.

The USSR has an interest in maintaining the stability, viability and durability of the East European region. The area has been a Soviet economic liability and promises to be even more so in the future, but it has been a Soviet political and military asset. In addition to Cuba, the six East European states are the only military and political allies the Soviet Union has. They contribute heavily to Soviet defense – in expenditures, men, weapons and geographic location – and they defend Soviet policies in international forums. They assist substantially in Soviet military and foreign aid to friendly developing nations and help the Soviet Union in Africa with money, technology, weapons and training. They also act as surrogates in areas where the Soviet Union prefers not to be directly involved (Triska, 1980, pp. 59–60).

Soviet economic neglect of Eastern Europe in the future would be much worse than the past economic exploitation under Stalin. It would be dangerous to the socialist system maintenance; it would cripple the local economies; inevitably, it would invite social disorder, which the respective governments would not be able to control; just as inevitably, the Soviet Union would have to intervene with military force.

Chances are that the Soviet leadership, present or future, will continue to minimize change. The choices are difficult, and risks are attached to innovation (Ross, 1980, p. 278). Cautious policies will keep frustrating workers' demands and will be costly economically, but, experience tells the Soviet leadership, it will not cause social turbulence and political crisis as long as the Soviet Union can afford to avert the trigger and the proximate cause of social upheavals, namely, the periodic, sudden worsening of acceptable minimum economic standards. Soviet economy assistance, the Soviets have discovered, makes the postponement of difficult policy decisions viable – as long as the Soviet Union can afford it. And this is where the East European workers enter into Soviet policy calculations.

The Soviet Union faces severe economic problems. Energy, manpower and raw-material shortages will tend to affect negatively Soviet industrial and agricultural production and the balance of trade. A significantly lower GNP and overall economic slowdown may be the result. The adverse economic development will place heavy constraints on Soviet assistance to Eastern Europe. The increasing demand ratios of legitimate Soviet domestic claimants, especially the military, will add to the pressure. The temptation to decrease the Soviet economic support of Eastern Europe will mount in direct proportion to the diminished Soviet economic capability. It will be difficult, more than in the past, to send emergency economic assistance to Eastern Europe. The interesting analytical question is going to be, not whether the Soviet Union will send the aid, but how it will be done, where the Soviet Union will get the funds.

The two major Soviet problems in the 1980s will be low agricultural productivity and investment shortage. To raise the former, and to increase the latter, the Soviet Union has only two sectors to draw upon: the military and consumers. High costs are attached to both. Reduced defense spending would stimulate economic growth and raise living standards but is without precedent in Soviet history. Decrease in the supply of consumer goods and services, on the other hand, would decrease labor productivity. Stepped-up foreign trade could conceivably provide the answer, or at least a good part of it (Goldman, 1979); in particular, opening up Siberia and the Soviet Far East for joint exploitation of oil, gas, and other raw materials with capitalist partners would bring in Western capital, technology and knowhow. But it would go against the grain of Soviet (and Russian) history to trade from a position of weakness, or worse, to become interdependent with the cunning capitalist world. Yet, the answer has to be found: Eastern Europe is just too important to let go down the drain (Ross, 1980, pp. 278–80).

Conclusion

Treatment of the working class in Eastern Europe has been embarrassing ideologically, retrogressive socially, and dangerous politically. Socialism has been exploited to legitimize the power of the ruling communist elites who have been systematically 'withholding from the workers the share of value they produce' (Konrad and Szelenyi, 1979, p. 155), and phony trade unions have failed to protect workers' interests and represent them as a class.

The workers have responded to this shabby treatment, whenever they could not longer tolerate it, by work stoppages and slowdowns, strikes, demonstrations, riots and even armed uprisings. In the process, they have emerged as a new social force with an occupational solidarity unknown in the past. The governments, East European as well as Soviet, have been unable to cope with this new phenomenon on any routine, sustained, institutionalized basis. Their reaction to the strikes and riots have been simple: punish the guilty, give the rest as much as possible of what they want, but do not rock the boat.

Up to now this uninspired 'crisis-management' patchwork has worked, and the workers have gone back to their jobs every time. But it has not been good practice. It is costly, risky and dangerous. The Soviet government, with its over-riding interest in social peace and political harmony in Eastern Europe, must of necessity be searching for a framework of order and stability which would eliminate such explosive, periodic political crises as workers' strikes and riots. In politics where one thing tends to lead to another, massive, violent social upheavals could have a cumulative effect. The Soviets do not need right now another unchecked source of trouble.

The fact remains that the Soviet leaders have not come up with any real solutions. Workers' riots in Eastern Europe reveal a deep, progressive alienation between the social forces in postindustrial socialist societies and obsolete political structures. Socialism has not abolished class antagonism, economic oppression and class struggle chiefly because it has failed to update and accommodate the functional requisites of its own development.

But pressures for change, which have been accumulating over the past decades, may well become cumulative in the 1980s. The situation will get worse. In addition to the increasing restiveness of workers, human rights activists and dissident intellectuals, though small in numbers, are making an impact on the East European societies. Nationalism, especially in its anti-Soviet variant, is on the upswing. The election of a Polish pope and the official visit of John Paul II in Poland, in 1979, made a deep impression on Eastern Europe. Stern economic measures, brought about by higher Soviet oil prices and other economic scarcities, signal an alteration in social income redistribution. Higher basic prices for fuel, energy and foodstuffs, together with gradual termination of state subsidies of basic consumer goods and services (Trend, 1979), are bound to severely affect the consumers, especially the lower strata. The stationing of large Soviet military forces, aside from their negative psychological impact on the population, places an added economic deadweight on the East European economies and threatens their development. When the ailing Brezhnev is replaced in the Kremlin, changes in East European leadership, following the historical pattern, are to be expected; this will destabilize East European polities still further. The collapse of détente is cutting many East European links with the West, the many avenues of trade, cooperation and tourism established in the 1970s, especially with Western Europe, leaving

Eastern Europe isolated once again, and even more dependent on the Soviet Union. And Chinese leaders, accusing the Soviet Union of predatory hegemony in Eastern Europe, continue to speak up for liberation of the region from 'large scale aggression, enslavement and slaughter' (Kux, 1980).

In the past, Soviet policy choices in Soviet-controlled Eastern Europe have been limited by Soviet fear of political change in the area. That has been the Soviet dilemma: how to deal with change in Eastern Europe without harming the Soviet-type socialist order. In the future, given the multiple pressures for change, the Soviet Union may well experience for the first time a serious *collective* threat to its rule in Eastern Europe, in more than one country and/or more than one social level at the same time.

References: Chapter 15

Andelman, David A., 'Romanian troops continue to patrol Jiu Valley', *New York Times*, 27 November 1977.

Apter, David, 'The premise of parliamentary planning', *Government and Opposition,* vol. 8, no. 1, 1973.

Bethell, Nicholas, *Gomulka: His Poland, His Communism* (New York and Chicago: Holt, Rinehart & Winston, 1969), esp. chapter XIV, 'October'.

Brezhnev, Leonid, *The World of Socialism – the Triumph of Great Ideas* (Moscow: Politizdat, 1978), p. 508.

Brzezinski, Zbigniew K., *The Soviet Bloc: Unity and Conflict* (Cambridge, Ma.: Harvard University Press, 1969).

Buletinul Official, No. 92, 26 August 1977, in Radio Free Europe, *Research Situation Report,* 11 October 1977, pp. 7–8.

Chekharin, E. M., and Kerimov, A. D., 'Socialist democracy in the contemporary state of communist development', 1973, cited in Jerry F. Hough, 'Political participation in the Soviet Union' (unpublished, 1975).

CMEA, 'The Council of Mutual Economic Assistance – 30 years', *Kommunist* (Moscow), 3 February 1979.

Connor, Walter D., *Socialism, Politics and Equality; Hierarchy and Change in Eastern Europe and the USSR* (New York: Columbia University Press, 1979).

Dudinsky, I., 'The present state of the CMEA countries' cooperation', *International Affairs* (Moscow), September, 1978.

Fejto, Francois, *A History of the People's Democracies* (New York: Praeger, 1971), p. 338.

Friedgut, Theodore H., *Political Participation in the USSR* (Princeton, NJ: Princeton University Press, 1979).

Goldman, Marshall I., 'Will the Soviet Union be an autarky in 1984?' *International Security, Spring* 1979, pp. 18–36.

Gordon, Jeren, citing two case studies, in RFE *Research,* RAD Background Report 44, 8 March 1978.

Huntington, S. P., *Political Order in Changing Societies* (New Haven, Conn.: Yale University Press, 1968).

Huntington, Samuel, 'Change to change: modernization, development and politics', *Comparative Politics,* vol. 3, no. 3, 1971.

International Herald Tribune, 17–18 February 1980, p. 1.

Kadar, Janos, at 10th Party Congress, 1970; *Nepszabadsag,* 24 November 1970, cited in William F. Robinson, ed., RFE *Research* ('What is a socialist society?'), 11 June 1971, p. 38.

Kecskemeti, Paul, *The Unexpected Revolution: Social Forces in the Hungarian Uprising* (Stanford, Ca.: Stanford University Press, 1961).

Konrad, Gyorgy, and Szelenyi, Ivan, *The Intellectuals on the Road to Class Power* (trans. from Hungarian) (New York: Harcourt, Brace, Jovanovich, 1979), pp. 255-6.

Kozlov, Iurii M., *Leninskii printsip uchastiia trudiashchikhsia v sovetskom gosudarstvennom upravlenii* (Moscow: Moscow State University Press, 1962).

KSS-KOR (Social Self-Defense Committee KOR), 10 October 1978, p. 4, in 'An appeal to the society', Radio Free Europe *Research,* RAD Background Report 236, 31 October 1978.

Kux, Ernst, 'Growing tensions in Eastern Europe', *Problems of Communism,* vol. 29, no. 2, 1980, p. 35, citing *Renmin Rihbao* (Beijing) of 1 November 1977.

Lewis, Flora, *The Polish Volcano: A Case History of Hope* (London: Secker & Warburg, 1959), esp. chapter IX on the Poznan riots, and chapter XI on the Poznan trials.

Lomax, Bill, *Hungary 1956* (London: Allison & Busby, 1976).

Molnar, Miklos, *Budapest 1956. A History of the Hungarian Revolution* (London: Allen & Unwin, 1971), esp. chapter 3, section on the Soviet bloc.

Nagy, Imre, *On Communism: In Defense of the New Course* (London: Waverly Press, 1957).

Oxley, Andrew, Pravda, Alex, and Ritchie, Andrew, *Czechoslovakia, the Party and the People* (London: Allen Lane/Penguin, 1973).

Pasic, Najdan, 'Socialism and modernization of politics', *International Political Science Association Roundtable,* 16-20 September 1968, p. 4.

Pullai, Arpad, secretary of central committee, *Nepszabadsag,* 24 November 1970, in W. F. Robinson, RFE *Research,* 11 June 1971.

Ramet, Pedro, 'Poland's economic dilemma', *New Leader,* vol. 58, no. 8, 1980, p. 5.

Robinson, William F., 'What is a socialist society?', RFE *Research,* 11 June 1971.

Robinson, William F., 'Hungary's NEM: a new lease on life?', Radio Free Europe, *Research,* RAD Background Report 275, 13 December 1979.

Ross, Denis, 'Coalition maintenance in the Soviet Union', *World Politics,* vol. 32, no. 2, 1980, pp. 258-80.

Stern, Carola, *Ulbricht: A Political Biography,* trans., A. Farbstein (London and New York: Praeger, 1965).

Trend, H. E., 'Consumer price increases in Eastern Europe', Radio Free Europe Research, *Background Reports,* no. 167, 26 July 1979.

Triska, Jan F., 'Citizen participation in community decisions in Yugoslavia, Romania, Hungary and Poland', in Jan F. Triska and Paul M. Cocks, eds., *Political Development in Eastern Europe* (New York: Praeger, 1977).

Triska, Jan F., 'Future Soviet-East European relations', in Robert Wesson, ed., *The Soviet Union: Looking to the 1980s* (Millwood, NY: Kraus, 1980).

Valenta, Jiri, *Soviet Intervention in Czechoslovakia, 1968* (Baltimore, Md.: Johns Hopkins University Press, 1979).

Vanous, Jan, 'The East European recession' (Discussion Paper, no. 78, Department of Economics, University of British Columbia, 1978), p. 18.

de Weydenthal, Jan B., 'The workers' dilemma of Polish politics: a case study', *East European Quarterly,* vol. 13, no. 1, 1979, pp. 95-119.

Wiles, Peter, 'Recent data on Soviet income distribution', *Survey,* vol. 21, no. 3, 1975.

16 Workers' Assertiveness, Western Dilemmas

CHARLES GATI

Occasional campaign oratory to the contrary notwithstanding, the activities of the governments of Western Europe and the United States indicate that they have come to accept the postwar *status quo* in Eastern Europe. Internationally, that *status quo* continues to feature the division of Europe into two political halves; domestically, it signifies one-party political systems in Eastern Europe in which competing ideas and organizations are strictly regulated. The main reason for Western acquiescence in this state of affairs is self-evident: the West lacks appropriate leverage – political, economic, or military – that could significantly reduce Soviet influence and bring the polities of the region closer to a Western orientation.

The apparent lack of appropriate *means* to change the East European *status quo* has served to define the limits of Western *objectives*. These objectives, therefore, have had to be modest, aiming at the maintenance of such contacts and interaction which would mitigate some of the harsher features of the East European dictatorial regimes and encourage a degree of diversity in the region. Time and again, however, the West has declined to provide active support to East Europeans seeking fundamental, systemic change. In 1956, when the Hungarians withdrew from the Warsaw Pact and introduced a multiparty political order, the West watched helplessly the brutal Soviet oppression of the Hungarian revolt. In 1968, when during the Prague Spring, Czechoslovakia experimented with a more lenient, humanitarian form of socialism, Soviet military intervention took place in the face of Western passivity. In 1980, when Polish industrial workers engaged in a persistent effort to obtain the right to organize free trade unions, the West declared that the issue was to be settled by the Poles without outside interference.

Such Western restraint – a marked disinterest to challenge Soviet preponderance in Moscow's frontyard – is based on a number of considerations and circumstances. One is the assumption that, as far as the Soviet Union is concerned, the political orientation of the East European party-states is non-negotiable. Therefore, any Western attempt to support systemic change in the region would be interpreted by the Soviet leadership as a challenge not only to its allies or dependencies in Eastern Europe, but to its own security. Hence, in the Soviet view, the West must refrain from assisting such indigenous political opposition as exists in Eastern Europe lest it is willing to renounce all hope for East–West accommodation. Put another way, acquiescence in the East European *status quo* is the price the West has been expected to pay to encourage prudence in Soviet behavior elsewhere (namely, arms control, Third World, etc.).

Another reason for Western restraint has had to do with the hopelessness of any direct East European confrontation with the Soviet Union. As demonstrated repeatedly, the Soviet leaders have been willing to resort to the use of military force to assure the survival of one-party regimes in Eastern Europe. Courageous and determined as the Poles or the Hungarians may be, they cannot hope to defeat the Soviet army, of course; they cannot extract meaningful concessions through militant confrontation. Under the circumstances, Western governments, anticipating strict countermeasures, have been reluctant to encourage the East Europeans to go so far as to invite Soviet intervention.

Thirdly, all Western governments have far more pressing priorities than the freedom and independence of Eastern Europe. Campaigns for human rights notwithstanding, Eastern Europe has been on the Western public agenda only in times of crises of potentially global consequence, that is, when there was a major buildup of the military arsenal of the Warsaw Pact (with its effect on the European balance of power), when Soviet armed forces were engaged, when Tito died. For the West, Eastern Europe is at best subsidiary to other, more immediate international concerns; at worst, it is a forgotten region.

Finally, Western restraint is due to the increasingly divergent interests of the 'West' as far as Eastern Europe is concerned. The most pronounced difference, apparent since the late 1960s, has been between the Federal Republic of Germany and much of the rest of the West, particularly the United States. It seems that the Federal Republic's *Ostpolitik* seeks not only the encouragement of East European semi-independence from the Soviet Union and the easing of dictatorial rule, but the creation of political conditions that would make it conceivable for East and West Germany to move toward some sort of confederal status. Although seldom acknowledged or discussed publicly, this objective has required a far more accommodating West German foreign policy toward both the Soviet Union and Eastern Europe than either the United States or other West European states have been willing to undertake. Yet, the American commitment to the Atlantic alliance has tempered US criticism of West German policies and resulted in an American willingness to follow West German leadership on Western policies toward Eastern Europe, if not the Soviet Union.

The resulting policy posture – cautious, some say fatalistic – inherent in the American approach to Eastern Europe has not been without its critics. A case in point was the controversy about the initial American position concerning the Polish workers' demands for economic and political rights in the summer of 1980. The official position was stated by the Department of State, according to which

> the domestic problems in Poland are a matter for the Polish people and the Polish authorities to work out. We do not believe that any further comment from the US government would be helpful as the situation is evolving in Poland.

Although the statement implied Washington's concern about Soviet intervention, *The New Republic* (30 August 1980) – a liberal weekly – sarcastically noted: 'Some human rights banner, this. It is all too typical of past administration behavior: big talk, no substance.' *The New Republic* editorial went onto suggest that the United States should let the strikers know that 'we're with you'. Why such a statement was not issued was then explained this way:

> American diplomats are rendered impotent by an Eastern European variant of the post-Vietnam syndrome. It might be called the post-Budapest syndrome. In 1956 the United States egged on Hungarian revolutionaries, gave them reason to think the United States might intervene on their side against the Soviets, only to leave them prey to tanks and the secret police. Never again, say American diplomats. Since we know we won't intervene militarily, we ought to keep our mouths shut. There is another syndrome at work here, too, which might be called post-Sakharov syndrome: the minute the United States intervenes in the internal affairs of a communist country, it makes things worse for those we are trying to help, as witness the Soviet crackdown on its dissidents after President Carter sent his letter to Andrei Sakharov. In this case, if we publicly side with the Polish dissidents, we may push the Soviets or the Polish regime to crack down, using 'outside agitation' as a pretext.

Thus, while the official position was that the United States ought not provide a 'pretext' for Soviet intervention, the critics suggested that if Moscow had decided to intervene it could always find some justification for its action – hence, the United States had nothing to lose by stating its support for the aspirations of the Polish people.

Controversy aside, it is clear that 1956 did mark a watershed in US rhetoric about Eastern Europe. For until then there had been a good deal of official talk about the 'rollback' of Soviet power from Europe and about the 'liberation' of Eastern Europe. The rhetoric was supplemented by extensive propaganda, based on the assumption that the United States could effect substantial, perhaps systemic, change in Eastern Europe. The confidence implied in that assumption was then shattered by the display of US passivity in the face of Soviet tanks on the streets of Budapest. Call it 'the post-Budapest syndrome', 'deliberate indifference', or 'prudent realism', since 1956 American foreign policy toward Eastern Europe has been low-key, only modestly activist, hopeful of gradual, long-term evolution. Relying almost exclusively on the presumed benefits of trade, credits and other economic instruments of policy, the United States has sought to assist those regimes which differed from the Soviet Union either in the foreign policy realm (Romania), or experimented in the domestic realm (Hungary and Poland).

Bluntly put, before 1956 the United States – and, indeed, the West – had not been reluctant to encourage regional instability in Eastern Europe. To the extent that such instability was thought to cause the Soviet leaders grave concern, it was a policy intended to distract Moscow from pursuing aggressive adventures in other parts of the world, notably Western Europe and the Third World. Since 1956, however, a different view seems to have emerged, according to which regional instability in Eastern Europe would constitute a threat to European security, ignite a hardline Soviet reaction against more liberal tendencies in Eastern Europe and against East–West accommodation – hence regional *stability* would serve the interests of Eastern Europe, the Soviet Union *and* the West. During the December 1970 Polish 'bread riots', for example, the West German government viewed the riots 'with alarm', noting its concern about their implications for the ratification of the recently concluded West German-Polish treaty. Helmut Schmidt, then the Federal Republic's Minister of Defense, worried that the riots might stall ratification of the 7 December 1970 'normalization treaty', observing that, 'I can imagine that political events in several Polish cities have turned the interests of the country's leaders to other problems rather than that of further progress of procedures for our German-Polish treaty' (*New York Times,* 20 December 1970).

A recent study by the Library of Congress, prepared for the US House of Representatives (1979, pp. 10–13), outlined four alternative Western approaches to Eastern Europe. One is based on Western acceptance of a Soviet sphere of influence in Eastern Europe. Those who advocate this approach contend that 'the primary American national interest is the prevention of thermonuclear war'; that Soviet withdrawal from the region would only lead to extreme instability; and that, therefore, 'it is in the American national interest to keep the Soviet Union in Eastern Europe' (Licklider, 1976–7). In general, proponents of this school of thought would seek to subordinate Western policies toward Eastern Europe to relations with the Soviet Union in order to avoid a possibly global confrontation with Moscow. In terms of specific policies, this approach calls for the extension of such economic or other benefits to the East European countries as would be granted to the Soviet Union itself.

The second approach aims 'at encouraging internal liberalization, a commitment to East–West interdependence in Eastern Europe and ultimately greater political, economic and foreign policy independence from the Soviet Union', but 'loosening Soviet-East European bonds [should be sought] only to the extent that these do not risk confrontation with the Soviet Union' (US House of Representatives, 1979, p. 11). This approach, which seems to be supported by the Department of State, relies on a policy of 'differentiation', giving preferential treatment to those East European countries which show signs of domestic liberalization or foreign policy independence from the Soviet Union. As former Deputy Assistant Secretary for European Affairs, William H. Luers, stated: 'We intend neither to leave our relations with Eastern Europe hostage to relations with the Soviet Union, nor conduct a policy that is reckless and destabilizing in Europe' (*U.S. Policy Toward Eastern Europe, 1979,* p. 35).

A third approach calls for a competitive Western involvement in Eastern Europe. Advocates of this approach (Gati, 1975) contend that (1) the Soviet Union is, and is likely to remain, the West's only significant adversary in the world; that (2) Soviet control over Eastern Europe is tenuous and the Soviet Union is vulnerable; and that (3) therefore the West should actively compete for influence in Eastern Europe, exploiting Soviet vulnerabilities in the region (the same way Moscow exploits Western weaknesses in Latin America, southeast Asia, and elsewhere). In the words of the Library of Congress study,

> This group sees a degree of unrest, instability and tension in the area as serving the security interests of the United States, although it stops short of recommending U.S. actions that might cause a Soviet backlash and bring East Europe under tighter Soviet control. (p. 12)

Finally, a fourth school of thought proposes policies which would seek to separate all East European governments from Moscow. Unimpressed by the import of 'diversity' within the region, advocates of this approach would treat the East European countries (with the exception of Yugoslavia) the same way as the West should treat the Soviet Union: limited economic contacts, curtailment of technology transfer, ideological confrontation. In short, the West should do nothing, they contend, to help these unpopular and, indeed, illegitimate regimes which were imposed on the people of the region by the Soviet Union. On the contrary, the West should encourage dissent and unrest, in the expectation that the Soviet hold over Eastern Europe could and should be ultimately eliminated.

These approaches – and the dilemmas they suggest—inform Western attitudes and approaches toward the trade unions and the industrial proletariat of Eastern Europe. In order to understand them, it is necessary to separate those held by Western governments, on the one hand, and by private and semiprivate organizations and institutions, on the other.

Western governments have had little or no occasion to develop formal relations with the party-run East European trade unions. Every now and then a delegation of East European trade union leaders would visit a Western country as part of a particular exchange agreement, but these visits normally entail no official contact. Nor is there any need for a Western 'policy', of course, toward blue-collar workers – except when riots or other disturbances create political tension, instability and, thus, the prospects for either incremental, or systemic change in an East European polity. Then and only then do Western governments take notice of the plight and aspirations of the East European industrial proletariat.

A case in point was Poland in 1980 – and the dilemma of Western governments was considerable. 'It's a cruel world', a West German official said. 'Our sympathy is fully with the strikers, but we must be realistic' (*Time,* 1 September 1980, p. 29). What it meant to be 'realistic', was explained by a US diplomat:

> We do not want to give the Soviets or the Polish authorities the slightest pretext for harsh action. It could be very dangerous for everyone, especially the Polish people, if the strike leaders were emboldened by suggestions of U.S. support. (*ibid.*)

The issue for the West was not one of supporting the workers against a Soviet military action; that, indeed, was not a 'realistic' option. The issue under active consideration was that of extending economic aid to the Polish government, which seemed willing to meet many of the workers' demands; which needed Western credit; which none the less was hardly representative, popular, or democratic. Put another way, the question was whether Western economic aid would help or hurt the workers' cause – their aspirations for better economic conditions and for free trade unions – or whether such aid would only strengthen the party's hold over the population, including the industrial proletariat.

Partly because the question entailed serious political and international complications, its resolution was postponed. In August, the nine members of the European Common Market, for example, could only note that the time was 'not right for taking either individual or joint positions', adding that 'there is absolutely no interest within the European Community to become involved in Poland's problems' (*New York Times,* 25 August 1980, p. 6). This view continued to prevail so long as the final outcome of the confrontation between the workers and the government was in doubt. For several weeks, Western governments refrained from assisting the Polish government (while it had not yet reached an accord with the workers), for such assistance at that time would have implied support for the government and, thus, the betrayal of the workers' cause. Conversely, any Western aid to the workers would have been seen as outside interference in Poland's internal affairs as well as the rejection of détente with the Soviet Union and its East European allies. As stated explicitly by Franz Josef Strauss, the Christian Democrats' candidate for the chancellorship of West Germany, Western loans to Poland should be withheld until such time when the country's government met the strikers' demands.

Once the Polish government had appeared to meet many of the workers' demands, Western reluctance began to give way to a willingness to assist the Polish government. By mid-September, the United States announced approval of an unprecedented $670 million worth of new credit guarantees for the purchase of grain, which was by far the largest such program for any country in the world. Mindful of the Western dilemma, President Carter declared that the credit guarantee was intended for 'the entire Polish nation – the workers, the government and the church' (*Albany Times-Union,* 13 September 1980, p. 1). In other words, the United States and indeed all Western governments still continued to try to act in such a way as *to aid the Polish government without appearing to hurt the workers' cause*

and to aid the workers without appearing to offend the Polish government.
All Western governments sought to maintain this cautious, diplomatic
posture and so did most of their political opponents. Typically, the
Republican nominee for President, Ronald Reagan, was silent. Only Lord
George Brown, a leading member of the British Labor Party, was quoted to
have asked:

> Why in heaven's name are we so craven about supporting the brave
> Poles? The Government is silent, the Labor movement and the
> Trades Union Congress, who above all should be supporting those
> who are opposing dictators and oppressors, are equally silent. We
> have to stand up and be counted. (*New York Times,* 25 August 1980,
> p. 6)

Lord George Brown's outcry seemed to express widely held Western
sentiments. After all, the Polish workers were seeking such elementary
rights – political and economic – which had long been obtained by most
Western workers and, indeed, promoted by their unions. The Polish
workers, moreover, pressed for their demands in an orderly and highly
disciplined way; there was no reported violence of any kind. Their leaders
were not only intelligent and reasonable, but politically astute and tactful
as well. In short, the Polish strike was an impressive performance by
Western standards, shattering a number of misconceptions and illusions
about the 'ultraromantic' nature of Polish political culture. Yet even this
impressive demonstration of working-class unity and discipline, combined
with substantive affinity with Western values, could only move public
'sentiments' in the West. For the governments of Western Europe and the
United States continued to prefer to deal with, and in a sense support, the
Polish government, expecting the government to retain its position once
the crisis abates and the old order, perhaps in a slightly modified form, is re-
established. Having long abandoned any hope for systemic change in
Eastern Europe, all Western governments assisted the process of gradual,
incremental, within-system change as the only 'realistic' alternative to
either doing nothing, or aiding the workers against their governments and
ultimately against the Soviet Union.

Non-governmental organizations and institutions in the West have
displayed more diversity of opinion in their assessment of the Polish
workers' demands than their governments have; some, such as the trade
unions in the United States, have been less circumspect, less inhibited.

The AFL–CIO has long refused to recognize East European trade
unions as legitimate representatives of the workers' interests; these unions
have been viewed as 'totalitarian labor front organizations'. Unlike most
West European trade unions which have occasionally engaged in a
dialog with East European trade union leaders, the AFL–CIO has
consistently and repeatedly rejected any contact with them. Its position was
explained at the 1975 AFL–CIO convention, for example, this way:

> The AFL–CIO rejects, as a matter of principle, the idea of free labor

sending delegations to any country which prohibits free trade unions, outlaws all free trade union activity and penalizes workers for advocating free trade unionism . . . The American labor movement must not compromise its organizational freedom by paying homage to so-called labor movements of totalitarian regimes through programs of exchange and cooperation. The dissolution of that resolve in Western European labor bodies, the last bastions of freedom in a disunited Europe, is cause for sadness and concern. (*Proceedings of 11th Constitutional Convention,* 1975, pp. 133–4)

Given this orientation, the reaction of the AFL–CIO to the 1970 Polish strikes and riots was logical and even self-evident:

The causes and consequences of the crisis in Poland are a powerful indictment of communism as an inhuman social and political order, as an incurably defective economic system . . . Only through freedom can the working people achieve greater well-being and genuine social progress. (*Proceedings of 9th Constitutional Convention,* 1971, p. 115)

In 1980, US labor leaders strongly criticized both the United States government's 'timid' approach and that of their West European colleagues. Albert Shanker, President of the United Federation of Teachers, for example, argued in his *New York Times* column (31 August 1980, p. E7) that,

It is one thing to say that we will not interfere (and we should also say that no other foreign power should interfere). But it is quite another to give the impression that, therefore, anything the Polish government decides to do – or the U.S.S.R. might do at the 'request' of the Polish government – is their own business.

Then, in an interesting passage, Shanker added:

If the Carter Administration hasn't been as strong as it should be on this issue, the Republicans are in much worse shape . . . It will be interesting to see how the Reagans, Hatches and Helmses, who claim to be warriors on the side of freedom against the Communist tyranny, will square their support for the Polish workers with their crusade to weaken unions in America.

Subsequent actions by the AFL–CIO did not quite match its adamant words. The International Longshoremen's Association once again refused to unload Polish vessels (as it did in 1970 and 1976); the AFL–CIO reportedly gave $25,000 to the families of Polish strikers; and Social Democrats, USA – a small party ideologically associated with the

AFL–CIO – organized a demonstration in New York in support of the striking Polish workers. Yet, on balance, American labor turned out to be far more active and vocal than its West European counterparts. In Britain, for example, a small-scale scandal developed when the British Trades Union Council (TUC) at first refused to cancel a long-planned visit with the official Polish trade unions. Although the visit was eventually called 'untimely' and then postponed, it is clear that the TUC approach to East European labor unions was, and remains, fundamentally different from that of the AFL–CIO; it is based on limited cooperation and 'quiet diplomacy'.

A confidential, fifteen-page policy statement by the TUC (Taylor, 1980) provides an unusually interesting insight into the British labor unions' assessment of East European conditions and of the most effective way Western labor can improve them. For one thing, the TUC maintains that it 'has no sympathy with any form of authoritarian regime, and no illusions about the involvement of national trade union centers in Eastern Europe in the apparatus of the Communist parties of the countries and of their governments, and about their subordinate role'. The best way the TUC seeks to influence them is through exchanges and other contacts. The policy statement emphasizes that the East European countries 'operate in a different political and economic environment from that in Western countries and it would be unrealistic to expect that environment to change rapidly'.

Accordingly, the TUC has apparently made a conscious distinction between 'trade union rights' and 'traditional political and civil rights'. It seeks to improve the former (including 'the right to work, to just and favorable conditions of work, to periodic holidays with pay', etc.), but is 'only exceptionally' concerned with the latter. It also believes – as all Western governments do – that informal representations to East European labor leaders about workers dismissed for political reasons are 'more likely to help the individuals concerned than would open and official representations'. That may well be true, of course; what some observers have asked, however, is why the British trade unionists favor such quiet diplomacy in Eastern Europe when they have traditionally refused to have any relations at all with the pseudolabor unions of right-wing dictatorships.

Finally, no survey of Western attitudes and approaches to blue-collar workers in Eastern Europe would be complete without taking a brief look at the so-called 'Eurocommunist' parties of Western Europe. For particularly for the Italian Communist Party (PCI), the oppressive quality of the East European political order has long presented a major dilemma. Should it approve East European oppression of dissidents and Soviet interventions, it would likely suffer electoral losses; it would be seen as Moscow's puppet. However, if the PCI were to join Western critics in their condemnation of the East European regimes, it would further weaken its already tenuous ties with what used to be called the international communist movement (Gati, 1977; Valenta, 1978). In either case, the PCI's reaction to the increasing assertiveness of the Polish working class has been seen as the litmus-test of its professed independence from the Soviet party line.

In 1980, during the Polish crisis, many of the 'Eurocommunist' parties expressed strong support for the striking workers. The PCI's foreign policy spokesman, Giancarlo Pajetta, said that East European 'unions should not be just transmission belts for the state administration' (*New York Times,* 25 August. 1980, p. 6). Pajetta pointedly endorsed the workers' most controversial demands – the right to strike and the right to form independent unions – when he stated: 'All liberties, including trade union liberties and the right to strike, must be firmly upheld in order to guarantee the rational development of society, to permit the correction of errors, and to ensure that each one obtains his proper share of work and coresponsibility' (*L'Unita,* 21 August 1980). This position was subsequently upheld by the· communist-run Italian labor federation (CGIL) as well, whose secretary-general, Luciano Lama, considered it possible that the Polish general strike would 'mark a stage in a gradual but irreversible opening up towards workers' participation and democracy' (Devlin, 1980, p. 3).

Most of the smaller communist parties of Western Europe followed the PCI's lead. Santiago Carillo of the Spanish party, for example, put his criticism of the Polish leadership this way:

It seems to me that in Poland, besides the economic problem, there is another very important issue, that of democracy. I repeat that I believe the political system does not correspond fully to the desires of a great part of the Polish working class. The solution, I think, must lie in a serious reform of the economic and political system, which will make socialism in Poland a more indigenous socialism, more linked to the personality of the Polish people. (Devlin, 1980, p. 5)

A spokesman for the Swedish Communist party argued that Poland 'needs a strong and democratic labor movement, both free and independent in its relation to the state and party apparatus' (*New York Times,* 25 August 1980, p. 6). The chairman of the Finnish Communist Party, Aarne Saarinen, concluded that 'something in socialist Poland must have gone completely wrong', while the Belgians took the position that the Polish workers sought a 'more active participation in choices and decisions' and that 'their expectations and hopes cannot be disappointed' (Devlin, pp. 5–7).

Somewhat more cautious assessments were issued by the French, British and Austrian communist parties, which sought to find a middle ground between endorsing the workers' demands and supporting the Polish government. French Politburo member Francette Lazard, for example, praised the Polish government, pointing out that it had responded to the strikes 'with the' will to conduct the debate democratically, with the will to negotiate, with no repression' (*L'Humanité,* 19 August 1980). In its apparent attempt to play down the significance of the Polish crisis, the Austrian communists offered the nebulous conclusion that 'socialist democracy is not yet as effective as it should be' (Devlin, p. 8). This quote, from the party's daily newspaper *Volksstimme,* may well be the understatement of the year.

For several decades now, Western influence on Eastern Europe has been indirect and quite modest. The West could *do* relatively little to either ease Soviet control, or oppression, yet what the West *is* – its freedoms, its prosperity – has not been lost on the region's people and leaders. Economic ties between the two halves of Europe have grown considerably, as has the indebtedness of Eastern Europe, but the political consequence of this state of economic affairs is unclear. In the face of the Soviet commitment to one-party hegemony neither the inviting example of the West, nor extensive economic relations, could significantly alter the East European political order.

Striking East European workers have evoked Western sympathy and moral support. Public opinion, in general, and the AFL–CIO in the United States and the communist parties in Western Europe, in particular, have identified with their cause. Yet, in the chancelleries of Western Europe and North America, where politicians and diplomats make the crucial decisions, the growing assertiveness of the East European industrial proletariat is invariably analyzed from the perspective of 'higher' considerations: from the perspective of its effect on Soviet foreign policy in other parts of the world and, thus, its effect on détente. The 1970 Polish riots, for example, were evaluated in the White House in terms of their impact on US-Soviet relations, with Henry Kissinger wondering what lessons Moscow might draw from them. In short, the East European workers' struggle for independent trade unions and higher living standards has brought Western applause and genuine expressions of solidarity, but behind the applause and the headlines looms the over-riding interest of the West in détente – and in its presumed precondition: the stability of Eastern Europe.

References: Chapter 16

AFL-CIO, *Proceedings of 9th Constitutional Convention,* Vol. II: Report of the Executive Council, Washington, DC, 1971.

AFL–CIO, *Proceedings of 11th Constitutional Convention,* Vol. II: Report of the Executive Council, Washington DC, 1975.

Devlin, Kevin, 'Western communist reactions to the Polish crisis', Radio Free Europe Research Background Report, no. 213, 26 August 1980.

Gati, Charles, 'The forgotten region', *Foreign Policy,* no. 19, Summer 1975, pp. 135–45.

Gati, Charles, 'The "Europeanization" of communism?', *Foreign Affairs,* vol. 55, no. 2, April 1977, pp. 539–53.

Licklider, Roy E., 'Soviet control of Eastern Europe: morality *versus* American national interest', *Political Science Quarterly,* vol. 91, no. 4, Winter 1976–7, pp. 619–24.

Taylor, Robert, 'British TUC takes soft line on rights in Eastern bloc', *New America,* June 1980, p. 7.

US House of Representatives (Library of Congress), *U.S. Relations with the Countries of Central and Eastern Europe* (Washington, DC: GPO, 1979).

US House of Representatives, *U.S. Policy Toward Eastern Europe* (Hearings Before the . . . House of Representatives) (Washington, DC: GPO, 1979).

Valenta, Jiri, 'Eurocommunism and Eastern Europe', *Problems of Communism,* vol. 27, no. 2, March–April 1978, pp. 41–54.

Notes on Contributors

JACK BIELASIAK is an assistant professor of political science and an associate of the Russian-East European Institute at Indiana University, Bloomington. He was educated in Poland, France and the United States, and holds a PhD in government from Cornell University. He is a contributor to the *American Political Science Review, Studies in Comparative Communism, East European Quarterly,* and several compendia. Professor Bielasiak is currently working on a book-length study of political leadership and political participation in communist states.

ELLEN COMISSO is an assistant professor of political science at the University of California, San Diego. She received her PhD from Yale University in 1977 and is the author of *Workers' Control Under Plan and Market* (1979). She is currently working on a comparison of labor unions' and workers' councils' ability to satisfy workers' interests, and on a project comparing the way in which communist and liberal democratic governments manage unprofitable industries.

WALTER D. CONNOR directs Soviet and East European Studies at the Foreign Service Institute of the Department of State. A frequent traveler in Eastern Europe and the Soviet Union, he is the author of *Socialism, Politics, and Equality* (1979), as well as other books and articles.

BOGDAN DENITCH is a professor of sociology and Chair of the PhD Program in Sociology at the Graduate School of the City University of New York and Queens College. He is also a visiting professor in the Columbia University Political Science Department and at the Johns Hopkins University Bologna Center. His more recent publications include: *The Legitimation of a Revolution: The Yugoslav Case* (1976), *The Legitimation of Regimes* (1979), and *Democratic Socialism in Europe* (1981). He is a former trade unionist and his interests center on working-class politics and institutions in Eastern and Western Europe.

CHARLES GATI is professor of political science at Union College. While coediting this book for publication, he was a senior research scholar at Columbia University's Research Institute on International Change. He is coauthor of *The Debate Over Détente*; editor of *Caging the Bear, The International Politics of Eastern Europe* and *The Politics of Modernization in Eastern Europe*; and author of a forthcoming book, *Stalin and the Hungarian Communist Party*. His articles have appeared in *Foreign Affairs, Foreign Policy, World Politics, Studies in Comparative Communism,* and other journals and edited volumes.

PAUL M. JOHNSON is assistant professor of political science at Yale University. He is author of *The Politics of Economic Reform in Eastern Europe* (forthcoming) and coauthor with Jan F. Triska of *Political Development and Political Change in Eastern Europe* (1976). Professor Johnson received his BA from Rice University and both his MA and PhD in political science from Stanford University.

GEORGE KOLANKIEWICZ was born in 1946, educated at Leeds University and is currently a lecturer in sociology at the University of Essex, England. He is the author of several works on contemporary Poland, including with D. Lane, *Social Groups in Polish Society* (1973). A regular visitor to Poland, he was on a British Academy exchange visit in Poland during the fateful months of July and August 1980.

SEYMOUR MARTIN LIPSET is professor of political science and sociology, and senior fellow of the Hoover Institution at Stanford University. Before going to Stanford in 1975, he was George D. Markham Professor of Government and Sociology at Harvard. Professor Lipset has authored or coauthored fifteen books and monographs. Translations of some of these have appeared in eighteen languages. In addition, he has edited twenty books, published over 200 articles and is also coeditor of the bimonthly journal, *Public Opinion*.

JOHN MICHAEL MONTIAS is a professor of economics at the Institute for Social and Policy Studies at Yale University. He is the author of *Central Planning in Poland* (1962), *Economic Development in Communist Rumania* (1967) and *The Structure of Economic Systems* (1976).

DANIEL N. NELSON obtained his PhD at Johns Hopkins University and is an associate professor of political science at the University of Kentucky. He is the author of *Democratic Centralism in Romania*, editor of *Local Politics in Communist Countries*, and several other books. His professional articles on communist politics have appeared in *World Politics, Journal of Politics, Soviet Studies, Slavic Review*, and in many other edited volumes and journals.

ALEX PRAVDA was born in Prague but educated in England. After obtaining his BA from Balliol College, Oxford, he completed a DPhil. thesis on Czechoslovakia in 1968 at St Antony's College. From 1972–3, he taught in the Department of History and Politics at Huddersfied Polytechnic; since 1973 he has lectured on Soviet and East European politics at the University of Reading. He is the author of *Reform and Change in the Czechoslovak Political System: January–August 1968* (1975) and coeditor of *Czechoslovakia: the Party and the People* (1973). In addition to several articles on East European politics, he has since 1978 contributed to five volumes on the politics and economics of the Soviet Union and Eastern Europe. At present he is completing a comparative study of workers, trade unions and politics in the Soviet Union, Hungary, Poland and Czechoslovakia.

JAN F. TRISKA is a professor of political science and international relations at Stanford University. Dr Triska received his education at Charles University in Prague (JUD), Yale (JSD) and Harvard (PhD). His most recent books include *Political Development in Eastern Europe* (1977), which he coedited with Paul Cocks, and *The World of Superpowers* (in press), which he wrote with Robert North and Nobutaka Ike. In 1980–81, Professor Triska was a fellow at the Wilson Center in the Smithsonian Institution, Washington, DC.

LAURA D'ANDREA TYSON received her BA from Smith College and her PhD in economics from the Massachusetts Institute of Technology. She has written numerous articles and monographs on economic conditions in Eastern Europe, with special emphasis on Yugoslavia. She is currently an assistant professor of economics at the University of California at Berkeley.

JIRI VALENTA is an associate professor and coordinator of Soviet and East European Studies in the Department of National Security Affairs at the US Naval Postgraduate School, Monterey, California. Previously, he was a research fellow at the Brookings Institute. Professor Valenta is the author of *Soviet Intervention in Czechoslovakia, 1968: Anatomy of a Decision* (1979), *The Communist States and Africa* (forthcoming) and coeditor of *Eurocommunism between East and West* (1980). He is a contributor to various scholarly journals, among others *Political Science Quarterly, International Security, Orbis, Problems of Communism, Studies in Comparative Communism, United States Naval Institute Proceedings* and *Political Quarterly* (London).

IVAN VOLGYES is a professor of political science at the University of Nebraska and the author or editor of eighteen volumes dealing with Eastern Europe. His most recent volumes dealing with Hungary are *Contemporary Hungary: a Profile* (1980), and with Peter Toma, *Politics in Hungary* (1977). He spent the academic year 1978-9 in Hungary, studying the modernization of the countryside.

JAN B. DE WEYDENTHAL obtained his PhD at the University of Notre Dame and is a senior analyst in the Radio Free Europe Research Department. He taught at the College of William and Mary in Virginia, as well as the University of South Carolina. He is author of *The Communists of Poland* (1978) and of *Poland: Communism Adrift* (1979). He has also written several articles for professional journals.

Index

Numbers printed in bold type refer to main entries, numbers printed in italic type refer to tables.